A Long Walk,
a Gradual Ascent

A Long Walk,
a Gradual Ascent

The Story of the Bolivian Friends Church in Its Context of Conflict

NANCY J. THOMAS
with a chapter by HAROLD R. THOMAS

Foreword by Pablo Alberto Deiros

WIPF & STOCK · Eugene, Oregon

A LONG WALK, A GRADUAL ASCENT
The Story of the Bolivian Friends Church in Its Context of Conflict

American Society of Missiology Series

Wipf & Stock
An Imprint of Wipf and Stock Publishers
199 W. 8th Ave., Suite 3
Eugene, OR 97401

www.wipfandstock.com

PAPERBACK ISBN: 978-1-5326-7975-9
HARDCOVER ISBN: 978-1-5326-7976-6
EBOOK ISBN: 978-1-5326-7977-3

Manufactured in the U.S.A.   NOVEMBER 11, 2019

The publisher gratefully acknowledges the use of material from the following sources:

Primary documents and photos from the archives of the Northwest Yearly Meeting of Friends, housed in the archival library of George Fox University, used by permission.

Primary documents and photos from the archives of the Evangelical Friends Church Southwest, used by permission.

Primary documents from the archives of the Iglesia Nacional Evangélica de Los Amigos in La Paz, Bolivia, used by permission.

Articles by Nancy Thomas originally published in the Evangelical Friend magazine ("Alto Lima: A Landmark for the Bolivian Church," 1979, and "Hard Hats in a Friends Church," 1985), used by permission of the Barclay Press.

Unpublished journal entries by Frank Laubach for December 21, 24, 25, 1942, and January 3, 1943, used by permission of ProLiteracy.

Cover art by Oscar Tintaya, @2014, used by permission.

Dedicated to the Quaker historians who were also our personal mentors and friends:

–Anna Nixon, author of *Centuries of Planting* (1985, Friends in India)
–Authur O. Roberts, author of *Tomorrow Is Growing Old* (1978, Friends in Alaska)
–Carmelo Aspi, author of *Los Amigos en marcha* (2007, Friends in Bolivia)
–Ralph Bebee, author of *Garden of the Lord* (1968, Friends in NWYM)
–Ronald Stansell, author of *Missions by the Spirit* (2009, Friends missiology)

And to the missiologists and historians who encouraged us along the way:
–Charles Van Engen, author of *Mission on the Way*
–R. Daniel Shaw, author of *Transculturation: The Cultural Factor in Translation and Other Communication Tasks*
–Pablo Deiros, author of *Historia de la Iglesia en América Latina*
–James E. Bradley, author of *Church History: An Introduction to Research, Reference Works, and Methods* (with Richard A. Muller)

Of all that was done in the past,
you eat the fruit, either rotten or ripe.
And the Church must be forever building,
and always decaying and always being restored.

O Father, we welcome your words,
And we will take heart for the future,
Remembering the past.

—T. S. ELIOT, FROM "CHORUSES FROM 'THE ROCK'" (1934)

Contents

Preface to the American Society of Missiology Series

The purpose of the ASM Series is to publish, without regard for disciplinary, national, or denominational boundaries, scholarly works of high quality and wide interest on missiological themes from the entire spectrum of scholarly pursuits, e.g., theology, history, anthropology, sociology, linguistics, health, education, art, political science, economics, and development, to articulate but a partial list. Always the focus will be on Christian mission.

By "mission" in this context is meant a cross-cultural passage over the boundary between faith in Jesus Christ and its absence. In this understanding of mission, the basic functions of Christian proclamation, dialogue, witness, service, fellowship, worship, and nurture are of special concern. How does the transition from one cultural context to another influence the shape and interaction of these dynamic functions?

Missiologists know that they need the other disciplines. And other disciplines, we dare to suggest, need missiology, perhaps more than they sometimes realize. Neither the insider's nor the outsider's view is complete in itself. The world Christian mission has through two millennia amassed a rich and well-documented body of experience to share with other disciplines.

Interaction will be the hallmark of this Series. It desires to be a channel for talking to one another instead of about one another. Secular scholars and church-related missiologists have too long engaged in a sterile venting of feelings about one another, often lacking in full evidence. Ignorance of and indifference to one another's work has been no less harmful to good scholarship.

The promotion of scholarly dialogue among missiologists may, at times, involve the publication of views and positions that other missiologists cannot accept, and with which members of the Editorial Committee do not agree. The manuscripts published reflect the opinions of their authors and are not meant to represent the position of the American Society of Missiology or the Editorial Committee of the ASM Series.

We express our warm thanks to various mission agencies whose financial contributions enabled leaders of vision in the ASM to launch this new venture. The future of the ASM series will, we feel sure, fully justify their confidence and support.

WILLIAM J. DANKER, CHAIRPERSON
ASM Series Editorial Committee

Foreword

As it is with love, the history of the Christian testimony is always the narrative of a two-sided experience. On the one side, it tries to reconstruct the experience of those who gave testimony of their faith. On the other side, it tries to recreate the story of those who received that testimony. The work of the Friends in Bolivia is such a narrative. However, the players on each side of the equation are unique and with very particular characteristics.

On the one side, there are the Aymara Indians, one of the most outstanding native peoples in the Andean area. They reside mostly around Lake Titicaca and on the high planes of Bolivia and Peru, but have expanded to the southeast of Bolivia and the northwest of Argentina. Their traditional religion is closely related to their rural activities. They are devoted to the earth spirit, *Pachamama*. However, today, the religion of the Aymara Indians is deeply syncretistic. It is interesting to note that a good number of their religious beliefs and values are similar to Christian values. Because of this, missiologists have seen in this culture open opportunities for the proclamation of the gospel, with excellent results. This book, written by two distinguished missiologists, offers an extended case study of this phenomenon.

On the other side, there are the various expressions of the Friends' testimony as brought by the missionaries from the Northwest which are also unique. As it is the case with the Aymara, Friends missionaries in Bolivia have shared, in singular ways, the richness of their extraordinary tradition. This is a marvelous combination of diverse elements.

Taken as a whole, the Friends missionary testimony in Bolivia has been a combination of piety and praxis. The Spanish proverb "*A Dios orando y con el mazo dando*" (To God praying and with the mallet hammering), has been fulfilled down through the years by the faithful witness of the Friends Mission in Bolivia, and today by the indigenous Friends Church.

As we go through the pages of this well-researched history of the Friends Mission in Bolivia and the development of the Bolivian Friends Church, we perceive groups of women and men becoming a community of authentic Christ-followers, compelled to change the world around them. Their intentional pursuit is to passionately reach out to those who do not follow Jesus.

In the beginning of the story, every possible effort was made to evangelize the Aymaras as a people group. This commitment to the proclamation of the good news is only understood as it is considered in the light of the deep valuing and love for the Aymara Indians on the part of the Friends missionaries. The goal of their sharing the gospel has been to create communities of connection and belonging, true communities of the kingdom of God.

As Aymara Friends believers began to develop as a church, they strove to combine evangelization with works of social significance, such as primary schools, literacy programs, medical assistance, and agricultural programs. In this regard, the Friends have perhaps exceeded other larger denominations. At times their sacrificial giving has been exemplary, stemming from gratitude and dedication. Seeing needs and responding to them practically, emotionally, and spiritually has not been the exception.

But none of this has been easy or automatic. The Bolivian context has always been complex. In geographic terms, there is not one but three Bolivias: the Andean region, the central valleys, and the jungle. In anthropological terms, there are also at least three indigenous Bolivias: the Aymara, the Quechua, and the Guarani. To this add the complexity of the mestizo and upper Spanish classes. The multiplicity of different languages is accompanied by a diversity of religious expressions. Worldviews vary from one region to another. For foreign missionaries or nationals moving from one region to the other, the task of contextualization is challenging. The only way to cope with this kaleidoscope is to be ready to learn in direct contact with people. Success in learning a different language, understanding diverse worldview perspectives, and building redeeming bridges between various ways of worshipping God is always the result of deliberate apprenticeship. The Friends missionaries have been responsibly involved in this kind of contextualization. But also, they have sought to form national believers in the knowledge, skills, and opportunities that have been entrusted to them as confessing Christians.

How can this small evangelical denomination celebrate with authentic Christian pride all these years of faithful witness in Bolivia? Growth has not been astronomical, the transformation of society on a national level has not been significant, recognition by those in power has been limited. However, their contagious enthusiasm is well evidenced when they are together. Their worship services show Friends believers experiencing laughter, joy, and fun. Of course, this is not a big issue when you are recognized, appreciated, and rewarded. But when your Christian testimony has been subject to trials, opposition, discrimination, and, at times, persecution, to keep worshipping is the expression of a great human spirit, a spirit filled with the Spirit of God. Bolivian Friends today seek to follow God with courageous innovation and a total commitment to the lordship of Christ. They may be a small denomination, but they are a great people of God.

This is the fascinating adventure that Nancy and Hal Thomas are inviting us to explore in this history of the development of the Friends Church among the Aymara people of Bolivia.

PABLO ALBERTO DEIROS
Historian, Educator, Missiologist
Author of *Historia del cristianismo en América Latina*, 1992, 2018
("History of Christianity in Latin America")

Acknowledgments

We wrote this book as part of a team and in the company of many to whom we owe our gratitude. Our first acknowledgment goes to Arthur O. Roberts, late Quaker philosopher, historian, professor, and poet. He was also our friend and mentor. Arthur encouraged us, many years before we began this project, to make our final missionary contribution as historians, to not let slip from memory the story of the development of the Bolivian Friends Church. The Oregon Yearly Meeting (now Northwest Yearly Meeting) had poured many lives into this effort and needed, not only to see the results, but to learn from all the successes and failures accumulated along the way.

We committed to using primary resources, and thanks to the universities, yearly meetings, and other organizations that gave us access to their archives, we were able to do this. In 2013 and 2014, Evangelical Friends Church Southwest superintendent, Stan Leach, opened to us their archives in Yorba Linda. In researching the beginnings of the work in Bolivia, we sorted through boxes of yearly meeting minutes dating back to 1898, mission board minutes from 1912–1958, early newsletters (the *Christian Workman* and the *Harvester*) and correspondence, records from the Ramona Friends Church between 1892–1904, and especially records of the mission to Guatemala. These gave us valuable information about William Abel and Juan Ayllón, the two men recognized as seed-planters and founders of the work in Bolivia.

Thanks also to Azusa Pacific University's Special Collections and its librarian, Ken Otto, for permission to access their archives back to the school's foundation as the Training School for Christian Workers in 1900, where William Abel was the second student to enroll. Through school records, copies of the *Quarterly Bulletin of the Training School for Christian Workers*, and US census records, we were able to clear up some of the mystery surrounding William Abel.

In 2014, we visited the headquarters of the Ramona Unified School District in Ramona, California, where William Abel attended grade school. We were also able to spend time in the Guy B. Woodward Museum, where we viewed copies of the town's newspaper, the *Ramona Sentinel*, dating back to the 1890s. We found news items about Abel and advertisements for his butcher shop, the Nuevo Meat Market.

While on the same trip to Southern California, we also visited the San Pasqual Indian Museum and Cemetery. Abel was born in San Pasqual in 1870 while it was still a federal reservation for the Kumayaay Indian group. The cemetery where his parents might have been buried had twenty-seven markers, only two of which were readable.

In Valley View, California, we met with Kumayaay tribal leader, David Toler, and the tribal historian, Wilda Toler. Neither of them had heard of William Abel but they were fascinated by our research. The historian gave us a clue about a man named Peter Abel who was murdered in 1870. He could have been William Abel's father or the rancher his family worked for.

That same year, 2014, we traveled to Indiana. In Westfield, we had access to the archives of the Union Bible College and the Central Yearly Meeting of Friends, where we researched the beginnings of the Friends missionary movement to Bolivia from 1919 to 1924. We also had a delightful interview with former Central Friends missionaries Imogene Hendrickson and Rachel (Enyart) Edwards Peters who gave us information about Juan Ayllón and Mattie Bount, as well as Carroll Tamplin.

In Marion, Indiana, the World Gospel Mission gave us access to old files of Peniel Mission, where we found some information about William Abel as he was sent out as a missionary from this group.

Tom Hamm, librarian of the Quaker collection in Earlham College in Richmond, Indiana, helped us find information in their archives of the Five Years Meeting in the late 1920s and early 1930s. This provided background for the Oregon Yearly Meeting's acceptance of Bolivia as its mission field in 1930.

From 2015 to 2018, our documentary research came mainly from two archival collections: the archives of the Bolivia Yearly Meeting (INELA) in La Paz, Bolivia, and the archives of Oregon/Northwest Yearly Meeting, held in the library archives of George Fox University in Newberg, Oregon.

I spent several years in the archives of George Fox University where archivists Zoe Clark (retired in 2015) and Rachel Thomas (2015 and following) helped me sort through the files and boxes of documents, information about the Friends Mission to Bolivia accumulated since 1930. Minutes of the mission board, field council minutes, reports, personal correspondence, stories for the various newsletters, and a vast collection of slides and photos provided a rich resource of primary documents for the years from 1930 to 2002.

When we began the project in 2013, the archives of the INELA in La Paz were not so neatly organized as those in George Fox University. But we were blessed to have one of our team members be a professional archivist, working at that time in one of the Bolivian government offices. Victoria Tazola is a third-generation Quaker from the *altiplano* community of Laja. The executive council (*mesa directiva*) of the INELA graciously gave the team permission to organize the boxes of documents, and Vicki took on this task. Documents were scarce during the first decades of the church's development, as it took place in an oral culture. But starting from the 1960s, the amount of official minutes and reports grew exponentially and almost threatened to overwhelm us. Thanks in large part to Vicki's help, we were able to work through it all, a valuable resource as this was input from the Bolivian national perspective, in contrast to the mission perspective.

The other key resource in our investigation came from personal interviews. Most of these took place in Bolivia as our Bolivian team members spoke with the grown children and grandchildren of former leaders who had died, as well as with former leaders still living. Some of these interviews happened in focus groups of people involved in specific decades in the development of the church. Over one hundred interviews were conducted, many of these filmed. These helped us triangulate with primary documents from the Bolivian perspective, primary documents from the mission perspective, and field interviews.

We were able to coordinate our research efforts because of an agreement between the NWYM and the INELA, reached in 2013 and 2014, to cooperate in the project, yearly meeting to yearly meeting. The NWYM Board of Global Outreach made available to us the ministry funds that had accumulated through our supporters up to the time of our formal retirement in 2014, thus allowing us to travel to Bolivia once a year for the duration of the project. They also made it possible for people in the Northwest to continue making contributions; these were designated to help with the expenses of the Bolivian team. The INELA *mesa directiva* fixed up a small apartment at their headquarters for us to use during our visits, and an office exclusively for the project. We're grateful for all of this.

Most of all, we're grateful for our Bolivian team members whose participation allowed us to approach the history of the church from a joint insider/outsider perspective. In 2014, the INELA approved the creation of a history commission, with the intention that its membership remain stable throughout the project, from 2013–2018.

Within the commission we organized ourselves, naming Hal Thomas as the overall coordinator, to serve as the liaison between the two yearly meetings. We named Reynaldo Mamani as the Bolivian coordinator, in charge of the field office; Humberto Gutiérrez as the writer for the book in Spanish, who was able to base a large part of his work on my investigations in English; Félix Huarina in charge of the documentary film; and myself, Nancy Thomas, as researcher and writer for the book in English. As mentioned above, Victoria Tazola served as the archivist. David Mamani worked as the technician, in charge of setting up and maintaining the computer system. David Tintaya was secretary and Marcos Mamani, treasurer. Arminda Tintaya also participated on the team, as did Dionisio Lucasi. At the level of personal commitment and enthusiasm, the team was outstanding, and this continued for the duration of the project, which extended into 2019. I can't imagine completing this project on my own. Our community made it possible.

We're grateful for another community, that of supporters in the Northwest who continued to encourage us, pray for us, and contribute financially, both as individuals and as churches. The Friends churches who made us a part of their regular offerings included North Valley, Reedwood, and Cherry Grove. Thanks also to Hal's parents, William and Esther Thomas (who died in 2015 and 2016), for their generous contributions that swelled our ministry fund and made possible our yearly trips to Bolivia. Thanks to Ron Stansell, fellow missionary to Bolivia during the 1970s and 1980s, for his help in reading and commenting on the manuscript. We also acknowledge those who loaned us letters and shared from their own time of service of Bolivia: Geraldine Willcuts, Martha Puckett, Gene and Betty Comfort, Ed and Marie Cammack, Quentin and Florene Nordyke.

We thank our families who encouraged us throughout this journey and provided us with the joy of their relationship: son David and Debby Thomas, with our grandchildren Bree (now married to Jade Becker), Aren, Gwen, and Alandra; daughter Kristin and Jon Gault, with our grandchildren Reilly, Paige, and Peter.

As the main author of this book in English, I want to acknowledge my husband, Hal, who actually headed up the whole history project. He accompanied me in each phase of the investigation, traveling with me to Southern California, Indiana, and Bolivia. He was my chief encourager and critic. His authorship of the chapter on the Aymara culture (chapter 2) and his cultural insights throughout the project helped all of us on the team interpret the history of the Bolivian Friends Church.

Most of all, we both give thanks to Jesus, the Head of the Church, the One who invited us on this wild adventure and who accompanied us each step of the way. To God be the glory.

List of Abbreviations

AFBFM   American Friends Board of Foreign Mission

ANDEB   *Asociación Nacional de Evangélicos Bolivianos* (National Association of Bolivian Evangelicals)

APU   Azusa Pacific University

BIM   Bolivian Indian Mission

BMC   Bolivian Mission Council

BQEF   Bolivian Quaker Education Fund

CALA   *Comisión de Alfabetización y Literatura en Aymara* (Commission of Literacy and Literature in Aymara)

CETI   *Centro de Educación Teológica Integral* (Center for Holistic Theological Education)

CIPCA   *Centro de Investigación y Promoción del Campesinado* (Center for Investigation and Promotion of Rural Populations)

COAL   *Comité Organizador para América Latina* (Organizing Committee for Latin America, a part of FWCC)

COB   *Central de Obreros Bolivianos* (Bolivian Workers Central)

COMIBOL   *Corporación Minera de Bolivia* (Mining Corporation of Bolivia)

CTA   *Centro Teológico de Los Amigos* (Friends Theological Center, part of the UEB)

CYM   California Yearly Meeting

EBAD   *Educación Bíblica a Distancia* (Distance Theological Education)

EFA   Evangelical Friends Alliance

EFCI	Evangelical Friends Church International
EFCS	Evangelical Friends Church Southwest
FWCC	Friends World Commission on Consultation
FYM	Five-Years Meeting
GFU	George Fox University
GPWM	Guy P. Woodward Museum (Ramona, CA)
INE	*Instituto Nacional de Estadística* (National Institute of Statistics)
INELA	*Iglesia Nacional Evangélica de Los Amigos* (National Evangelical Friends Church)
IQA	International Quaker Aid, an arm of the FWCC
ISETA	*Instituto Superior de Educación Teológica Los Amigos* (Friends Institute for Theological Higher Education)
MAS	*Movimiento al Socialismo* (Movement Toward Socialism)
MD	*Mesa Directiva*, executive body of the INELA
MIR	*Movimiento de la Izquierda Revolucionaria* (Leftist Revolutionary Movement)
MNR	*Movimiento Nacionalista Revolucionario* (Nationalist Revolutionary Movement)
NGO	Non-Governmental Organization
NHMS	National Holiness Missionary Society
NWYM	Northwest Yearly Meeting
OYM	Oregon Yearly Meeting
QBL	Quaker Bolivia Link
SEAB	*Sociedad Evangélica de Amigos Bolivianos* (Evangelical Society of Bolivian Friends)
SEAN	*Sociedad Evangélica de Amigos Nacionales* (Evangelical Society of National Friends)

SETALA	*Sociedad Evangélica de Tecnología Apropiada de Los Amigos* (Friends Evangelical Society for Appropriate Technology)
TEE	Theological Education by Extension
TSCW	Training School for Christian Workers
UAC	*Universidad Autónoma Católica* (Autonomous Catholic University)
UBC	Union Bible College, in Westfield, Indiana
UCB	*Universidad Católica Boliviana*
UEB	*Universidad Evangélica Boliviana*
UEELA	*Unidad Educativa Evangélica Los Amigos* (Friends Evangelical Educational Unit)
UFINELA	*Unión Femenil de INELA* (Women's Union of Bolivian Friends)
UJELAB	*Unión de Jóvenes Evangélicos de Los Amigos de Bolivia* (Union of Evangelical Friends Youth of Bolivia)
WTSN	*The Witness and Training School News*

Glossary of Spanish and Aymara Terms

acapacha	Ay., realm of the present earth
Actas de la Junta Anual	Yearly Meeting Minutes (INELA)
Actas de la Mesa Directiva	Executive Committee Minutes (INELA)
allaxpacha	Ay., realm of the heavenlies
altiplano	high plain; the area between the eastern and western arms of the Andes in western Bolivia
Awki	Ay., God the Father
ayllu	Ay., old Aymara communities interconnected by complex kinship ties
Buen Amigo	Good Friend
Buen Samaritano	Good Samaritan
cargo	task; a community service role and the way an individual or couple participates in a traditional Aymara community
catequista	catechist in the Catholic Church
ch'amakani	Ay., shaman, specialist who deals with the darker powers
cholo	an urbanized indigenous person; a *mestizo* who is more indigenous than Spanish
chuyma	Ay., heart, place of the emotions and will
colonos	Indians that lived as serfs on the haciendas
comité jurado	pastoral oversight committee

comunitarios	Indians cultivating land in a free community
conquistadores	Spanish conquerors
corregidor	Spanish official appointed to represent the king in a rural town
cursillo	short course
departamento	state (of the country) or department (of an organization)
encargado	someone given a temporary pastoral leadership role in a local church
encomendero	Spanish settler who lived on an *encomienda* as the governor
encomienda	Spanish land grant that governed relations between the colonists and the indigenous peoples
Estado Plurinacional de Bolivia	Plurinational State of Bolivia
estatutos	statutes; the constitution of the church
evangelistas	evangelists; the Catholic term for Protestants in the early twentieth century
gorro	knitted wool cap with ear flaps worn by Aymara men
hacienda	large ranch belonging to a Spanish overlord who managed the serfs who lived on it for agricultural production in the years between the Spanish conquest in the 1500s and the revolution of 1952
jaqechasiña	Ay., to marry, to become a complete person
jaqi	Ay., the complete person, a good person
jilakata	Ay., political and ceremonial leader of a community
Junta Anual	Yearly Meeting, referring either to the annual sessions or to the denomination, a Quaker term
Kollasuyo	Ay., extensive region of the Incan Empire south of Cuzco

kuraka	Ay., leader of the upper part of an Aymaya community (the nobility)
layka	Ay., specialist who deals with the darker powers
mallku	Ay., Aymara leader of a large geographical region
malo	bad
manqhapacha	Ay., realm of the underworld
mesa directiva	executive council; sometimes referred to as *mesa*, and sometimes as *directiva*
mestizo	mixed Spanish and Indian race, edging toward the middle class
mita	in the colonial period, the system of forced labor of Indians, especially in the mines
nayrapacha	Ay., the ancient past
obrero	lay leader, usually someone in pastoral training with a few years left; an official title on the local church level
originario	original (native) inhabitants of a country; synonymous with "indigenous"
Pachamama	Ay., "Mother Earth," important Aymara deity directly involved with agricultural production
padrinazgo	system of god-parents or sponsors
pueblo	town
q'ara	Ay., the irresponsible person
qulliri	Ay., curer
rutuche	rite of the first haircut
salteña	Bolivian vegetable-meat pastry
señorita	young unmarried woman
taypi	Ay., the center, the place of equilibrium and balance

umasuyo	Ay., eastern mountains, *altiplano*, and valleys in the times of the Aymara kingdoms and the Incan Empire
urkosuyo	Ay., western mountains, *altiplano*, and valleys in the times of the Aymara kingdoms and the Incan Empire
usos y costumbres	practices and customs; a reference to whatever cultural customs members of a particular community practice
yatiri	Ay., diviner

Introduction

The Aymara people have a proverb that goes, "*K'achat k'achat wali jayaruw sara-ñani*" (Slowly, slowly, we can journey a long distance). The image that comes to mind is a group of people, perhaps a family, walking up and down a mountain trail, herding a few sheep. They are dressed for the cold with their layers of sweaters, their ponchos and shawls, the *gorros* that cover their heads and ears. Their possessions bundle on their backs. Heads down, they face into the wind. Slowly and steadily they plod onward and upward. They have a great distance to travel, and they know the journey will take a long time.

The saying and the image convey persistence, patience, and hope. They serve as a metaphor for the development of the Friends Church among the Aymara peoples of the Bolivian Andes. Although the story contains its share of drama and some miraculous events, by and large it chronicles "a long walk, a gradual ascent" to maturity. This book aims to tell that story.

The book's subtitle, "The Story of the Bolivian Friends Church in Its Context of Conflict," sets the stage. Conflict, instability, and, at times, violence, have characterized Bolivia's history from the time the church began up to the present. In addition, the culture in which the church grew, the Aymara people, is recognized to be a culture of conflict, as will be seen as the story unfolds. It may be an irony that this should be the setting for the development of a "peace church" such as the Quakers; or it may be a sign of grace.

The particular church this book chronicles goes by the acronym INELA, standing for *Iglesia Nacional Evangélica de Los Amigos* (National Evangelical Friends Church). Other Friends denominations also rose up in Bolivia, coming from different missionary roots, and developing separately. This book focuses on the INELA, although the other groups enter the story. It also tells the story of the mission that accompanied the INELA for seventy-one years of its journey (1931–2002), the Friends Mission from Oregon Yearly Meeting (OYM), now Northwest Yearly Meeting of Friends (NWYM).

The beginnings of the INELA go back to the years between 1915 and 1924 as the first congregation rose up spontaneously and mysteriously on the shores of Lake Titicaca. The first officially recognized Friends church was established in 1924 in La Paz by missionary Juan Ayllón. Today the INELA spreads out into fifteen districts and has somewhere around two hundred congregations. It is an independent yearly meeting with a broad roster of ministries. The INELA is still predominantly Aymara, although it is reaching into other cultures and even other countries.

Our interest in this project began many years ago, but it wasn't until our friend and mentor, Arthur O. Roberts, urged us with his perception that not only did the history of the INELA need to be written, but that we were the ones to do it, did we actually take on the task. We were still under the sponsorship of NWYM as missionaries, with little free time for another project. But the sense of urgency grew until in 2012, the Board of Global Outreach gave permission for us to add this to our job description and we began making plans. After our formal retirement in 2014, we were able to devote more time to the research and writing. We entered this project aware of its demands and the time it would take, but also sensing the call of God to give ourselves to this task.

At the time we began the project, we were seconded by the mission board to an educational organization that offered a PhD in theology to leaders across Latin America (PRODOLA, *Programa Doctoral Latinoamericano*). The job required frequent travel and enabled us to regularly visit Bolivia. We shared with the brethren our task of writing the history of the INELA for the people back home in the Northwest, and their instant response was the recognition of a need for such a history in Spanish for the INELA's constituency. The church's young people represent the fourth and fifth generation of Bolivian Quakers, and most of them do not know the story of their own church. The conversation was spurred on by the fact that the church would soon be celebrating its centennial.

So we began planning together. The idea quickly gained the enthusiasm of the leaders of the INELA. In 2013 and 2014, the INELA and the NWYM (through the Board of Global Outreach) formally agreed to cooperate in the project of writing the history of the INELA. In their annual representatives meeting in January of 2014, the INELA named a history commission to work with us (Hal and Nancy Thomas) in a five-year project, running from 2013 through 2018.

Teamwork defined our methodology throughout the project and allowed us to present the story from both insider (INELA) and outsider (mission) perspectives. Hal and I traveled to Bolivia once a year for a two-month (or longer) stay where we shared our research, discussed the results, and planned the next steps. The commission met once a month throughout the year and included us, while we were in the United States, via Skype. We maintained regular contact.

We defined our research methodology as follows: "The basic research will be documentary, supported by extensive interviews and placed in the historical and cultural contexts in which the INELA has developed. The data collected will be submitted to a process of analysis and interpretation in community."[1]

---

1. Bolivian Friends History Project Proposal, 2013.03.

While in Bolivia, we gathered with our team to check and verify the facts we had gleaned from the archives and field interviews. It was an arduous but necessary task. We included many different leaders in our times of reflection, asking questions of the text, noting the patterns, trying to determine significance and meaning. We attempted to do the work of historical interpretation as a community. It proved a rich and stimulating experience.

We defined our purposes, what we hoped to achieve, for this book in English as follows:

- That readers would come to an understanding of the development of the INELA in its historic and cultural context and thus to a deeper understanding of this church today, as well as insight into the vital role of context in the planting and growing of a church.

- That readers would come to an understanding of the mission's role in the development of the church and how this might apply to an ongoing mission outreach in other parts of the world.

- That readers would appreciate and understand the complexities of denominational emphasis (in this case, Quakerism) in raising up a church in another context.

- That readers would experience a sense of gratitude for all that God has done and a renewed faith in what God is doing and will do in building the church around the world.

As we met together with our Bolivian colleagues to reflect on the different periods of the church's development, we brought four questions to the text, chapter by chapter. These reflected our specific objectives for the book in English. The Bolivian leaders also brought their own questions, reflecting the issues in each decade. The four basic questions were as follows:

- How did the history of the country and/or the Aymara culture affect the development of the INELA in this period?

- What missiological principles or strategies do we see in this period, as reflected by the relationship between the mission and the national church?

- How did the theology and practices of the Friends affect the development of the INELA in this period?

- Where do we see the Spirit of God at work in the development of the INELA in this period?

Some of the results of these rich and challenging discussions come out in the sections entitled "Reflections on the Decade," at the end of each chapter, and in the conclusion to the book.

The meditations on the last question of the movement of the Spirit of God were especially revealing. In the midst of all the struggles, it was often hard to recognize the presence of God building the church. It would have been easy to turn cynical, reflecting on different conflictive periods of the history. But by deliberately asking for wisdom and insight, we were able to discern the slow, steady hand of God on God's people. We were able to recognize growth and transformation through the years, along with the challenges the church still faces. Seeing God's faithfulness in the past, in spite of the hard times and failures, gives courage to face the future, knowing the church belongs to God, and God accompanies God's people as they continue the long walk to maturity.

Before jumping into the history in chapter 1, we need to explain some of the terms used in the book. The first is the word "Indian" in reference to a person or a people native to an area. The Bolivian government refers to them as "original inhabitants" *(orginarios)*, and in the United States we've been taught to use the term "Native American." This is changing, at least in the United States. While "Native American" is still politically correct, many of the tribal people prefer to call themselves Indians, with respect and in recognition of their heritage. All the mission documentation from the 1920s through the 1950s refers to the Aymara Indians. We've chosen to vary the terms as we refer to the Aymara and other original groups in Bolivia.

"Indigenous" is another word important to this story, and we use it in two different senses. The first is a reference to a person or tribal society native to a context. The Aymara, Quechua, and Guarani are all indigenous peoples of Bolivia, having inhabited the land for centuries before the coming of the Spaniards.

But the word "indigenous" also refers to a missiological theory important to the story of the Friends in Bolivia. A mission that adopts the indigenous principle of church planting intends to develop an independent national church that is self-governing, self-supporting, and self-propagating. The theory applies whether or not the recipients are the original inhabitants of a country.

We trust the context makes clear which meaning the word "indigenous" carries.

In a work of this size, covering so many periods and handling so many details, there will be errors. We take full responsibility for those. But we hope that the overall picture this story paints will be true and will serve to encourage the church and glorify that church's Lord.

1

Amacari, Abel, and Ayllón

The Beginnings of the Bolivian Friends Church (1915–1924)

In the community of Amacari, nestled on the eastern shores of Lake Titicaca, a series of unusual events took place between the years 1915 and 1924; these resulted in a gathering of believers unrelated to any denomination or missionary outreach. In Southern California, William Abel, a young man from the Kumeyaay Indian tribe, converted to Christianity in a Friends Church and began in 1900 to prepare for missionary service. Meanwhile, a boy named Juan Ayllón of mixed Aymara/mestizo background migrated from the Yungas valleys in Bolivia to the city of La Paz and encountered Christianity in a life-changing experience. The believers in Amacari, William Abel, and Juan Ayllón would later converge, and the Bolivian Friends Church (INELA) would be born. This chapter explores the joining of these three narrative streams.

HISTORICAL OVERVIEW

The Bolivian Friends Church was not born in a vacuum. Events and movements taking place early in the twentieth century in Bolivia and, indeed, in the rest of the world, would influence the shape this new work would take.

Historians have identified the period between 1880 and 1932 as one of radical political transformation in Bolivia.[1] The most dramatic event of 1880 was Bolivia's defeat to Chile in the War of the Pacific, resulting in the loss of her Pacific coast. Related to that disaster, in the same year the government changed from a military caudillo regime to a system that "represented the first viable republican government of a civilian oligarchic nature."[2] A small group of elite citizens would make the laws and govern the country, and this would remain the norm up through 1934.

---

1. See especially Klein, *Concise History*, locs. 2635–3228, and Gotkowitz, *Revolution*, 1–130.
2. Klein, *Concise History*, loc. 2638.

As historian Herbert Klein observes, "In terms of the Indian peasant masses there was nothing democratic or participatory about the republican governments that existed after 1880."[3] The Bolivian indigenous peoples, although composing a majority of the country's total population (estimated at 51 percent in 1900)[4] played no part in its government. By law they were not even considered citizens; they were not literate, did not own land, and did not earn money for their labor, all requirements for citizenship.

For the first twenty years, government was controlled by the conservative political party, and it took a civil war in 1898/99 for the liberal party to gain the upper hand. In order to succeed, the liberals decided to arm the Indians and, with promises of future justice, encourage the masses to join the revolt.

Shortly after taking over, the new government disarmed the Indians and basically reneged on all their promises. Under the liberal government, suppression of the indigenous populations continued as strong as ever;[5] however, under the surface, Indian resistance was growing, occasionally expressing itself in bursts of violence.

The political development of the country was intimately tied to its economic development. The rise of the twentieth century saw Bolivia's mining industry pass from silver to tin, in a period of prosperity. Bolivia's indigenous populations (mainly Aymara, Quechua, and Guarani) made up most of the mines' working force, and the government was concerned with maintaining and controlling this resource. Regard for civil and human rights was not a priority. In fact, during this period the hacienda system, which used Indian serfs "owned" by the landowner, expanded, while the free Indian communities diminished.[6]

Concurrent with these political and economic changes, Protestantism began making inroads. Although a few attempts had been made in the late nineteenth century, especially with the British and American Bible Societies, at the ascendancy of the liberal government around the turn of the century, five pioneer mission groups began work in Bolivia, these being the Methodists, the Brethren Assemblies, the Canadian Baptists, the Bolivian Indian Mission, and the Seventh-day Adventists.[7] In 1906 the Bolivian constitution was amended to include religious liberty, and for a time, religious persecution was at a low ebb. That would change in 1920. The years between 1920 and 1935, when the INELA experienced its beginnings, saw a return to conservative politics and, at times, strong persecution of the Protestant church. Yet the constitutional guarantee of religious freedom was still on the books.[8]

---

3. Klein, *Concise History*, loc. 2709.

4. Klein, *Concise History*, loc. 2704.

5. Klein, *Concise History*, loc. 2720.

6. Klein, *Concise History*, loc. 2991. See the next chapter concerning the differences between hacienda Indians and free community Indians.

7. H. Thomas, "Bolivia," *Evangelical Dictionary of World Missions*, 136–37.

8. For more detail on early Protestant missions in Bolivia, see chs. 2 and 3 (16–92) of Peter

On a larger scale, in the early part of the twentieth century World War I was raging in Europe (1914–1918). Bolivia was relatively isolated from the rest of the world at that time. The conflict negatively affected the tin economy for the duration of the war, but prices rose again a few years afterward.

This is the context surrounding the beginnings of the Friends work in Bolivia among the Aymara-speaking indigenous people. A certain amount of mythology swirls around all three narratives that form these beginnings: the events in Amacari and the figures of William Abel and Juan Ayllón, the two men considered to be the founders of the Bolivian Friends Church (INELA). Sifting fact from fiction is one of the first tasks of the historian.

THE AMACARI STORY

Amacari is an Aymara fishing and agricultural community on the eastern shores of Lake Titicaca. In the early twentieth century the small Catholic chapel occupied a place of honor in the central plaza, but a priest only rarely visited, and the people were free to practice their traditional animistic customs. Small subsistence farm plots dotted the hills around the village. As a free community, never part of the oppressive hacienda system of the time, people in Amacari were accustomed to making their own decisions. Though relatively isolated, they were free to travel as they wished.

This village is the scene of the first church in what would one day become a group of congregations known as the Bolivian Friends Church (INELA). The descendants of that early gathering in Amacari remember the stories their grandparents handed down. As is typical with oral history several versions of the events compete.

According to one version, the story of the Friends Church in the lake region began perhaps as early as 1915 when Cruz Chipana, a local community leader, made a trip to La Paz, heard the gospel message preached on the street, and experienced conversion. The messages of the preaching evangelist made such an impression that Chipana remembered and repeated them to himself in the following years. He returned to Amacari, told his wife about his experience, but decided to hide it from others for fear of reprisals.[9] Slowly news spread and a small group began to secretly gather.

Wagner's *Protestant Movement in Bolivia.*

9. Carrillo, *Los Amigos*, 31–33.

A community on Lake Titicaca (NWYM)

A different version of the Amacari story begins earlier with a boy named Sebastián Ticona, who traveled with his parents from Amacari to the highland city of Oruro sometime around 1905. While in Oruro, young Ticona heard the gospel story. He memorized some Scripture and learned to read and write. At the age of seventeen, Sebastián Ticona returned to Amacari and privately shared his knowledge of the gospel with Cruz Chipana. Chipana, deeply impressed by this message, became a Christian at that time and secretly began sharing the message with others, gathering a clandestine group of worshipers in his home.[10]

At some time between 1918 and 1924, a crisis forced Chipana out into the open. In an annual fiesta in the large town of Tiquina, where the active participation of the surrounding communities was obligatory, the citizens of Amarcari gained first place in the traditional dance competition. Chipana himself was the leader of the dance and apparently the dancers were the members of his secret church.[11] The people of Tiquina responded to Amacari's triumph with envy and the two groups broke out

10. Juan Ticona, interview with Harold Thomas and Nancy Thomas, January 9, 2015, La Paz.
11. Carillo, *Los Amigos*, 31–33.

in a rock-throwing fight. In the melee, one of the Amacari men broke the foot of the political leader, the *corregidor*, of Tiquina, and people fled back home in fear.[12]

There are several versions of what happened next. One report is that the dance troupe returned to Amacari the next day, were apprehended, and spent time in jail.[13] Another version has the troupe leaders paying a fine and being released to go home.[14] Whether jailed or merely fined, all those involved talked it over, deeply regretting their actions in Tiquina. They together affirmed, "We should change our behavior. We should no longer drink alcohol, get drunk or participate in fiestas because all this brings on consequences of punishment and suffering. Rather we should more firmly convert to the gospel that teaches us not to get drunk or go to fiestas and warns us that the Day of Judgment will come soon and God will destroy evil-doers."[15]

At that point the group formed an open congregation, naming Cruz Chipana as pastor. A group met in Chipana's home and other congregations soon opened in the lake communities of Calata and Chicharro.[16] They met without any relation to an established church or mission.[17]

According to Juan Ticona,[18] concurrently with the story of Cruz Chipana's conversion (whichever version), in the nearby village of Chicharro, Manuel Alvarado Cañawakito was serving as a *catequista* in the Catholic Church and as a helper to the priest in the central town of Tiquina. Alvarado's parents had migrated from Tacna, Peru, to Chicharro when Manuel was still a boy. As a *catequista*, Alvarado was learning much from the Word of God, but things about the Catholic practice and doctrine bothered him, and he decided on his own to separate himself from the Catholic faith. Alvarado seems to have been a natural theologian, and through his study of the Scriptures he developed his belief in the sovereign power of God, who is greater than all the animistic forces that filled the Aymara cosmos and inspired fear in the people, who protects his people and frees them from curses and disease. He also came to believe that people should not worship idols or the images of saints and virgins, that these were merely man-made statues and carried no power. He insisted that followers of

12. Carrillo, Ticona, and Aruquipa coincide in this incident in Tiquina and its importance, although the details vary.

13. Carillo, *Los Amigos*, 31–33.

14. Juan Ticona, interview with Harold Thomas and Nancy Thomas, January 9, 2015, La Paz.

15. Carillo, *Los Amigos*, 32.

16. Carillo, *Los Amigos*, 32.

17. An alternate version has Cruz Chipana, not yet a Christian and deeply shaken by the Tiquina incident, going to La Paz in 1919, and becoming a Christian at that time in an open-air meeting. This version also has him purchasing his first Bible from William Abel (Cirilo Aruquipa, quoting his grandfather, Baltazar Yujra, in an interview with Harold Thomas and Nancy Thomas, January 20, 2015, La Paz).

18. This part of the story comes from my interview with Juan Ticona in La Paz (January 9, 2015), as well as from an unpublished manuscript by Ticona (no date) given to Humberto Gutiérrez in 2015. Ticona himself gives contradictory versions of some of the details.

Jesus should not participate in the ritual drunkenness that was part of the syncretistic blend of Aymara animism and Catholicism.[19]

Manuel Alvarado and wife, ca. 1930 (NWYM)

Several versions of the connection between Manuel Alvarado and the believers in Amacari exist. One has Alvarado coming to Amarcari around 1917 to preach the

19. Details about Alvarado's theology and messages come from Humberto Gutierrez's interviews with the adult children of Baltazar Yujra (Josefina Yujra), Nicolás Cáceres (Celso Cáceres), and Manuel Poma (Andrés Poma), who were part of the early church in Amacari. The interviews were conducted on May 20, 2015, in Amacari. INELA archives.

gospel, leading to the conversions of Sebastián Ticona and Cruz Chipana.[20] Another version has it that Alvarado heard about the believers who were already gathered in Amacari and came to visit them. He began teaching them some of what he had learned about the Bible from his time as a *catequista*. It was Alvarado who told the believers of Amacari that they needed to give up chewing coca as part of their worship, along with some of their other cultural customs.[21]

However it happened, the ministry of Manuel Alvarado in Amacari contributed to the stability of the group of new believers. Several conversion stories strengthen this conclusion. Baltazar Yujra was one of the early leaders of this church. He became a believer thanks to the message of Alvarado, who told him he need not fear the evil spirits that were threatening to kill him, that God was all-powerful and could protect him against any threat.[22] Another testimony comes from Nicolás Cáceres, one of the early believers, who claimed to have seen the devil, which always resulted in death, but Alvarado told him to go to the believers in Amacari for prayer, and he would be healed from the curse.[23]

Alvarado was a gifted evangelist, and, according to INELA historian Humberto Gutiérrez, "Manuel Alvarado's participation was fundamental in the diffusion of the message of the gospel"[24] in the whole area around Lake Titicaca. According to the testimony of Josefina Yujra, daughter of Baltazar Yujra, Alvarado spent years evangelizing, mounted on his grey donkey and wearing his wide-brimmed hat. Rumors have it that he lived to a very ripe old age; some say he was around 145 years old when he died.[25] His influence extended beyond the Friends, but certainly included them.

In spite of differing versions and dates, part of the nature of oral history, what we can glean is that God was clearly at work in Amacari and other areas around Lake Titicaca before the appearance of missionaries. The names Cruz Chipana, Sebastián Ticona, Baltazar Yujra, and Manuel Alvarado appear in many of the stories, as well as in other documents of the early Friends Church in Bolivia. The Spirit was preparing the way, drawing people to God, getting ready for the planting of the Friends Church in Aymara soil.

THE STORY OF WILLIAM ABEL

The second narrative stream in the beginnings of the Friends Church in Bolivia takes us north to a Native American tribe in Southern California, and a series of events that would lead to La Paz in 1919. Although William Abel's actual time as a missionary in

---

20. Juan Ticona, unpublished manuscript, n.d., INELA archives.

21. Juan Ticona, interview with Harold Thomas and Nancy Thomas, January 9, 2015, La Paz.

22. Josefina Yujra, interview with Humberto Gutiérrez, May 20, 2015, Amacari. INELA archives.

23. Celso Cáceres, interview with Humberto Gutiérrez, May 20, 2015, Amacari. INELA archives.

24. Humberto Gutiérrez, interview with Harold Thomas and Nancy Thomas, January 26, 2016, La Paz.

25. Josefina Yujra, interview with Humberto Gutérrez, May 20, 2015, Amacari, INELA archives.

Bolivia was less than a year, Bolivian Friends consider him one of their founders and a hero of the faith.

Cultural-Historical Background

William Abel was born around 1870[26] in San Pasqual, California, a village that had been reserved for members of the Kumeyaay tribe.[27] At the time of his birth there were estimated to be about 195 members of the tribe living in the village,[28] along with some Euro-American and Mexican squatters. Within a decade all the Indians would be gone from San Pasqual.

The Indians had inhabited this land for centuries.[29] Traditionally, the Kumeyaay tribe was believed to have been composed of different bands living in semipermanent settlements near water sources during certain seasons and dispersed for hunting and gathering during other seasons.[30]

Beginning in the mid-eighteenth century, three succeeding conquering forces would disrupt and forever change the Kumeyaay culture. In 1769, the Spanish *conquistadores*, followed by the Catholic missions, entered what is today Southern California, dominating and subjugating all indigenous tribes in the region. The Franciscan Mission established at San Diego had jurisdiction over the San Pasqual Valley, and many Indians were forced to live at the mission and work the lands, while others continued on their original lands, but not as free people. As historian Bernard Duffy notes, "This missionization process disrupted all aspects of [Indian] culture,"[31] and, along with the foreign diseases, resulted in a high death rate.

Historian Richard Carrico adds that, "in spite of the efforts of the Spanish missionaries to convert the Kumeyaay to Christianity and of the presidial military forces to subdue them, large segments of the Kumeyaay population resisted and resented the European intrusion."[32]

---

26. In the 1880 national census, the man he was living with in Ballena, California, identifies Abel as being twelve years old, thus putting his birthdate at 1868. The 1890 census for California was destroyed in a fire. In the 1900 census, Abel, then living in Whittier, California, identifies himself as being thirty years old, putting his birthdate at 1870. Several years earlier, in 1897, he reported being "about" twenty-five years old, with a birthdate in 1872. Obviously, he didn't know exactly when he was born. Based on the fact that the 1870 census bears no record of a child named William Abel, we have some basis to conclude that he was probably born after June of 1870.

27. They are also referred to as "Mission Indians" or "Northern Diegueño Indians." For a history and description of the Kumeyaay, see Carrico, *Strangers*; Peet, *San Pasqual*; or Roberts, *San Pasqual*.

28. Carrico, *Strangers*, 84.

29. Archeological evidence indicates that the area has been inhabited for 9,500 years. Evidence for the Kumayaay tribe dates back 2,000 years (Carrico, *Strangers*, 1–17).

30. For a more complete description of Kumeyaay life before 1769, see Carrico, *Strangers*, 1–17.

31. Bernard Duffy, unpublished manuscript, n.d., 161, GBWM archives. See also Carrico, *Strangers*, 19–49.

32. Carrico, *Strangers*, 31.

The people entered a new historical period in 1821 when the Mexican republic overthrew the Spaniards. The years between 1821 and 1848 saw a decreasing of the influence of the missions. In 1838, the Mexican overlords had declared San Pasqual an Indian *pueblo*, and many of the mission Indians returned to live there.[33] Yet under Mexican government, "the Indians became serfs, trespassers on their own lands, rebels, or fugitives."[34]

The period of Mexican domination was followed by that of the United States at the end of the Mexican-American War in 1848. Under neither of the two groups did the fate of the Indians improve for long.

In 1850 the State of California passed a series of state regulations known as "An Act for the Government and Protection of Indians," also referred to as the "Statute for the Punishment and Protection of Indians," or, simply, "The Indian Act." Section 3 of the statute legalized indentured servitude of Indian children, a custom already being practiced. Another section of the statute prohibited mistreatment, but this provision was hard to enforce. The statute did nothing to guarantee Indian land rights. This statute was the law of the land for more than thirty years.[35]

The Common School Act of 1855 legalized the exclusion of minority children from public schools. In 1866 the law was modified to allow schooling for mixed-blood Indians and for Indian children living as indentured servants with white families. An 1874 law provided for separate Indian schools, with a provision that if no such school were available, an Indian child could attend a white school.[36] These various laws would directly affect William Abel as he grew up.

When he assumed office as president of the United States in 1869, U. S. Grant began to put into action an Indian Peace Plan, an attempt to rectify past injustices. He instituted a Board of Indian Commissioners to help establish reservations and disburse funds. Interestingly enough, this included "placing many of the Indian Agencies in the hands of Quakers, eliminating much of the patronage that had led to the spoils system being rife in Indian affairs, and lessening the power of the military in Indian affairs."[37]

On January 31, 1870, President Grant signed an executive order establishing the San Pasqual Indian Reservation, including four thousand acres in the San Pasqual Valley. During the rest of the year, California newspapers and legislators campaigned heavily against the reservation, responding to the demands of the settlers. As a result, on February 25, 1871, Grant revoked his order, placing more than sixty-nine thousand set-aside acres throughout the United States in the public domain, open to the land

33. Carrico, *Strangers*, 43.

34. Bernard Duffy, unpublished manuscript, n.d., 161–62, GBWM archives.

35. Carrico, *Strangers*, 53–57.

36. Carrico, *Strangers*, 57–58.

37. Carrico, *Strangers*, 109.

claims of any settler.[38] Duffy reports that "immediately after the executive order was revoked, non-Indian settlers moved in and filed homestead claims on Indian lands in the San Pasqual Valley and surrounding regions. The settlers then had the sheriff evict the Indians from their adobe homes, farms, orchards and grazing lands."[39] While some Indians left immediately, there is evidence that the eviction gradually took place throughout the 1870s, but by the end of the decade, no Indians were left in the San Pasqual Valley. In 1910, a reservation for the San Pasqual Kumeyaay Indians was established in Valley Center, north of the San Pasqual Valley, in land that is hilly, rocky, and much less fertile than their ancestral lands. Today it continues as a reservation and tribal center.[40]

In 1870, in the midst of this turmoil and trauma, William Abel was born in San Pasqual.

Ethnicity and Family Origins

In the literature William Abel is usually referred to as an "Indian," and, in fact, this is how he self-identifies.[41] However, other sources refer to him as a "half-breed Indian,"[42] a "Mexican,"[43] or a "Mexican-Indian." A few secondary sources refer to a "Dutch Jewish" father.[44] The name William Abel is neither Mexican nor Indian.

Both Bernard Duffy and Mary Rockwood Peet, historians, record the presence of a settler in San Pasqual named Peter Abel during the years immediately preceding William Abel's birth. Duffy affirms that he was a non-Indian American "squatting on the public lands in San Pasqual" in 1869.[45] Peet entitles one chapter in her history of San Pasqual, "Who Killed Abel?" Peter Abel owned a horse ranch, and he was killed in a squabble with another settler around 1870. The name of the killer remains a mystery (hence the chapter title) and there exist several versions of the story of his death. One version has it that a neighbor's cows jumped the moat Abel had built around his vegetable garden, thus ruining his broccoli and cucumbers. As Abel ran in the house to get his gun, the neighbor shot him in the back.[46]

---

38. Bernard Duffy, unpublished manuscript, n.d., 156–57, GBWM archives; Carrico, *Strangers*, 108–13.

39. Bernard Duffy, unpublished manuscript, n.d., 157, GBWM archives.

40. For more information on the current situation, visit the tribal web site at http://www.sanpasqualbandofmissionindians.org.

41. For example, in a letter from the Philippines back to K. C. Beckwith of the Ramona Friends Church in 1911, he calls himself "Your Indian brother in Jesus" ("Philippine Islands," *Pacific Friend* 20, no. 7 (1911) 8, EFCS archives.

42. CYM Minutes, 1930, 53, EFCS archives.

43. Tilman Hobson, "Church Work, Ramona," *Christian Workman* 7, nos. 2–3 (1899) 10, EFCS archives.

44. "Through His Grace," *Friends Minister*, October 14, 1920, 6, UBC archives.

45. Bernard Duffy, unpublished manuscript, n.d., 156, GBWM archives.

46. Peet, *San Pasqual*, 56.

Was there a relationship between Peter Abel and William Abel? William Abel claimed that by the age of eight he was an orphan. If Peter Abel was his father, William could have been born and bereft of one parent in the same year, with his mother dying several years later. Or it could have been that the Indian lad was indentured to Peter Abel and took his last name (or had it given to him) from the white family.

We can conclude that his ancestry largely stems from the San Pasqual Kumeyaay tribal group, with perhaps some Mexican blood in his background. In a testimony he wrote in 1900, Abel differentiated himself ethnically from the "Americans." He wrote that, "living as I did among the Americans, and my studies all being in English, I forgot for the most part my own language."[47] When writing of "my language" or "my people,"[48] he was referring to his Indian heritage.

Childhood

William Abel was born and lived in San Pasqual for at least some of his childhood years. By the time he was eight years old, he was orphaned. This time span corresponds to the revoking of the land treaty in 1871 and the gradual eviction of the Indians.

Historian Elizabeth Judson Roberts came from a family of settlers that moved into San Pasqual in 1875. She was a child at the time, and her memories of the Indian village paint a picture of what would have been William Abel's childhood experience. She described the Indian village as consisting of small adobe houses on the slopes of the hills and brush huts on the flat land. Writing of the Indians, she noted, "I was never afraid of the Indians and a favorite diversion was to mount the pretty black pony Father had given me and gallop down to the Indian Rancheria. Tying my pony to a willow tree, I would then wander from hut to hut through the village, watching the brown, more or less naked, children play or the squaws as they washed their clothes on a stone at the edge of the lagoon, or pounded acorns and grain into meal in their stone *metatas*."[49]

We don't know where William Abel lived—on the slope of the village in an adobe house, in the flat places in a brush hut, or on the settlement of a white squatter. Judson Roberts also mentions a small Catholic chapel in the village and the priest, Father Uback, who came once a month to hold services for the Indians.[50]

47. William Abel, "Work among the Spanish People," *Christian Workman* 1, nos. 5–6 (1900) 7, EFCS archives.

48. William Abel, "Work among the Spanish People," *Christian Workman* 1, nos. 5–6 (1990) 8. This testimony was originally published in a magazine called *Spanish Evangel* in 1900 and reprinted in the Friends magazine, *Christian Workman*. It may have represented the concern of the Rev. A. B. Case, a missionary with the Spanish Missionary Society of California and teacher of Spanish in the Training School for Christian Workers at the time when William Abel was a student. Case would naturally have focused on the Mexican side of Abel's ethnicity.

49. Roberts, *San Pasqual*, 19.

50. Roberts, *San Pasqual*, 20, 23.

William Abel had lost both parents by the age of eight and found himself living for a time with his grandfather in the mountain village of Julian. He noted that he "was left mostly to look after myself."[51] In his 1900 testimonial, written semi-anonymously as "A Goat Herder,"[52] he gave a brief picture of his ten years in the area around Julian and his work herding first goats, then pigs, and finally, cattle. In his first job, herding goats, he said he made his living, "such as it was," and earned $5 a year. This corresponds to the conditions and customs of an indentured child servant. Summing up his misadventures as a child goatherd, Abel wrote,

> But I didn't know how to herd goats, and the American for whom I worked was hard on me, oftentimes my flock would wander away from my care. The goats would climb up the mountain, on and on to the highest rock and there lie down. I would follow and by the time I was with them at the top, I would think it was a good place to lie down too. I was tired and while the goats were resting I would go to sleep.[53]

He added that once upon waking and finding the goats escaped, he became frightened of the consequences and ran away, thus ending two years as a goat herder.

Abel tells of his next two years herding pigs, noting, "I didn't know how to herd hogs any better than I did goats."[54] This probably was from 1880 to 1882 and corresponds to the US Census records for the township of Ballena, in a valley near Julian. The 1880 census states that William Abel, a twelve-year-old Indian, was part of the household of Lyman and Rose Graves, ages twenty-eight and twenty-two, with no children of their own at that time. Lyman was a farmer, Rose a homemaker, and they record Abel as being a herder. The recorded age is obviously a guess, as Abel did not know the date of his birth. He was more likely ten years old at the time of the census.[55]

He goes on to explain the details of being fired from this job after two years: "The occasion of my leaving them [the hogs] was this: I had let them run into the dry foxtail so much that, strange as it may seem, the eyes of many had become destroyed, the eyeballs emptied by the barbs which had pierced them. My master, when he discovered this, accused me of having punched out their eyes with my thumb, and so he fired me."[56]

---

51. William Abel, "Work among the Spanish People," *Christian Workman* 1, nos. 5–6 (1900) 7, EFCS archives.

52. William Abel, "Work among the Spanish People," *Christian Workman* 1, nos. 5–6 (1900) 7–8, EFCS archives.

53. William Abel, "Work among the Spanish People," *Christian Workman* 1, nos. 5–6 (1900) 7, EFCS archives.

54. William Abel, "Work among the Spanish People," *Christian Workman* 1, nos. 5–6 (1900) 7, EFCS archives.

55. US Census of 1880.

56. William Abel, "Work among the Spanish People," *Christian Workman* 1, nos. 5–6 (1900) 7, EFCS archives.

William Abel would then have been about eleven or twelve years old, and here he notes that his life changed for the better. He got a job herding cattle and was given a horse to ride. And "yet," he writes, "I was still a child, and didn't well understand my business for occasionally my charge would get into the unfenced grain fields. I always had to stand the blame, and lots of it."[57]

During his ten years as an indentured servant herder, he had not gone to any school. But by the time he was eighteen years old and free, William Abel had saved enough money to move to the nearby town of Ramona and begin his education. This would have been around 1888. At that time, Ramona was a town of between five hundred and six hundred people, known as a farming, fruit, and stock raising region.[58]

In Ramona William Abel obtained room and board with "an American family" and enrolled in the first grade. He described this experience: "I did not know my letters, but entered the public school. I was put in the first grade with the little children. I was ashamed, but I staid by and in three years I had passed the sixth grade, leaving the little ones behind, but I worked for it, studying almost night and day."[59] He would have graduated around 1891.

We don't know what Abel's relationship to the American family was, but there is some indication he may have been apprenticed to a butcher. Copies of the Ramona newspaper, the *Sentinel*, between the years of 1893 and 1897 carry an advertisement for the Nuevo Meat Market. (Nuevo was the original name of Ramona.) The ad informs: "Fresh meat always on hand. Fresh sausage every week. Meat delivered at San Pasqual, Poway and the surrounding country. Give me your patronage. Main Street, Nuevo, Cal. Wm. Abell, Prop."[60]

It's worthy of note that this young man had come from an Indian village and a childhood of indentured servanthood, without schooling, to become the owner of a respectable business in town, a position that he held for at least seven years, until he moved from Ramona in 1900. The news column of an issue of the *Sentinel* in June of 1897, "Here and There," notes simply that "William Abel is in San Diego."[61] The rest of

57. William Abel, "Work among the Spanish People," *Christian Workman* 1, nos. 5–6 (1900) 7, EFCS archives. An undocumented biography of Abel, published in the *Friends Minister*, of the Union Bible College, Westfield, Indiana, in 1920 gives a different version of Abel's childhood. This version of the story has Abel leaving Julian after only one year, not mentioning a grandfather, and has him returning to live in San Pasqual with a cousin, Thomas Curo, until he was fifteen, at which time he goes to Ramona ("Through His Grace," *Friends Minister*, October 14, 1920, 6–7, UBC archives). Given the fact of the eviction of Indians from San Pasqual, this doesn't seem likely.

58. Q. A. R. Holton, "Ramona," *Christian Workman* 5, nos. 2–3 (1897) 11, EFCS archives.

59. William Abel, "Work among the Spanish People," *Christian Workman* 1, nos. 5–6 (1900) 7, EFCS archives.

60. *Sentinel*, newspaper of Ramona, California, July 27, 1893; February 15, 1894; February 22, 1894; June 24, 1987. Other editions of the *Sentinel* were not available. Abel's name was spelled in a variety of ways: Abel (the most common), Abell, and Able. GBWM archives.

61. *Sentinel*, June 24,1897, GBWM archives.

the column is filled with similarly brief tidbits about local Anglo citizens. It seems that William Abel had become an accepted member of Ramona society.

Apparently problems with drinking and gambling interfered with his work.[62] In a 1911 letter sent from the Philippines to Friends in Ramona, he remembered that "Ramona is the home town of my young days and where I spent my life, mostly in pleasure and sin."[63] This picture of drinking and carousing, part of his conversion testimony, needs to be balanced with the picture of William Abel, proprietor of the Nuevo Meat Market.

Conversion

The history of the Ramona Friends Church dates back to 1883 with the arrival of the Q. A. R. Holton family to the town. They were joined in 1887 by a Quaker minister from Kansas, W. E. Mills, along with J. H. Thomas, James Williams, and their families. They made plans to establish a Friends work in Ramona, beginning with a Union Sunday School open to Christians of all denominations. The first regular Friends meeting was established in 1891, under the leadership of Mills, and in July of 1892, Ramona Friends Church was recognized as a monthly meeting, under the Pasadena Quarterly Meeting of the California Yearly Meeting of Friends Church.[64] All of this was simultaneous with William Abel's move to Ramona and his educational experience in the public school. There seems to have been little contact between Abel and the church up to 1897.

In September of 1897, Levi Gregory, superintendent of evangelism for California Yearly Meeting, held a three-week series of evangelistic meetings in the Ramona Friends Church. He was accompanied by Tilman Hobson of Pasadena Monthly Meeting. In the subsequent literature, these meetings are referred as the "Ramona Revival." Fannie Kirkman of Ramona described the experience:

> During their stay here [Gregory and Hobson], they visited most of the families and held 48 meetings, besides working in the Sabbath School and Christian Endeavor Meetings.
>
> The attendance was very good at these Meetings. There were about twenty conversions and renewals and fourteen persons gave in their names to become members of the church. There has been such plain and earnest teaching. The gospel was truly preached in its fullness.
>
> The leaven is working and it is our earnest prayer that the good work will go on. We believe the Christian people were awakened to their responsibility, as never before and will unite their efforts to build up Christ's kingdom in this place.

62. "Through His Grace," *Friends Minister*, October 14, 1920, 6, UBC archives.

63. William Abel, "Philippine Islands," *Pacific Friend* 20, no. 7 (1911) 7, EFCS archives.

64. Q. A. R. Holton, "Ramona," *Christian Workman* 5, nos. 5–6 (1897) 11, EFCS archives.

Bro. Gregory's teachings to the Christians and helps over hard places in the day meetings were very much appreciated. He seemed to leave nothing unsaid and we believe the work done by these earnest and faithful ministers will bring an abundant reaping by and by.[65]

There is little doubt that William Abel is one of the twenty some converts referred to, although we have yet to find the details of the experience in his own words. We do find several general references to his conversion through Ramona Friends in 1897.[66] One of these comes from a letter Helen Oakley sent to Laura Trachsel in 1977. Oakley, veteran Friends missionary to Guatemala, recounts a conversation between Lavina Rice, Viola Walton, and herself about William Abel. These three women grew up in California Yearly Meeting, and they were recalling things their parents had told them about Abel (the parents having heard first hand when Abel preached in one of the Friends churches). Oakley writes that the three women remembered that Abel "was an Indian of southern Calif., living back from San Diego. He understood not too much English, probably spoke some Spanish; he entered the little Friends Church in Ramona, during some special meetings; drunk and not understanding much, he accepted the Lord; but the next morning he found his desire for liquor was gone, and knew something had happened."[67]

The revival lasted for several years. In 1898, Levi Gregory revisited Ramona to encourage those who had decided to follow Christ. Tilman Hobson, newly appointed pastor to the Ramona Friends Church, writes about Gregory's visit, "His time was largely spent in visiting families during the day and in preaching with mighty power at night."[68] Hobson reports again in 1899, "We frequently have overflow meetings. . . . No time for preaching but spontaneous prayers, praise, and testimonies, and hands raising for prayers. Oh such wonderful love!"[69]

In that same 1899 report, Hobson notes special offerings given toward the new parsonage project: "Donations were solicited. One friend put in fourteen acres of grain for the Lord's work. Another gave the use of twenty acres of ground and plowed it. Others contributed grain and work and planted it. A Methodist gave a horse, a young Mexican who was converted at the revivals gave $5. Some tithed, others gave work, etc., etc. Some gave money, many prayed and *all* are interested."[70]

---

65. Fannie Kirkman, "Good Work," *Christian Workman* 5, no. 11 (1897) 7, EFCS archives.

66. William Abel, "Work among the Spanish People, *Christian Workman* 1, nos. 5–6 (1900) 7; "Philippine Islands," *Pacific Friend* 20, no. 7 (1911) 7–8, EFCS archives.

67. Helen Oakley, letter to Laura Trachel, n.d. (1977), EFCS archives.

68. Tilman Hobson, *Christian Workman* 6, no. 12 (1898) 7, EFCS archives.

69. Tilman Hobson, "Church Work, Ramona," *Christian Workman* 7, nos. 2–3 (1899) 10, EFCS archives.

70. Tilman Hobson, "Church Work, Ramona," *Christian Workman* 7, nos. 2–3 (1899) 10, EFCS archives.

The generous "young Mexican" was probably William Abel. It's interesting to note that $5 would have been his annual wage several years back when he worked as a goat-herder. The amount sounds small, but for some reason Hobson found it significant enough to include in his report. Abel continued to earn his living at this time as a butcher in Ramona.[71]

William Abel's conversion was genuine and the two following years found him still among Friends at Ramona, maturing as a new Christian.

The Training School for Christian Workers

For many years leaders in California Yearly Meeting had been talking about the need for a Bible training school for the formation of pastors and missionaries.[72] On March 3, 1899, seven California Quaker leaders and one Methodist evangelist met in Whittier to wait on the Lord for guidance and formulate plans. Among those Quaker leaders was Levi Gregory, still yearly meeting superintendent for evangelism and the pastor who had led in the Ramona revival meetings where William Abel became a Christian.[73]

The group met again on September 19 and December 26 and drew up a constitution for the new training school. Doctrinal matters were paramount, with an emphasis on the Trinity, the authority of Scripture, the sinful state of humanity and the need for the Savior, "entire sanctification" of the believer, and, as the final point, the "speedy evangelism of the world."[74]

Although the intent from the beginning was to make this an interdenominational school, the founders were predominantly Quaker. The first chairman of the board was Irvin H. Cammack, also the superintendent of missions for California Yearly Meeting. The first classes were held in Philena Hadley's home in Whittier (Philena was the vice president of the yearly meeting's Women's Foreign Missionary Society). Mary A. Hill, a Quaker from Ohio was invited to be the first president.

At this point it would be good to note the influence of the American Holiness Movement on this new training school. Affected by the Second Great Awakening of the late eighteenth century, this movement took form in the mid-1880s. Theologically Arminian in nature, it emphasized complete sanctification, the authority of Scripture, and involvement in world missions. Its appeal crossed denominational lines and included evangelical Friends. Around the turn of the century (1900), a number of Bible training schools rose up in its wake, and these focused on the preparation of consecrated Christian workers on the local and international level. As we will see later in this book, the holiness ethos and doctrines, especially as they flowed out of the Bible

---

71. R. Esther Smith, "Beautiful Story," *Harvester* 17, no. 1 (1923) 2–3, EFCS archives.

72. *Christian Workman* 7, nos. 4–5 (1899) 2, EFCS archives.

73. Jackson, *Azusa Pacific University*, 4.

74. Jackson, *Azusa Pacific University*, 5.

training schools, would profoundly affect missionary work in Bolivia and the nature of the church that rose out of it.[75]

When the Training School for Christian Workers opened in February 1900, William Abel of Ramona was one of the first two students to enroll. By the end of the first term, the school had twelve students, and these numbers would slowly grow over the next few years. (Today, the seed that was planted as the Training School for Christian Workers has grown into Azusa Pacific University. But that's another story.)

The 1900 US Census for the city of Whittier records William Abel as thirty years old (born in 1870) and living as a boarder in the home of Jesse and Esther Butler.[76] While Abel was a nonresident student, most of the students lived in the school. Abel probably participated in most of the activities. An account of the daily routine gives insight into the formation he received. After breakfast at 6:00, 6:30–7:00 was spent in worship, a Scripture lesson and prayer. This was followed by a work hour; students did all the cleaning, thus bringing down living expenses to $1.50 per student, per week. From 8:00–9:00 students had personal devotions in their rooms. The rest of the morning was given to faculty lectures and study time. Afternoons and evenings were devoted to study and different ministry opportunities.[77] Class content centered on Bible, theology, and practical ministry.

The school presented a strong focus on preparation for missionary service, with special emphasis on China, Central America, and local ministry among Native Americans. The school's first catalog and prospectus states that the objectives of the school included "to impart information concerning mission fields; to inspire missionary enthusiasm; and to cultivate a passion for winning souls. . . . We would see this school as a hotbed of germinating missionaries."[78] R. Esther Smith, one of Abel's classmates, would soon leave to become a missionary leader of the Friends work in Guatemala (and a figure in the history of the INELA). His teacher and school principal, Mary Hill, also left to begin a missionary work in China. J. Hudson Taylor was one of the chapel speakers in 1900 or 1901.

William Abel's experience at the training school was profound. In the school's newsletter we read that in 1900 when the school first opened, "William Abel was perhaps the first student to receive the Pentecostal Baptism, if we remember correctly, at the first Monday night prayer meeting, and it soon became evident the hand of God was placed upon him for blessed and fruitful service in winning souls."[79] The same news article mentions that during the school break, Abel "has gone to the mountain

75. For more detail on the "Holiness Movement," see the article by that name by H. E. Raser. Concerning the effect of the holiness movement on Friends missions in the first half of the twentieth century, see R. Stansell, *Missions by the Spirit*.

76. US Census of 1900.

77. "Day in the School," *WTSN* 1, no. 2 (1901) 7, APU archives.

78. Jackson, *Azusa Pacific University*, 7.

79. *WTSN* 1, no. 2 (1901) 12, APU archives.

regions of San Diego County to carry the good tidings of a Savior's love to his Indian brethren."[80] Quaker historian Sheldon Jackson notes that "he dedicated his life to Christ during the first Training School sessions in Hadley's Whittier home. Full of enthusiasm, he organized the school's first Gospel team."[81]

Abel occasionally preached in Friends churches in California, and he spoke in the manner of Friends, perhaps influenced by the example of Amos Kenworthy, a frequent speaker in the Training School's chapel services. In an article written several years later, Quaker Dana Thomas remembers "seeing many large audiences composed of cultured, intelligent people, who were moved in a wonderful manner by this simple native. He was a true Friend, refusing to address meetings where he did not feel the Spirit's leading."[82]

During those early years of the training school, a certain informality predominated, at least in terms of any degree completion program. At any rate, William Abel did not finish the school's program, but left after two years, swept up in the passion for missions that would take him to the Philippine Islands for the next eleven years.

Missionary Experience in the Philippines

On April 8, 1902, having joined the Peniel Mission of California, William Abel set sail for the Philippine Islands. He was accompanied by C. G. Carlson, "a Swede from California."[83] R. Esther Smith reported that "they go out with the Lord's anointing and at His sending. It was indeed a precious time to the 100 who stood on the wharf to wave them farewell. Tears stood in many eyes and songs of hallelujahs rang from many hearts as these two spirit-filled young men stepped out for Him to tell Christless creatures about Christ."[84]

Dana Thomas (later missionary to Alaska) recalls the send-off: "Hundreds of church and mission people gathered at the pier to bid him Good-speed on the day when his steamer sailed. I recall humble William Abel trying to escape from the seeming plaudits of the people, shrinking behind some of the freight piled upon the vessel's deck."[85] He sailed carrying 1,500 Spanish New Testaments with him.[86] While Abel was not officially a Friends missionary, the yearly meeting was aware of him and his missionary work, even providing some financial support.[87]

---

80. *WTSN* 1, no. 2 (1901) 12, APU archives.

81. Jackson, *Azusa Pacific University*, 11.

82. Dana Thomas, "Voice from the Philippines," *WTSN* 6, no. 5 (1907) 5–6, APU archives.

83. R. Esther Smith, "Missionary Department," *Christian Workman* 10, no. 4 (1902) 3, EFCS archives.

84. R. Esther Smith, "Missionary Department," *Christian Workman* 10, no. 4 (1902) 3, EFCS archives.

85. Dana Thomas, "Voice from the Philippines," *WTSN* 6, no. 5 (1907) 6, APU archives.

86. *Friends Missionary Advocate* 18, no. 4 (1902) 54, Earlham College archives.

87. CYM Minutes, 1902, 42, 48, EFCS archives.

Details of Abel's eleven years in the Philippines are scant, coming mainly from the few letters he sent to the Training School for Christian Workers or to friends in California Yearly Meeting. Peniel Mission historian Paul A. Hittson notes that for a time Abel and Carlson worked together as the only Peniel missionaries in the country, and that soon Abel served alone; he admits that there is little or no information about those years,[88] although Abel seems to have written letters to Manie Ferguson, cofounder of Peniel Missions.[89] He also seems to have kept contact with the Ramona Friends Church, as evidenced by a letter he wrote to that congregation in 1911. The financial records of the congregation show that the Ramona Sunday school consistently sent Abel offerings.[90]

Abel wrote a letter to the Training School for Christian Workers on February 1, 1903. While not giving any details about his work, he writes a great deal about the importance of prayer and referred to the difficulty of the context and the "hate of the natives toward the American."[91]

On May 14, 1903, Abel wrote a long letter to I. H. Cammack that mentions his ministry of Bible distribution and notes that many people were coming to faith in Christ out of Roman Catholicism. He wrote that "no one ever came here with the gospel. We are their first visitors."[92] He was ministering among Spanish speakers.[93]

In several letters back to the training school, Abel acknowledged his mistake in not completing his course of studies.[94] He warned training school students with the following words:

> Men and women who come as missionaries should be well equipped.
>
> There is no greater mistake than to suppose that a man needs less preparation for Philippines than for England. If it be difficult to maintain a ministry in one's mother tongue, how much more so in acquired language? All the call that would be made on him in a home church will be made on the missionary here and more—He will have to meet and answer men of all shades of

---

88. Hittson, *History of Peniel Missions*, 75.

89. We learn of these letters in an article that appeared in the *Friends Minister* in 1920 ("Through His Grace," 6, UBC archives). The letters themselves have been lost.

90. The *Ramona Friends Journal* (record book) for 1901 indicates that the Sunday school was supporting him while he was still in the Training School (a total of $4.48 for July through November). The minutes of the meeting for January 17, 1904, record the decision to divide the year's missionary offerings between William Abel and one Alice Jimmer (possibly a misspelling of Zimmer, a missionary to Guatemala). The annual Sunday school report for 1904 records a total of $15 sent to William Abel (January 1, 1905). The church's treasurer's report for the period between March 31, 1911, and March 31, 1912, shows a total of $10.80 sent to William Abel. That was his last year in the Philippines. Other records for the church were not available. EFCS archives.

91. William Abel, "From the Philippines," *WTSN* 2, no. 6 (1903) 5, APU archives.

92. William Abel, "From the Fields," *WTSN* 3 (1903) 2–3, APU archives.

93. Dana Thomas, "Voice from the Philippines," *WTSN* 6, no. 5 (1907) 5, APU archives.

94. Dana Thomas, "Voice from the Philippines," *WTSN* 6, no. 5 (1907) 5; W. Abel, "Wm. C. Abel," *WTSN* 3, no. 5 (1904) 6, APU archives.

opinion—his whole future success in a new town may be influenced by his ability or inability to answer fully those who will try to trip him up.[95]

In 1911, Abel sent a letter to K. C. Beckwith, secretary of the Ramona Sabbath School, thanking Friends in that congregation for their continued support of his work. He reported that in the nine years he had been in the Philippines, he had distributed more than nine thousand Scriptures and that in this labor he had the help of "many natives." He also reported, "We are holding open air meetings from village to village as best we can. Some are receiving and some are getting farther away from the truth."[96]

In the same letter, Abel wrote that he hoped to be in California the following year and followed this statement by a startling assessment of his own condition: "I am dying up, it seems to me, in my spiritual life as well as in my body."[97] ("Dying up" could be a typo for "drying up." Both are serious conditions.)

Training School for Christian Workers, 1913–1916

Sometime in 1913 William Abel left the field in the Philippines and returned home to California, weakened by malaria and his years of service.[98] He returned to the Train-

William Abel, 1916 (E. Comfort)

ing School for Christian Workers, now located in Huntington Park, California, studied from 1913 to 1916, and graduated with the 1916 class.[99]

The training school had changed since Abel first attended in 1900 and 1901. Yet the school's missionary zeal had remained strong, and its purpose continued to be "the immediate preparation of students for entering upon the important and interesting work of spreading the Gospel and winning souls to Christ."[100] A new emphasis was on mission work in Latin America, prompted in part by the successful missionary venture in Guatemala, now under California Yearly Meeting and led by Abel's old classmate, R. Esther Smith. In a 1912 edition of the Training School Bulletin, an unnamed author (probably editor W. P. Pinkham) issued a special call for mission work in

95. William Abel, "Word to the Wise," *WTSN* 3 (1904) 9, APU archives.

96. William Abel, "Philippine Islands," *Pacific Friend* 20, no. 7 (1911) 8, EFCS archives.

97. William Abel, "Philippine Islands," *Pacific Friend* 20, no. 7 (1911) 8, EFCS archives.

98. "Through His Grace," *Friends Minister*, October 14, 1920, 6–7, UBC archives.

99. TSCW, Catalog 1913–1914, 32; Catalog 1914–1915, 28; Catalog 1915–1916, APU archives. (Abel's classmates included Mary Kellogg and Clyde Thomas, later to become parents of David Thomas and grandparents of Harold Thomas, who would both become missionaries to Bolivia.)

100. *TSCW Bulletin* 1, no. 8 (1912) 4, APU archives.

Spanish-speaking countries. The writer pointed out, in addition to Spanish-speakers, the needs of indigenous peoples on the continent, referring to them as "neglected and shunned by their Spanish neighbors, . . . perhaps as much to be pitied as any class of persons in the world."[101] This atmosphere and emphasis undoubtedly influenced Abel, as probably did R. Esther Smith's visit to the school while Abel was a student, presenting the need for more workers in Latin America.[102]

One of the teachers in the training school, Florence R. Smith from Kansas Yearly Meeting, may also have exerted an influence on Abel. The School invited Smith, known for her ability as a Bible teacher and evangelist, to become a part of the faculty in 1913.[103] Along with president William P. Pinkham, she was one of the main teachers,[104] and William Abel would have been in her classes. She resigned her position as teacher in the fall of 1914 in order to devote herself to evangelism.[105] Within a few years she went as an independent missionary to La Paz, Bolivia, where she and Abel met up again in 1919.

After his graduation on June 9, 1916, Abel continued living in Huntington Park. The Training School Bulletin reported that he was working to pay his school bills and made another plea for financial support, noting that Abel was planning to go as a missionary to South America. The Bulletin praises his character and his missionary zeal.[106] He spent 1916 to 1919 in the greater Los Angeles area, where he preached in the streets at night, and worked as a milk truck driver by day until he was able to cancel his school debt.[107]

Missionary to Bolivia, 1919

Sometime toward the end of his time in Los Angeles, Abel received a letter from the Philippines, inviting him to come and pastor the church that had formed in a village where he had preached. When he discovered that the village was now under the jurisdiction of a New York mission board, he wrote to that board concerning the possibilities. But he could not afford to travel for an interview, and the board turned him down.[108]

So Abel renewed his relationship with Peniel Mission and was sent to Bolivia in 1919, arriving sometime in February or March. Although he was not in any official relationship with a Friends board or church, a news item sent from California Yearly

101. "Spanish Speaking Countries," *TSCW Bulletin* 1, no. 8 (1902) 6, APU archives.

102. Ray Lewis, "Opening of the Fifteenth Year," insert in *TSCW Bulletin* (1914), APU archives.

103. *TSCW Bulletin*, 2, no. 4 (1913) 1, APU archives.

104. *TSCW Bulletin*, 3, no. 4 (1913) 4, APU archives.

105. *TSCW Bulletin*, 4, no. 4 (1914) 6, APU archives.

106. *TSCW Bulletin*, 6, no. 1 (1916) 4, APU archives.
R. Esther Smith, "Beautiful Story," *Harvester* 17, no. 1 (1923) 2–3, EFCS archives.

107. "Through His Grace," *Friends Minister*, October 14, 1920, 7, UBC archives.

108. "Through His Grace," *Friends Minister*, October 14, 1920, 7, UBC archives.

Meeting to the Five Years Meeting makes it obvious that Friends in California were aware of Abel's mission assignment to Bolivia and still considered him one of their own.[109]

We know very little about William Abel's work in Bolivia. He lived and served primarily in La Paz, while waiting for the way to open for him to work among Aymara Indians at the Peniel Hall Farm on the shores of Lake Titicaca.[110] While in La Paz his ministry consisted of Bible distribution and street preaching. He accompanied himself on the guitar.

Abel's appearance in La Paz coincided with that of several other Friends. As we saw above, Florence Smith, formerly a Quaker teacher at the Training School for Christian Workers, had gone to Bolivia as an independent missionary and had been living in La Paz for about two years when Abel arrived. At the same time, the Union Bible Seminary of Westfield, Indiana, another Friends training school for Christian workers, sent out its first missionaries to Bolivia: Emma Morrow and Mattie Blount. Florence Smith had been instrumental in getting Morrow and Blount to Bolivia. When they arrived on May 14, 1919, Smith met them at the train station and then let them stay in her home.[111]

Eventually, Abel connected with the three women, all of them Friends missionaries new to this part of the world. On August 21, 1919, Morrow wrote home a description of a three-week series of street meetings in La Paz where the four ministered together, after having obtained an official permit from the local government. Morrow wrote,

> We have been out in the "Prado," one of the main streets of the city every night except two since Aug. 8th, and during that time hundreds of people have heard the Gospel. I believe there has been an average of a hundred people each night that would stand for a full hour, and sometimes longer, to listen, while many came and went, and the attention has been remarkably good. . . .
>
> We have given away thousands of tracts and have sold 100 New Testaments during the three weeks. . . . Mr. Able [sic] and Florence Smith do the preaching, and Mattie and I pray and help sing. Mattie preached one night and Mr. Able [sic] interpreted.[112]

109. *Friends Missionary Advocate* 35, 6 (1919) 187, Earlham College archives.

110. Emma Morrow, letter to Westfield, IN, August 21, 1919, printed in *Friends Minister*, October 26, 1920, 5, UBC archives.

111. Emma Morrow, letter to Westfield, IN, August 21, 1919, printed in *Friends Minister*, October 26, 1920, 4–6; Emma Morrow Langston, unpublished manuscript, "History of the Opening of the Missionary Work in Bolivia," 1968, UBC archives. Concerning Florence Smith, Emma Morrow Langston writes that "five months after their arrival [Blount and Morrow] she had a nervous breakdown and returned to the States. . . . She was never able to return. They found that she had been seeking the gift of tongues and saw that it was of the Lord that she left before starting a work with her" (1–2).

112. Emma Morrow, "Some Street Meetings in La Paz," *Friends Minister*, October 6, 1919, 6, UBC archives.

Abel apparently made several converts and influenced several other young Christians, among them Juan Ayllón, a young mestizo Christian. He joined with Abel in the street ministry and was deeply influenced by Abel's spirit and zeal for the work.[113]

Upon his arrival in La Paz, Abel had written home, "I have a strange feeling that somewhere around these parts I shall end my days."[114] And, indeed, William Abel died of small pox only eight months after his arrival, on October 12, 1919. Ayllón and Morrow cared for him in his final illness, and Ayllón arranged for the funeral and burial in La Paz. The verse on the marble slab marking his niche reads in Spanish, "Whether living or dying, I am the Lord's."[115]

THE STORY OF JUAN AYLLÓN

The next person to play a major role in the beginnings of the Bolivian Friends Church (INELA) is the Bolivian mestizo Juan Ayllón, disciple of William Abel.

Family, Childhood, and Youth

Juan Ayllón was born in 1897 or 1898 in the mountainous town of Apolo, north of La Paz.[116] His mother, Rosaura Herrera, was a traditional Aymara woman of mixed blood, but his father, Hipólito Ayllón, was of Spanish descent, and both parents were merchants. The family was strongly Catholic, and his mother actually was the daughter of a Catholic priest[117] (which would not have been seen positively in the community). Juan himself was the legitimate son of his parents.

When Ayllón was still a small child, he moved with his parents and a younger brother to a town in the Yungas valleys, where both his father and brother soon died. His mother kept a small store in town and united in common-law marriage with another man. She apparently practiced a syncretistic version of Catholicism, common among Aymaras. In a letter about Ayllón's life, Carroll Tamplin quotes him in saying his mother was a "skull worshipper"; she kept the skull in a prominent place in the store and relied on it to find lost objects and to keep both the store and her son safe.[118]

In his boyhood, Ayllón served as a sacristan in the local Catholic church. Along with the rest of his family, he thought that Protestants ("*evangelistas*") came straight from the devil. On one occasion, as his son remembers the story, Ayllón and a group

---

113. R. Esther Smith, "Beautiful Story," *Harvester* 17, no. 1 (1923) 2, EFCS archives.

114. "Through His Grace," *Friends Minister*, October 14, 1920, 7, UBC archives.

115. R. Esther Smith, "More from La Paz," *Harvester* 22, no. 7 (1929) 5–6, EFCS archives.

116. Most of the information in this section comes from an interview by the INELA history commission with Juan Ayllón Valle, the son, in La Paz on February 10, 2014, in La Paz, and a letter written by Carroll Tamplin to Chester Hadley in 1933. At the time Tamplin was working with Ayllón and so would have known his story.

117. R. Esther Smith, "Beautiful Story," *Harvester* 17, no. 1 (1923) 2–3, EFCS archives.

118. Carroll Tamplin, letter to Chester Hadley, February 10, 1933, NWYM/GFU archives.

of other young people stoned the Baptist Church on the Prado in downtown La Paz, then ran away.[119]

Having finished primary school in the Yungas, Ayllón desired to attend a good high school in La Paz, so he moved to the city.

Conversion and Early Discipleship

Ayllón was accepted into the Methodist American Institute, a well-known high school in the city, and he found employment as an apprentice in the school's carpentry shop. This apprenticeship proved providential in the transformation of this young church stoner into a disciple of Jesus. Juan Jr. recalls well his father's story.[120] It so happened that one day an old man selling *salteñas* (a Bolivian pastry) approached the shop. The master carpenter was out at the moment, and the other young apprentices took advantage of the old man, taking his *salteñas* and sending him off without paying him. As the old man began to cry, an American appeared, learned what had just happened and, out of pity, he comforted the old man, paid him what his *salteñas* were worth, and sent him on his way.

Ayllón watched from the sidelines and felt deeply moved. He got up his nerve to approach the American and ask why he acted in that way. The two conversed for some time, and the American, possibly a Protestant missionary connected with the school, left a New Testament with Juan.

Ayllón read the Testament and, again, felt deeply moved, so much so that he decided to become a Christian. So he found a Salvation Army hall and during an evangelistic service, he took the steps to convert and become a disciple of Jesus. It was a life-changing decision, involving acts of restitution, such as returning some ceramic planters he had robbed from a nursery. He began regularly attending a Baptist congregation in La Paz, learning all the songs, entering into the life of a Protestant Christian. He spoke with his friends about his new life. He even began preaching and singing as a street evangelist, experiencing rejection and persecution from time to time. This was indeed a change of life.

The Methodist American Institute had offered Ayllón a scholarship, and he studied there until his graduation. Knowing Juan's desire for further education, his Methodist friends offered him the possibilities of studies in Chile or North Dakota, an offer that included support for both college and seminary. Even the local Methodist bishop became involved, insisting that Ayllón accept and begin his preparation for further service among the Methodists.[121] The attraction must have been great, for, as his son remembers, Ayllón wanted to study in the United States.

---

119. Juan Ayllón Valle, interview with the INELA history commission, February 10, 2014, La Paz.
120. Juan Ayllón Valle, interview with the INELA history commission, February 10, 2014, La Paz.
121. Juan Ayllón Valle, interview with the INELA history commission, February 10, 2014, La Paz.

But in the meantime and as part of his Christian service, Juan had continued his ministry of preaching on the streets of La Paz. One day, Ayllón attended a public service where the newly arrived William Abel prayed. Carroll Tamplin writes that "Juan immediately felt that he was a man of God and sought him out."[122] The year was 1919, and Ayllón would have been in his early twenties. R. Esther Smith[123] writes that Juan Ayllón joined William Abel in his street ministry. "He imbibed William Abel's spirit, received his advices and when he died Juan helped to lay him away."[124] I imagine that Abel's strong insistence on an adequate preparation for Christian service, born of his own experience in the Philippines, also influenced Juan Ayllón, part of the "advices" he received.

As we have seen, the year 1919 was also the year the Union Bible Seminary, with headquarters in Westfield, Indiana, sent out their first missionaries to Bolivia. Ayllón probably first connected with Mattie Blount and Emma Morrow through the street meetings in which William Abel participated. In their reports home, Blount and Morrow write of his help and encouragement in their efforts to begin a mission work.[125] Another interesting aspect of this period of early contact is the development of a romantic interest between Ayllón and Mattie Bount. This was apparently more one-sided on the part of Blount, and Ayllón broke it off, but misunderstandings persisted and would have future repercussions.[126]

R. Esther Smith wrote about Ayllón's decision to become a Friend and pursue further study: "This young man became acquainted with Friends who were just beginning their service in Bolivia and felt constrained to ally himself with them in interest and work. He wanted to continue Bible study, feeling the hand of the Lord upon him for His service."[127] It's interesting to note that Ayllón, evangelized by a Methodist, converted in a Salvation Army service, and attending a Baptist church, should decide to align himself with Friends. The fact that Abel was a Quaker was undoubtedly part of the attraction, as were the connections with Blount, Morrow, and Florence Smith. Ayllón's commitment to the Quaker expression of Christianity would prove to be deep and enduring.

In the spring of 1920, Emma Morrow wrote a letter to R. Esther Smith in Chiquimula, Guatemala, telling her about Juan Ayllón and asking if there were a Bible training program on that field that could be helpful in Juan's preparation for future service

122. Carroll Tamplin, letter to OYM, February 10, 1933, NWYM/GFU archives.

123. R. Esther Smith, "Beautiful Story," *Harvester* 17, no. 1 (1923) 2–3, EFCS archives.

124. R. Esther Smith, "Beautiful Story," *Harvester* 17, no. 1 (1923) 2–3, EFCS archives.

125. Emma Morrow, "Trip on Mule Back," *Friends Minister*, September 30, 1920, 5, UBC archives.

126. Carroll Tamplin, letter to OYM, June 8, 1931, NWYM/GFU archives; Rachel Edwards Peters, interview with Harold Thomas and Nancy Thomas, October 14, 2014, Winchester, IN. It's interesting to note that news of the "romance" even reached Chiquimula, Guatemala; in a letter to R. Esther Smith on furlough in California, Matilda Haworth writes that Juan had responded correctly to Mattie Blount (letter to R. Esther Smith, March 4, 1922, EFCS archives).

127. R. Esther Smith, "Beautiful Story," *Harvester* 17, no. 1 (1923) 2, EFCS archives.

among Friends.[128] The Westfield missionaries obviously had strong expectations that Ayllón would join them in their work upon his return.

Formation as a Friends Minister and Missionary

In 1906, R. Esther Smith had gone to Guatemala as a missionary under California Yearly Meeting.[129] Since that time, she had had contact again with William Abel after his return from the Philippines. She knew of his assignment to Bolivia and of his death in La Paz in 1919.

By 1920, Smith had become field superintendent of the Guatemalan Friends Mission and also served as the editor of the *Harvester*, the missionary magazine of California Yearly Meeting. The years between 1918 and 1920 saw a revival movement of the Spirit among Friends in Chiquimula,[130] and closely related to this was the growing conviction that the mission needed a training school for Christian workers. Smith was undoubtedly envisioning something along the holiness line of her alma mater.

In writing for the *Harvester* in 1923, Smith recalls the dramatic events leading up to the formation of what would come to be called the Berea Bible Training School: "God was speaking to His servants in Central America telling them on the 3rd of May, 1920, that He would have them organize for Him a Bible Training School. At once they said, 'This is born of the Spirit.' On the 10th of May the letter . . . written at La Paz, Bolivia [from Emma Morrow] arrived at Chiquimula and the missionaries said, 'This is a seal to the indications of the Spirit.'"[131]

In another publication Smith explained, "We took this as seal of the Spirit upon the work and rejoiced in the opportunity to work for Jesus in South America. We wrote him [Juan Ayllón] to come, suggesting to the Mission at that place [Westfield Friends in La Paz] that if they would pay his expenses to and from Guatemala that we would be responsible for his education in the proposed Bible School. The young man replies that he will start North in November."[132]

So, feeling led by the Spirit, with a scholarship and an invitation from the Friends Mission in Chiquimula and the blessing of the Westfield missionaries in La Paz, young Juan Ayllón left on the journey of a lifetime. The date was November 25, 1920. The journey itself proved to be quite an adventure with unexpected twists and turns. After his arrival in Chiquimula on March 9, 1921, Ayllón wrote out the details of the trip as a testimony to God's provision and faithfulness. He wrote of traveling by train from La Paz to Arica, Chile, waiting there eight days and then sailing by steamer to Callao, Peru. He was detained twenty-three days in Peru, searching for a steamer that would let him work for his passage north. Finally, through the help of a Salvation Army

128. R. Esther Smith, "Born of the Spirit," *Harvester Supplement* (1920), EFCS archives.

129. Later California Yearly Meeting directly took on the supervision of the mission in Guatemala.

130. Stansell, *Missions by the Spirit*, 101–13.

131. R. Esther Smith, "Beautiful Story," *Harvester* 17, no. 1 (1923) 2–3, EFCS archives.

132. R. Esther Smith, "Born of the Spirit," *Harvester Supplement* (1920), EFCS archives.

captain, he secured the needed passage on a boat, only to find himself headed south to Caldera, Chile, where the boat loaded up its cargo of metals before heading north with New York as its destination.

Feeling frustrated at so much delay, Juan approached the captain with the idea of disembarking in Panama, rather than going on to New York. The captain was willing, but legal problems in Panama involving permits forced Ayllón to remain aboard all the way through the Panama Canal and then up the east coast to New York City. He wrote, "My disappointment was keen. I prayed much. The work on the vessel was very hard such as I have never been used to. It was now already past the time when I should have been in Chiquimula. It seemed like the last straw to have to take that additional trip to New York and the whole matter almost made me sick physically. But I prayed much and I cannot tell you how God comforted me and conformed me to the conditions. It was wonderful."[133]

God's providence followed him in his adventures in New York. Arriving on February 14, the ship's captain let him continue to occupy his room on board for five days while the ship reloaded. After that time, on a Sunday morning, Ayllón gathered his belongings to leave at a police station while he attempted to arrange for his passage to Guatemala. A policeman at the station, upon learning that Ayllón was a Quaker, "just happened" to know of a Friends meetinghouse nearby and gave him directions.

Ayllón was the first to arrive at the meetinghouse and he prayed in silence for someone to help him. After the meeting, people were interested in Ayllón's story, and for the next few weeks Friends from New York and New Jersey took him under their wings. Paul Furnas of New York and Frederick Swan of New Jersey hosted him, even contacting California Friends about his case, and between them all they arranged for his trip by train to New Orleans, and then by ship to the east coast of Guatemala.[134] He embarked on the Coppename on March 4, arriving in Port Barrios on the 8th, and then traveling by land to Zacapa. The last leg of the journey, from Zacapa to Chiquimula, was by "beast," probably mules, putting him in Chiquimula on the evening of March 9, late for the beginning of classes, but welcomed with open arms and much relief by both students and faculty. Ayllón concluded his travel testimony, "I am very, very happy indeed to be here. God put it strongly on my heart to come to this Bible

133. R. Esther Smith, "Arrival of Juan Ayllón," *Harvester* 15, no. 1 (1921) 4, EFCS archives.

134. On February 22, 1921, Benjamin Coppock, superintendent of the Department of Missions of California Yearly Meeting wrote a letter to R. Esther Smith in Guatemala, confused and upset about the request from Paul J. Furnas, a New York Quaker, about "one Juan Ayllon Herrera from Lapas [*sic*], Bolivia," and asking for $100 to help get Herrera to Chiquimula. Coppock writes that he is "'at sea' about that Herrera stranded in New York. It is no small trouble to me. I am personally over borrowed at the banks just at this time. I have no funds. The board has none for that purpose. Suppose we send it who will back us. Is the whole thing a fraud or fake?" Coppock decides to send the money despite his doubts, and over the next year letters are exchanged between Guatemala, California, and Bolivia, as people try to figure out how California can be repaid. Eventually the Westfield missionaries send Coppock the $100 (Juan Ayllón, letter to Benjamin Coppock, May 1921; Coppock, letter to Juan Ayllón, July 14, 1921; Matilda Haworth, letter to Mabel Adell, September 4, 1922; EFCS archives).

School, and though I knew I would have hard provings of one kind or another, I praise Him that He has brought me. During my long journey I have rested on His promise, 'They that wait upon the Lord shall renew their strength.' I am here to study the Bible and return to give my life to my people in South America."[135]

In an article the following year, R. Esther Smith referred back to Ayllón's arrival and their meeting, dramatically observing that "it was a red-letter day when South America met North America in Central America to study the Bible."[136]

The Berea Bible Training School

Juan Ayllón's experience in the Berea Bible Training School was positive, giving him the type of biblical and ministerial formation William Abel would have approved. He studied three years, beginning in March of 1921 and graduating in November of 1923. The fifteen students that first year included Tomasa Valle, a young Quaker woman from Ocotepeque, Honduras, who would later become Juan Ayllón's wife.

Students followed a well-planned course of studies that focused on Bible knowledge, sound holiness doctrine, and practical ministry. Scripture memorization was emphasized; that first year, students committed some two hundred verses to memory.[137]

All students worked to help with their expenses, the boys serving in the Friends primary and secondary schools. Students also participated in teams that did ministry projects in the city of Chiquimula, as well as in other places in Guatemala where Friends had work. An article in the 1923 Harvester notes that Ayllón and two other students conducted three days of meetings in the "Indian parish" of San Jacinto.[138] All this practical training contributed to Juan Ayllón's formation as a future missionary.

In November of 1923, Juan Ayllón and Tomasa Valle were two of seven students in the first group of graduates from the Berea Bible Training School. The November issue of the Harvester notes of the graduation ceremony that "the orations, to which perfect attention was given throughout, were remembered with grace and power. We should be glad to describe each if it were possible, but space forbids. However, we wish to speak of the thrilling words of Juan Ayllón, the Boliviano, who called upon Central America to help him preach the Gospel to the Indians of his country. The people were not asked to respond, but they sat on the edge of their benches, with tears in their eyes, saying with all their being, 'We will help.'"[139]

---

135. R. Esther Smith, "Arrival of Juan Ayllón," *Harvester* 15, no. 1 (1921) 5, EFCS archives.

136. R. Esther Smith, *Harvester* 16, no. 4 (1922) 6, EFCS archives.

137. R. Esther Smith's frequent reports on the school in the *Harvester* included details of curriculum and activities.

138. *Harvester* 16, no. 8 (1923) 7, EFCS archives.

139. "Our Schools Close," *Harvester* 17, no. 5 (1923) 2–3, EFCS archives.

Missionaries to Bolivia

As early as July 1923, an idea born in the heart of R. Esther Smith was searching for its path to reality. Smith appealed to California Yearly Meeting to seriously consider supporting a new mission work in Bolivia, with Juan Ayllón as its first missionary. When California Yearly Meeting, mainly for financial reasons, responded negatively to this challenge,[140] Smith found another way to fulfill the dream and support Ayllón's call to his homeland. The Central American Friends Mission joined the new Central American Friends Church, under Smith's strong influence, as the official supporters of the new work in Bolivia. In January of 1924, we find these words (undoubtedly written by the *Harvester's* editor, R. Esther Smith herself): "We never chose Bolivia, but God has chosen for us service in Bolivia. We feel that it is no man-made plan. We dare not falter on the threshold of the open door. . . . North American has given to Central America, and Central America will in turn give to South America."[141]

On January 26, 1924, Juan Ayllón and Tomasa Valle were married in Chiquimula, Guatemala, during the yearly meeting sessions of the Central American Friends Church. Then the gathered church consecrated the young couple for missionary service. The yearly meeting unanimously adopted the new mission field, pledging to support the Ayllóns as their missionaries. The official minute reads as follows:

> WHEREAS, God wondrously led Juan Ayllón from La Paz, Bolivia, to this place to study in our Bible school; during his three years here, he has proved his aptness, honesty, worth and spirituality and the mission recognizes the hand of God in the young man's coming; and
>
> WHEREAS, the church has known Tomasa Valle as student in the Girls' school and later in the Bible school from which she graduated in the same class with Juan Ayllón, and also when she was a worker in the churches of Guatemala and Honduras; and
>
> WHEREAS, the marriage of Juan Ayllón and Tomasa Valle took place in Chiquimula, Jan. 26, 1924, in the presence of the representatives assembled in annual meeting; and

---

140. CYM mission board superintendent, Charles S. White, informed Smith that they had discussed the possibility of sanctioning the new work in Bolivia, but saw problems in "dividing the income of the native church for other fields when your own is just being opened up, getting on your hands a work that would drain funds as badly needed nearer you, the spreading out too thinly rather than husbanding our strength in closer quarters where it could be more carefully looked after. . . . The romance of sending . . . the young man back to his own people . . . [is] appreciated by us, and those people do need the Gospel. But we cannot reach everybody" (letter to R. Esther Smith, October 8, 1923, EFCS archives). White also expressed his understanding that Ayllón was somehow "a product of the mission in Bolivia and under the care of the school at Westfield, Ind." He encouraged White to coordinate the new work with Westfield (White, letter to R. Esther Smith, November 17, 1923, EFCS archives).

141. "Bolivia Beckons," *Harvester* 17, no. 7 (1924) 5, EFCS archives.

WHEREAS, the churches and the missionaries have clearly comprehended the will of God in separating Juan and Tomasa Ayllón for the work in Bolivia,

HEREFORE, BE IT RESOLVED, that the native church herein constituted recognizes its privilege and obligation to sustain with prayer and money these two workers in Bolivia and commends them to the love and communion of all Christians where they may go.[142]

Juan and Tomasa Ayllón wedding, 1924 (SWYM)

From February through mid-April, the Ayllóns traveled around Guatemala, speaking in churches, raising enthusiasm for the project. The missionaries themselves seemed to thoroughly enjoy helping the young couple get equipped for their adventure. An article in the *Harvester* enthusiastically informs that

142. "Report of Annual Meeting, Missions," *Harvester* 17, no. 8 (1924) 4, EFCS archives.

treasures (?) have been brought from the missionaries' trunks.... Three woolen dresses have been provided, a warm coat, a rain coat, other semi-warm garments, and some cotton dresses and aprons. The missionaries presented them with two table cloths and six napkins, with an "A" embroidered in the corners by the school girls. A new riding suit with divided skirt is provided; also a poncho for rain and snow; a pretty brown leather bag for her is yet to be made, and she must have a hat, and he must have another umbrella.... These young people are not rich nor do they go with a beautiful outfit, but they go with abounding love and prayers of our native church.[143]

An outstanding aspect of this mission venture is the fact that it was supported by the indigenous Central American Friends Church, still a mission field themselves. In the yearly meeting sessions in 1924, an eight-person committee of Central American Friends, representing the eight church districts, was named. This committee was to work in cooperation with the expatriate missionaries to care for the work in Bolivia. By the end of January 1924 offerings from the national church had amounted to $165,[144] and the church pledged $60 a month to the missionary couple.[145] This level of care and support would continue through 1930, continually encouraged and publicized by Smith. In another *Harvester* article, she comments to her supporters back in the California Yearly Meeting, "The heart of the mission is comforted in that those who were cared for once now rise to care for others."[146]

After several worship gatherings in Chiquimula during the previous week, a crowd accompanied the couple out of town on April 15. Smith describes the scene: "It was a wonderful morning when a beautiful company gathered to sing the last farewell and accompany them to the edge of the city. During their last preparations and mounting the mules the schools sang farewell choruses and songs of harvest fields. Finally all were ready, and with bowed heads, standing between the mules where Juan and Tomasa were mounted, one led in prayer, again committing them to the care of the Lord of the harvest."[147]

Then Juan Ayllón, along with his bride, Tomasa, left Chiquimula the same way he had entered over three years previously—on mule back. The Ayllóns traveled by mule to Zacapa, and from there by train to Guatemala City. The send-offs, at each stage of their journey through Guatemala, were understandably warm and tearful.

On April 26, at the last goodbye as the couple readied to board the ship from the port of San José, Guatemala, Smith handed Tomasa a bouquet of a dozen pink carnations and to Juan a box of marshmallows. Thus equipped, the Ayllóns departed.[148]

143. "Outfitting Missionaries," *Harvester* 17, no. 10 (1924) 6, EFCS archives.

144. "Report of Annual Meeting, Missions," *Harvester* 17, no. 8 (1924) 4, EFCS archives.

145. "Our Parrish in Bolivia," *Harvester* 19, no. 11 (1925) 2–3, EFCS archives.

146. R. E. Smith, "Off to Bolivia!," *Harvester* 17, no. 11 (1924) 6, EFCS archives.

147. R. E. Smith, "Off to Bolivia!," *Harvester* 17, no. 11 (1924) 4, EFCS archives.

148. R. E. Smith, "Off to Bolivia!," *Harvester* 17, no. 11 (1924) 6, EFCS archives.

From San José they sailed to Cristóbal, Panama, then down to Mollendo, Peru, where they took a train across the Andes Mountains, and a boat across Lake Titicaca, finally arriving by another train in La Paz, Bolivia, on May 18, 1924.[149]

Within days of their arrival in La Paz, both Juan and Tomasa wrote back to Friends in Chiquimula, giving details of their trip and news of their arrival. Especially sweet was the reunion with Juan's parents (mother and stepfather) who apparently had both become Protestant Christians. Tomasa writes, "We were received as princes in the home of Juan's parents. Juan's father presented us with a beautiful bed that he had made, and his mother some blankets of pure wool, new sheets, etc., etc. They are precious in the Lord, and our family prayer daily is filled with much comfort."[150] She also comments on the high altitude: "The atmosphere here is very light, and sometimes I can hardly breathe."[151]

They had arrived, and a new work was waiting to be born.

REFLECTIONS ON THE BEGINNINGS OF THE CHURCH

The historical context of the period set the stage on which this unique drama would be played out. The liberal triumph of the 1899 civil war, while it did nothing to improve the conditions of Bolivia's indigenous populations, served in many ways as a wake-up call. It led to a growing awareness of social injustice and the beginnings of an indigenous resistance movement. These deep social stirrings often serve to make a people receptive to new ideas. A Christian gospel message that offered, not only relief from suffering in a future heaven, but also a new and better way of life in the here-and-now would have its deep appeal. Free communities like Amacari that had no history of being under the power of the hacienda system would be especially receptive.

Perhaps the part of the liberal agenda that would most profoundly affect the planting of a Friends church in Bolivia was the 1906 constitutional amendment that made religious freedom the law of the land. This opened the door to the whole Protestant movement.

The date 1919 has importance for the whole Quaker movement in Bolivia, not just the family of Friends that would become the INELA. The convergence in La Paz of the missionaries sent from the Union Bible Seminary of Westfield, Indiana with California Quaker William Abel and finally with Bolivian Quaker convert Juan Ayllón would have repercussions beyond what any of the sending agencies planned. From this convergence the seeds planted would eventually grow up into the different Quaker yearly meetings in Bolivia today, the two largest being the Holiness Friends and the INELA.

---

149. R. E. Smith, "Off to Bolivia!," *Harvester* 17, no. 11 (1924) 4; Tomasa Ayllón, letter to Guatemala, *Harvester* 18, no. 1 (1924) 3–4, EFCS archives.

150. Tomasa Ayllón, letter to R. Esther Smith, *Harvester* 18, no. 4 (1924) 4, EFCS archives.

151. Tomasa Ayllón, letter to R. Esther Smith, *Harvester* 18, no. 4 (1924) 4, EFCS archives.

A major question we are asking in each period of the development of the INELA is, "Where was the Spirit of God at work in all of this?"

Early evidence of the Spirit's movement comes through the conversion stories emerging from the community of Amacari. Although the details vary with the different versions, it is evident that people such as Cruz Chipana, Sebastián Ticona, and Manuel Alvarado heard the gospel message and responded in Christian conversion. They began gathering together, although secretly at first, searching the Scriptures, and sensing that this was a message to be shared with others. Over time, the community took note of the transformation in the lives of these believers. The emphasis of their conversion process was directly related to Aymara cosmology: the breaking of curses which signaled confrontation with spiritual powers, the frequent experience of physical healing and changed circumstances, and the change of loyalty expressed in the turning of Christian conversion.

We may never know all the details of this story, but the fact is that this small group of believers, with no input from an outside church or mission, was planted on good soil and grew for a hundred years, provided much of the leadership for the INELA during those years, and is today an active district of the INELA. Surely, this is the work of the Spirit of God.

Another evidence of the Spirit's work can be seen in the conversion stories of William Abel and Juan Ayllón, both young men who had shown no previous interest in the gospel. Their conversion surprised both of them, and in both cases it resulted in a complete transformation. Both were unlikely candidates for mission work, being marginal people in their own contexts. Yet both felt called of God for service, and both were led to prepare for that service in sacrificial ways.

In William Abel's case, his seemingly tragic death after so short a time in Bolivia is interpreted by Bolivian Friends today as illustrative of the words of Jesus that "unless a grain of wheat falls into the ground and dies, it will not bear fruit" (John 12:24). They consider that Abel's sacrificial death in La Paz was the seed of the church, and many claim 1919, the year of his coming to Bolivia as well as his death, as the founding date of the INELA, even though the first official Friends Church would not be planted until 1924 with the mission work of Juan Ayllón. It was also in 1924 that Ayllón first made contact with the believers in Amacari.

Perhaps the very convergence of these three streams is, in itself, evidence of the work of the Spirit of God. God's "Triple A": Amacari, Abel, Ayllón. Who but the Spirit could have engineered the coming together of three such unique stories? Who but the Spirit could have so prepared the soil, gathered the laborers, and planted a church that would grow and spread across the high planes of Bolivia?

2

From the High Plains of Bolivia

A Brief Overview of the Aymara People

BY HAROLD R. THOMAS

Three streams converged in the historical narratives that the previous chapter identified as the Triple A's of Amacari, Abel, and Ayllón. A fourth stream would merge in 1931 with the entrance of Oregon Yearly Meeting of Friends to support and augment these original streams in the formation of the Bolivian Friends Church (INELA). However, there were other equally significant influences as well. Down through the years, as we shall see, the Bolivian Friends Church grew and developed almost exclusively among the Aymara people.

To presume to describe the major patterns of Andean Aymara culture is like trying to understand the sun by viewing its halo in a near total annular eclipse as reflected in a rain puddle. We did this as a family in August 1980. We did not have eclipse glasses, but we did have cardboard and various sizes of needles to punch experimental holes. We also had the lenses from an old pair of welding goggles.

We gathered these few implements into the jeep and headed out onto the *altiplano*. At a convenient point we left the highway and ventured onto a muddy track that wandered toward an Aymara community. When we found a clear-surfaced rain puddle, we pulled off the track and parked. We stood around the puddle, trying to find the right positions to view the eclipse.

Soon the sky darkened, stars appeared, roosters began to crow in the distance, dogs barked. We watched and felt the moon's shadow progressively block the brilliant high-altitude sun and chill its warmth. We focused on the reflected image of the sun in the water at our feet as what appeared to be not only a small ring of light, but the faint flaring corona of the sun's surface outlining the dark moon for three or four minutes.

All of this we watched through the protection of pinholes in cardboard and through the lenses.

This chapter is only an introduction and certainly carries none of the danger of gazing directly at the sun and its corona, even in a total eclipse. But we hope that, as incomplete as it is, the chapter can give insight into the shape of important patterns of Aymara life and perception and help the Western reader understand how this has formed the Friends Christian movement in Bolivia.

The chapter introduces the Andean Aymara people themselves—their history as a pre-Columbian millennial people, their present populations and trends, their cultural traditions, and their enduring values in worldview perspective. It concludes with a brief reflection of how becoming Christian interacts with these values and perspectives.

HISTORICAL OVERVIEW

The Aymara-speaking people of the Bolivian and Peruvian Andes have inhabited the mountain pastures, high plains, and the breakaway valleys of what is today Bolivia and southern Peru as a significant social and cultural presence for more than nine hundred years. Their presence spans from well before AD 1100, during the final centuries of the Tiahuanacan civilization to the present. Klein observes: "The development of the Aymara kingdoms marks the beginning of the historic period of Bolivian history. It is the Aymara who dominated the central highlands of Bolivia from the end of the twelfth century until the arrival of the Spaniards in the sixteenth century."[1]

The Decline of Tiahuanaco and the Rise of the Aymara Kingdoms

The immediate social context of the rise of the Aymara-speaking people, from about the twelfth through the fourteenth centuries AD, was the decline of the Tiahuanacan civilization. Evidence for the pre-Columbian civilization of Tiahuanaco dates back to about 1000 BC. The actual site of Tiahuanaco flourished as an urban center from about AD 600 through 1200, expanding in centers around Lake Titicaca and widely influencing surrounding societies through trade, cultural assimilation, and religion. In contrast to the later Aymara dominions and the Incan Empire, Tiahuanaco does not appear to have expanded primarily through military conquest.[2]

At the height of its influence, Tiahuanaco was a major multiethnic urban population of about forty thousand people. Its dominant language was Puquiña, which persisted even to the time of the Spanish Conquest in the fifteenth century. Today the Puquiña language has disappeared, except for traces in some surrounding languages. The ancient Huruquilla was the language of the Uru fisher folk, who lived on the shores and islands of Lake Titicaca, and to the south, the Desaguadero River and Lake

1. Klein, *Bolivia*, 15; Klein, *Concise History*, loc 397.
2. Klein, *Bolivia*, 13–14; Klein, *Concise History*, locs. 375–81.

Popoo. Today a small and diminishing population of Uru-Chipaya communities continues to use the Uru language, along with Aymara and Spanish. The "proto-Aymara Jaque" language added to the mix in the final centuries of Tiahuanaco. This was the language of the complex and mobile cultures of the camelid herders from the surrounding Andean mountain pastures, who also established agricultural communities around the lake and throughout the *altiplano*. Their colonies extended beyond both the eastern and western ranges into the lower valleys. The incursion of the Quechua languages from the northern Andes came with the Incan conquests and was reinforced by Spanish conquest and mission. Yet today Aymara remains by far the most significant language that spans from the last centuries of Tiahuanaco to the present.[3]

Between AD 900 and 1200 the Tiahuanacan civilization entered a period of decline. Bolivian historian Teresa Gisbert suggests that the evidence now available of three centuries of decreasing rainfall and drastically falling lake levels, followed by an intense drought from 1250 to 1310 in its final years meant that its centers and technology could no longer provide sufficient food for its concentrated populations. Its people dispersed rapidly in the final decades of drought, to merge into smaller sustainable settlements and lifestyles.[4]

The final centuries of Tiahuanaco were times of increasing tension and conflict. The characteristic walls and community defenses, as well as the burial structures of this period, give evidence to the extension of Aymara communities around Lake Titicaca and across the high plains and mountains of the *altiplano* to the south. During the decades of the final collapse of Tiahuanaco, the "rather warlike and aggressive" Aymara-speaking communities and dominions had moved into positions of significant power.[5]

The greatest economic development and cultural contribution of the Aymara herders and farmers from this time was their successful adaptation to the climate extremes of altitude, weather, drought, and the relative infertility of the land.[6] These climates ranged from the high mountain pastures of camelid herding communities to the *altiplano* plains and descending valleys where Aymara farmers adapted a variety of crops to diverse ecological niches, developing sustainable societies. In addition to the variety of crops that niche farming made possible for trade, various communities specialized as fisher folk, salt producers, miners, weavers, potters, and metalworkers. These communities prospered, producing the wealth the Incan and Spanish *conquistadores* would find and exploit. Today, trucks and a cash economy have largely replaced the llama pack trains traveling from zone to zone with goods to barter, but even this custom continues in remote areas.

3. Gisbert, "*Libro I: Período prehistórico*," 18. Linguists debate the origins of the Aymara language and its relation to the Quechua language.

4. Gisbert, "*Libro I: Período prehistórico*," 17–18, 24–25.

5. Klein, *Bolivia*, 15.

6. Gisbert, "*Libro I: Período prehistórico*," 29.

The greatest social development of the Aymara-speaking peoples from about AD 1200 to 1400 was their formation into at least seven major kingdoms, each with a ruling nobility and a serving peasantry. Each larger kingdom divided into two independent parts, the *urkosuyo* and *umasuyo* sectors.[7] The *urkosuyo* kingdom divisions of the western Andean Cordillera were mountain herding communities in the high pastures, with their related farming communities spilling onto the western *altiplano*. The *umasuyo* kingdom divisions of the eastern Andean Cordillera also had their farming communities on the eastern side of the *altiplano*, and herding communities rising into the high mountain pastures. Each kingdom also established sustaining agricultural colonies that followed the dry valleys to the Pacific Coast, or to the semitropical *Yungas* valleys and jungles to the east.[8] The governments and territories of each kingdom were interrelated through ties of actual and fictive kinship (*allyus*), but a single maximum ruler governed each half-kingdom independently.

The Aymara were never a peaceful people, and fighting occurred between the different kingdoms. By the end of the fourteenth century, through the different battles and power struggles, the combined Lupaca and Colla Kingdoms, united under the Lupaca ruler Cari, had become one of the largest and most powerful empires in South American to that time.[9] That position of dominance would soon be challenged.

The Aymara regional communities, like their kingdoms, divided in two parts, related by kinship but distinguished by the superior/inferior social rank of nobility and peasants. The regional rulers of the Aymara nobility, whom Klein identifies as the *kuraka*, had both the right to private ownership of land and free labor from the peasant community. The *kuraka* administered the peasant communities more or less indirectly through the mediating *jilakata*, a respected elder leader of the peasant community.[10] It is significant that this millennial term continues to be used to the present time with either the traditional title of *jilakata*, or the Bolivian civil authority title of *secretario general*. The position combines both civil and traditional ritual responsibilities, which vary from community to community.

The Incan Conquest

The Incan Empire arose in Peru, to the north of Tiahuanaco, and began to grow in power in the mid-1300s. The Aymara kingdoms and their resistance to outside

7. The *urkosuyo* (*urko* meaning masculine) was generally the drier lands to the west, while the *umasuyo* (*uma* meaning water, a feminine concept in Andean thought) occupied territory to the east.

8. I note Teresa Gisbert's use of the Orcosuyo (Urcusuyo) and Omasuyo (Umasuyo). The second spelling follows the unified alphabet of three vowels, which is now generally accepted as better reflecting Aymara and Quechua phonetics. The first follows the traditional use of the distinctions of the Spanish vowels. Klein uses the unified alphabet, which I will follow.

9. Klein, *Bolivia*, 15, 19; Gisbert, *Libro I: Período prehistórico*, 32.

10. The title *kuraka* is Quechua, not Aymara. I am not sure the title is correctly used to describe the original authority structure between the nobility and peasants in the trational Aymara communities. But the *jilakata* is an actual Aymara term that is currently used in many Aymara communities.

domination were the major challenge to the Incan expansion southward from Cuzco into what became the *Kollasuyo* region of the empire. The Incan conquests ended the independence and dominance of the Lupaca and Colla Aymara kingdoms. Incan expansion eventually reached into what is today a major part of southern Peru, Bolivia, Chile, and northern Argentina.

Incan expansion meant wars of resistance and conquest between the Incas and the other indigenous peoples of South America. It meant pitched battles between huge Stone Age armies in bloody hand-to-hand conflict, their warriors equipped with slings, stone- and bronze-tipped spears, battle axes, knives, and protective clothing. The commanders fought with strategy and endurance. Conquest brought power and tribute to the conquerors.

It is generally believed that the Aymara kingdoms had the superior military power, but the fact that they were divided and warring among themselves gave the advantage to the Incan forces. Through a strategy of deceit, broken treaties, and massacres, the Inca Pachacuti brutally overcame the united Aymara-speaking Lupaca and Colla kingdoms in 1438. Sometime shortly after 1470 at his death, the leaders of the Colla and Lupaca Aymara kingdoms united in one last effort to reestablish their independence. After three and one-half years of siege and battle, an Incan army of 120,000 warriors gained the final victory.[11] This defeat opened the southern Aymara kingdoms to Incan conquest in the decades that followed and marked the greatest *Kollasuyo* expansion of the empire.

Upon defeat, Aymara sacred places and objects of supernatural power (such as sacred stones, a variety of fetishes, and symbols of authority) were covered by symbols of Incan power. The conquering Incas removed the most important of these objects to Cuzco, incorporating them into their own syncretistic system. Defeat also meant death for the maximum governing ruler and his military commanders, and the humiliating subjection of the regional rulers and nobility of the Aymara kingdoms who had opposed the Incas.[12] The young leaders of the noble class were taken to be educated in Cuzco.[13]

During the one hundred years of the Incan conquest and dominance, the Aymara people were subject to the political and economic organization of their conquerors. But Incan and Aymara ways of life were similar, and Aymara communities resisted rapid assimilation into the Incan systems, keeping their language and traditional way of life intact. As long as they were submissive under the new organization of authority, and produced the tribute of crops, products, and labor demanded by their rulers, they lived much as they always had.

11. Gisbert, *Libro I: Período prehistórico*, 32.

12. Gisbert, *Libro I: Período prehistórico*, 31.

13. Klein, *Concise History*, loc. 472.

The Spanish Conquest and the Colonial Period

With the coming of the Spanish *conquistadores* in the sixteenth century, the Aymara people entered a new era in their history. Because of their resistance to their Incan oppressors, other indigenous Andean peoples at first considered the Spanish as liberators and allies. Several Aymara kingdoms around Lake Titicaca gave significant military support to the *conquistadores* as they sought to overthrow the Incas. The Spaniards penetrated the western Andes in 1532, and by 1538 they had effectively subjugated the Incan Empire.[14] Ironically, because of initial Aymara support, the subsequent conquest of what is now Bolivia proved relatively easy.[15]

The initial rule of the *conquistadores* consolidated the Incan towns, cities, and territories under Spanish control. By 1538 they had established the city of Lima, secured Cuzco, and controlled the Incan resistance. The first wave of Spanish settlers arrived, looking for land and wealth. But governance rapidly degenerated into conflicts of power that challenged even the authority of the Spanish king. Initial respect for the status of Aymara leaders and communities who had cooperated with the Spanish deteriorated into abject exploitation of their land, stored resources, and labor. And Aymara communities responded to mounting injustices and intolerable situations with many local uprisings from the early colonial period on.

The Spanish king sent his first viceroy in 1544 primarily to impose official Spanish rule in order to control the abuse of the indigenous peoples. In 1542 Bartolomé de las Casas, Bishop of Chiapas among the Mayans in lower Mexico, had exposed exploitative practices of the Spanish conquest through his book *A Brief Account of the Destruction of the Indians*, publishing it in Europe. Las Casas, himself a former *encomendero* in Cuba, who had become a Dominican priest, early on became a primary defender of the Indians. His book, documenting the conquest from 1500 to 1542, caused extreme political embarrassment to the Spanish crown, making it possible for rival European nations to question the legitimacy of Spanish colonization. That same year, 1542, the critique and discussion resulted in the "New Laws," known as the *Ordenanzas de Barcelona* that attempted to correct the long-standing abuses.[16]

It was in this context that the Spanish king Felipe II appointed Francisco Toledo as the fifth viceroy (1569–81). His charge was to consolidate the rule of the Spanish crown through well-organized and effective government administration, a task which had not yet been accomplished. He was also to form an industry that would be able to profitably exploit the 1545 discovery of silver in the *Cerro Rico* of Potosí in what is today Bolivia. Finally, he was to investigate and resolve the issue of the legitimacy of the Spanish rights by conquest of the West Indies (the Americas). He ultimately defended the claim of legitimacy of the Spanish conquest, not on the basis of armed

14. For detail of the Spanish conquest of the entire Incan Empire, see Gisbert et al (*Libro II: El Choque*, 83–92) and Klein (*Bolivia*, 31–38).

15. Klein, *Concise History*, locs. 653–59.

16. Mesa et al., *Libro II: El choque*, 94–95.

force, for which he concluded that the *conquistadores* were no more justified than the Incas, but on the justification of Christianizing the indigenous peoples. Thus, the activities of Catholic Christian mission justified the Conquest.[17]

The innovations Toledo introduced would plague the Aymara communities for the next two hundred years. A major problem for Toledo was to provide a stable source of income for colonial government to function. To do this he needed to be able to consistently tax both the population and production of the Aymara communities. He also needed to provide an adequate source of plentiful free labor to make the silver mines in Potosí profitable. At this time slave labor in the Spanish colonies was already well established, and the *mita* system left a measure of control with the communities.

For Toledo, "the only solution was a reorganization of the social and economic basis of Andean life. To this end, he decided to 'reduce' the Indians into permanent fixed villages and attempted to convert the remaining *ayllus* into nucleated communities."[18] These reductions, as the new towns were called, attached to fixed and contiguous lands, effectively doing away with the traditional movement for planting and harvest between upper and lower ecological regions. For Spanish control and administration, it made it easier to tax, manage, and attempt to Christianize the Indians. But the forced social reorganization not only threatened the traditional Aymara way of life, but their prosperity and survival as well.[19] In addition, as had taken place throughout the Americas, frequent and devastating epidemics of European diseases drastically diminished the indigenous populations. Among the Andean communities, a rapidly growing number of families and persons abandoned their lands to escape the steadily increasing burden of exploitive taxation and the quotas for forced labor in the mines.

To provide the large labor force needed in the Potosí silver mines, Toledo adapted the *mita* system of forced labor for the mines from previous Incan practices. But with the decreasing population, this practice become abusive. By the end of the sixteenth century, one-seventh of the adult males in each town were obligated to give a year's service in the mines, with the year of service coming up once every six or seven years. Many died in the mines and others from lung diseases after their time of service. Local community government in the free communities of the reductions continued in the hands of indigenous leaders, but the Spaniards maintained indirect control through appointed *corregidores de indios*, magistrates who oversaw these community leaders.

The introduction of the Catholic missions in 1538 included Dominicans, Franciscans, Augustinians, Merecedarians, and, after the mid-century, Jesuits. The missionaries came both to minister to the needs of the *conquistadores* and to convert the Indians. They built churches, evangelized, and attempted to plant Spanish Christianity in Bolivia. By 1584, following the publication of Quechua texts, the first Aymara catechism texts were published, followed by the first Aymara grammars and dictionaries.

17. Mesa et al., *Libro II: El choque*, 101–2.

18. Klein, *Concise History*, loc. 774.

19. Klein, *Concise History*, locs. 774–79.

But there were not enough priests to keep contact with such a large and spread-out constituency, and this, with wide cultural differences, prevented the church from putting down deep roots. As Klein notes, "This creation of the outward forms of Christianity does not mean that precontact religion disappeared, or that the clergy had universal success in its evangelization among the Indians. . . . Every reduced town and older settlements now had a church, but most Indians saw a priest only rarely. Thus, traditional beliefs, especially as related to family and work, were preserved to a large extent."[20]

Throughout the 1600s, with the continued decline of the indigenous populations and the constant reorganization of their social systems, land became available for purchase, and the hacienda system arose. Rich Spanish landowners developed a system of Indian serfs who eventually belonged to the hacienda and provided the necessary labor. Although the free Indian communities remained dominant in terms of population, these still had to pay the tributes and provide forced labor for the mines.[21]

Despite the oppression, the Aymara managed to remain a cohesive people, and from time to time they attempted to rise up against their oppressors. As Klein notes, "The innumerable Indian rebellions in the period after Toledo, which lasted well into the middle of the twentieth century, were never disorganized individual affairs but were always movements of united communities led by their principal elders."[22] Most of the rebellions originated in the free communities.

The rebellion of 1780 to 1782 was different. Beginning in Cuzco, Peru, to the north, under a Quechua leader named Tupac Amaru, it spread south among indigenous peoples. Two Aymara leaders, Tomás Katari and Julián Apaza, along with Apaza's wife, Bartolina Sisa, gathered people and attacked the haciendas. Eventually, Spanish forces put down the rebellion and brutally executed its leaders. Klein writes that "the destruction of human life and property during the rebellion had been massive, especially around La Paz and the Lake Titicaca region. But general economic and demographic growth—quite pronounced in this decade—enabled most of the haciendas to be rebuilt by the end of the 1700s."[23] The rebellions ultimately had little effect, but their leaders are honored today.

Independence and the Republic

Political changes in Europe, including the overthrow of the imperial government in Spain, and the successful wars for independence in Haiti and the North American colonies did not go unperceived by ruling classes in Bolivia, who by the early 1800s were more Bolivian in outlook than European. And it was people in the upper and

20. Klein, *Concise History*, locs. 942–47.

21. Klein, *Concise History*, loc. 1018.

22. Klein, *Concise History*, loc. 888.

23. Klein, *Concise History*, loc. 1511.

middle classes, not her indigenous populations, who would lead in Bolivia's sixteen-year battle for independence (1809–25).[24]

Bolivia's declaration of independence from Spain on August 6, 1825, followed years of civil war, including "serious loss of life, and severe economic and social dislocation."[25] Bolivia's indigenous populations, estimated at roughly eight hundred thousand in 1827,[26] experienced an economic uplift immediately following the war, but they did not experience any notable alleviation from the oppressions they had suffered under previous overlords. Although in the first year of independence, the new government abolished the taxes all Indian males had paid to the Spanish rulers, in the second year, the tribute tax was reinstated. Klein notes that "with a stagnant international trade, declining silver production, and a bureaucracy incapable of collecting land or business taxes from the whites and *cholos*, the government came to depend on the Indian head tax as its most lucrative source of income and was to maintain that tax until the end of the century."[27] The hacienda system continued intact, thus ensuring the virtual slavery of thousands of Indians. Free Indian communities continued to pay the tribute.

Into the 1840s and beyond, 89 percent of the population of Bolivia continued to be rural; most of these people were indigenous and remained both illiterate and monolingual, not speaking Spanish, which was the language of the political and economic life of the nation. The majority of these people lived in the free communities,[28] but with a growing population of landless Indian peasants.

As was mentioned in chapter 1, the indigenous people played a significant role in the civil war of 1899, with their participation ensuring the victory of the liberal party that replaced a conservative government. But the victorious liberal politicians reneged on their promises and continued a program that disregarded the human rights of the growing lower classes on into the early years of the twentieth century. It is at this point that the history of the Bolivian Friends Church among the Aymara begins.

PRESENT AYMARA POPULATIONS

Aymara speakers are the third largest language group of the Bolivia, following Spanish and Quechua. Today most Aymara speakers also speak Spanish, and a significant percentage Quechua as well. According to the national census of 2012, at least 11 percent of the Bolivian population of 10.06 million people speak Aymara, and 16 percent, though they may no longer speak the Aymara language, identify themselves as coming from Aymara roots.[29]

24. Klein, *Concise History*, loc. 1511, locs. 1684–91.

25. Klein, *Concise History*, loc. 1850.

26. Klein, *Concise History*, loc. 1942.

27. Klein, *Concise History*, loc. 1953.

28. Klein, *Concise History*, locs. 2228–34.

29. INE, *Características de la población*, 2.

For a better time perspective of language and ethnic trends, we note that in 1992 Aymara speakers registered at 23.5 percent of a total Bolivian population of 6.4 million. Combined with the culturally and historically related Quechua-speaking populations, these two major indigenous language groups made up 57.7 percent of the population of Bolivia.[30] This combined percentage, according to the census response in 2012, had dropped by half to 27.8 percent. It is obvious that Bolivian populations who identify themselves as speaking Aymara and/or Quechua are decreasing significantly.

But the census of 2012 created a new category of the population who directly identified their Aymara and Quechua roots. It showed self-awareness of indigenous origins, apart from language use, at 34.3 percent. This was significantly greater than 27.8 percent but still only half of the combined language category of nearly 60 percent recorded in 1992.[31]

Three major reasons suggest themselves. First, the phenomena of avoiding language and/or ethnic identification because of perceived social discrimination in Bolivia has been a common response to census questions in urban areas.[32] But the far more significant second category of reasons reflects the growing integration of indigenous peoples into national life. This includes what has become near universal education, the economic pressure for both survival and increasing prosperity, and the wide access to mass media, which brings cultural alternatives directly into the homes. The Spanish language facilitates all these contacts.

But beyond these reasons it seems more significant to recognize that present generations who are descendants of these millennial pre-Columbian peoples are moving away from five hundred years of Spanish conquest and dehumanizing exploitation to identify themselves primarily as Bolivians in a multiethnic and multicultural society. My own research, this portion not published, shows major change in self-identity among my informants within four generations of migration to La Paz from their rural communities.[33] Whether this comes from a process of cultural rejection and assimilation of popular mestizo identity, or from a more appreciative process of recognizing and building on the strengths of their millennial heritage as well, these people are, and will increasingly be, a significant social and cultural presence in Bolivia.[34]

TRADITIONAL AYMARA CULTURE

This section introduces Aymara culture from the perspective of its traditional cultural type and five principal subsystems.[35] It focuses on the rural culture that still character-

---

30. INE, *Censo de la población*, 8, 36, 126, 131. See also H. Thomas, "Cultural Themes," 162–86.

31. H. Thomas, "Cultural Themes," 60, 63, 77.

32. H. Thomas, "Cultural Themes, 163n12. See also Albó et al., *Chukiyawu*, 81.

33. H. Thomas, "Cultural Themes," 60, 63, 77.

34. H. Thomas, "Cultural Themes," 179, 181–82.

35. I am following R. Daniel Shaw, anthropologist and linguist, with reference to T. Wayne Dye (Shaw, *Transculturation*, 23–43).

izes a large portion of the Friends movement in Bolivia, similar to the culture at the beginning of the twentieth century when the movement began. It also highlights a culture that is changing with greater self-awareness, participation in national government, universal education, and professionalization. With the movement of rural migration, especially to the central cities of La Paz and El Alto, traditional Aymara culture continues to renew itself as a strong influence in these urban centers.

From a social perspective, the Aymara society has been a peasant, rather than a tribal culture, in the context of a dominant elite culture. At its height where two dominant Aymara kingdoms became a major South American culture, it developed according to its own internal social hierarchy. But since the time of the Incan and Spanish conquests, Aymara society has existed within the context of another dominant culture that largely replaced its own hierarchies of political and social power. Aymara communities since the Spanish conquest have been subjugated and exploited. Since the Agrarian Reform both free communities and former haciendas have increasingly incorporated into national life through community syndicates. They continue to live today within the larger context of national life, with local government being subject to the laws and authorities of the country. But an Aymara community enjoys increased local autonomy as well. Aymara families are strongly oriented to their community traditions and values.

The economic base of an Aymara community, rather than the subsistence of hunting and gathering tribal cultures, has been the cultivation of the land, the development of a variety of food and artisan products, and the exchanges of products through a market economy.

The five cultural subsystems we will consider here are the economic system, the social group system, the kinship system, the political system, and the ideological system. Separating the subsystems is somewhat artificial as they all interrelate, with the spirit world (the ideological subsystem) penetrating every aspect of life and tying everything together.

The Economic Subsystem

The economic subsystem of traditional Aymara culture centers in the land, and the basic unit of production is the family. There are two types of landownership since the Agrarian Reform of 1953: the lands owned through legal titles and passed down through inheritance, and communal lands in the free communities where plots can be assigned to individual families but are not owned by them.

Farming follows the seasons for times of planting and harvesting, with some fields left to lie fallow. Typical *altiplano* crops are potatoes of many kinds, habas (a broad bean), quinoa, oca (a root crop), barley, and wheat. The upper and lower valleys produce corn, vegetables, and fruits. A family plants for its own subsistence needs, but also to take to the community market for trade or cash. When not in a labor-intensive time of the crop cycle, men often travel to the lowlands or the city to find other means of earning money for the family. The women usually stay home to care for family property, crops, the animals, and small children.

The different subsystems intertwine, with animistic rituals involved in each phase of the crop cycle, part of the ideological subsystem and underlying worldview perspectives. Reverence for the land (the *Pachamama*) predominates. Even those who pay the weekly fees to the labor syndicates and the municipality for the right to sell their products in stalls on the streets of La Paz and El Alto also each year renew the dedication of their small businesses to the *Pachamama* for her blessing.

The market place figures in both the economic and social subsystems. As Libermann (et al.) notes, "The market is a place of commerce, but it is also a meeting place and a source of information. The importance of the market system is huge, as much for the development of capitalization and its applications, as for the social relationships that are not capitalistic. These reinforce each other and permit the flourishing of the family economy."[36]

Families that have migrated to the cities have, of course, a different economic

Harvesting wheat on the altiplano (H. Thomas)

basis in their jobs. They are no longer rural farmers. They become merchants, artisans, employees, or laborers. But they maintain ties to their communities, traveling back for the community fiestas and for planting and harvesting crops, depending on this to help sustain their lives in the cities.

The Social Group Subsystem

The social group subsystem is a complex series of connections between families in a community. Many of these interconnections within and outside of the community come through the *padrinazgo* system where selected couples agree to sponsor baptisms, weddings, or other life-cycle events and thus enter into permanent sponsoring and advising relationship with the family, with reciprocal obligations and privileges.

Other interconnections form through the reciprocal borrowing-lending relationships (*ayni*). For example, a young man who takes on the formation of a dance troop to preform in community celebrations, a first step in establishing his prestige,

36. Libermann et al., "Mundo rural andino," 38.

will borrow money and contributions from friends and neighbors. He then becomes indebted to these sponsors and will in the future pay them back in like manner. Even wedding gifts are traditionally considered to be *aynis*. I have seen many gifts of plates, cups, silverware, and blankets carefully noted, then put aside in their original wrappings to be returned later at the wedding of a son or daughter of the family who first gave it.

The strength and complexities of a community's social ties are especially seen in its *cargo* system. This is "a sequence of public service obligations to the [community] through which all adults are expected to pass," a series of ascending "ladders of public service," a road traversed by the couple, although "the man is often the most public face of cargo leadership positions."[37]

Upon marriage, the new couple (the complete person or *jaqi*) is expected to take on its first major cargo and thus participate in the system of work roles in the community that will continue throughout life, often culminating in carrying out the highest responsibilities of public service. Speaking of the married couple, Albó says,

> In reciprocity, the new couple enters the "long road," the road of growing responsibilities in the community which they will carry out as a sacred obligation. These are social tasks (*cargos*) that increase from minor obligations, such as helping in the local school or in participation in certain ritual practices, to greater responsibilities, such as taking their turn as a local government authority (who cares for his people as a pastor) and as the sponsor of a community fiesta.... The characteristic seal of each cargo should be generosity and service to others in the community during the year of fulfilling the cargo.[38]

A family's right to use communal land depends on its successfully completing the *cargos*, and the ascending of the ladder of *cargos* guarantees the person's or the family's status in the community.

The Kinship Subsystem

The kinship system refers to family life. The basic unit in the Aymara family is husband and wife. In the traditional cultural ideal, the man and woman join in marriage as equals. In fact, the old Aymara word for "to marry," *jaqechasiña*, literally means, "to become a complete person." A man, even more than a woman, is not recognized as a mature, responsible, or trustworthy person until he marries. The apparent, but not always realized, equal state of the woman is lived out within the tensions of marriage.

Traditional Aymara marriage is a state of many negotiated tensions. There is often the tension of the wife who, under normal circumstances, moves with her new husband to his parents' patio and land, with her mother-in-law treating her as an interloper. There is also the tension of a young man who, without the resource of land,

37. Orta, *Catechizing Culture*, 50–51.
38. Albó, "La experiencia religiosa Aymara," 101.

marries a young woman whose family has land and possessions; he usually assumes a secondary role within that family. There is the continuing tension between the two kinship systems that come together when people marry.

Young people who escape to the city to be free of family domination face unique tensions, such as the difficult condition of single mothers who lose their community and kinship support. A high incidence of abused women contrasts to the cases where the wife rejects the husband, refusing to cook or to wash his clothes, eventually forcing him to leave.

In the communities, roles within the family are delineated, with the man generally tending to the larger animals, fields, and community responsibilities, and the woman in charge of the children, cooking, washing clothes, tending sheep and smaller animals, and doing the housework. Both participate in preparing the land, planting, and harvesting.

The culture is more patriarchal than matriarchal, but reflects tensions that defy clearly distinguished categories.

Children are welcomed and highly valued. As they grow, they find their places in the family, with the boys helping their father in the fields and the girls helping their mother in her domestic tasks. In the early twentieth century, Aymara children did not go to school, but today, with universal education, there is a primary school in every community, and children go for half days, with an option to migrate to the city or travel to a larger community if they wish to attend high school. More recently, with increasing migration to the cities of El Alto and La Paz, some communities no longer have many children, and consolidated schools serve multiple communities.

An altiplano family (H. Thomas)

The three most important rites of passage in the life of an individual are birth, marriage and death,[39] and these are observed in the context of both the extended family and the community. Birth and marriage offer the opportunities to increase the family's networks through *padrinazgo*, or the god-parent system, building reciprocal relationships that are nearly as binding as those of parent and child. Marriage itself is a complex series of steps that can last up to a few years and often does not culminate until the couple has several children.

The mother is the main socializer as she spends time with the small children in the home. "Deliberate or spontaneous teaching that is being given to children orients them toward a sense of work, of responsibility, and cooperative behavior and collective tasks."[40] Until they are seven, even little children are given tasks to carry out in the home and are expected to respect and obey their elders. Between the ages of five and seven children enter their second rite of passage (*rutuche*), the ritual of a first complete haircut, the assigning of godparents, the gifting of resources and animals they become responsible for, and, in general, the recognition that they are old enough to assume family responsibilities.

Extended family, neighbors, god-parents, the community fiestas, and the schools also join in the task of socializing the children. Extended family units usually include three to four generations, with the grandparents exercising a special role of formation that includes telling the folk tales to the children. The school system is a more recent factor and has its positive as well as negative effects in passing on cultural values. Carter and Mamani, looking at the overall enculturation of children, state that "the combination of house chores, games, and wise sayings that make up the base of the education of children would be sufficient and complete if the child were to become an adult and follow the traditional Aymara life, but formal school instruction has become more and more universal, and this prepares the child to be a leader and, in the majority of cases, encourages his/her later migration to the city."[41]

The Aymara kinship subsystem is facing the changes brought by education, urbanization, and modernization, along with the rest of the culture. In the urban context, it is especially obvious where many parents no longer teach traditional values but encourage their kids to acculturate toward a mestizo way of life.

The Political Subsystem

The political subsystem, the means of social control and communal decision-making, closely relates to the social subsystem and the assigning of *cargos*.

Before the Spanish conquest in the 1500s, Aymara communities were independent, self-governing units interconnected by complex kinships ties, known as *ayllus*.

---

39. Libermann et al., "Mundo rural andino," 85–86.
40. Libermann et al., "Mundo rural andino," 85–86.
41. Carter and Mamani, *Irpa Chico*, 162.

The conquering Spaniards took the land they wanted for their land-grant *encomiendas* and their purchased haciendas, in both cases subjecting the people living in these communities to the control of the Spanish landlord. This abolished traditional community life and self-government. The "free communities," organized as reductions (later redefined as community *ayllus*), were not affected by the hacienda system, and continued to self-govern much as they always had, but subject to national authority.

Altiplano community of Yaurichambi (H. Thomas)

Since the political reforms of 1953, especially in communities that have always been "free," local government combines the traditional ways of assembling and making decisions with the national laws that set up local syndicates and elected or appointed officials. Libermann (et al.) notes that "in reality in many original communities there is a coexistence of the traditional system of authority (with names like *jilaqata, mallku, kuraka,* . . . and other local terms) alongside the new syndicate organization, not as competing entities, but rather as an integrated system. In the majority of places where the maximum authority role is now called 'secretary general,' sometimes this is just a new name for the old *jilaqata*."[42]

The communal assemblies have maximum authority, and decisions usually take several meetings, with ample time for all to voice their concerns and opinions. Men attend these meetings (with some women substituting for a husband who has traveled), but they go home to discuss all issues with their wives before any decision is

42. Libermann "Mundo rural andino," 52.

made. The process is highly participative and democratic, with most decisions made by consensus, unless a very serious issue is dividing the community and a vote needs to be taken.[43]

Political organization extends beyond the basic unit of the community. Several communities in an area surround a central *pueblo* (town), and several of these *pueblos* group around a dominant *mestizo* provincial town (the province being equivalent to a county in the Western system). The towns have a more Spanish structure with a central plaza and government buildings grouped around it. The provinces then make up the state. Aymaras progressing through the *cargo* and syndicate systems in local government may advance to hold roles at provincial levels.

The Ideological Subsystem

The ideological—or belief—subsystem permeates every other aspect of life in Aymara culture. Aymaras are animistic, and for the Aymara person, "the world of the spirits is as real and pervasive as the world of people. His community is not just surrounded by spirits, it is totally invaded by them."[44]

The pantheon of the spirit world is complex, some spirits being more powerful than others. Some are related to geography, inhabiting the mountains, the passes, the rivers, and sections of the communities. There are ancestor spirits and the spirits of babies who died unbaptized. Some come from the mixing of traditional beliefs and Catholic Christianity, such as *Awki* (God the Father, Creator), Jesus the Son, the different virgins, the devil, and various saints. Some spirits are relatively benevolent, such as the *Pachamama* and the *Condor Mamani*, and others are evil. All spirits demand attention from humans.

Carter and Mamani observe that,

> for the most part, the majority of the spirits are ambiguous. If treated with affection and respect, if they are remembered, they pour out blessings on the individual. But if they are ignored and forgotten, they seek revenge and pour out punishments and disasters. Just as the individual cannot live in the community without respecting others and, in certain occasions, serving them, so neither should one forget his obligations to the world of the spirits. The person always has to act as a social being. If he doesn't, he only invites total disgrace.[45]

Religious specialists include the diviners (*yatiris*) who are known as "touched by God" by living through close encounter with lightning. Aymara curers (*kuriris*) are famous for their specialized knowledge of herbs, bone setting, and massage. The shamans (*ch'amakanis*) are greatly feared and operate in both socially beneficial and malevolent magic; they work directly with the spirit world. The *laykas* are most like

43. Libermann "Mundo rural andino," 49–51.
44. Carter and Mamani, *Irpa Chico*, 287.
45. Carter and Mamani, *Irpa Chico*, 293.

witches in the European tradition, persons who have been marginalized by some strange physical characteristic; people secretly contact them to curse enemies or to produce charms or potions. At their best, all of these specialists help persons, families, and communities keep this world in balance, carrying out the proper rituals for reciprocity with the spiritual powers.

Elaboration of the ideological subsystem continues in the next section on worldview.

AYMARA WORLDVIEW AND CULTURAL VALUES

Beneath the everyday complexities of the cultural subsystems, with all their intertwined customs, lies the realm of worldview perspectives and values. These are the underpinnings, the reasons and causes, for the Aymara way of life. Many of these perspectives and values are unconscious to the people themselves, things that when brought to their attention would cause an underreaction such as, "Well, of course. That's just the way it is."

Worldview Perspectives

Worldview is the philosophic and anthropological term used to describe a culture's perception of reality, of what's real and what isn't. It is subjective, not scientific, perception. It has to do with the relationships between person and group, the self and all that impinges from outside on the self, linguistic and other symbolic systems of classification, causation, and orientations to time and space. It has to do with all the assumptions handed down through the generations about what makes the world function.[46]

At the macro level the Aymara people perceive reality as a three-tiered universe: *alaxpacha*, the realm of the sky, sun, moon and stars; *manqhapacha*, the underworld and realm of evil; and *acapacha*, the here-and-now, the middle realm where day-to-day life takes place. With the coming of the Spanish conquistadors and their missionaries, people began associating *alaxpacha* with the Christian heaven and *manqhapacha* with hell, although the correspondences are not exact. The resulting realms in this adapted worldview reflect Aymara animism more than they do Christianity; they are universally held in traditional rural culture. The urban tendency is toward secularization, but with a continuing fear of the traditional supernatural world.

The creator God in *alaxpacha* is distant and aloof, unless he is visiting deserved punishment on humans, through the agency of the ancient power of the lightning and thunder, identified with the Christian Saint James. He is often referred to as *Awki* ("Ancient Father"), but he bears limited similarities to the God of the Christian Scriptures. The sun, moon, and constellations are part of the ancient *alaxpacha*. Jesus,

---

46. Kearney, *World View*, 41–47; Kraft, *Christianity in Culture*, 25–29; Kraft, *Anthropology for Christian Witness*, 51–68; H. Thomas, "Cultural Themes," 25–28.

the various virgins, and the saints have become part of the hazy border between the *alaxpacha* and the *acapacha*, along with other more traditional spirits, such as the ancestors and the spirits of the wind and the mountains. These can be appealed to for blessing, but if not attended to, they can cause various misfortunes.

A host of evil beings inhabits the *manqhapacha*, the underworld. These spirits, if not appeased in the proper way, are ever ready to waylay and harm humans. The devil is associated with the *Tío* (literally "uncle" in Spanish, a term of respect), the ancient bull-headed, human-bodied spirit of the mines, the gateway to the underworld.

The task of humans in the middle realm, *acapacha*, is to make the proper offerings at the proper times, as they attempt to maintain equilibrium, to balance and take advantage of the good and evil forces that surround them. Many spiritual beings and powers, able to act benevolently or malevolently toward humans, inhabit the *acapacha* itself. These include the overarching *Pachamama*, the loved and feared feminine spirit of the earth and fertility. She inhabits and acts in all three realms of reality. Different spirits protect the house, the corrals and animals, and the potato fields. The list goes on.

Aymaras perceive reality as hostile. People expect conflict and danger, because "that's the way it is." This sense of danger is attached to what Carter and Mamani say is "a general orientation that can only be described as a negative fatalism." They go on to state that "the destiny of an individual has already been determined. If he discovers what is to be his destiny and can convince those who have influence over him to co-operate with him, he can change that destiny to some degree, but the powers, be they temporal or spiritual, are capricious. The person is practically indefensible, remaining obligated to accept the inevitable; and because of this he is not responsible nor does he feel guilt nor does he make recriminations."[47]

Within such a perspective, the Christian concepts of grace and gratitude do not make sense; there are no direct vocabulary words in the language for them. Punishment is a strong theme, not necessarily connected with guilt, but more seen as the actions of a perpetually angry pantheon of spirits, including the *Awki*, the distant Father God. Related to this is the concept of "limited good," an anthropological construct that fits the Aymara culture. It's an unconscious sense that there is only so much prosperity or good luck available, and one must struggle to protect and obtain one's share. Someone else's obvious prosperity is suspect and must be appropriately spread out through the rest of the community. This introduces a competitive spirit and is one of the sources of conflict between families or sections of a community.[48]

Concerning time, traditional Aymara culture is orientated to the past, to the times of the ancestors. The Aymara word for "eye," *nayra*, matches the word for the distant past, *nayrapacha*, indicating that the person is facing the past. The culture is basically conservative, valuing the old traditions and threatened by change. The present is also

---

47. Carter and Mamani, *Irpa Chico*, 365.

48. Foster, *Traditional Cultures*, 52–53; *Traditional Societies*, 34–36.

emphasized, as this is the time and the place to placate the spirit world. But more and more, as young people migrate to the cities and become educated, an orientation to the future is growing. This is a current tension today, one of the differences between adults and youth, and also between rural and urban Aymaras.

Another worldview perspective has to do with the relationship between person and group. At first glance, one would be tempted to classify the Aymara culture as communal, but the reality is much more complex, given the highly competitive nature of life and the need for the person to secure his or her measure of good luck. And yet, community is indeed a strong value, with relationships in the family and the community providing the glue that holds life together.

Xavier Albó, a key anthropologist of the Aymaras, has classified the culture's person/group orientation as being one of "communal individualism."[49] An example of this is how the boundaries of who is included and who is excluded in a group are continually shifting. A family as a basic unit can act as an individual if involved in a feud with another family. But if two sides of a community are in conflict, all the families on either side unite as one. And if two communities enter into conflict (such as disputes over land boundaries or water rights), all the members of each community act as one, even formerly feuding families. And in the smallest instance, each person knows he or she must fend for himself, although doing this alone is a source of despair.

Another of the sources of conflict in the Aymara culture is the sense that reality is full of contraries, such as the above contrast between communal and individualistic values. Dealing with the contraries is conflictive, until equilibrium is found. Libermann (et al.) states that "those who don't intimately know the rural context tend to idealize the beauty and harmony of community life; those who live well within this life tend to emphasize the opposite: the internal conflicts. A more adequate interpretation, taking into account Andean logic, would see solidarity and conflict as the two poles of a dialectic reality. . . . One of the most recurrent themes in Andean social organization and symbolic organization is the union of two contraries."[50]

The value of the center between two contraries, the *taypi* (a word also used to describe the central design in an Aymara weaving), and the search for equilibrium and balance are among the highest values of the culture. The ideal "progress" report is that nothing new has happened.

The unity of life is one of the most positive aspects of Aymara worldview. Again, this is largely unconscious and unexpressed. And while we've divided our description of the culture into subsystems and worldview perspectives, for the people themselves, there are no such neat divisions. Life in the family, the fields, the marketplace, the community, and in the face of the all-pervasive spirit world is of one piece, combining the various threads into one whole fabric. This is all in the context of the Aymara people's great love and respect for the earth. Albó states that "everything is treated as

49. Albo, "La paradoja aymara," 26–34.

50. Libermann et al., "Mundo rural andino," 57–58.

if it were alive and deserves to be spoken to with respect and affection. Even a rock or a worm. One must walk without crushing, sit down gently, cultivate the land while talking with it and kissing the seeds, without causing them fear or damage."[51]

While life may be hostile with dangers abounding on every hand, it is also beautiful, and both the land and the community are to be cared for with responsibility and affection. Planting, harvesting, and courtship are among the most beautiful times of life and celebration.

Cultural Values

Cultural values are closely related to worldview perspectives and stem from them. Related to the view of the universe as hostile and to the competitive nature of human relationships, values or cultural themes such as mistrust, suspicion, deception, and vengeance are considered positive.[52] These values reflect attitudes toward whites, mestizos, and Aymaras of a different group or community. Mistrust and suspicion are the proper attitudes toward those outside of one's immediate family or community circle.

These values are characterized by the terms *jaqi* and *q'ara*. The *jaqi* is the good person, the man or woman who responsibly serves the community, upholding the traditions, customs and rituals necessary to placate the spirits and maintain equilibrium. The *q'ara*, on the other hand refers to "that person who doesn't fulfill the minimum social conventions (reciprocal work), indispensable to behaving like a human being. . . . The term applies mainly to the exploitative class of white people and mestizos in the towns and cities; but an Aymara person who has abandoned his community and assumes the same attitudes can also come to be seen as a *q'ara*."[53]

Andrew Orta states that "*q'ara* is perhaps the strongest racialized epithet in Aymara. The term often refers to whites, but more precisely denotes outsiders without social ties. The term means 'peeled,' connoting not only physical difference but also differences in costume. The term also suggests barrenness, as in an empty, uncultivated field."[54] The proper responses to *q'aras* are mistrust, suspicion, deceit, and vengeance.

The Aymara have other strong values that would be seen more positively by Westerners. Connected with the worldview perspective of the conflictive nature of the universe, *alaxpacha* and *manqhapacha*, and the continual search for equilibrium, the values of mediation and reconciliation stand out. The *taypi*, the mediating person or place in the center that works to reconcile the two sides of a conflict, is highly valued. The culture has ancient, pre-Christian, rites of reconciliation that work on the level of the spirit world or between communities in conflict. While conflict is accepted as a fact of life, people seek to resolve it, aiming for harmony and peace.

---

51. Albó, "La experiencia religiosa aymara," 126.
52. Carter and Mamani, *Irpa Chico*, 180–82.
53. Albó, "La experiencia religiosa aymara," 107.
54. Orta, *Catechizing Culture*, 250.

On the level of interpersonal relationships, hospitality and generosity are highly valued, at times to the point of conspicuous giving. The value of reciprocity comes in at this level. Orta notes that "reciprocity is like a pump at the heart of Andean life. . . . Reciprocal exchange is a principal template for interactions among Aymara and between Aymara and the gods. . . . [And] things that are authentically (and effectively) given are given from the *chuyma* ['heart'].''[55]

Aymaras value community, generosity, and hospitality (H. Thomas)

55. Orta, *Catechizing Culture*, 163.

Hard work, responsibility and sacrifice are other traits that Aymaras highly value. The good person, or *jaqi*, is one who takes seriously his community responsibilities, his or her *cargos*, works hard and makes sacrifices for the good of the family and of the community. These link with the value of solidarity, an emphasis on community.

The Aymaras also have strong aesthetic values. As Carter and Mamani attest, "The Aymara . . . highly respect aesthetic excellence in weaving, care for the fields, music, clothes, the dance and courtesy."[56] This artistic excellence comes out in the community fiestas, in the dances and music, the costumes, and the food served. Aymaras are renowned for their colorful and intricate weavings, skills that are passed down from generation to generation.

Carter and Mamani go on to address the fact of conflicting values in the culture.

> Some values appear to be in direct conflict with others, and the same person appears to embrace one value on one occasion and another on another occasion. The Aymara is utilitarian, but he is also aesthetic; he is mistrustful, but he can also be an optimist; he is full of anxiety and apt to interpret everything according to supernatural terms, but he also can be totally empirical in his orientation and can work rationally to obtain a desired goal. . . . This kind of conflict between basic themes tends to be the rule rather than the exception in human cultures.[57]

We have seen this kind of conflict between communal and individualistic orientations and between rural and urban Aymaras. The changes brought by education and urbanization make the whole subject of cultural values more complex.

REFLECTIONS ON AYMARA CULTURE AND THE GOSPEL

It's at the level of worldview and values that the gospel message needs to penetrate if a genuine Christian church is to arise within a culture. The topic of how the gospel and culture interrelate is complex. Missiologists have observed that in a given culture, certain factors provide bridges or natural entry points for the Christian message. Other aspects of the culture, especially at the worldview level, put up barriers to an understanding of the gospel. Most customs at the level of the subsystems are neutral.

Aymara history, with its centuries of oppression and injustices suffered, and with its resistance, often violent, to those injustices, contributes to deeply entrenched attitudes of suspicion and mistrust toward outsiders. This ensured that any contact between the Aymara culture and a Christian missionary endeavor, Catholic or Protestant, would be more complex and negatively charged than either side could possibly recognize. In hindsight, these barriers are easier to identify.

Another possible barrier coming from the history of this people is their syncretistic adaptation of Catholic Christianity, combining it with traditional animism.

---

56. Carter and Mamani, *Irpa Chico*, 180.

57. Carter and Mamani, *Irpa Chico*, 184.

Familiarity with the terms at least—Father, Jesus, Holy Spirit, and a whole subset of saints—might breed indifference or even contempt at a new interpretation. It would at least cause interference in reception of the Protestant presentation of the gospel.

The deeper worldview perspectives of a hostile reality, a distant but punishing God, and a limited amount of available good or luck all run counter to the Christian message. We've noted the absence of words—or concepts—for grace. An acceptance of the conflictive nature of human life and relationships also runs counter to a focus on love and unity within the church. A singular conversion experience is usually not enough to change these deep underlying, if unconscious, perceptions of reality.

Competitive human relations, so natural in the culture, also enter the church and make maturity difficult. The need to exclude and to define relational boundaries continually challenges harmony within the body of Christ; love seems too idealistic. These changes need time and the active work of the Holy Spirit.

And yet, transformation does take place. It happens because of the work of the Holy Spirit. It also takes place because the Aymara culture itself contains multiple bridges to the gospel.

Perhaps the greatest bridge is the holistic view of reality which leaves the Aymara person and community open to spiritual activity in all areas of life. This would certainly include physical healing, a universal area of need and a common motivation for Christian conversion.[58] This holistic perspective also leaves the community receptive to supernatural messages and other phenomena mentioned in the Christian Scriptures, but not widely practiced in Western Christianity. (Examples would be the seriousness with which people consider their dreams and the reality of demonic spiritual beings that need to be dealt with.)

The values the culture places on family, community, and belonging can serve as both barriers or bridges, depending on circumstances. Fear of rejection by family or community certainly could be a deterrent to Christian conversion,[59] but in instances of group conversion experiences, the resulting church is stable, the formation of a new community.

Some aspects of the culture make Quaker Christianity appealing: these include participatory ways of decision-making, a horizontal model of leadership, and a focus on equality of gender and persons. The dual values of community and individualism also find an echo in Quaker values, while they repeat the inherent tensions.

Some of the cultural themes have a complex relation to the Christian gospel, as is the case with reciprocity, a deeply ingrained Aymara value. For those outside the Christian faith, the idea of reciprocity, helpful between humans, makes nonsense of the concept of grace. The felt need to earn favor from God, a being more likely to punish than bless, can stay with a person after a conversion experience. It can enter the life of the church and challenge a clearer understanding of the Christian message.

58. H. Thomas, "Cultural Themes," 226–28.

59. H. Thomas, "Cultural Themes," 261, 287.

On the other hand, research into Aymara conversion experiences shows that many who have a life-changing experience of encounter with God, resulting in conversion, respond in a positive sense of reciprocity. According to their understanding, "On the part of God this means blessing, protection, active guidance, and purpose. On the part of person and church community it means gratefulness, faithfulness, single allegiance, and response to God's call."[60]

The ancient Aymara values of sacrifice (as seen in the offerings to the spirits and the commitment to community responsibility), mediation, and reconciliation also provide bridges to an understanding of the Christian gospel. These help make sense of the story of Jesus and his sacrifice as the one in the middle who reconciles God and humanity, person and person, community and community.

Another key to understanding what happens when Aymara people convert to the gospel is what some Christian anthropologists have referred to as "power encounter."[61] This was obvious in the message and ministry of Manuel Alvarado, the man who brought the group of believers together in Amacari. Power encounter has been described as what happens when the leaders of a group of people recognize the superior power and authority of Creator God and challenge the traditional powers of their animistic systems. Power encounter is not conversion but the realization that the traditional powers are no longer to be feared and placated, but to be put aside and replaced by the sovereign power of the Christian God. It can be seen as a rite of confrontation and leaving.

I have seen this occur spontaneously at various times in Aymara communities and families. But to end with these confrontations, even in dramatic moments of liberation or healing, is not in itself sufficient. People also need encounter with the truth of the living and written word of God, and the encounter of loyalty in a deliberate decision to change allegiance.[62] This enables the level of paradigm shift that in time is able to transform worldview, while enriching rather than destroying the treasure of culture.

Conversions that result from these combined encounters are behind the development of Friends churches that aim for contextualization and incarnation in the Aymara world. This calls to mind the difference between ideal and actual cultural practice. The overall reality of the development of the Bolivian Friends Church took twists and turns that were less than ideal, as we shall see in the following chapters.

The cultural tensions, both the bridges and barriers, plus the conflictive history of the Aymara people all helped shape the development of the Bolivian Friends Church. The story is incredibly complex and layered, but rich with insights for the whole Christian church.

---

60. H. Thomas, "Cultural Themes," 266–67.

61. Tippett, *Introduction to Missiology*, 82–85; Kraft, *Christianity in Culture*, 243; Kraft, *Anthropology for Christian Witness*, 452–54.

62. Kraft, *Anthropology for Christian Witness*, 452.

3

A Church Is Born

The Bolivian Friends Church from 1924 to 1940

In 1924 Juan Ayllón planted the first officially Friends congregation of what would one day become the Bolivian Friends Church (INELA). This was shortly after his arrival back in his homeland. In 1930, Oregon Yearly Meeting adopted the work in Bolivia as its own mission field, and the rest of the decade saw the arrival of the first North American missionaries, the fourth stream of influence that would form the church. Come to work alongside Ayllóns were Carroll and Doris Tamplin, Helen Cammack, Esthel Gulley, and Howard and Julia Pearson. These were all rugged pioneer missionaries, and the barriers they struggled to break through were significant. This period also saw the early development of Aymara leadership in the church in such persons as Cipriano Mamani, Pedro Choque, Bernardo Paredes, and Mariano Medrano.

HISTORICAL OVERVIEW

The decade of the 1920s had seen the rise of new political parties attuned to social issues. In 1921 the first national socialist party was founded and began to discuss injustices to the Indians and their rights. This decade also saw the beginning of the labor movement, with the first general strike in 1922. Radical student groups formed, influenced by the Marxist thought popular in neighboring Peru.[1]

The situation of the indigenous population had changed, with an increase in the numbers of landless Indians, those whose communal lands had been purchased by rich landowners, according to government policy. There remained a small number of free Indians who continued to live on communal lands (*comunitarios*), as well as the hacienda Indians (*colonos*).

The Catholic Church participated in the growing concern for social justice and in the 1920s instigated an educational drive devoted to bettering the lot of indigenous

1. For a complete political/social overview of this period of Bolivian history, see Klein, *Concise History*, chs. 6–7, and Gotkowitz, *Revolution*, chs. 1–4.

peoples. In 1926 the government passed a law granting Protestant missionaries the right to preach and to teach among the Indians. This underreported event, criticized by the Catholic Church and not always honored, would facilitate all Protestant work going forward.

Events taking place in the larger world would soon divert attention from social issues within the country. According to Klein, "the extraordinarily open nature of the national economy would mean that Bolivia was one of the first nations in the world to feel the full effects of the great crisis in the world economy known as the Great Depression."[2] As early as 1930, and on into the decade, the popular uprisings were weakened by the onslaught of the Great Depression; people had to focus on work and survival rather than on strikes and protests. The expansion of the haciendas was also coming to an end, as heavy land investments became more and more difficult.

On July 18, 1932, a war between Bolivia and Paraguay was declared, focused on disputes over the petroleum-rich territory known as the Chaco in the southeast corner of Bolivia. From July of 1932 until a peace treaty was signed in May of 1935, the Chaco War devastated the populations of both countries. Those most profoundly affected were the indigenous peoples, whose young and old men were placed on the front lines of the battles. In Bolivia, government agencies entered Aymara villages on the *altiplano*, in forced recruitment campaigns. It's hard to overestimate the traumatic effects of this war on Bolivia. Klein writes that "in the Chaco conflict, the losses were phenomenal. Over sixty-five thousand were killed, deserted, or died in captivity, or roughly 25 percent of the combatants on the Bolivian side. These out of a total population of just about two-million persons created war losses equal to what the European nations had suffered in World War I."[3] With both nations exhausted and devastated, it would be hard to name a "winner," but the title should probably be assigned to Paraguay. Bolivia had lost valuable territory to her enemy, although retaining the petroleum fields.

Sectors of the indigenous populations, in the aftermath of their sufferings during the Chaco War, were more prepared than ever to join with the newly forming radical political groups to force change and bring justice. Klein says that "Bolivia entered the Chaco War as a highly traditional, underdeveloped, and export-dominated economy and emerged from that conflict with the same characteristics. But it changed from being one of the least mobilized societies in Latin America, in terms of radical ideology and union organization, to one of the most advanced."[4]

Into this tumultuous context came the Friends, with their testimony of peace and social justice through the reality of Jesus Christ, Prince of Peace.

2. Klein, *Concise History*, locs. 2985–91.

3. Klein, *Concise History*, loc. 3313.

4. Klein, *Concise History*, locs. 3222–27.

JUAN AYLLÓN AND THE LAYING OF THE FOUNDATION
(1924–1930)

From 1924 through 1930, Juan and Tomasa Ayllón worked alone as missionaries to the Aymara people who would one day form the Bolivian National Evangelical Friends Church (INELA). The Friends Mission and Church in Central America continued to support the new work up to 1930.

The First Crucial Year (1924)

Juan Ayllón was never one to sit around waiting for life to happen. Within the first few weeks back in Bolivia in May of 1924, he was preaching in Aymara in Baptist and Methodist churches. He wrote of the Aymara believers, "How we love them! I told them that the believers in Central America were praying for them. Hallelujah! They saluted us with much love, and some of them knelt before us."[5] In a letter written in June to his supporters in Central America he shared his plans to visit some neighboring Indian churches and to take an extended trip to visit the villages around Lake Titicaca.[6] In July Ayllón announced his first convert: "A sick Indian has accepted our message and another Indian under conviction in one of our Thursday meetings sought the Lord. . . . An Indian has promised to take us to his village."[7]

It would be well at this point to comment on Ayllón's use of the term "Indian." Although he had Aymara blood on his mother's side, he was a mestizo and did not self-identify as "Indian." There is a clear us/them perception in his reference to the people to whom he was called to minister.

Juan and Tomasa kept up a steady stream of letters back to Guatemala, telling of their activities and the results. From these we learn of Juan's exploratory trips during the rest of 1924.

Sometime in June or July, Ayllón traveled north to the village of Sorata where the Friends missionaries from Westfield, Indiana, had a center. The Sorata missionaries asked Ayllón to honor polity arrangements and avoid overlap in areas where they were already ministering. Apparently, the conversation was friendly and the Sorata missionaries recommended that the Ayllóns explore the lake region.[8] Throughout the rest of the 1920s, Ayllón maintained friendly relationships with the Friends missionaries from Indiana.

In August 1924 Ayllón did colportage work in the area around Cochabamba, mostly selling New Testaments in the Quechua language, possibly under the encouragement of the American Bible Society, who harbored hopes that he would work for

---

5. The letters written by Juan and Tomasa Ayllón and published in *Harvester* were all sent to R. Esther Smith, who translated them from Spanish into English. Juan Ayllón, letter written on May 26, *Harvester* 18, no. 1 (1924) 4, EFCS archives.

6. Juan Ayllón, letter written in June, *Harvester* 18, no. 2 (1924) 3–4, EFCS archives.

7. Juan Ayllón, letter written on July 1, *Harvester* 18, no. 2 (1924) 6, EFCS archives.

8. Tomasa Ayllón, letter written on August 2, 1924, *Harvester* 18, no. 4 (1924) 4, EFCS archives.

them.[9] The assignment was to have been for several months, but Ayllón, although finding the people needy and responsive, returned after only sixteen days. Tomasa observed in a letter, "There were good results, but there was not liberty to remain among them as our supreme thought and deep responsibility are for the Aymaras."[10] Tomasa also wrote that while on this trip, Juan "found a map—how strange—which represented a place that we have had in mind for some time. It was a map of Lake Titicaca and surrounding country where live a great mass of Aymara Indians. The owner did not want to sell it, so by the light of a candle, Juan made a copy."[11] God was confirming the call to minister among Aymara-speaking people.

Ayllón made his first exploratory trip to Lake Titicaca sometime between August and October of 1924.[12]

In a letter written in September 1924, we see the beginnings of two activities that would continue to be fleshed out in the Ayllóns' ministry: the development of an Aymara hymnody, and aggressive witnessing. The Ayllóns wrote of two Aymara seekers who came to their home one evening. Juan taught them three hymns he had translated into Aymara, all of an evangelistic nature: "Why Not Now?"; "Sinner, Come to Jesus"; and "Jesus Loves Me." The letter also mentioned that "the other night when Juan was witnessing to a multitude some boys threw stones at him but they did not even touch him. God protected him."[13]

The highlight of that first year in Bolivia was the formation of the first congregation (other than his family meeting) in the section of La Paz known as Tembladerani. One of Ayllón's contacts introduced him to "an Indian in Tembladerani who was a believer and who was seeking a pastor or someone to help him in that place."[14] The man was Pedro Choque, soon to become one of the first leaders in the new Friends church.

Tembladerani and neighboring Llojeta were Aymara communities, and Ayllón referred to Pedro Choque as the "chief" of both.[15] He was a person of influence in the context and had already become a Christian, perhaps through contact with the Adventist community. Ayllón mentions having to persuade him that it was fine to worship on Sunday, "for he had been influenced by the Adventists."[16]

---

9. Just after the Ayllóns left Chiquimula, Dr. W. F. Jordan of the American Bible Society visited that city and encouraged the mission to have the Ayllóns focus their ministry on Bible distribution among the Quechua people of Bolivia (R. Esther Smith, "Off to Bolivia," *Harvester* 17, no. 11 (1924) 4–6, EFCS archives).

10. Tomasa Ayllón, letter to written on August 22, *Harvester* 18, no. 5 (1924) 2, EFCS archives.

11. Tomasa Ayllón, letter written on August 22, *Harvester* 18, no. 5 (1924) 2, EFCS archives.

12. Juan Ayllón, letter written on November 14, *Harvester* 18, no. 7 (1924) 3–4, EFCS archives.

13. Juan and Tomasa Ayllón, letter written on September 9, *Harvester* 18, no. 5 (1924) 2, EFCS archives.

14. Juan Ayllón, letter written on October 27, *Harvester* 18, no. 6 (1924) 4–5, EFCS archives.

15. Juan Ayllón, letter written on November 14, *Harvester* 18, no. 7 (1924) 3–4, EFCS archives.

16. Juan Ayllón, letter written on October 27, *Harvester* 18, no. 6 (1924) 2, EFCS archives.

Ayllón first visited Tembladerani on October 7, 1924, and he suggested to Choque that they have a meeting for worship, there and then. Apparently Choque had already been attracting interested people in the zone, willing to listen to teaching about the Christian way. Ayllón writes about this meeting that "the Lord spoke, blessing us richly. We made an altar of some chairs, and nearly all came forward, seeking the Lord with tears."[17] He returned the following Sunday, and again "God spoke afresh to our souls, and nearly all came to the altar. There were about 30 Indians besides children. Of course some did not understand what it meant to be justified, but the Lord will make them understand."[18] Along with his preaching, Ayllón used the hymns he had translated into the Aymara language. This meeting was followed by five more Sunday services, "and not a meeting passed without an altar call."[19]

Ayllón considered this contact with Tembladerani a breakthrough in the work of the mission, along with the potential contacts on Lake Titicaca. He wrote back home, "We are praying about Tembladerani as a center for our work. From this open door we could reach many villages, and by a trip of two days on train and boat, we could reach Amakeri [sic] and have it for our main station on the Lake. We plan to make a second journey there soon."[20]

On December 2, 1924, Juan and Tomasa Ayllón moved to a room in Tembladerani, at the urging of Pedro Choque. By the end of the year, in addition to church services, Ayllón was conducting literacy classes for adults. He sums up the developing ministry in Tembladerani in a letter: "We are having regular meetings as follows: Sundays, Sunday-School in the morning, and meeting in the afternoon and evening; Wednesday evenings, meeting; Friday evenings, prayer meeting. Mondays, Thursdays and Saturdays we have night school for the Indians. We have 17 enrolled."[21]

Thirty-five people attended the Christmas night service where three men became Christians and everyone received a "little bag of candy." The Ayllóns expressed their deep gratitude to God for this beginning.[22]

Early Development under Ayllón's Leadership

Certain activities and patterns stand out in the succeeding years in the early development of the work, 1925–1930. These include strong emphases in evangelism and church planting, organizational development, discipleship and leadership training, and general education.

---

17. Juan Ayllón, letter written on October 27, *Harvester* 18, no. 6 (1924) 4–5, EFCS archives.

18. Juan Ayllón, letter written on October 27, *Harvester* 18, no. 6 (1924) 4–5, EFCS archives.

19. Juan Ayllón, letter written on October 27, *Harvester* 18, no. 6 (1924) 4–5; letter written on November 14, *Harvester* 18, no. 7 (1924) 3–4, EFCS archives.

20. Juan Ayllón, letter written on November 14, *Harvester* 18, no. 7 (1924) 3–4, EFCS archives.

21. Juan Ayllón, letter written on December 20, 1924, *Harvester* 18, no. 9 (1925) 3, EFCS archives.

22. Juan Ayllón, letter written on December 25, 1924, *Harvester* 18, no. 9 (1925) 3–4, EFCS archives.

The young church in Tembladerani grew through Juan Ayllón's strong preaching ministry; he regularly reported new conversions.[23] The congregation also reached into its community through the evangelistic efforts of some of the new believers, and through follow-up with the family relations of the believers. In a letter back to Guatemala at the end of 1925, Ayllón told the story of one of his converts, which, in addition to information about the people coming into the church, gives insight into Ayllón's own prejudices:

> Here in our meetings God is making of the hardhearted, superstitious and idolatrous, saved beings, and all by "the foolishness of preaching" of the spilt blood of Jesus. Let us take Andrew Huanca for an example. He is a gardener, with a face far from pleasing, bronze-colored, and long coarse hair; he is of medium height, and poorly dressed. Before he was saved he lived the life of a dog and the whites and others treated him as if he were less or equal to a burro. He tells that he was a great drinker, without hope in the world, nevertheless a lover of the dance, and as all Indians are generally, a thief and consequently deceitful and lying.[24]

Ayllón continued to tell how Huanca, through an accident he suffered as a result of drunkenness during a fiesta, sought the Lord at the altar of a church and became a Christian. Since that time, claimed Ayllón, he was a changed man and a faithful attender of the congregation.

Along with salvation messages, Ayllón was concerned with the organizational growth of the church and the maturity of the believers. He taught the new believers basic Christian duties, such as tithing and taking responsibility for the life of the church. In his annual report for 1925, he writes that ten believers are tithing, and that "from the tithes and offerings the church has paid the rent of the room where we hold meetings, bought nine benches, a pulpit, two lamps, some ordinary carpet, wood for a platform, etc."[25] Total offerings from the new congregation in 1926 came to $214.85, a considerable amount for the times.[26] The congregation in Tembladerani was organized officially as a monthly meeting[27] before the end of 1925.[28]

Examples of Ayllón's emphasis on discipleship and leadership training can be seen in the various weekly meetings in the church, including Sunday school, Bible classes for adults, and even music classes. Juan and Tomasa received some of their teaching materials from Central America—tracts, lessons, and songbooks. But much

---

23. Juan and Tomasa Ayllón, letter written on January 12, *Harvester* 18, no. 9 (1925) 4; August 31, *Harvester* 19, no. 4 (1925) 2, EFCS archives.

24. Juan Ayllón, letter written on December 7, 1925, *Harvester* 19, no. 9 (1926) 5–6, EFCS archives.

25. Juan Ayllón, letter written on December 7, 1925, *Harvester* 19, no. 9 (1926) 5–6, EFCS archives.

26. R. Esther Smith, "Missions," *Harvester* 19, no. 8 (1926) 3–4, EFCS archives.

27. In Friends jargon, a "monthly meeting" is a fully recognized church. The term comes from the practice of holding monthly business meetings.

28. Juan Ayllón, letter written on December 7, 1925, *Harvester* 19, no. 9 (1926) 5–6, EFCS archives.

of this training was probably informal, through relationships. In a letter home in early 1925 Ayllón writes about spending the morning talking with Pedro Choque about "law, grace and the second coming, etc.," mentioning that "even Pedro forgot about his lunch."[29]

It is clear that early on Ayllón began training the believers to carry out the various leadership roles of the church. In a letter written in August of 1926, he reports, "The prayer meeting on Monday one of the brethren usually directs. Last Monday I went to the meeting which was led by Inocencio Choque. I sat in the back and just listened. One Indian gave an exhortation, another a promise, and Inocencio spoke on some verses found in Romans 8, inviting to prayer. What a precious moment that was! All knelt and began to pray, some with sincere tears. After a short time it seemed all were through, but then the heart cries increased. May God hear their prayers. After singing a chorus the meeting was dismissed."[30]

The educational ministry moved ahead, coming to include women and children, as well as men. Classes in reading and writing were conducted at night in Tembladerani, and by the end of 1926, some sixteen men, women, boys, and girls were receiving education in literacy and other subjects.[31]

In addition to the congregation in La Paz, Juan Ayllón continued his exploration of the region around Lake Titicaca. In these trips, he was always accompanied by men he was discipling and training as leaders in ministry. Tomasa, now mother to Dorcas (July 22, 1925) and Juan (September 20, 1926), and more susceptible than her husband to the harsh Bolivian climate, stayed home and carried on the ministry in the local church, assisted by believers there.

After that initial exploratory trip to Lake Titicaca in 1924, Ayllón began traveling regularly to the villages around the lake. As he began his ministry there, he was again building on a foundation already laid. As in the case with Pedro Choque in Tembladerani, the gospel had already arrived in Amacari and the resulting church was being led by local leaders such as Cruz Chipana and Manuel Alvarado. Juan Ayllón stepped onto ground that had been prepared.

In May of 1925, Juan Ayllón traveled to the lake, and he again visited Amacari. He writes home about this trip: "On entering the village some recognized me and welcomed me more or less with these words: 'Did you come? Finally you decided to come and teach us? Don't you come to stay with us now?' I went to room with Esteban Chipana. He received me lovingly, giving me a bed of mud and some sheep-skins which served as a mattress. I was able to visit several places in this section."[32]

---

29. Juan and Tomasa Ayllón, letter, n.d., *Harvester* 18, nos. 11–12 (1925) 12, EFCS archives.

30. Juan Ayllón, letter written on August 11, *Harvester* 20, no. 4 (1926) 6, EFCS archives.

31. Juan and Tomasa Ayllón, letter written on February 5, *Harvester* 18, no. 10 (1925) 6, EFCS archives.

32. Juan Ayllón, letter written on June 3, *Harvester* 19, no. 2 (1925) 5, EFCS archives.

Ayllón continued traveling to the lake, always accompanied by a national worker. In 1926 alone, he made seven trips, all evangelistic in nature.[33] A description of the trip he made in March gives a picture of his evangelistic ministry during these years:

> Committing ourselves to the grace and power of God, the 27th of last month, Inocencio Choque, his wife and I left for the white fields of Lake Titicaca. After riding on train and boat we arrived the following day at Chicharro. We had many opportunities to talk to the Indians of that place about salvation. Inocencio was so eager to give his testimony. In the evening we had a meeting in the home of Coronel, who is convinced of the Gospel.
>
> . . . On the 29th we went on foot to Challapampa [probably Challapata]. There we stayed in the house of the parents of Inocencio's wife. We spoke to several old Indians and beggars. Some friends from a nearby town came to see us, so we had a short time to again talk to them about their souls' need. We borrowed a guitar and sang and played songs which they enjoyed. . . .
>
> The following day we returned to Chicharro. We got started rather late, but surely the Lord thus ordered, for had it not been so we would not have met a company of about 35 Indians who were going to their farm work. We took their picture, then told them our message of salvation. They listened without losing a word, now nodding affirmatively as we spoke. After receiving an exhortation, they were going, but some stayed on to know more; when they finished asking questions they also went, but one, seemingly more decided, remained longer. This young man of about twenty years told us his sad and unfortunate condition because of witchcraft, and with desperation like one who is dying with hunger he asked us: "What shall I do? What shall I do?" We told him how Jesus had died for him and how he could be free from condemnation. Not understanding, he continued to ask us: "And what shall I do now?" "Believe what He has done for thee and thou shalt be saved," we told him, and he said: "I believe." We knelt and prayed, and then so as to be more sure, in his simplicity he said: "I do it again," but he knew that the work was done in his heart. We instructed him how to pray, and told him that hereafter the bad spirits need not have anything to do with him. At last we said goodbye, and he left satisfied.
>
> At the Port we had to wait a couple of days for the train so decided to visit the town of Tiahuanacu. There six accepted the Lord.[34]

From this account, we note that Ayllón took advantage of all opportunities to evangelize, with individuals or groups, in homes and in the open air. He followed the family networks of believers when possible (as with the parents of Inocencio's wife) and took with him those believers he was training in ministry, encouraging them to

---

33. Juan Ayllón, annual report for 1926, *Harvester* 20, no. 9 (1927) 4–5, EFCS archives.
34. Juan Ayllón, letter written on April 12, *Harvester* 19, no. 12 (1926) 6–7, EFCS archives.

actively participate. Among those that worked under Ayllón were Inocencio Choque (possibly a relative to Pedro Choque), Antonio Chambi, and Carlos Espinoza.[35]

In June of 1927, Juan Ayllón, accompanied by Pedro Choque, made his first evangelistic, exploratory trip to the North Yungas valleys. The two visited Santa Rosa, Coroico, Coripata, Chulumani, and Irupana, along with other towns, and, according to Ayllón, "personal evangelism . . . occupied most of our time," along with the distribution of tracts and the sale of Bibles and Testaments. It's also interesting to note that offerings from the Tembladerani church of $19.50 covered half of the trip's expenses.[36]

Although Ayllón expended much energy and prayer on these exploratory evangelistic trips, planting churches in the lake area and the Yungas valleys would require more time and trained workers. In the annual report for 1927, the Ayllóns write,

> More than ever we feel the need of workers. We are asking the Lord for them. Practically we have no other work outside of this City. Although with great burden we have prayed and waited on the Lord concerning this matter, to our sorrow the doors have remained closed. Under the present conditions to go to any other place would mean to abandon this precious work which God has given us. Nevertheless we have sowed the seed in the Lake region and in the Yungas provinces. We also hope to extend our work here in this city. We are waiting on God.[37]

New believers in La Paz, 1928, Tomasa Ayllón standing far left (INELA)

35. *Harvester* 20, no. 8 (1927) 5; Juan Ayllón, annual report for 1927, *Harvester* 21, no. 9 (1928) 3–5; Tomasa Ayllón, letter written on June 5, *Harvester* 21, no. 2 (1927) 5, EFCS archives.

36. Juan Ayllón, letter, n.d., *Harvester* 21, no. 4 (1927) 4–6, EFCS archives.

37. Juan and Tomasa Ayllón, letter written on December 10, 1927, *Harvester* 21, no. 9 (1928) 3–5, EFCS archives.

Ayllón tended to be upbeat in his reports back to Central America, according to the expectations of the times and the religious rhetorical styles. Nevertheless, we get hints that the work was hard and discouragement a temptation. The reports of slow growth and closed doors, the occasional mention of "hardness of lack of blessing in the meetings"[38] in the Tembladerani church, the recounting of converts who had fallen away because of persecution or other reasons,[39] and his mention of the surrounding hostile environment that saw evangelical Christians as being "like frogs or snakes . . . with horns and a tail"[40]—these give some idea of the difficulty of the task. Added to all this, the Ayllón family suffered personal tragedy in the birth and death in 1930 of their third child, Beulah.

From the statistical reports that we have, we see the church growing from thirty believers at the end of 1926, to fifty at the end of 1927, and up to seventy by December of 1928. Annual offerings rose from $253.00 in 1926, to $334.82 in 1927, leveling out to $331.19 in 1928. In the annual report for 1930, the Ayllóns reported eighty believers, two organized congregations that included Sunday schools, six students in the Bible class, and twelve students in the evening literacy class. Reflecting on the offerings of the people, in light of the social problems in the country in general, the Ayllóns report that "almost all of the expenses of the Mission were paid with the tithes and offerings given out of their poverty. These expenses include rent of two meeting places, light, trips, medicines and charity of which under the circumstances indicated above, there was special need."[41]

The two organized congregations in the report were those in Miraflores and Chijini, both areas of La Paz. Apparently Juan and Tomasa had moved back with his parents for financial reasons, and the congregation that had gathered in Tembladerani was now meeting in Chijini. The annual report also mentions evangelistic trips to Viacha in the Ingavi Province, with ten converts, and further work in Achocalla, with the information that the new believers in that village "were expelled . . . for having chosen to follow the Lord Jesus."[42] The Ayllóns had also begun gathering believers from all areas into larger meetings twice a year, a precursor to Quaker yearly meeting sessions.

It seems that the legacy of those first seven years was two established congregations in La Paz, a slowly growing body of native leaders, the beginnings of a yearly meeting structure, and small groups of Aymara believers scattered in different areas of Bolivia, groups waiting to be discipled.

---

38. Juan and Tomasa Ayllón, letter, n.d., *Harvester* 20, no. 1 (1926) 4, EFCS archives.

39. Juan Ayllón, letter written on March 10, *Harvester* 20, no. 11 (1927) 5, EFCS archives.

40. Juan Ayllón, letter, n.d., *Harvester* 21, no. 1 (1927) 5–6, EFCS archives.

41. Juan and Tomasa Ayllón, annual report for 1930, to the OYM mission board, December 15, 1930, NWYM/GFU archives.

42. Juan and Tomasa Ayllón, annual report for 1930, to OYM mission board, December 15, 1930, NWYM/GFU archives.

During the years the Ayllóns served as sole missionaries on the Bolivian field (1924–1930), the support of the Central American Friends Church and Mission proved crucial and the couple frequently expressed their gratitude in letters to Guatemala.[43] The encouragement went both ways. Having Bolivia as a mission field also impacted the Central American Friends Church. The special 25th anniversary edition of the *Harvester* in 1927 (celebrating the twenty-five years of the Friends Mission work in Central America) reported on the work of the eight-member national mission board, and went on to say, "Of the influence of the work in Bolivia on the church in Central America, too much cannot be said. It calls them to prayer, to regular giving, and to a love for those beyond their own borders. The work in Bolivia is Central America's thank offering to God for the Gospel. The general interest and faithful giving of the native church has made this, their foreign mission, a blessing in their spiritual life."[44]

TRANSITION IN SPONSORSHIP

The connection between Central America and Bolivia was undeniably crucial to the early work in establishing the church. But the time was quickly approaching when the limitations of that connection would have to be recognized and changes made.

Visit of R. Esther Smith to Bolivia

In October of 1928, R. Esther Smith fulfilled a long-held dream as she traveled from Chiquimula, Guatemala, to La Paz, Bolivia, via boat and train, to spend a little less than four months among Friends in Bolivia. While there she was able to see firsthand the work the Central American mission and national church had supported since 1924. She gave an emotional accounting of that trip in a booklet published in 1930, *In Aymara Land*. She tells how she spent time with her beloved Juan and Tomasa Ayllón, and let them accompany her as she met believers, worshiped in congregations, and traveled out to some of the preaching points.

A highlight for Smith was a visit to the grave of her old schoolmate in the Training School for Christian Workers and a planter of seeds for the Friends Church in Bolivia, William Abel. She writes of the experience:

> In this historic place [the National Cemetery] I stood in front of the grave of William Abel. . . . He lived to preach and sing on the streets but eight months and died of smallpox in the Government Hospital where he passed out alone in the midst of high fever and delirium. I saw one or more of his converts, his over coat with fur collar and his fine guitar. After some seeking we found a marble slab up in the fourth or fifth row of niches that contained his name, the

---

43. E.g., Juan Ayllón, letter sent on November 5, *Harvester* 19, no. 7 (1925) 5–6; Juan and Tomasa Ayllón, annual report for 1930, to the OYM mission board, December 15, 1930, NWYM/GFU archives.

44. "Brief History of the Work," *Harvester*, special edition (December 1927) 12, EFCS archives.

two dates and a suitable scripture. There we hung a green wreath and bowed our heads in prayer, thanking God that the mantle of this His servant had fallen on another to preach and sing and carry on, on one who stood in that solemn presence that day, Juan Ayllón.[45]

Smith's visit was not just for tourism and ministry. In her annual field report for 1929, she includes a list of "blows that have not been easy to bear," among which is "a possible change in the work in Bolivia."[46] Smith had seen the challenge of the Bolivia field, put that together with the financial limitations of the Central American mission and national church, and come to the hard conclusion that it was time to pass the work to another sponsor.

After unsuccessfully attempting to transfer the work to the Union Bible Seminary in Westfield, Indiana,[47] Smith turned to Oregon Yearly Meeting. While on furlough in June 1930, Smith visited Oregon Yearly Meeting and presented the following letter to the board of foreign missions:

> To the Missionary Board of Oregon Yearly Meeting:
>
> The Friends Mission, Chiquimula, Guatemala, offers to Oregon Yearly Meeting the work and workers at La Paz, Bolivia, South America.
>
> It consists of Juan Ayllón and wife, Tomasa, a congregation of some seventy Indians of the Aymara race, and a few of the Cholo Class beginning to believe. There is an organized Monthly Meeting and a larger established meeting held annually in November that in time will become a Camp or Yearly Meeting.
>
> The work is sound in doctrine, evangelistic in spirit, maintains a small Bible Training school, night school, a Bible depository, a small medical department, and other church activities in addition to renting two chapels in the city.
>
> The work is five years old and has come to its present state and condition at a total cost of about $4,500, contributed in most part by the native churches of the Central American field, accompanied by their tears and prayers.
>
> If assumed by Oregon Yearly Meeting it is very probable that the Central American churches will wish to make a monthly offering to the Ayllóns, but this cannot be well determined until their annual meeting next January.
>
> Under God we make the offer of this work to Oregon Yearly Meeting for its direction and care, in which the mission in Guatemala will maintain no part in future management. We do this believing in the integrity of Oregon Yearly Meeting as to soundness in the Quaker faith and the doctrine of Holiness. We take this step in the fear of God and with confidence in our brethren

45. R. Esther Smith, *In Aymara Land*, 20.

46. R. Esther Smith, "Report of the Chiquimula Mission," CYM Minutes 1929, 77, EFCS archives.

47. Westfield accepted the proposal but Ayllón protested that he could not work with that mission (OYM Minutes 1930, 36, quoting from a letter from Ayllón to Smith, NWYM/GFU archives).

and co-laborers of Oregon Yearly Meeting, believing that, if you enter Bolivia as a mission field, you can better care for the future development of the growing interests there.

On behalf of the Mission,
Signed, R. Esther Smith, Supt.
Newberg, Oregon, June 11, 1930.[48]

Behind the Decision

R. Esther Smith's letter did not fall into a vacuum. Since the official establishment of the Oregon Yearly Meeting (OYM) of Friends Church in 1893, evangelical Quakers in the Northwest were involved in mission outreach. In the first yearly meeting session, the assembly adopted Kake Island, Alaska as its field, in cooperation with other yearly meetings. It maintained this work until 1911 when it was agreed in yearly meeting sessions to hand this work over to a Presbyterian mission board.

OYM was one of the original yearly meetings who had joined to form Five Years Meeting (FYM) in 1902. This association of yearly meetings, with headquarters in Richmond, Indiana, included a missions branch, the American Friends Board of Foreign Missions (AFBFM). Between 1911 and 1926, OYM actively supported Arthur and Edna Chilson's pioneering work in Kenya, under the AFBFM.

The possibilities of rift between OYM and FYM rose up through the 1920s, part of the Christian scene throughout the United States during those years. A division between the more conservative evangelical churches, influenced by the holiness movement, and those reputed to be more liberal theologically affected groups across all denominational lines. Finally, in the 1926 yearly meeting sessions, OYM decided to sever its relations with FYM. That included all OYM support of the AFBFM fields, although they continued to support the Chilsons in Kenya for a time.

The mission board then turned its attention to the need to find its own mission field. As late as April of 1930, the mission board was deliberating on whether to unite with Ohio Yearly Meeting in their missions work, or to find its own field in either Africa or South America (country unspecified). In early June, R. Esther Smith's invitation arrived, requesting that Oregon Yearly Meeting become the new sponsors of the work in Bolivia. The timing was right, and people seemed to sense the Spirit opening the way for this adventure. The mission board unanimously recommended to the yearly meeting the acceptance of the work in Bolivia.[49]

Oregon Yearly Meeting Adopts Bolivia

In the June 1930 yearly meeting sessions, Oregon Yearly Meeting officially adopted the Bolivian work as its own mission field and appointed Carroll and Doris Tamplin

48. OYM Minutes 1930, 29, NWYM/GFU archives.

49. The Minutes of the OYM Board of Foreign Missions provide details of the process of a search for a new mission field, especially during 1928–1930, NWYM/GFU archives.

as the first missionaries to be sent from the Northwest to Bolivia. R. Esther Smith was present in these sessions. Part of the transfer included the services of Juan and Tomasa Ayllón, now to become paid field staff under the OYM mission board. A letter from the board to the Ayllóns welcomed them into the new relationship.[50] They began receiving $75 a month as early as September 1930.[51] The board also agreed to accept regular offerings of $17 a month for the Ayllóns' support from the Friends Mission in Chiquimula.[52] At the time, Chester A. Hadley was superintendent of OYM and Frederick J. Cope was president of the mission board.

Carroll and Doris Tamplin, Oregon Quakers steeped in the holiness tradition from their studies at Cascade College in Portland, had been moved by the need in Bolivia and called to that land several years previously. As the way had not yet opened, they agreed to serve as missionaries under California Yearly Meeting in Guatemala and did so from 1925 until 1930 when invited by OYM to go to Bolivia. Their years in Guatemala were always understood by R. Esther Smith and their supporters to be years of training for future service in Bolivia. And now the time had come.

On January 31, 1931, the mission board again wrote to the Ayllóns. After assuring them, "As you already know the Tamplins are very nice and friendly, full of the Holy Spirit, and we know that you will greatly enjoy working with them," they informed them that in a board meeting on January 5, they had appointed Carroll Tamplin as field superintendent and his wife, Doris, as secretary/treasurer.[53] One wonders what the Ayllóns, pioneer missionaries and founders of the work, thought of this arrangement.[54]

EARLY YEARS OF GROWTH AND DEVELOPMENT (THE 1930S)

Carroll Tamplin and Juan Ayllón worked together in Bolivia for only one year, 1931, when Ayllón left for medical reasons. Throughout the rest of the 1930s, other OYM missionaries joined the Tamplins in the new work.

Juan Ayllón and Carroll Tamplin

On January 6, 1931, Carroll and Doris Tamplin, along with sons David and Jonathan, left Oregon by boat for the long journey to La Paz, Bolivia, a journey that included a stopover in Chiquimula, Guatemala, and a train trip over the Andes from Arica, Chile. They finally pulled into the train station in La Paz on the evening of February

---

50. OYM Board of Foreign Missions, letter to Ayllóns, July 7, 1930, NWYM/GFU archives.

51. Juan Ayllón, receipt to OYM, November 1930, NWYM/GFU archives.

52. Mabel F. Adell, letter to OYM, October 1930, NWYM/GFU archives.

53. OYM Board of Foreign Missions, letter to the Ayllóns, January 31, 1931, NWYM/GFU archives.

54. In an exchange of letters in 1929, Charles White and R. Esther Smith express their concerns about the Ayllóns being willing to work with any North American missionaries. Smith assures White that Juan Ayllón is indeed willing "to have missionary helpers" (R. Esther Smith, October 7; see also letters by White written July 25, August 8, August 22, and October 5, 1929, NWYM/GFU archives).

28 to a crowd of believers, along with Juan and Tomasa Ayllón, there to welcome them home.

Tamplin's ten-page report back home to the mission board is highly entertaining. He graphically describes every stage of the journey, highlighting their reception at journey's end:

> At 5 p.m. we drew up to Alto La Paz on the "rim of the kettle" and looked upon an immense Statue of Christ with hand stretched out over the city below. . . . How anxiously we looked down into the city! It took us a full hour to wind our way down to the city, a thousand feet below. As we neared the station I put my head out the window. Flocks of young Indians boarded the train and pled for our suitcases but we waved them all aside. As the train slowed down I recognized Juan's stepfather, Félix Hermosa. He exclaimed, "Don Carlos," and grasped me by the hand. Then came Don Juan. He also exclaimed, "Don Carlos!" "Don Juan!" I replied. He jumped up and we embraced through the window. I passed our suitcases out thru the window, struggling continually with those young ruffians to keep them from carrying them off. . . .
>
> Once off the train we had another time of embracing. Tomasa, Juanito and Dorcas were there. Jonathan and David had an apple apiece for them. Willing hands took our suitcases and carried them out to the street. There we found about twenty or more of the believers waiting for us. There more embraces and handshakes but few words for we could not understand them. We walked the half mile to the house, accompanied by the Indians. We had to stop frequently to breathe, but oh, how happy we were and how happy they were![55]

The "house" was an old six-story building on Los Andes Street in the Chijini barrio, a building that belonged to Juan's stepfather, Félix Hermosa, and his mother, Rosa. The Hermosas, the Ayllóns, and two other families lived there; the building also served as mission headquarters, chapel for the congregation that formerly met in Tembladerani, and classrooms for the Bible school and literacy classes. This would also become the Tamplins' temporary home.

Later that same evening, people gathered in the chapel for a spontaneous worship service, and among those gathered was a delegation of believers from the lake area. On Sunday, believers came from all points where the Ayllóns had made contacts, some 105 people, there to welcome the new missionaries and receive words of encouragement from faraway Oregon. Carroll Tamplin wrote home that "our first impressions of the work were of its definitely evangelistic character, good discipline, deep spiritual experience of the Indians and the solidity of it all."[56]

Another observation from this early letter home is worthy of note, having to do with the work on Lake Titicaca, where Juan Ayllón had extensively visited. Tamplin reported that

55. Carroll Tamplin, letter to OYM, March 20, 1931, NWYM/GFU archives.
56. Carroll Tamplin, letter to OYM, March 20, 1931, NWYM/GFU archives.

Monday night, after prayer meeting, the eleven Indians from Tiquina [probably from the meeting in Amacari] on the Lake near Copacabana, asked for a conference also. There is a large congregation there. The spokesman of the group, speaking in Spanish, stood and took his Testament in his hand and directed his remarks to me, "Pastor, it is true we have received this New Testament in Tiquina and we believe the Gospel to be true; but we need someone to come and teach us to read it, and to explain it to us. We have a chapel ready and a house for a pastor. We will come and help him move. We have waited long for you to come and resolve the problem for us. Pastor Juan began the work of the Gospel in our District and we have come first to you. Can you and will you send us a pastor or must we look elsewhere for one? There we are persecuted and threatened and we need someone to teach us and animate us. Tomorrow we must return. Shall we expect a pastor?" I wish you could have seen them. I asked Juan if he had anyone we could send. His answer was quick and frank—"Yes, we have several from the Bible School." Then I said, "Tell them we will send them a pastor within three weeks or a month." We didn't know how it would be accomplished but it was a Macedonian cry.

In conference with the rest of the missionary body we decided that Cipriano Mamani should go. He and his wife are steady, earnest Christians and he has a definite call to the work. The native church will support them in part with their offerings.[57]

Carroll Tamplin and Juan Ayllón (NWYM)

This major decision was made on Carroll Tamplin's third day in La Paz. He was clearly a mover and shaker. It appears that the believers had already begun to recognize him as the authority figure in the mission.

For the next several months, Juan Ayllón and Carroll Tamplin worked side by side as Tamplin began learning about the ministry among the Aymaras. They traveled together several times to the lake area, in response to the needs and requests of people Ayllón had been working with.

The relationship between the two very different men seems to have gotten off to a good start. Each wrote back to Oregon, expressing appreciation for the other.[58] Tamplin recommended that the mission board consider officially

---

57. Carroll Tamplin, letter to OYM, March 20, 1931, NWYM/GFU archives.
58. Juan Ayllón, letter to OYM, April 8, 1931, NWYM/GFU archives.

presenting Juan Ayllón for recording as a Friends pastor, observing that "he is a good preacher and excellent pastor, his work and the salvation of souls giving evidence of a real gift in the ministry."[59]

But it soon became clear that Tomasa's poor health hindered Juan's contribution to the ministry. She continued to struggle with altitude-related heart problems, and with the birth of Ruth Esther on May 14, 1931, her struggles increased.

In addition, Tamplin discovered that the Ayllóns had been struggling financially for years, with never quite enough money to pay the rent for their quarters and cover ministry expenses. The two families joined their resources to pay all the back bills. Tamplin wrote home that "the Ayllóns have sacrificed much for the work. How they were to carry on so long I do not know, except that God's blessing was upon it."[60]

In October of 1931, the OYM mission board wrote to the Ayllóns, giving them permission to take a leave of absence so that Tomasa could recover.[61] The family traveled to Arica, Chile, to be out of the altitude, with the provision of funds from the board.[62] They ended up staying in Arica until June of 1933, over twenty months, more than anyone had anticipated. OYM continued their monthly support, plus medical expenses, at considerable sacrifice to those in the north in the midst of the Great Depression.

While in Arica, the Ayllóns participated in a local Methodist church, and Juan spent time translating hymns into Aymara and putting together a Spanish/Aymara songbook.[63] He was able to make several trips back to Bolivia, at the end of 1931 when his mother died and in 1932 when he paid a surprise visit to the yearly meeting sessions, as well as once in 1933. At the time of the yearly meeting visit, Tamplin wrote home, "It was next to seeing an angel from heaven (almost) to see him there before our eyes. We certainly praise the Lord because He enabled him to come to us at this time. He is fine, and a great help. The Indians are glad to see him also."[64]

The two years that the Ayllóns spent in Arica turned into an agonizing period of indecision and uncertainty, with many letters going back and forth between Oregon and Bolivia. In July of 1932, Tamplin reported a generous offer from R. Esther Smith to host the Ayllóns in Chiquimula, Guatemala, letting Tomasa heal and giving Juan a teaching position in the Bible school. Smith assured Tamplin that the Ayllóns would be considered "Oregon's missionaries," free to return to Bolivia when health was recovered.[65]

---

59. Carroll Tamplin, letter to OYM, June 8, 1931, NWYM/GFU archives.

60. Carroll Tamplin, letter to OYM, June 8, 1931, NWYM/GFU archives.

61. OYM Board of Foreign Missions, letter to the Ayllóns, October 20, 1931, NWYM/GFU archives.

62. Bertha Haworth, letter to Carroll Tamplin, October 20, 1931, NWYM/GFU archives.

63. Carroll Tamplin, letter to OYM, February 24, 1932, NWYM/GFU archives.

64. Carroll Tamplin, letter to OYM, March 24, 1932, NWYM/GFU archives.

65. Chester Hadley, letter to Carroll Tamplin, October 5, 1932, NWYM/GFU archives.

The beginning of the Chaco War with Paraguay complicated the decision. Juan Ayllón was particularly vulnerable, susceptible to inscription into the army or to arrest for having "evaded" his civic duty by going abroad.

An interesting letter about the situation that Tamplin sent to Oregon gives insight into the religious expectations and pressures of the times, reflecting a stern holiness theology, and a tendency to judge others by a harsh standard. Tamplin wrote to Hadley,

> I feel that I must tell you something. You will know how to be careful about the use of this. We feel that doña Tomasa bears the responsibility of this decision (though Juan has not stated it so), and that her own lack of faith in God and lack of a vision of the field are responsible for her not desiring to return to this altitude though we must not forget that she has suffered much up here. However, being short of faith for her healing, lacking the vision of the work, being sickly and enemic, we fear for their ever returning here from the pest-ridden clime of Guatemala.[66]

By June 1933, the Ayllóns had received tickets to Guatemala, thanks to an anonymous donor, and they set out on their trip, arriving in Chiquimula on September 15.[67] Their friends in Guatemala gave them a joyous reception, and their journey toward healing continued. They were to stay in the home provided them in Chiquimula by the Friends Mission for the next six years. The three children enrolled in the Friends school in town, while Juan took on various teaching and preaching ministries in the Central American Yearly Meeting. By the end of his six-year stay in Guatemala, Juan had become pastor of the large Friends Church ("The Tabernacle") in Chiquimula and one of the teachers in the Bible school.[68] Tomasa slowly gained ground physically and began to enter into ministry again with her husband. Juan Ayllón Valle, the son, remembers fondly his school days in Chiquimula, considering it an excellent education. He also remembers traveling around the country with his father, visiting different Friends churches as his father preached and taught. His childhood memories of this time are positive.[69]

Challenges to the Establishment of the Church

Several difficulties made the decade of the 1930s a challenging time for the new mission staff to begin a work, even building on the solid foundation laid by Juan Ayllón. One of Tamplin's early tasks had to do with clarifying relationships with Friends who had previously established a presence in Bolivia. We have already seen how Friends

---

66. Carroll Tamplin, letter to OYM, April 27, 1933, NWYM/GFU archives.

67. Chester Hadley, letter to Carroll Tamplin, May 13, 1933, NWYM/GFU archives; "Ayllóns Arrive," *Harvester* 32, nos. 3–4 (1933) 3–4, EFCS archives.

68. *Harvester* 31, no. 6 (1937) 7; *Harvester* 31, no. 7 (1938) 5–6, EFCS archives.

69. Juan Ayllón Valle, interview with INELA history commission, February 10, 2014, La Paz.

sent out from the Union Bible Seminary (Westfield, Indiana) in 1919 befriended Juan Ayllón and facilitated his education in Guatemala.

In late 1930 or early 1931, before the Tamplins arrived in Bolivia, the OYM mission board received a letter of deep concern from Walter Langston and other Friends missionaries in the town of Sorata. They had apparently separated themselves from the Union Biblical Seminary in Westfield, and some of them may have also renounced their US citizenship. Hadley tried to smooth the way for both groups to work in Bolivia. He promised to respect their work, while he affirmed OYM's sense of call to also work in Bolivia. He concluded his letter by assuring these Friends, "We sincerely hope that there can be the heartiest cooperation there between you and our missionaries. Surely there [is] room in so large a field as Bolivia represents, for all who preach a full gospel."[70]

In one of Carroll Tamplin's letters home to Oregon, we learn of another issue that clouded the relationship between the two groups. Back around 1919 Juan Ayllón apparently had a brief romantic relationship with Westfield missionary Mattie Bount. Ayllón broke off the relationship before leaving for Guatemala, and Blount harbored some resentment over the years.[71] Tamplin noted the difficulties this led to in the work: "As to Mattie Blount Marca and her husband—they are now in Guaqui. Guaqui was Juan's territory and he had believers there. When she went in that district Juan reminded her that it was his work, to which she replied, '*Acaso tú eres Dios*' [Who do you think you are? God?], insinuating that he was not the one to tell her where she could or could not go."[72]

In several letters home Tamplin mentions hosting most of the Sorata Friends missionaries (some of whom had relocated to the village of Achacachi) in their home, and listening to their stories of financial hardship and illness. The Tamplins offered friendship to such as desired it.[73] The relationship continued to be uneasy, but it was not a major problem for the OYM mission staff or work. In fact, several times during the 1930s, a Sorata missionary was invited to preach in the church's annual conference.

Along with the medical crisis of the Ayllóns and the need to negotiate the claims of the Sorata Friends, the decade of the 1930s brought the international challenge of the Great Depression and, on the Bolivian scene, political and social instability that would culminate in the Chaco War.

These were difficult times in which to begin a new work, and the fact that the OYM accepted the challenge in the middle of the Depression seems a miracle in

70. Chester Hadley, letter to Sorata Friends, January 22, 1931, NWYM/GFU archives.

71. Verification of this story comes through an interview with Rachel (Enyart) Edwards Peters (by Harold Thomas and Nancy Thomas, October 14, 2014, Winchester, Indiana) whose mother, Mary Bernard Enyart, served as a Central Friends missionary to Bolivia and was a companion to Mattie Blount.

72. Carroll Tamplin, letter to OYM, June 8, 1931, NWYM/GFU archives.

73. Carroll Tamplin, letter to OYM, August 1, 1931, NWYM/GFU archives.

itself. The subject came up frequently in the exchange of letters between Tamplin and Hadley, and it produced insecurity about finances and the development of the work. Tamplin frequently expressed his concern that the mission needed to purchase property for a headquarters that would also serve as a church, a school, and missionary living quarters. Possibilities and descriptions of lots in La Paz were sent home. Added to this discussion were the pleas for more missionaries, especially after the Ayllóns' departure.

The OYM mission board responded to Tamplin's concerns with the news that in spite of the Depression, mission giving in OYM was good; people were enthusiastic and responsive, going beyond their means to give to such projects as a motorcycle for the field.[74] At one point the board decided that the $1,800 designated for property purchase in La Paz should instead go toward sending down more missionaries. The James and Mildred Raymond family and Milo Ross were the current candidates.[75] Tamplin confirmed that the sending of more missionaries had priority above property.[76]

In September 1932, Hadley wrote to Tamplin about the effects of the Depression. The board had stepped out again and Helen Cammack was on her way to Bolivia as the next missionary:

> If it were not for the sure conviction that it is the thing to do, I would hesitate to send her out under the present conditions. We are beginning to feel the depression as never before. The 1st National Bank of Boise and 10 other banks in the surrounding towns including Caldwell, went under last week. This leaves only one bank in the whole city of Boise. Other conditions are worse than they have been and we are finding it hard to meet the finances of the Y.M. But I believe that if we step out on faith He will see us through. But the only thing that we can hope to do at the present time is to keep your salaries up. And if Central America can take Juan for a time it will relieve us much.[77]

In spite of the hardships and the additional expenses of a new missionary, Hadley encouraged Tamplin to continue searching for the ideal property for a mission headquarters in La Paz.[78]

The other major challenge the mission staff and the young Friends Church faced in the 1930s was widespread social and political unrest. The slow and rocky shift to a more liberal political orientation, set against the background of the Great Depression and its effects on Bolivian economy, was only acerbated by the territorial conflicts with Paraguay over the oil-rich fields of the Chaco area in southeastern Bolivia. The interests of both Argentina and the Standard Oil Company of New Jersey complicated

---

74. Chester Hadley, letter to Carroll Tamplin, September 30, 1931, NWYM/GFU archives.

75. Chester Hadley, letter to Carroll Tamplin, January 1, 1932, NWYM/GFU archives.

76. Carroll Tamplin, letter to OYM, March 17, 1932, NWYM/GFU archives.

77. Chester Hadley, letter to Carroll Tamplin, September 4, 1932, NWYM/GFU archives.

78. Chester Hadley, letter to OYM, December 18, 1932, NWYM/GFU archives.

matters, and on July 18, 1932, war was declared between Bolivia and Paraguay. The Chaco War, which lasted until June 1935, profoundly affected both the mission and the church, as well as the populations of both countries.

As mentioned above, the onset of the Chaco War complicated Juan Ayllón's possible return to Bolivia from Chile, and later, from Guatemala, even after the war ended, as the possibility of his arrest for "evasion" of responsibility was considered a danger.[79] Beyond the war's effect on mission personnel, the church itself was feeling the stress. Tamplin wrote home in November of 1932, asking the board to "pray for our young men who have been taken to the war and those who are about to go—undoubtedly will before this reaches you. There is little to be done for exemption for an INDIAN. Between those who have gone into service and those who are in hiding we do not have enough to carry on the Bible school. As soon as possible we shall open it."[80]

In May of 1933, Tamplin reported on an evangelistic trip to the village of Aigachi on Lake Titicaca, where ten people became Christians. He wrote that "soon after this trip five of these were sent to the Chaco where two have been killed. What if we had not gone with the message?"[81]

A letter written at the end of 1933 gives details of the effects of the war on Friends. These details include a stand taken by some believers on their conscientious objection to war, persecution of believers by Catholics in the military, the strong testimony maintained by some, and the loss to the churches:

> One of our boys returned some time ago with a wounded arm. He said that during the year God had kept him from blood-shed, though as a believer and conscientious objector he had been placed repeatedly at the front of the battle, rifle in hand. One day he was kneeling in prayer with another believer, the bullets flying about them, when this boy was wounded in the arm and was taken to the hospital. He does not know what happened to the other man but believes that he was killed for he never saw him any more. . . .
>
> From one of our boys who has been at the front almost from the beginning we have heard nothing for over 3 months. We do not know if he is dead or alive. We do know that he was in the section where the fighting has been the heaviest and where the Paraguayans have advanced considerably. Two other of our boys were in the section that was reported this morning taken by the Paraguayans after the armistice was supposed to have taken effect. A wounded soldier, recently returned from the Chaco, says, "When I went to the war I was a staunch Catholic. But I met F____ P _____ (our believer boy) [probably Félix Paredes] and was thoroughly converted through his testimony and prayers." So we feel that this boy is standing true to Jesus under difficulties, *tremendous* difficulties. Because not only the Paraguayans seek his life but also

79. Carroll Tamplin, letter to OYM, January 5, 1934, NWYM/GFU archives.

80. Carroll Tamplin, letter to OYM, November 1932, NWYM/GFU archives.

81. Carroll Tamplin, letter to OYM, May 1, 1933, NWYM/GFU archives.

his own fanatical catholic countrymen. But Aymara material, thoroughly converted, is stubborn material. Their natural tenacity and stubbornness when sanctified becomes firm determination and the Aymara would rather die than give in. . . .

As to the Bible School—as a missionary body we have resolved not to re-open until the conflict in the Chaco ceases. Our prospective material is either at the front or in hiding.[82]

In his 1934 field report back home to the Board of Foreign Missions, Tamplin wrote that

of some 18 young men (12 of whom were preparing definitely for the work of the Gospel) not one remains. Some have entered the service as soldiers; one of them has returned wounded and at least one is known to be a prisoner of war in Paraguay. From the others we have not heard for several months. Some could not withstand the persecution and bloodshed and so deserted from the army. Others could not muster the courage to answer the call to arms and take their stand as conscientious objectors, and have taken to hiding.[83]

The war would actually drag on a year and a half beyond the date of this letter, ending in June 1935. All the work of the mission during the years from 1930 to 1935 was carried on in the tension of this war and profoundly affected by it.

One positive and unexpected effect of the war was that it encouraged leadership among the lower classes who had been forced to participate, and this in turn further stimulated the social unrest that eventually led to revolution and reform in the country. All this would serve to encourage the development of indigenous leadership in the church.

Early Strategies and Activities of the Mission

Before the Ayllóns left the country, Juan Ayllón and Carroll Tamplin worked closely together, with Tamplin gradually moving into the leadership role. The meetings in La Paz continued, but Tamplin's enthusiasm was gravitating toward building up the work around Lake Titicaca. Acting on the decision taken in February 1931 on Tamplin's third day on the field, the mission and small body of believers in La Paz dedicated Cipriano Mamani and his wife, Petrona, to the Lord's service on March 22. In early April the Mamanis accompanied a group of believers back to the lake, and Cipriano took up his work as pastor of the congregation. The town of Amacari was designated as the center of the Friends work in that area of the lake, based on the existence of that small group of believers whose stories were referred to in chapter 1.[84] Tamplin

---

82. Carroll Tamplin, letter to OYM, December 12, 1933, NWYM/GFU archives.
83. Carroll Tamplin, OYM Minutes, 1934, 27, NWYM/GFU archives.
84. Carroll Tamplin, letters to OYM, April 15, 1931; May 1, 1931, NWYM/GFU archives.

appointed Cipriano Mamani as pastor of the group, thus bringing it clearly under the umbrella of the Friends.

Tamplin attempted to back the establishment of the Friends on the lake legally, and together with Ayllón secured protection from persecution and obtained legal permission to open a Friends primary school. He informed the mission board,

> We have secured an order from the Supreme Government to the officials of that district to grant the religious liberty to the Indios Evangélicos according to the articles of the constitution. We have also secured government authority and supplies for the establishment of a school for the Indians of that region. Juan and I plan to go tomorrow to the Lake and show our papers to the authorities and open up the work formally. It will relieve matters a great deal there when the Indians of that free colony realize that there is a foreign organization behind the business, and that we have the protection of the government.[85]

The primary school that opened in Amacari alongside the church in 1931 began with forty-five children; Mamani served as teacher.

The strategies Tamplin employed during those early years in the 1930s to build up the work in the lake area included the following: (1) building, where possible, on the foundation laid by Juan Ayllón and those who preceded him, such as Cruz Chipana; (2) appointing national pastors and leaders, such as Cipriano Mamani; (3) sponsoring conferences for Friends in a larger area with special preaching and teaching; (4) traveling with national evangelists, such as Máximo Loza and Antonio Chambi, both in visitation of areas with a Friends presence and for evangelization in new areas; (5) encouraging the education of the children of believers through schools.

A letter sent home in May of 1931 illustrates Tamplin's evangelistic strategies. At that time he traveled with Juan Ayllón on an extended visit to the lake. He wrote that

> while we were at Amakari [sic] holding meetings . . . an Indian chief came 18 miles to ask us to come over to his village, Kalata, to hold a meeting. We went, accompanied by some twenty Indians (men and women) from Amakari [sic]. The trip over the terraced mountains with the lake always in view was beautiful indeed. Descending a stony trail we came into a picturesque little valley, dotted with barley fields and mud-walled, reed-roofed huts. In the center of the valley was this picturesque Roman Church. It is the property, not of the clergy, but of the community of Indians. Straight to the church we were led. We passed under the arched gateway. Five Indian headmen were there with their silver-adorned canes. The mayor (an Indian) was there and had the door opened for us. We went in and the people sat on the floor for there was no bench. We sang some gospel songs and then don Juan preached a gospel sermon to more than a hundred Indians in a Roman C. Church. When the altar call was given the mayor and other headmen were the first to come, and

---

85. Carroll Tamplin, letter to OYM, April 15, 1931, NWYM/GFU archives.

behind them all the 100 gathered on their knees with tears and heart-prayers. For at least once that old mud church felt its walls resound with the gospel songs and message, and the cries of hungry souls seeking God.[86]

Tamplin continued to describe the evangelistic contact of the following Sunday, still on the same trip to the lake:

> On Sunday these came to us, after the meeting, saying that they wanted us to preach in their village also. They tho't the village was small and we would not want to go, but they said that there were many who wanted the gospel there and that if we would go and preach many would accept the gospel and Christ. So on Monday we went to preach there and were received as princes. The mayor was there also. Sure enough as the message was given they began to cry and as the altar call was given the mayor led the way and many flocked to the altar and testified to having found pardon. How they hung to us and wanted us to not forget them! We called a meeting of the heads of the congregation on the Lake and decided to celebrate conferences there in June! Pray for the conferences.[87]

It's important to note the presence of community officials in these evangelistic meetings. This particular trip typifies the type of traveling ministry, and the importance of Juan Ayllón's presence in the early trips that Tamplin undertook. By the end of 1931, still Tamplin's first year on the field, he estimated that there were now some three hundred believers in the lake area alone.[88]

In spite of going to the trouble of securing government documentation for the rights of evangelicals, and in spite of attempts to work through local officials, the persecution of believers continued. In a letter home in July of 1931, Tamplin relates that Cipriano Mamani in Amacari was "beaten with sticks & kicked, and the school building was attacked with stones."[89] The persecution continued through the 1930s.

The ministry focus in the first half of the 1930s continued to be in evangelism, both on the part of the mission and on the part of the growing body of national workers, usually working together. Sometimes Tamplin and the workers he was training visited places where they had contacts and a small group of believers. Sometimes they set out on their own and entered completely unreached areas. The purchase of a launch christened "Ambassador," made in spite of the depression back home, helped facilitate this evangelistic work around the lake.[90]

In 1933 the Tamplins spent six weeks living in Puerto Pérez, where a small congregation was growing. They purchased property there and considered making it their

---

86. Carroll Tamplin, letter to OYM, May 1, 1931, NWYM/GFU archives.

87. Carroll Tamplin, letter to OYM, May 1, 1931, NWYM/GFU archives.

88. Carroll Tamplin, letter to OYM, December 31, 1931, NWYM/GFU archives.

89. Carroll Tamplin, letter to OYM, July 6, 1931, NWYM/GFU archives.

90. Carroll Tamplin, letter to OYM, October 24, 1933, NWYM/GFU archives.

home base on the lake.[91] This never developed, but national workers used the property as a base for their ministry and outreach. Later it became a temporary home to Helen Cammack and Esthel Gulley.

One conversion story illustrates the fact that, while Carroll Tamplin's influence was crucial to these early efforts at raising up a Friends Church, God was also working through the growing core of national leaders. In a letter home at the end of 1931, Tamplin tells the story of a man from the lake town of Pucarani whose wife had died, leaving him with two young children. When his mother became sick, the man began spending time and money with the local animistic healer ("witch doctor" is the term Tamplin uses), but to no avail. Having learned of a famous healer in Tiquina, the man decided to seek him out. As Tamplin tells it,

> He took a boat across the lake and landed at Amakari [*sic*]. There he sought out the house of [two community leaders] to tell him where the witch-doctor lived. These two Indians were among the principal persecutors there. But they told this man not to look for the witch-doctor, but to accept the gospel for they had seen that the believers did not get sick, were fat and healthy, dress well. It was a loss of time and money to deal with the witchdoctor. They gave him our direction here [La Paz] and he came immediately to accept. . . . I instructed him and gave him a Testament. That night he accepted publicly. He said he was going back to Pucarani and read his Testament to his relatives and tell them to come to the Gospel also. So you see how God has made even His enemies to glorify His name.[92]

Tamplin does not give the name of the man from Pucarani, but this may have been the genesis of the Friends Church in that community. It's important to note the strong testimony of the believers in Amacari. Even so, at the time of this story, some believers seemed to feel that the presence of the missionary was necessary for the conversion "to take," but that sense was soon to pass as people matured in their own Christian experience.

Growth of the Mission Staff

Along with the growth of numbers of believers and congregations, the mission staff increased as others came to share the load with the Tamplins. Helen Cammack arrived in 1932 and took on as her first task teaching in the primary school in La Paz, dedicated to the children of believers. This was building on the work begun by Juan Ayllón and encouraged by Carroll Tamplin. Cammack went on to develop a Bible-based curriculum to be used in literacy work with both children and adults in the three Friends primary schools that grew up in La Paz, Amacari, and Pongon Huyo by the end of the 1930s. In the 1940 annual conference, Cammack was recognized for her

---

91. Carroll Tamplin, letter to OYM, August 16, 1933, NWYM/GFU archives.

92. Carroll Tamplin, letter to OYM, December 31, 1931, NWYM/GFU archives.

contribution and named by the Missionary and Native Church Council as Director of Biblical Studies for children and adults.

Helen Cammack evidenced a positive initial attitude toward the Aymara people she felt called to minister to. One senses the stance of a learner. In 1935/36, she served as temporary field superintendent while the Tamplins were home on furlough. As part of the 1936 annual field report she requested special prayer "that the missionaries may more fully understand the viewpoint and life of the people so they may know better how to present the gospel to them" and "for the special help of the Lord for the missionaries in learning the Aymara language."[93]

In Tamplin's 1937 annual field report, he writes about Cammack that "a request from the Indians at the Lake states that during the time she has been among them (about two months) she has come to understand them and talk to them in their dialect, and that they do not want her to go home to Oregon,"[94] a reference to her upcoming furlough.

Esthel Gulley arrived in 1935, bringing her medical skills to add to the contributions of the mission staff. For a time Gulley and Cammack lived together in Puerto Pérez. This became their base as they traveled around the lake and to areas on the *altiplano* in evangelistic, educational, and medical ministries. The 1939 annual field report states about Gulley that "her ministry to the physical needs of the people about the port is playing a large part in the breaking down of the prejudices against the mission there."[95]

Howard and Julia Pearson joined the mission staff in 1936. Like the Tamplins, they had felt a call to Bolivia, but first experienced missionary service in Guatemala before coming under the umbrella of OYM for deployment to Bolivia.[96] For their first four years of service they lived in the mining community of Corocoro. Sometime between 1936 and 1937 the mission had received permission from the Methodist-Episcopal Mission, who had polity rights in the Corocoro region, to begin a work, passing on to Friends the base of a few believers in the town. After doing a survey of the area, the mission rented a house and a hall for meetings, and sent the Pearsons to live there. Their work consisted mainly in hosting meetings in Corocoro, attempting to disciple the believers and organize a church. They had notable success with large numbers of children in town attending their Sunday school. They also traveled some to do evangelistic work in surrounding villages, especially Santo Tomas and Pucarani.

Carroll Tamplin continued on as field superintendent during the 1930s, but with the arrival of new mission staff, his work more and more became administrative, rather than evangelistic. Most of his time during that later part of the decade was tied up with purchase of property in La Paz and oversight of the construction of the chapel.

93. OYM Minutes, 1936, 30, NWYM/GFU archives.

94. OYM Minutes, 1937, 38, NWYM/GFU archives.

95. OYM Minutes, 1937, 25, NWYM/GFU archives.

96. Charles S. White, letter to R. Esther Smith, June 1, 1926, EFCS archives.

As early as 1934, the American Bible Society, under the leadership of John Ritchie, invited Tamplin to be the treasurer of its Bolivian branch.[97] In 1938 the ABS organized a team to work on a translation of the Gospels and Acts in Aymara. Along with a core of Aymara speakers, the Baptist, Methodist, and Friends missions participated, and Carroll Tamplin accepted the invitation to lead the team. For much of 1939, Tamplin lived and worked at the Baptist farm headquarters in Huatajata, on Lake Titicaca, traveling back to La Paz on weekends to be with family and oversee the Friends work. The ABS invited Juan Ayllón to come from Guatemala and contribute to the project, which he did, leaving Tomasa and the kids back in Central America for a time.

The Indigenous Ideal

With Tamplin focused on administration, the evangelistic work of the mission was carried on by the Pearsons in Corocoro, and by Helen Cammack and Esthel Gulley in the lake area, along with their other tasks. But while the intensity of the evangelistic thrust on the part of the missionaries was diminishing, the Aymara believers were growing in their own sense of call and efforts to reach out in their communities and beyond.

Actually, the increasing evangelistic activity of the national church fits with the vision Carroll Tamplin had since the beginning of his work in Bolivia. As early as 1933, Tamplin was explaining to Chester Hadley his vision of the indigenous church, taken mainly from a book written by John Ritchie, *The Indigenous Church in Peru*. Ritchie was the same ABS missionary under whom Tamplin would later serve in the Aymara translation project. Tamplin encouraged Hadley to have the mission board read the book aloud together and become convinced of the vision of "a truly indigenous church in Bolivia." He expressed some of his philosophy of mission strategy in this letter:

> With a Yly. Mtg. with as limited resources as Oregon has, it seems to me an extremely important thing for us to carry on our work on purely native resourcefulness and sacrifice as is possible. Frankly, I am not a partisan to the idea that the home church should hold deed and title to *all* the native church structures. . . . I plan to ask the homeland for as little as possible for the building of chapels etc. in the villages. . . . A recent proposed law in congress . . . (restricting the establishing of new religious orders, regulating the number of foreign dignitaries in proportion to natives, and providing for a complete inventory of all furniture as well as property) makes me feel that we must build from the start on the purely *native* plan.[98]

Although this letter gives finances and political astuteness as reasons for an indigenous strategy, we know from Tamplin's practice of encouraging national leadership

97. Carroll Tamplin, *Harvester* 28, nos. 1–2 (1934) 6, EFCS archives.
98. Carroll Tamplin, letter to OYM, October 9, 1933, NWYM/GFU archives.

that his vision had a deeper basis. He tried to prevent dependency on the mission, convinced that the church needed to stand on its own. In a sense Tamplin was ahead of his times, for this was not yet accepted missiological practice among other missions in Bolivia, but in other ways his ideals clashed with his own tendency to exercise strong leadership and control outcomes of ministry. Added to this was the dark view most North American missionaries seemed to take of the native culture, and their suspicion that the new believers needed lots of care and supervision before they could be trusted to stand on their own. The early work went forward in the context of these tensions.

These tensions found expression within the missionary team. In a 1939 letter to Chester Hadley, Tamplin reinforces the importance of what he is now calling the mission's "Indigenous Church Plan," and complains that "it might be frankly stated that Pearsons are not in full-hearted support of the Indigenous Church idea. It would be a good idea to be sure that future candidates for the field understand that this is the *Board's* policy as well as the Mission's."[99] Hadley responded, reassuring Tamplin that the board indeed affirmed the policy and would so instruct future candidates.[100]

During the decade of the 1930s, the mission was involved in the training of local leadership as part of its strategy. Much of this training happened informally as various workers accompanied Tamplin and then other missionaries on their evangelistic trips. The formal Bible school in La Paz made up another key training strategy. Tamplin again built on the foundation laid by Juan Ayllón but had his own thoughts about the development of the school. As he was planning to reorganize the school in 1932, he mentioned emphases in Bible, trades (such as carpentry), physical exercise, and spiritual depth; he saw missionaries as the main teachers.[101] This description gives some of the flavor of the Bible school experience:

> We have now had the school going for two weeks. We are on a full schedule. We have ten Bible School students and twelve children in the Grammar school. We have a teacher helping us—paying him 20 bolivianos per month. We have purchased a carpenter's bench and large wheel for a turning-lathe and four of the Bible School boys are working there trying to earn their way. . . . Last week two of the Bible Students went to Obrajes to distribute tracts and evangelize. They reported, in chapel, that they had been threatened with stoning, and some asked them, "Why have you come to trouble us here?" . . . This week two others are to go to Achocalla . . . where we have a few believers. Next week I hope we can send them to Laja where we have a congregation of 20 who are begging for a pastor. Then to Viacha, an important railroad and

---

99. Carroll Tamplin, letter to OYM, September 11, 1939, NWYM/GFU archives.
100. Chester Hadley, letter to Carroll Tamplin, September 29, 1939, NWYM/GFU archives.
101. Carroll Tamplin, letter to OYM, December 31, 1931, NWYM/GFU archives.

military center on the Arica line. . . . Our school for children is full to capacity and we have had to turn away some.[102]

Tamplin actively engaged students in his evangelistic and outreach plans for expansion of the work. This effort at formal training through a Bible school fell to the side during the time of the Chaco War, as we have seen, when so many young men of the indigenous peoples were forced to serve in the military. The Bible school did not open again until January of 1939. At that time, the program ran for three months, with a different missionary teacher in charge each month, and a student body that varied between six and fifteen people, one of whom was a young woman. The outside work demands on students, some of whom traveled to La Paz from their rural communities, made consistent attendance and serious study a problem.

The La Paz Friends Church

The mission followed the organizational form of Oregon Yearly Meeting and other Friends churches around the world. Organized churches were called monthly meetings, in reference to the custom of having one business meeting a month. Newer groups came to be referred to as dependent congregations.

One of these monthly meetings stands out during this period and serves to illustrate some of the dynamic of the growth and development of the Bolivian Friends Church during the 1930s. This was the congregation in La Paz.

The congregation in La Paz dates back to 1924, as we read earlier in this chapter, when Juan Ayllón first visited Tembladerani. It was recognized as a monthly meeting in 1925. The congregation changed locations several times, all within the same general area of La Paz. Ayllón himself served as pastor.

The arrival of Carroll and Doris Tamplin, and the departure of the Ayllóns for medical reasons, both in 1931, changed the leadership of the congregation. Tamplin assumed the pastoral role, as well as oversight of the expansion of the work. At times, as Carroll traveled, Doris Tamplin served as pastor of the church, always relying on the developing local leadership. The congregation moved to another building in Chijini in 1932 or 1933 when the Tamplins themselves moved out of the house owned by Ayllón's stepfather, Félix Hermosa.

The annual field report to the mission board in 1936 reported that Félix Hermosa was leading the work in La Paz, that church attendance was increasing, that children now had their own program, that people were being trained as Sunday school teachers, and that even a few women were serving as teachers for girls.[103]

The annual field reports for 1937 and 1938 speak about the evangelistic outreach of believers from the congregation and the formation of "Gospel teams" who traveled out to areas around La Paz, entirely under local leadership. In the 1938 report

---

102. Carroll Tamplin, letter to OYM, January 22, 1932, NWYM/GFU archives.

103. OYM Minutes, 1936, 27–28, NWYM/GFU archives.

Tamplin notes of these leaders that "they have willingly sacrificed time from work to hold evangelistic services on the street, in the plazas of Villa Victoria, Laja, Achocalla, and Tambillo. Trips were made regularly every week-end (two teams in different places) when weather would permit."[104] The report also mentions some persecution by Catholic priests and local authorities on these trips.

The 1939 field report informed that from this congregation a group of twelve people have given themselves to the work of evangelization, and that from this group the congregation has separated two men: Justo Tabel, a "self-supporting pastor," and Mariano Medrano, "a travelling evangelist with partial salary and expenses paid by the La Paz congregation." Tamplin went on to state that "this congregation is setting the pace for the entire field, carrying their local expenses and supporting two native workers, Cipriano Mamani and Mariano Medrano, with their offerings."[105]

Construction of Friends meetinghouse on Max Paredes Street, 1938 (NWYM)

A key piece in the story of the La Paz congregation in the 1930s concerns the purchase by the mission of property on the corner of Max Paredes and Santa Cruz Streets in a developing area of La Paz. Carroll Tamplin was heavily involved in the property purchase in 1937 and the construction of the first church building during 1937 and 1938. Although the major financial contribution came through the mission, local believers gave generously of their money and active participation on the building crews. They

104. OYM Minutes, 1938, 26, NWYM/GFU archives.
105. OYM Minutes, 1939, 25, NWYM/GFU archives.

constructed a meeting room for three hundred, with a basement that included an apartment, and classrooms that could accommodate Sunday school, as well as a Bible school and general education classes. The site would also house the mission head-quarters and, later, yearly meeting headquarters for years to come. While Tamplin's concern for indigenous development of the work held that funds for church proper-ties should come from the people themselves, the expense of property in the city and the hope for a headquarters for the work made this case an exception.

The official dedication of the chapel took place on August 28, 1938. Julia Pearson describes this event in a letter home to her sister. Julia herself led a special service for children in the morning with forty in attendance. People spent the afternoon in a praise service, and the main service began at 7:00 p.m.

> The evening service was the formal dedication. The Baptists and the Method-ists dismissed their services and joined the dedicatory service. We had bor-rowed benches from them as we haven't near enough. . . . We jammed 400 people in the auditorium that night. The aisles were full and the walls lined with those standing up and the front around the platform filled with "mamas" sitting on the floor. It was a great service. Several prominent doctors, lawyers and business men of La Paz came too and it was a mixed crowd, with lowly Indians and high class Spanish sitting side by side. We started at 7 pm and closed at 10:30 pm. . . . Helen was royally welcomed by the believers.[106]

Pearson reports that Helen Cammack, just returned from her year of furlough in the United States, had brought an organ for Corocoro. They had unpacked it and inaugurated it in the dedication service. In the invitation, the chapel is referred to as the "Templo Evangélico 'Amigos'" (Friends Evangelical Temple).

In 1940, the congregation came full circle when it invited Juan Ayllón to become pastor. Ayllón had come from Guatemala to serve with the American Bible Society's translation project, directly under the leadership of Carroll Tamplin. The Friends Mis-sion extended the invitation to the Ayllóns to stay in Bolivia as national workers. They agreed, although they would not have their former status, or salary, as missionaries. Happy to be back home in Bolivia, Juan and Tomasa Ayllón took up their pastoral role at the La Paz Friends Church in December of 1939. The mission gave them an annual salary as national workers. The La Paz congregation also contributed to their support.

The Emergence of National Leaders

The names of several individuals come up in the various reports as developing Friends leaders throughout the decade. Most of these names belong to men. (Tamplin ex-pressed his sense of the need to develop "a vision on the part of the women of the possibilities of service for the Gospel by them" in 1934.)[107] The intentional discipling

---

106. Julia Pearson, letter to OYM, August 30, 1938, NWYM/GFU archives.

107. Carroll Tamplin, letter to OYM, February 1934, NWYM/GFU archives.

efforts of the early missionaries bore fruit. Bolivian Quaker leaders who were active during the decade of the 1930s include Antonio Chambi, Félix Hermosa, Cipriano Mamani, Bernardo Paredes, Mariano Medrano, Máximo Loza, and Félix Guanca, among others. Most of the leaders that Tamplin worked with, with the exception of Félix Guanca, had first been discipled and trained by Juan Ayllón.

Cipriano Mamani

The other congregation that stands out in this developing period of the church is that in the lake town of Amacari; this is the group that originally formed between 1915 and 1924. With the continual visits of Juan Ayllón in the 1920s, the group began to identify itself with Friends. In 1931, as we read earlier, the new OYM mission staff, under Carroll Tamplin, appointed Cipriano Mamani as pastor. Mamani had been initially discipled under Juan Ayllón as part of his small Bible school. Throughout the 1930s, as Cipriano Mamani and his wife, Petrona, gave indigenous leadership to the growing work around the lake, the mission supported this work with frequent visits, leadership training courses, and annual conferences that gathered all the groups in the area for worship and teaching.

Cipriano and Petrona Mamani, 1930s (NWYM)

Even though it's clear that the presence of the missionaries was crucial and even dominant during this period, the Bolivian church was growing in maturity and leadership. The congregation at Amacari exemplifies this growth. Cipriano Mamani served as pastor, schoolteacher, and evangelist in the whole lake region. In his 1934 field report to the mission board in Oregon, Tamplin wrote about the congregation in Amacari:

In Amacari the records show a steady increase in attendance on the Sunday services. During the week Cipriano Mamani holds services in the neighboring villages. The believers of that region are zealous and are doing very nicely with carrying their own burdens. Each member designates a certain number of rows of potatoes, habas, barley and ocas in his harvest field, to be turned over to the support of the pastor. A council of five faithful Indians arranges and settles church matters and disputes. Each Sunday offerings and tithes are received and the pastor keeps a very neat and faithful record. These offerings have been used to purchase a small land-site for the pastor and build a three-room house for him adjoining the school-room. All of their expenses have been taken care of by themselves. It is their hope to build the big chapel building during this next dry season, which will seat between three and four hundred. Pray for them. Frequent journeys of evangelization are made by them, even into Peru.[108]

This shows a congregation of believers learning to govern themselves, support their pastor, finance their own building projects, and reach out into the surrounding area, with a minimum of supervision by the mission. The leadership of Cipriano Mamani was probably a key factor. In the same 1934 report Tamplin commented on Mamani's leadership in Amacari:

> About him has grown a thoroughly native Aymara work which is already much larger than the parent congregation here in La Paz. His methods are his own. He is an exhorter and faithful circuit "rider" though he makes his circuits on foot. He is not eloquent nor of an outstandingly intelligent type; but he is a man of sterling good character, honest, zealous, a plodder. . . . His work as teacher, pastor, and settler of disputes among the inhabitants of that section, has established him in the hearts of his enemies as well as of his friends. All speak well of him.[109]

The annual field reports through the end of the 1930s increasingly mention Petrona Mamani, now included with her husband Cipriano as pastors at Amacari. The Mamanis continued to be supported both locally and by offerings from the La Paz congregation. The Amacari Friends school received all its support from the local congregation. Although the Mamanis were growing older, they continued through the decade serving the congregation and reaching out in evangelism. Cipriano was also recognized as a leader on the national Friends level, invited by the mission to teach or preach at the annual conferences in April.

Bernardo Paredes

Bernardo Paredes became part of the Friends movement in 1926 or 1927 under the influence of Juan Ayllón in Sopocachi (La Paz). He originally became a follower of Jesus through the preaching of the Seventh-day Adventists in La Paz in 1924, and attended a Methodist congregation until his contact with Ayllón. His parents were "fanatical Catholics," in his own words. In 1927, under the ministry of Ayllón, he came

108. Carroll Tamplin, OYM Minutes, 1934, 30, NWYM/GFU archives.
109. Carroll Tamplin, OYM Minutes, 1934, 31, NWYM/GFU archives.

to an experience of "certainty that God had pardoned *all* my sins." From that time on, he identified with Friends.[110]

Paredes's personal testimony is full of stories of God's provision through tragedies that included two work-related accidents that put him out of commission for months, a robbery that depleted the family resources, and persecution for his faith. He developed a warm relationship with Carroll Tamplin and served as pastor of the small congregation in Sopocachi for several years during the 1930s. In his 1934 field report to the Board of Foreign Missions, Tamplin writes of Paredes that "his smiles and firm faith in the midst of suffering and need have brought blessing to us many times as we have knelt and prayed by his bedside. A man of judgment, faith, and vision."[111]

Mariano Medrano

Mariano Medrano from the lake district was frequently mentioned in field reports as a gifted evangelist. Tamplin includes one interesting story in his 1934 report. The context is the Chaco War and the various nativistic uprisings that were occurring:

Mariano Medrano, 1930s (NWYM)

> And so it is, that while the workers have been few and our young men taken from us (in large measure) our hearts have been cheered by the substantial, unwavering character of our older men. Take this one from the rank and file: Mariano Medrano, unlettered Indian, fisherman, burden bearer, mason's helper, former chief, drunkard, dancer, fighter and rebel against the "whites." He travels by foot and evangelizes tirelessly. He has been taken up as a draft-evader on several occasions, though he is much too old to be taken. He has improved the opportunities to testify of the change that God has wrought in him both to officials and soldiers.[112]

Tamplin went on to describe a time when Medrano was arrested and jailed. By the end of the first day, two other prisoners had become Christians. Spending several

110. Bernardo Paredes, letter to OYM, probably translated from Spanish to English by Carroll Tamplin, 1934, NWYM/GFU archives.

111. Carroll Tamplin, OYM Minutes, 1934, 31, NWYM/GFU archives.

112. OYM Minutes, 1934, 31, NWYM/GFU archives.

days in jail until his release, "he testified to the guards and fellow-prisoners, and God comforted him with visions in the night."[113]

In his 1935 field report, Tamplin reports that "Mariano Medrano was the Indian with whom I was travelling when the storm overtook us and shipped so much water that we became doubtful of making land. He prayed and the storm was stilled."[114] In his 1936 report, Tamplin writes, "Outstanding among the believers in evangelism is Mariano Medrano. He sees the opportunities and tries not to lose them. When at the station to bid Tamplins good-bye the believers sang a farewell hymn. Some standing near began to make fun. When we turned to go I found Tata Mariano giving the gospel to quite a group of those who had sneered."[115]

By 1939, Medrano had moved to La Paz and was supported by that congregation as a traveling evangelist in the area around the city. Tamplin mentions that at age sixty, Medrano was finally learning to read.[116]

THE YOUNG CHURCH AT THE END OF THE DECADE

Along with the development of congregations and indigenous leaders, we see structural development taking place during the decade of the 1930s. The mission sponsored the annual meetings of all Friends gatherings in April, held in La Paz, and another annual gathering in the lake area in November. These were important times of encouragement, teaching, fellowship, and consolidation of identity as a community of Friends.

Another important step toward structural development took place during the 1939 annual conference. Tamplin describes this development in the field report: "Among some other important forward steps in the development of the Aymara church was that of a studied plan of nationalization. As a proper development of the movement already in operation a united council of missionaries and Aymaras was appointed—to consist of four missionaries and four Aymaras. This council is called The Missionary and Native Church Council. We trust that this work may be carefully guided of the Lord."[117]

This was an early attempt to encourage the eventual self-government of the national church. Concerning that same annual conference where this decision was taken, Tamplin observes the growing respect the people have for their own leadership: "There was this year a decided willingness on the part of the people to listen to their own Aymara workers preach and report, whereas in other years they seemed to prefer only the ministry of the foreigners. This shows, not a drifting away from the missionary, but an increased respect for their own fellowmen as pastors and men of God. Our

113. OYM Minutes, 1934, 31–33, NWYM/GFU archives.
114. OYM Minutes, 1935, 31, NWYM/GFU archives.
115. OYM Minutes, 1936, 29, NWYM/GFU archives.
116. OYM Minutes, 1939, 25, NWYM/GFU archives.
117. OYM Minutes, 1939, 29, NWYM/GFU archives.

respect to these men gave them a place of confidence which in former years they had not enjoyed. It is our hope that from year to year the ministry of these native brethren may be much enlarged."[118]

A statistical report for this period is difficult. The Aymara culture of the times did not value numbers and the believers didn't bother counting themselves. While the mission desired to give positive reports of growth to supporters back home, we have no record of how the statistics were gathered. But some of the numbers from the annual field reports can at least give an idea of the growth of the church.

In 1930, the Ayllóns reported the existence of two congregations in La Paz, the original meeting in Chijini and a small group meeting in Miraflores. They also referred to regular contact with groups of believers in twelve villages. The 1940 field report records three fully organized monthly meetings (with resident pastors and Sunday schools) in La Paz, Amacari, and the newly acquired Pongon Huyo congregation. This report also mentions twenty-six "outstations" and a total of fifty-six "points under constant visitation." Some of these would be the equivalent of dependent congregations.[119]

The 1930 report noted six leaders-in-training in night Bible classes, while the 1940 report acknowledged eleven "native workers," including pastors and evangelists. The two primary schools existing in 1931 (La Paz and Amacari) expanded to include the school in Pongon Huyo by 1940. Church membership is reported for the first time in 1940, with a figure of 250.[120] The number of attenders would have been higher.

REFLECTIONS ON THE PERIOD

During this early period the church developed exclusively in the Aymara culture, with the first churches in Amacari and La Paz being planted among free Aymaras, rather than among those who had belonged to the hacienda system. As representing free communities, the people would have more ability to choose and were thus relatively more receptive to a new message, even though facing persecution.

The historic events that most impacted the development of the church were the Great Depression and the Chaco War with Paraguay. The Depression naturally limited the size of the mission and the funds at its disposition, both of which were probably beneficial in forcing a light footprint. The Chaco War, while drastically affecting the indigenous population of Bolivia, had its positive effects in awakening the people to the injustices of the times and to their own potential to influence history. This population is that from which the leadership of the Friends church would come.

In considering the missiological significance of the early practices of the mission, it is helpful to look at the strategies Juan Ayllón established from his very first year as

---

118. OYM Minutes, 1939, 29, NWYM/GFU archives.

119. Juan and Tomasa Ayllón, report of 1930, to OYM; OYM Minutes, 1940, 31–36, NWYM/GFU archives.

120. Juan and Tomasa Ayllón, report of 1930, to OYM; OYM Minutes, 1940, 31–36, NWYM/GFU archives.

a missionary to Bolivia, most of which Carroll Tamplin would later continue to carry out. Several factors in those first few years, 1924–1930, point to reasons for the firm foundation that was laid for the future development of the INELA. Juan Ayllón fleshed out some sound missiological practices well before the time when these would be taught in seminaries for the preparation of missionaries:

1. An attitude that permitted experimentation in different methods and ministries: The ministry of colportage was common among missions around the world at that time and had been an emphasis of William Abel. The American Bible Society had an interest in Juan Ayllón's serving with them in this capacity among the Quechua-speaking peoples of Bolivia. Ayllón gave it a try, and then decided this was not what God was calling him to do.

2. A focus on a specific people group: Ayllón was able to say "no" to work among the Quechuas because he felt a strong call to the Aymara people. Although this was part of his own heritage, through his mother, he did not identify himself as Aymara, and he saw the need for cultural preparation. We know that he spent time that first year reading the novel *Raza de bronce* (Race of Bronze, 1919), by *mestizo* author Alcides Arguedas, an artistic attempt to tell the story of the oppression and suffering of the Aymara peoples. We also know that Tomasa was concerned with learning to speak the language, along with her husband. They were totally focused on this one people group.

3. Aymara worship services: Although Ayllón was probably more proficient in Spanish than in Aymara, he began right away to preach in the Aymara language. He also began translating hymns into Aymara, and he used these in the first worship service in Tembladerani.[121]

4. Firsthand contact with many people: Juan Ayllón occupied much of his time that first year talking with people, meeting his neighbors, following up all the contacts that came his way. His strength was in person-to-person relationships. These contacts took him out to locations that would later become centers of the Friends Church, places such as the community of Amacari on Lake Titicaca and Tembladerani on the outskirts of La Paz.

5. Identification with the people: Although there does not seem to have been an attempt to "go native," the Ayllóns evidenced their desire to understand and relate to the Aymara people in their move to Tembladerani, an Aymara community, where they lived close to the level of others in that community. This went hand in hand with what appears to be a growing understanding of the leadership and kinships systems of the culture.

121. The movement to write original hymns in Aymara, rather than make translations from Spanish or English hymns, was to come several years later, prompted by missionaries with Wycliffe Bible Translators. Bolivian Friends were among these early composers, but that comes later in the story.

6. A focus on leadership training: Whether formally through the Bible school that met in the evenings, or informally as different men accompanied him on his evangelistic trips, Ayllón was actively training people to lead in the church and reach out in ministry. Most of the leaders that Tamplin later worked with in establishing the church were those whom Ayllón had trained.

7. Holistic ministry: In addition to evangelism and discipleship, Ayllón's adult literacy classes would soon expand to include general education classes for the children of believers. As he traveled he always carried a simple first aid kit and frequently used it.

8. Sowing the seed among people of cultural influence: While this may not have been a deliberate strategy on Ayllón's part, the fact that the first Friend in that first congregation in Tembladerani was an influential leader in his sociocultural setting is significant. This prepared the way for the receptivity of many Aymara people to the gospel message.

9. Respect for the work of others: Ayllón made contact with Friends missionaries in Sorata, some of whom had been his friends previous to his years in Guatemala. He respected their feelings concerning mission polity and followed their advice as to where to focus his work. Although the relationship between the different groups of Friends would get complicated in the future, Ayllón respected those who came before him.

10. Strong relationship with supporting churches: The many letters that went back and forth between their Guatemalan supporters and the Ayllóns provided needed encouragement. Frequent communication, and the assurance of constant prayer support played a role that can't be measured.

Those first years of Juan and Tomasa Ayllón in Bolivia helped lay a firm foundation upon which to build the Friends Church.

We have seen how Carroll Tamplin carried on some of these same strategies, such as his focus on enabling national leadership, and his combination of evangelism with service (as evidenced in the schools). One of Tamplin's main contributions was his insistence on the indigenous philosophy for mission work, with the purpose of eventually facilitating an independent national church. This contrasted to other mission groups in Bolivia at the time, and although the actual application of this philosophy would prove complicated, as the rest of this book will show, it remained the standard. Tamplin was the one who first articulated the philosophy that would guide the Friends Mission work down through the years among the Aymara of Bolivia and Peru.

The indigenous church concept of the times focused on the three selves, seeing the goal of mission as the formation of a national church that was self-governing, self-supporting, and self-propagating. These became the goals of the OYM mission in Bolivia, with Juan Ayllón's work as a precursor. The focus was on independence from foreign ownership. Today it is widely recognized that the three-self concept does not necessarily lead to a mature church in the biblical/theological sense, nor does it automatically result in a contextually appropriate church. These were issues that the mission and the church would wrestle with in the future.

The attempt to plant a Friends church in these early years was subordinate to planting a Christian holiness church. We've seen the strong influence of the holiness movement on William Abel, Juan Ayllón, and Carroll Tamplin. Indeed, the evangelical Friends churches in the United States were all impacted by this movement. Some of the holiness doctrine and practice coincided with the essence of the Quaker Christian faith, stemming from the seventeenth century, with its emphasis on the person and work of Jesus, the guidance of the Holy Spirit directly and through the Scriptures, and the various testimonies that fleshed out the faith in daily life. The missionaries obviously taught the peace testimony, as seen in the various reactions the believers had to serving in the Chaco War. And their activity showed the value of service combined with evangelistic outreach, a Quaker perspective. But by and large, the focus was on the forming of a Christian church with a holiness emphasis, not on forming a Quaker community.

The early missionaries were growing in their understanding of the Aymara culture, seeing the importance of the kinship and social structures. On the other hand, they probably did not sense the depth of the animistic worldview perspectives, tending to identify beliefs and customs as "superstition," needing only a conversion experience to be eradicated. This proved to be a secularizing influence in the early Friends church. Aymara converts themselves would continue to hold their deep convictions about the reality of the spiritual world and the need to face it. It seems that the mission focused its message on an expectation of holiness and personal transformation, while the new Aymara believers put more expectation in God's power and protection in the community.

One of the things that stands out about these early missionaries was the ways they tried to identify with the Aymara people. Obvious, too, was the way they gained the trust and appreciation of these people, in spite of their differences. We see the work of God's Spirit in this.

The work of the Spirit throughout these early years can also be seen in the fierce commitment of the missionaries whose lives of service planted seeds that would one day result in abundant harvest. And we see the Spirit's work in the receptivity of the Aymara people and the development of men and women who would themselves become the leaders and ministers of their church.

4

Inner Turmoil

The Bolivian Friends Church in the Decade of the 1940s

On the national scene, the decade of the 1940s was a period of political and social unrest, punctuated by seasons of violence. The Friends Church experienced its own internal conflicts as well as conflicts with the mission; in spite of all this, the church continued to develop.

Throughout the decade, as the mission staff grew, strategies changed. Yet the commitment to the indigenous ideal held steady. The story of the church and the story of the mission intertwine, all against the background of turmoil on the larger political and social scene.

HISTORICAL BACKGROUND

During the decade of the 1940s, Bolivia's political leadership fell to a succession of short-lived governments ranging from military regimes to elected officials. These governments represented both conservative elements as well as the variety of new leftist political parties that were rising up. Some of the governmental changes were violent.

The decade witnessed major struggles over labor issues and the rights of indigenous peoples. Klein notes that "with the progressive radicalism of the middle-class whites, there came a more profound radicalization of the laboring classes, and especially of their most powerful and revolutionary vanguard, the mine workers."[1] In light of major strikes in the mines, including what became known as the "Catavi Massacre" in 1942, union leader Juan Lechín rose to prominence. In 1944, sixty thousand mine workers and union organizers gathered at Huanuni to organize the *Federación Sindical de Trabajadores Mineros de Bolivia* (the Federated Union of Mine Workers of Bolivia), and Lechín assumed leadership of the country's labor movement.

The labor movement was closely aligned with the movement for indigenous rights, especially in regards to the land and to the system of forced labor on the

1. Klein, *Concise History*, locs. 3620–26.

haciendas. Since the Chaco War in the 1930s, the move to expand the haciendas had died down, due mostly to the economic hardships following the Great Depression. The peasantry now found itself divided into three groups: the *colonos* still tied to the hacienda system, the *comunitarios* or free Indians still living on communal land, and the newest group, landless Indians who had been removed from their homes and fields by the government policy of enabling land purchases on communal land. All these groups of indigenous peoples now became involved in the spirit of unrest and rebellion that was moving through the nation.

Another significant event early in the decade was the birth of a new political party known as the *Movimiento Nacionalista Revolucionario* (MNR, or Nationalist Revolutionary Movement), which would soon emerge "as the most popular party on the left and the single most powerful political movement in the nation."[2]

The year 1947 was especially chaotic, with armed assaults against hacienda landlords and uprisings of free Indians as well. The government responded with armed repression, killing hundreds of indigenous people. Gotkowitz observes that "while state repression struck a powerful blow against rural leadership in all regions, and ruptured a movement uniquely based on rural-urban ties, it did not fully suppress indigenous mobilization. Rural unrest persisted until the 1952 revolution."[3]

On the international scene, World War II raged, coming to an end in 1945. Bolivia continued to remain relatively isolated. One change was the few Nazi leaders who made Bolivia their country of refuge, along with a larger number of Jews who, ironically enough, also claimed the country as their new home.

THE MISSION AND THE CHURCH IN THE 1940S

During the 1940s, the mission staff grew from two couples and one single woman at the start of the decade, to a robust team of five full-time couples at the beginning of the 1950s. The purchase of a three thousand–acre hacienda in the Copajira region of the *altiplano* in early 1947 marked a change of strategy on the part of the mission, one that would profoundly affect the development of the national church. One wonders how the new believers and their communities perceived the foreign missionaries, now owners of a hacienda during this time of unrest that had both racial and social class origins.

Overall attendance in the national church grew from a community of roughly 250 people in 1940 to over 700 attenders[4] meeting in nineteen recognized churches in 1951. This slow but steady growth was accompanied by a series of internal conflicts that focused attention away from outreach, and possibly even away from what was happening in the nation at large. These tensions had to do with significant differences

2. Klein, *Concise History*, locs. 3676–81.

3. Gotkowitz, *Revolution*, 261.

4. OYM Minutes, 1951, 4, Bolivian Field Report of 700 attenders in yearly meeting sessions; actual attendance in churches would be higher.

of perspective among the mission staff, as well as conflicts between missionaries and nationals, and between Aymara Quakers themselves. The tensions and their resolution, or lack of resolution, played a significant part in the history of this era and reflected the larger tensions of the context.

THE JUAN AYLLÓN STORY CONTINUES

The American Bible Society invited Juan Ayllón to come from Guatemala back to Bolivia in 1938, in order to participate in the project of revising the translation into Aymara of the four Gospels and the book of Acts. Carroll Tamplin had been invited to direct the Bolivian team as different denominations worked together on the Baptist Mission farm in Huatajata, on the shores of Lake Titicaca.

As noted in the previous chapter, this provided an opportunity to reincorporate Ayllón into the work of Friends in Bolivia. Carroll Tamplin advocated this reincorporation in letters to the mission board. In late 1939, the missionary council voted unanimously "to recommend to the Board that the Ayllóns be returned to the field as workers. An understanding has been reached with him on the unfolding of the indigenous church plan."[5]

Juan Ayllón returned to Bolivia in 1938, followed the next year by Tomasa and the children. The mission began paying Juan a worker's honorarium of $330 a year;[6] this was about a third of what the North American missionaries received and less than what he had previously received as a full missionary years earlier.

While Ayllón outwardly expressed joy at being back in Bolivia in 1939 and seemed to accept his reduced position, one wonders what was going on inwardly. This change of status occurred during a period when the mission was making the decisions and administering the development of the very church Ayllón had founded.

The Ayllóns's Work from 1940 to 1944

The church in La Paz issued a formal invitation to Ayllón to become pastor, a task he took on in December 1939. In addition to the stipend he received from the mission as a native worker, the local church also agreed to give him $5 a month, soon to be raised to $10.[7]

---

5. Tamplin, letter to OYM, September 11, 1939. See also Tamplin, OYM Minutes, 1940, 33; NWYM/GFU archives.

6. OYM Minutes, 1940, 36, NWYM/GFU archives.

7. Carroll Tamplin, letter to OYM, September 9, 1939, NWYM/GFU archives.

Juan and Tomasa Ayllón and children (NWYM)

The Ayllóns were happy to be back in Bolivia, in whatever capacity, and their work went well for a while. Juan Ayllón juggled pastorship of the La Paz Friends Church with his work on the translation team. In 1941 the mission gave the Ayllóns the task of administering the whole La Paz District,[8] and Juan frequently preached and taught throughout the field.

That first year Ayllón lived in the same house as his stepfather, Félix Hermosa, and worked with him on the ABS translation project. This proved difficult. According to a previous agreement with the ABS, as long as Hermosa continued to serve on the translation revision committee the mission would pay him the compensation he had been receiving as their "native worker." But for various reasons the mission decided not to continue the formal relationship with Hermosa.[9] The amount designated in the

8. OYM Minutes, 1941, BFM Annual Field Report, NWYM/GFU archives.

9. Carroll Tamplin cites Hermosa's "lack of clearness on sanctification," bad behavior, an un-healing leg ulcer, the Revision Committee's dissatisfaction with his "senseless bickering and misconceptions of Scripture," and "un-Christlike actions in working with Juan on a settlement of the estate"; letter to OYM, September 11, 1939, NWYM/GFU archives.

mission budget for the "native worker" was then transferred from Hermosa to Ayllón. It was, at best, an awkward beginning for this new phase of ministry.

In fact, within a few months, the resulting awkwardness was so great that Ayllón felt forced to sell the portion of the house he had inherited from his mother and move to another section of town.[10] The awkwardness extended to the relation between Tamplin and Ayllón.[11] Other leaders in the church wanted to know why Hermosa had fallen into disfavor and why Tamplin was advising them to no longer listen to Hermosa's advice.[12]

In 1941 mission board president A. Clark Smith wrote to Ayllón asking his advice involving a situation with Helen Cammack and his opinion of single missionaries in general. Ayllón's response expresses surprise at being treated with such dignity: "I was very much surprised indeed to receive your letter of June 10th. What surprises me more is your strange attitude to ask for the viewpoint of a native worker, in such a serious case. That is too much a good thing for us natives who are accustomed not to be consulted in such a sincere way."[13]

In the same letter, he had some harsh complaints about the Tamplins, generalizing about what he called their inability to see anything from the perspective of a native person. In reference to his low compensation of $30 a month, he states that although he and Tomasa had decided to be content with that amount from the mission board, "down here they make us feel that they are the ones who are paying us, and that that amount may be too much for us to receive. We feel as if we were not workers with a holy calling, but hirelings."[14] Ayllón's complaints were limited to the Tamplins; he spoke highly of both the Pearsons and Helen Cammack.

At the beginning of 1943, Juan Ayllón was released from his pastorate so he could work fulltime with the New Testament revision committee. In his absence the La Paz church called Tomasa de Ayllón as pastor. Julia Pearson reported in a prayer letter that "she has entered into her labors and we are all happy for she is a capable woman and a true pastor for the flock."[15] Tomasa actively involved herself in other aspects of the work, as evidenced by her visit to the congregation in Pongon Huyo in 1943.[16]

Not only did Ayllón struggle in his relationship with the mission, relationships were not smooth with the national church.[17] Sometime early in 1943, four men from the La Paz Church[18] wrote a letter to A. Clark Smith, clerk of the Board of Foreign Mis-

---

10. Helen Cammack, letter to OYM, April 20, 1943, NWYM/GFU archives.

11. Juan Ayllón, letter to OYM, June 19, 1941, NWYM/GFU archives.

12. Juan Ayllón, letter to OYM, June 19, 1941, NWYM/GFU archives.

13. Juan Ayllón, letter to OYM, June 19, 1941, NWYM/GFU archives.

14. Juan Ayllón, letter to OYM, June 19, 1941, NWYM/GFU archives.

15. Julia Pearson, letter to OYM, January 20, 1943, NWYM/GFU archives.

16. *News Flash*, August 30, 1943, NWYM/GFU archives.

17. Helen Cammack, letter to OYM, April 20, 1943, NWYM/GFU archives.

18. Justo Tabel, Pascual Mamani, Feliciano Sirpa, and Antonio Condori.

sions, with some serious accusations against Juan Ayllón involving sexual harassment against several Aymara women in the church around 1939. This was before Tomasa joined Juan in La Paz.[19] In concluding the letter, church secretary Justo Tabel informed the board that he was hiding the monthly meeting minutes in his house, so no one could misuse them.[20]

With a copy to the mission staff, Smith replied with a gentle letter encouraging the brothers to confront one another in a spirit of love and humility, and to return the monthly meeting minutes to the church. He also promised an investigation into the more serious accusations in the letter,[21] something a team of visitors to the field carried out within a year. The accusations against Ayllón apparently proved to be groundless, as no further mention is made of them, but the letter demonstrates divisions within the church over Ayllón's ministry and character.

In February of 1943, the same year the four men sent the accusation against Ayllón to Oregon, the La Paz congregation in their monthly meeting session decided to remove three of the accusers[22] from membership for immoral conduct.[23] This incident further highlights the tensions within the local community.

Juan Ayllón spent most of his time in 1944 on the New Testament revision project, and Helen Cammack joined him part of the time as a proofreader. In one of her last letters home Cammack speaks highly of Ayllón's work and informs that she is gathering information to write a biography of Juan and Tomasa, in part to correct certain rumors.[24]

But the beginning of 1944 proved stormy for Ayllón and the Friends Mission. Carroll Tamplin returned from furlough in January, but now on loan from OYM to the National Holiness Missionary Society (NHMS) and no longer a part of the Friends Mission. He was joined by Marshall and Catherine Cavit, also with the NHMS, and their plan was to help begin a new holiness mission to work among lowland tribal groups in Bolivia. They were also planning to cooperate with Friends and others in opening a new interdenominational Bible school in La Paz for training national workers.

The Cavits had been named to stay in La Paz and work with Friends in beginning the new Bible school. But various conflicts would prevent this from happening, and Juan Ayllón played a part in this drama. On a surface level, disagreement over whether or not Juan Ayllón should be director of the proposed Bible school caused a rift that

19. The letter also accused the Pearsons of laziness and Helen Cammack of indiscretion.

20. Tabel, Mamani, Sirpa, and Condori, 1943. The copy is included in a letter from A. Clark Smith to the INELA, sent on April 1, 1943, NWYM/GFU archives.

21. A. Clark Smith, letter to the INELA, April 1, 1943, NWYM/GFU archives.

22. Mamani, Tabel, and Sirpa.

23. *Registro de Miembros*, 1943–1951, INELA archives.

24. Helen Cammack, letter to OYM, March 3, 1944, NWYM/GFU archives.

was never able to be resolved.[25] All sorts of conflicts swirled under the surface. Difficulties between the Tamplins and the Friends Mission were the subject of an exchange of letters between George Warner of the NHMS in Chicago and Joe Reese, superintendent of OYM, arriving at the conclusion that Tamplin should be forced to stay away from La Paz.[26] In addition, conflict developed between Pearsons and Cavits to such an extent that Cavits were forced to cancel their plans to cooperate with Friends.[27] They eventually relocated to a lowland region of Bolivia under the NHMS. Juan Ayllón was somehow barely managing to survive in the middle of all the conflict. (Helen Cammack's death came as a surprise in April of 1944 and increased the sense of crisis and tension in the field staff. Ayllón, a close friend of Cammack's, preached her funeral sermon.)[28]

In the spring of 1944, Gene Hamby of the NHMS paid an official visit to Bolivia and spent some time with Friends missionaries, as well as with the Tamplins and Cavits. He was able to attend the Friends annual conference and get a sense of the church as well as the mission. He mentioned the conflicts between Pearsons, Cavits, and Tamplins, and expressed his doubts about the possibility of cooperation in a Bible school or any other project.

Interestingly enough, Hamby expresses great appreciation for Juan Ayllón: "Your native leadership seemed unusually good to me. Despite some bad reports I heard about Juan Ayllón from the Cavits having to do with relations between Juan and Tamplin, I can say that I was deeply impressed with Juan and believe that he is a man of God. He is very gifted, efficient and spiritual. He is looked up to by the other workers, who seem to follow him very readily and without question. To my mind Juan is one of the best, if not the best, national worker that I met on my entire trip."[29]

This positive perspective of Juan Ayllón was corroborated by Helen Cammack and Howard Pearson in various letters. In the June 1944 annual meetings of the Bolivian Friends Church, Ayllón was honored as the people celebrated the twentieth anniversary of his coming to Bolivia as their first missionary in 1924.[30]

25. Brown, *Sent to the Heart*, 28–29.

26. Reese, letter to George Warner in Chicago, January 8, 1944; Warner, letter to Joseph Reese, July 3, 1944. Warner and Reese exchanged other letters on this topic between 1943 and 1945, NWYM/GFU archives.

27. Marshal Cavit, letters to OYM, January 24, 1944; February 14, 1944; March 2, 1944; Howard Pearson, letter to OYM, March 7, 1944. Other letters at this time contain further accusations and counteraccusations, including declarations by both Pearson and Cavit that it would be impossible to each to work with the other; NWYM/GFU archives.

28. Julia Pearson, letter to OYM, April 29, 1944, NWYM/GFU archives.

29. Gene Hamby, letter to Joseph Reece, May 25, 1944, NWYM/GFU archives.

30. OYM Minutes, 1944, 23.

A Painful Separation

Yet Ayllón continued to struggle under what he perceived to be the "control" of the mission over the national church. Sometime in 1944, he wrote a general, unofficial letter to all the churches, expressing his opinion that the church should be independent, free of all influence of a foreign mission.[31]

In the fall of 1944, George Warner of the NHMS and Joseph Reese and Walter Lee of OYM joined in a visit to Bolivia, partly to see if they could help resolve some of the conflicts.[32] While the visitors were there a conflict among the brethren of the La Paz church over Juan Ayllón became evident; Ayllón was again serving as pastor. Angel Tintaya, a young man at the time, remembers that Ayllón and Tamplin began yelling at each other in English in the middle of a church gathering. When he asked afterward what they were saying, Tintaya was told that Tamplin had seen Ayllón drinking beer in Copacabana, and Ayllón, in turn, had witnessed Tamplin come out of a movie house in Arica. They were challenging each other's holiness.[33]

The situation came to a head in November, just before Reece and Lee were to return to Oregon. Reece, Pearson, and Ayllón reluctantly agreed to call a meeting of the active members and take a vote as to whether Ayllón could stay on as pastor. Reece moderated what proved to be a very strange meeting:

> At this meeting Howard did the interpreting in Spanish and Máximo Loza into Aymara. After repeating several times what was expected to be voted on, we made the following suggestion—that Walter would sit in one corner of the room near the platform behind a screen and as the names of the active members were called they would go there and tell Walter "yes" or "no" to the question—Do you want a change of pastors? . . . Of the nearly active 60 members—I believe they have 56—40 of them voted. 18 voted for a change and 17 voted for no change and 4 were willing for their vote to go with what was considered the most necessary.
>
> Walter left before we could talk with Juan and I had that job to do alone. I went over I believe that afternoon Sat. and talked with both Juan and Tomasa. They seemed to have a very fine spirit and felt that under the situation that he should resign.[34]

Reece quotes Ayllón's letter of resignation, addressed to the Friends Mission and dated November 20, 1944:

Beloved Brothers in Christ:

31. Jesús Tórrez, interview with Harold Thomas and Nancy Thomas, February 10, 2015, La Paz.

32. During the years between 1942 and 1945 of conflict between missionaries who would eventually belong to two different mission groups (the NHMS and OYM Friends), Warner and Reese maintained a warm, mature friendship as their correspondence demonstrates.

33. Angel Tintaya, interview with Humberto Gutiérrez, October 30, 2015, La Paz.

34. Joseph Reece, letter to George Warner, April 9, 1945, NWYM/GFU archives.

By means of this letter I present to you my resignation, irrevocable and voluntary, as pastor of the Friends Church at 479 Max Paredes Street, in this city; and also my position as an employee of the Friends Mission in this same city, and under the direction of Oregon Yearly Meeting.

On making my resignation of these positions or responsibilities which I have held, it is not superfluous that I take the liberty to mention that I have given to this Evangelical Mission under your care in this part of Bolivia, for some 13 years, my services performed on my part with all abnegation and devotion to my divine call.

With this motive I sign myself always
Your attentive brother in the faith,
(signed) Juan Ayllón H.[35]

The mission paid Ayllón three months' severance salary and rent, a sum of $217.50. Reece wrote to Ayllón, "We trust that this is not breaking the bond of fellowship and Christian service which has been ours for the past 13 years. You have made a wonderful contribution to the work of the Gospel in Bolivia. We pray that under the leading of God we may again be united for the cause of Christ among our beloved Indians."[36]

That reuniting would never take place.

Word soon got out, and rumors abounded. Sometime in early 1945, the Assembly of Bolivian Pastors and Brothers wrote to Joseph Reece in Oregon to protest the action taken against Ayllón, as they understood it. They noted that this action "will be of fatal consequences for the future of the evangelical work in our father land," and they said that they backed Ayllón with a vote of complete confidence.[37] The news even traveled to Guatemala, and missionaries there wrote to George Warner asking why "Juan Ayllón and family had been put out of the Mission and everything they had taken away from them," an allegation that was not true.[38]

Juan Ayllón Valle, the son of Juan Ayllón, was a teenager during this time and doesn't remember much about the conflict, only that his father stopped receiving support from the mission and began to work in a shop that repaired electrical appliances. He also remembers that after quite a long time, Carroll Tamplin came to ask his father forgiveness for his part in the conflict.[39]

Juan Ayllón proved problematic for Friends for several years. Some of the flock of the La Paz church followed him when he left. For a time he worked with the Nazarene Mission[40] and later with the Bolivian Holiness Mission. In both cases he experienced

35. Joseph Reece, letter to George Warner, April 9, 1945, NWYM/GFU archives.

36. Joseph Reece, letter to George Warner, April 9, 1945, NWYM/GFU archives.

37. Joseph Reece, letter to George Warner, April 9, 1945, NWYM/GFU archives.

38. George Warner, letter to Joseph Reece, April 5, 1945, NWYM/GFU archives.

39. Juan Ayllón Valle, interview with INELA history commission, February 10, 2014, La Paz.

40. Jesus Tórrez, interview with Harold Thomas and Nancy Thomas, February 10, 2015, La Paz.

conflict working with foreign missionaries and left.[41] At the time he also repudiated the Friends position on the ordinances.[42] He ended up focusing his attention on the creation of his own denomination, known as the Bolivian Evangelical Church, about which he claimed that this was indeed a "national" work, whereas the Oregon Friends had planted an "international" church, under foreign influence and control.[43]

Mention of Juan Ayllón and his possible threat to the Friends work continued to surface from time to time during the 1940s in reports and correspondence. During his first year of missionary service Ralph Chapman wrote to the board that the problems Ayllón was causing gave him his "biggest headache."[44] A. Clark Smith, in one of his letters in 1946 to NHMS director George Warner, mentioned the problem of "Juan Ayllón and the power of his leadership."[45] Gradually, however, the sense of threat, as well as the mention of his name, would die away.

THE HELEN CAMMACK STORY

The 1940s saw an increase in the missionary staff sent from OYM to Bolivia, replacing those who had come during the 1930s. While we can't detail the contributions of each missionary, some specific stories shed light on the larger picture. Helen Cammack's is one of these stories.

Helen Cammack was the third North American to join the mission staff, coming in 1932. She spent much of her first term (1932–1937) learning the culture and language of the Aymara people, serving in the primary schools in both teaching and curriculum development, and in evangelistic outreach around Lake Titicaca. She evidenced from the beginning the spirit of one willing to learn from the people she had come to reach. The Aymara Quakers responded by requesting that she not be allowed to go home on furlough, because here was one who understood them and spoke their language.[46]

But by the end of her first term, Cammack was tired and had suffered the many health problems common among the mission staff. It was time to return to Oregon, and she arrived back in May of 1937.

After a year of reuniting with family and friends, of reporting to her supporting board and churches, Helen Cammack gave her farewell speech in the 1938 yearly meeting sessions in Newberg. Part of her speech is as follows:

Apparently the INELA congregations in Corocoro, Huarina, and Pongon Huyo switched to the Nazarenes at the time. Ayllón worked with Nazarene missionary John Briles.

41. Jesús Tórrez, interview with Harold Thomas and Nancy Thomas, February 10, 2015, La Paz.

42. Ralph Chapman, letter to OYM, December 28, 1945, NWYM/GFU archives.

43. Ralph Chapman, letter to OYM, March 16, 1945, NWYM/GFU archives.

44. Ralph Chapman, letter to OYM, March 11, 1945, NWYM/GFU archives.

45. A. Clark Smith, letter to George Warner, November 1, 1946, NWYM/GFU archives.

46. See chapter 2 for a brief overview of Cammack's first term in Bolivia.

I go back knowing somewhat of what I face. The glamour is gone, yet the pull and the urge is strong and compelling. I cannot explain the desire, but the call has been reemphasized in my heart. . . .

I go not knowing what is before me in the way of experience, but God has whispered John 12:24, 25 to me: "Verily, verily, I say unto you, except a corn of wheat fall into the ground and die, it abideth alone; but if it die, it bringeth forth much fruit. He that loveth his life shall lose it; and he that hateth his life in this world shall keep it unto life eternal."

. . . The missionary work of Bolivia is at the stage that we as ambassadors must give our lives completely, forgetful of self in order that others may live. "In journeys oft" must be said of us—seeking out the homes and villages where Christ is not known, to bring the light of the world to them. The world says that we are throwing away our lives, but I go back to die that others may live.[47]

"I go back to die that others may live." Little did Helen Cammack know that her words would prove prophetic.

Helen Cammack (NWYM)

Cammack arrived back in Bolivia in August of 1938, just in time to attend the dedication of the new church building on Max Paredes Street in La Paz. She had brought in her luggage a new organ for use in the mining community of Corocoro, and it was inaugurated in the La Paz church dedication. Julia Pearson wrote home that "Helen was royally welcomed by the believers. They were all glad to see her, and she has been a blessing to us as well."[48]

Her job assignments were twofold at the beginning of her second term: to do evangelistic work around Lake Titicaca and to oversee the educational work with the primary school program, a task that included adult literacy. For much of the following six years she would serve in Bolivia, the mission council assigned her to work in other capacities, as a fill-in for missionaries taking sick leave or home on furlough. This would include time in La Paz, working in the church and school there

---

47. F. B. Baker, ed., "Helen Cammack Gives Farewell at Yearly Meeting," taken from "Missionary Flash" (July 1938) 1–2; NWYM/GFU archives.

48. Julia Pearson, letter to OYM, August 30, 1938, NWYM/GFU archives.

and time in Corocoro,[49] overseeing the work when Pearsons traveled. But her heart was especially drawn to visitation and evangelization in the churches and communities around Lake Titicaca, and she did that as she was able, traveling by truck, boat, or mule.

In the Bolivian church's annual meetings in June of 1940, the Missionary and Native Church Council, newly formed in 1939, appointed Helen Cammack as the new Director of Biblical Instruction, a program of primary education for both children and adults. Her task was to develop a curriculum that would teach literacy and promote Bible knowledge, following the "each-one-teach-one" principles of Frank Laubach. At the end of the session, an Aymara woman rose to thank Helen and the whole group for a plan that would raise them from their misery.[50] By 1941, Cammack's primers had been published in both Spanish and Aymara and were being used in the primary schools in La Paz, Amacari, and Pongon Huyo;[51] she continued to develop this work through the first half of the 1940s.

On a personal level, events were taking place that would profoundly affect Cammack's future.

Helen Cammack, along with the other early Friends missionaries, suffered physically from the altitude and the challenging conditions on the field. During her first term, several times she needed to get out of the altitude for periods of rest. One of the resting places for mission staff was the lower city of Cochabamba. Cammack spent time at the guest quarters of the Bolivian Indian Mission (BIM) where she developed a friendship with that mission's director, George Allan.

Allan and his wife, Mary, had founded the BIM in 1907. His specialty was work among the Quechua peoples, and one of his greatest contributions was the translation of the New Testament into the Quechua language.[52] By the time of Allan's friendship with Cammack, he had been widowed for several years.

In the spring of 1940, as Cammack was preparing to travel to Cochabamba for a time of rest, Allan approached with a proposal of marriage that took her by surprise. She wrote in a letter home a year later, "My immediate reaction was negative, but the thing was such a surprise to me that I consented to pray about it as that seemed only fair and as I have always prayed concerning everything in life. I didn't expect to change my reaction however even thus."[53]

Cammack entered into a season of intense struggle, seeking the mind of the Lord, even as she was coming to realize that she did, indeed, love George Allan.[54]

49. Julia Pearson, letters to OYM, July 11, 1939; August 21, 1939, NWYM/GFU archives.

50. OYM Minutes, 1940, 32, NWYM/GFU archives.

51. OYM Minutes, 1941, 35, NWYM/GFU archives.

52. Wagner, *Protestant Movement*, 73–78. Wagner dedicated this book to George Allan, among others.

53. Helen Cammack, letter to OYM, May 26, 1941, NWYM/GFU archives.

54. Helen Cammack, letter to OYM, May 26, 1941, NWYM/GFU archives.

Her assignment at the time was to oversee the evangelistic work in Corocoro, during the Pearsons' year of furlough in the United States, and to continue to facilitate the development of the school curriculum; she lived alone in Corocoro, with frequent trips back to La Paz. The struggle went on for a little under a year. During that time she wrote, "Now I have been facing the greatest crisis in life I have ever faced and my Lord knows my heart. I do not want to make a mistake. I want to be an instrument in His hands in coming days to win souls. I am willing to continue working alone if that be His first plan."[55]

The reasons for her hesitation included Allan's age (he was much older than she was), the disappointment she might cause the Friends by leaving the work among the Aymara and joining with the BIM, and, of course, the possibility of making a mistake. She resolved to talk to no one, except for her mother in letters home, until she and Allan, as well as the BIM, felt clear as to God's will.

While for months Cammack did not feel free to accept Allan's proposal, neither was she released to say, "No." But in good time, Cammack acknowledged that "from the beginning . . . the thought which went along with the thought of marriage has been that there is a work which Mr. Allan and I can do together for souls in Bolivia which neither of us can do alone,"[56] and on that basis Helen Cammack agreed to marry George Allan. Not yet knowing how the BIM would respond, she decided that if Allan's mission were to reject her, she would call off the marriage and resign from the Friends Mission as well, so as to prevent any hint of scandal.[57] The couple agreed to keep all this secret until the BIM gave its approval.

But circumstances would force the situation into the open sooner than Cammack wanted. In February of 1941, when Allan was in La Paz on mission business, he took it upon himself to let Carroll and Doris Tamplin know about his relationship with Cammack. The Tamplins were miffed that it had been going on for some months and that Cammack had told them nothing. Cammack was also in La Paz at the time, and at one point she attended a worship service in the La Paz Friends Church with Allan; according to Tamplin, the fact that she had taken Allan's arm as they entered the church caused a scandal among the believers. But the worst was yet to come.

When it was time for Cammack to get on the train to go back to her post in Corocoro, the Tamplins accompanied her to the train station. They had said nothing to her about Allan, and the air between them must have been tense. It so happened that that very day was Cammack's birthday. George Allan suddenly appeared at the end of the station platform, running toward them to say goodbye. He robustly proclaimed, "Happy Birthday, Helen!" and proceeded to give her a big, public kiss. Several of the Friends believers were in the background, and they saw it all. The train was about to

---

55. Helen Cammack, letter to OYM, May 26, 1941, NWYM/GFU archives.
56. Helen Cammack, letter to OYM, May 26, 1941, NWYM/GFU archives.
57. Helen Cammack, letter to OYM, May 26, 1941, NWYM/GFU archives.

leave, so, without another word to anyone, Cammack boarded, and the train pulled out of the station.[58]

Shortly after arriving in Corocoro, Cammack received a letter from Tamplin, demanding that she immediately return to La Paz and give a thorough explanation for her unseemly conduct. He also wrote home to the mission board informing them of the romantic relationship.[59] Cammack complied and returned to La Paz. At that time, she also wrote home long letters detailing to the board her experience in seeking God's will in this matter.[60]

In the meantime, Tamplin had managed to cool his emotions. George Allan's friendship with him and Allan's sterling reputation for godliness must have helped. Eventually the BIM gave their permission for Cammack to join them after the marriage. The OYM mission board and staff responded with understanding, giving their blessing. So Allan and Cammack proceeded with plans for an October 1941 wedding in La Paz at which Tamplin would officiate. Of the Friends believers, Cammack wrote home, "I have greatly appreciated the believers here, their love, and their tears at my going. After they heard me tell my testimony, give the promise the Lord gave me and how I had prayed for months over it, they were very nice, even though they dislike to see me go."[61]

At this point the story takes a strange and tragic turn. The wedding party gathered in La Paz and plans went forward for the October 23 ceremony. On the night of the 21st, Allan fell sick with a hemorrhage of the lung. He struggled for several days, with Helen and others constantly at his side. It soon became apparent that his heart would give out, and on the afternoon of October 26, 1941, George Allan died.[62]

The next day Cammack wrote several lengthy letters, one to Allan's colleagues in Cochabamba and one to the mission board in Oregon. She shared details of the crisis and of his strong testimony during his last days. She shared with the mission board her own strong faith in God, saying, "I know now what real love is and also the sorrow of losing the loved one. Just why I have had to have the experience I do not know, but God knows and will use it someday to help someone else who needs comfort." She expressed her desire to stay on with Friends as their missionary to the Aymara people: "As far as I am concerned I would rather go right on working. Work will be the best panacea for sorrow, and to work among the Indians and carry on the much needed work here would give me much more satisfaction than to leave it for a time and think of it from a distance. . . . I plan to go to the Conference in Amacari this week-end and help in the classes."[63] With no thought for a time-out for grief, Cammack went on to

58. Helen Cammack, letter to OYM, April 20, 1943, NWYM/GFU archives.

59. Helen Cammack, letter to OYM, April 20, 1943, NWYM/GFU archives.

60. Helen Cammack, letters to OYM, May 2, 1941; May 26, 1941, NWYM/GFU archives.

61. Helen Cammack, letter to OYM, October 16, 1941, NWYM/GFU archives.

62. Helen Cammack, letter to Joseph Reece, October 27, 1941, NWYM/GFU archives.

63. Helen Cammack, letter to Joseph Reece, October 27, 1941, NWYM/GFU archives.

speak of her desire to perfect her Aymara language skills and of a special burden she had for Aymara women.[64]

In another letter to the mission board, asking for a response to her request to continue with the mission, Cammack wrote, "My testimony will mean much more to the natives and to the other missionaries in all the missions, if they see me victoriously go right on with my work, and that is the spirit I feel."[65] In their November meeting, the mission board reissued a call to Helen Cammack to serve as their missionary to Bolivia.[66]

From 1942 to 1944, Helen Cammack continued in her role as head of the primary school and adult literacy program. She lived for the most part in La Paz and also helped in the main La Paz church and in a new church plant in the *barrio* of Sopocachi. Her role in the school program gave her opportunity to travel out to the rural schools, especially in Amacari and Pongon Huyo. In addition to curriculum development, she emphasized the training of native teachers. She wrote in a prayer letter in 1942 that "altho [sic] I am eager to be out in the evangelistic work or in Bible classes, yet I feel that I am doing the right thing now in getting this primary school work organized."[67] She mentioned in the letter that Dorcas and Juanito Ayllón, two of Juan and Tomasa's children, were teachers in the La Paz school. This long newsy letter is full of reports of the work of the church and her own activities, making no mention of her recent loss or her grief.

In 1943, the mission board was struggling over some placement issues involving Carroll and Doris Tamplin, currently at home on furlough. The board wrote to Cammack, asking for her assessment of the Tamplins' ministry and character. It was like an invitation to open the floodgates. Cammack rarely criticized other missionaries or nationals in her letters home. Her personal journal, written during her first term, is full of spiritual wrestling, asking God to make her more submissive, more thoughtful of others, less concerned to make her own opinion known, and similar relational struggles. But this request from the board gave her the opportunity to express concerns that had been weighing on her and that she claimed were in large part responsible for her nervous disorders.[68]

In a long letter back to the board, Cammack detailed her observations about how the Tamplins had mistreated her: refusing to take her ideas or opinions seriously, assigning her to tasks regardless of her wishes or sense of call, speaking negatively of her to the nationals or other missionaries, accusing her of sexual sin, being jealous of

64. Helen Cammack, letter to Joseph Reece, October 27, 1941, NWYM/GFU archives.

65. Helen Cammack, letter to OYM, November 8, 1941, NWYM/GFU archives.

66. OYM Board of Foreign Mission, Minutes, Nov. 29, 1941, NWYM/GFU archives.

67. Helen Cammack, letter to OYM, February 10, 1942, NWYM/GFU archives.

68. Helen Cammack, letter to OYM, April 20, 1943, NWYM/GFU archives.

her ability in the Aymara language and of her good relationships with the people, and the list goes on, with detailed incidents to illustrate.[69]

This letter needs to be taken seriously, but with discernment. Cammack did admit in the letter that things had not been so bad in previous years and that Tamplins were currently suffering physical ailments. We also need to realize that Cammack herself was extremely tired and still struggling with grief at the time she wrote. But this, as well as other documents, illustrates some of the hardships of the first twenty years of OYM's mission work in Bolivia.

A great deal of the struggle had to do with interpersonal relationships among the mission staff. This partly stemmed from certain personality characteristics, realizing that the beginnings of a new work require adventurous, strong, aggressive pioneer types. Carroll Tamplin certainly, Howard Pearson, and, to some extent, Helen Cammack herself were genuine pioneers; that they should sometimes clash seems natural.

But another aspect of the hardship of the early years, also illustrated in Cammack's letter, was the mission leadership system itself, and the expectations that system carried. The field superintendent system was the norm for missions organizations all over the world at the time Friends were beginning their work in Bolivia. When OYM accepted Bolivia as their new field, they appointed Carroll Tamplin as field superintendent. While it may have been understood that other missionaries were to be consulted in planning and decision-making on the field, the superintendent had executive authority to act on his own. Tamplin took this role seriously.

Cammack was scheduled to leave for her year of rest and furlough in the United States in mid-1943. In order to complete the school year and prepare the educational work for whoever would take her place, she asked for an extension, thus delaying her return to the United States almost a year. The mission board granted the request, with consequences no one could have foreseen.

In April 1944, Cammack was in La Paz for the annual church conference. The day after the last meeting, she went to bed sick, and the doctor soon diagnosed typhoid fever. It was barely a month until she was to begin her journey home to Oregon, something she had been looking forward to. In a letter written home to her mother on April 13, she reports, "Dr. says my heart is fine so don't worry. It is a matter of patience. . . . It is a great disappointment to us all to think of the summer plans possibly being disrupted but 'let's keep our heads up' and try to find the hidden blessing. I am resting in the Lord for 'my times are in His hands.'"[70] That was the last letter Helen Cammack wrote home.

Her condition rapidly deteriorated, and on April 28, 1944, Helen Cammack died in La Paz, Bolivia. Julia Pearson, one of those who were by her side, wrote to the Cammack family the next day, telling of her last moments: "I think she understood we were praying for her but couldn't talk as she was laboring to breathe, but she smiled the

69. Helen Cammack, letter to her mother, April 20, 1943, NWYM/GFU archives.

70. Helen Cammack, letter to OYM, April 13, 1944, NWYM/GFU archives.

most heavenly smile just before she closed her eyes. It was as if she were already within the gates of Heaven."[71] Many people attended the funeral service where her dear friend Juan Ayllón preached. She was buried in a cemetery for foreigners in La Paz.

According to Friends historian Ralph Beebe, "Helen's death had a tremendous impact upon Oregon Yearly Meeting. One result was that one of the dreams she had held for many years was soon to be realized; this was the establishment of a Bible training school in Bolivia, which was constituted as a memorial to Helen Cammack."[72]

CHANGES TO MISSION STAFF AND STRATEGY

Another evidence of the impact of the life and death of Helen Cammack was the response of new missionary candidates for the work in Bolivia. Before the end of the decade, four new couples would join the mission team.

A New Mission Council

Ralph and Marie Chapman, newly appointed missionaries under OYM, arrived in La Paz in October of this tumultuous year, 1944. In Marie's newsy letters home those first few months, another picture of missionary relationships emerges. We find the Cavits and Tamplins still living in La Paz, although now not formally cooperating with Friends. Yet they joined with the Pearsons in welcoming the new couple, and all four families celebrated Thanksgiving and Christmas together. Marie told how helpful all the other couples were to her and, in general, painted a picture of mutual fellowship and help.[73]

Yet the tensions were real. In November Juan Ayllón resigned, and Julia Pearson went home to Oregon with a nervous breakdown (owing in part to the trauma of Cammack's illness and death). Howard followed her in February 1945, leaving the Chapmans as the sole OYM missionaries in La Paz, with Ralph acting as field superintendent; they were still in the language learning and cultural adjustment phase. In spite of having asked the Tamplins to keep their distance from the OYM mission work in La Paz, circumstances moved the mission board to reverse their position and ask them for help. Tamplins responded graciously and the NHMS placed them on loan back to OYM for a limited time. Carroll Tamplin agreed to pastor the La Paz Friends Church, following Ayllón's resignation, direct the day and night schools in La Paz, and organize the 1945 annual conference. But his main task was to come alongside the Chapmans in an advisory capacity.[74] In November of 1945, the OYM mission board terminated the Tamplins' pastoral and advisory work with the Friends mission and

---

71. Julia Pearson, letter to OYM, April 29, 1944, NWYM/GFU archives.

72. Beebe, *Garden of the Lord*, 175.

73. Marie Chapman, letters to OYM, October 21, 1944; November 26,1944; December 30, 1944, NWYM/GFU archives.

74. OYM Minutes, 1945, 27, NWYM/GFU archives.

released them back to the NHMS fulltime, with expressed appreciation for their help-fulness in the transition.[75]

The second half of the decade saw the missionary team increase by the arrival of Roscoe and Tina Knight in October of 1945; the return from a year of furlough of Howard and Julia Pearson in November of 1946; and the arrivals of Jack and Geral-dine Willcuts (July 1947) and Paul and Phyllis Cammack (February 1948). The new mission council was bursting with the energy of five couples, four of them new to the field.

In response to the many tensions on the field since 1930 when OYM first became involved, in the 1946/47 church year, the mission board came up with a new "Hand-book of Rules and Regulations" that changed the leadership system on the field. Ralph Chapman summarized this change in his annual field report, sent to OYM in June of 1947:

> In accordance with the new Handbook of Rules and Regulations, shortly after the arrival of the Pearsons, our field personnel was organized under the Field Mission Council. Ralph Chapman was elected chairman and Howard Pearson as secretary. The office of Field Superintendent was abolished, and the man-agement of the field was undertaken by the Mission Council, officiating as one body through its departmental secretaries. We feel that the merit of this form of mission policy already has been evidenced in the exercise of unity among the missionaries and in our relationship as a missionary body to the national church.[76]

This significant systemic change not only made the administering of the mis-sion work more democratic and participatory, it brought it into line with the Quaker testimonies of equality and unity. Although this change did not erase the possibility of interpersonal tension that comes whenever human beings work together, it would make a positive difference in the future development of the work. In addition to chair-man, secretary, and treasurer, the different roles shared among the missionary team in the remainder of the decade were secretary of evangelism, secretary of education, secretary of agriculture, secretary of construction, and editor of the publication *Soul Cry of the Aymara*. Some missionaries carried more than one role.

Carroll Tamplin continued receiving some support from OYM for his work on the American Bible Society team's revision of the Aymara New Testament, an arrange-ment that was finally terminated in 1948.[77]

75. OYM Board of Foreign Missions, Minutes, November 8, 1945; see also the Minutes for Febru-ary 6, 1946; NWYM/GFU archives.

76. OYM Minutes, 1947, 50, NWYM/GFU archives.

77. OYM Board of Foreign Missions, Minutes, September 23, 1948, NWYM/GFU archives.

The Farm

Although as early as 1936, the idea of a farm had been proposed to the mission board, at that time the idea was more that such a work at a lower altitude would give missionaries a break from the harsh conditions on the *altiplano*. When the idea resurfaced in the mid-1940s, it was discussed more as a new strategy of ministry, a possible venue for a Bible training school that would prepare the future pastors and leaders of the church. In 1945 and 1946 OYM leaders promoted the idea of a farm and began raising funds among Friends in the Northwest.[78]

On the field, Chapmans and Knights explored various possibilities and at the end of 1946 settled on three thousand acres of farm and grazing land some forty miles from La Paz, a hacienda called Copajira. Enough money had been raised to make the $23,800 purchase[79] in early 1947.

Copajira (NWYM)

Although much work needed to be done to remodel the buildings already on the property, in February of 1947 the Pearsons and Knights moved to Copajira, and on March 25 they opened the new Helen Cammack Memorial Bible School with nine students. As students ranged in preparation from basically illiterate to those with a fifth-grade education, their education challenged the missionary teachers. Classes

78. OYM Minutes, 1945, 30, NWYM/GFU archives.

79. OYM Minutes, 1947, 57, NWYM/GFU archives. With additional costs, such as lawyer fees and other legal incidentals, the total cost came to $26,197.

included basic education (reading, math, geography) and Bible in the mornings, and trades such as hat-making, tailoring, and masonry in the afternoons. In further years, only students with some education would be accepted in the Bible school, and another grade school at Copajira would care for the general educational needs of children.[80] As the farm itself developed, students would give the afternoons to farm work to help support their education; they were not charged tuition. Sundays were spent in ministry, with some students involved in the chapel at Copajira and others fanning out in evangelism or church visitation. The 1949 school year ended with fifteen students who represented all but one of the existing Friends churches.[81] Howard Pearson's report to the Board summarized the hopes for the Bible school:

> We are glad to say that after three years of existence of the Bible School, it is beginning to play an important part in the spiritual life of our field. The boys made a big impression during the annual conference in La Paz and have helped in our regional conferences during the year. We realize more and more that our pastors look to us to train their young people to help, our churches look to us to supply them with pastors and workers and the boys look to us to get them ready for service in the field. It is no longer necessary for us to urge them to attend but it is getting to be a privilege.[82]

Running the farm increasingly became a major missionary task, and when Paul and Phyllis Cammack arrived on the field in 1948, Paul was named secretary of agriculture and stationed on the farm, along with the Bible school missionary teachers. Developing the soil, raising and selling crops, maintaining the machinery, and raising stock were all necessary tasks to keep the farm running. Annual reports back to the board regularly began to include accounts of specific crops, state of the machinery, kinds and numbers of livestock, and so on. In addition, major time and effort needed to be inverted in construction at Copajira, to have adequate facilities for the Bible school, for storage and maintenance of farming equipment, and, not least, for missionary residences.

One aspect of the mission ownership of the farm was the fact that it had formerly been part of the hacienda system and that upon purchase of the land, the mission also acquired "ownership" of the thirty-two Indian families that had belonged to the hacienda. They were referred to as "peons." (We will refer to them as *colonos*.) While the mission may not have understood all the historical weight of oppression that was part of the hacienda system, from the beginning of their ownership, the missionaries had determined to give the *colonos* their freedom, and they actively pursued this policy. This involved some complicated legalities, in addition to the fact that not all of

80. See the annual Bolivian Field Reports in the OYM Minutes for 1947, 1948, and 1949, NWYM/GFU archives.

81. OYM Minutes, 1950, 54, NWYM/GFU archives.

82. OYM Minutes, 1950, 55, NWYM/GFU archives.

the *colonos* wanted freedom, preferring the security of the old system. Mistrust of the foreigners was part of the package. This whole relationship was to prove troublesome, even dangerous, to the mission for years to come. Acting according to the dictates of justice would require more than good intentions.

In February of 1947 when the missionaries first occupied Copajira, Roscoe Knight insisted that the former owner inform the *colonos* that the mission now owned the farm. These people immediately began bowing before the missionaries and addressing them as *mi partrón* or *mi patrona* ("my lord" or "my lady"). The situation was awkward at best. In the first called meeting between the missionaries and the *colonos*, the missionaries presented gifts of pictures, sugar, and candy. It was not enough. The *colonos* also wanted the traditional gifts of coca leaves and whiskey, which the missionaries assured them they would never give. On the first fiesta day, missionaries locked drunk *colonos* out of the compound, something unheard of. The possibilities for misunderstanding seemed vast.[83]

The mission intended to convert the Catholic chapel on the grounds (part of any hacienda system) to a Friends meetinghouse, but they gave the *colonos* permission to remove their sacred statues first, which they did in a formal procession, having covered the statues in black to symbolize mourning. The mission refused a request to build a new Catholic chapel on the back of the property, noting that "the Evangelical part" was the most difficult of the changes for the people to accept.[84]

In the 1949 field report, Paul Cammack made reference to an uprising of the *colonos* that constituted the major crisis of the year. Apparently the police had to be called in to give protection and help settle the uprising. He noted that "God protected and brought peace ultimately. The peons on the whole seem friendly and cooperative now. We praise the Lord for the change of attitudes. . . . Twenty-one of the thirty-two peon families eligible for freedom have accepted the freedom plan and are working to complete it. It is possible that in six months the first people will be freed and given title to their property under the plan."[85]

The following year, in the 1950 field report, after giving the crop and livestock statistics, Cammack noted that "the peons have shown friendliness to us throughout the year and will listen to gospel exhortations but the greater part of them still do not attend our services. Thirteen now have been freed and are no longer called 'peons' but 'farmers.' More of them are putting their children in our day school. We feel that God is dealing with their hearts and that there will be a day of turning if you with us intercede effectually for their souls."[86]

A major turning of the Copajira *colonos* to the gospel never happened. Until they obtained their freedom, the *colonos* worked for the mission three days a week and

83. Roscoe Knight, letter to OYM, February 18, 1947, NWYM/GFU archives.
84. Roscoe Knight, letter to OYM, April 5, 1947, NWYM/GFU archives.
85. OYM Minutes, 1949, 57, NWYM/GFU archives.
86. OYM Minutes, 1950, 58, NWYM/GFU archives.

raised their own crops on the other days. Problems between the missionaries and the farm Indians would continue through the 1950s.

Developing Relations between Mission and National Church

From the coming of Carroll Tamplin in 1931, the goal of the mission had been the development of an indigenous church that was self-governing, self-supporting, and self-propagating. Although the strategies for accomplishing this goal would change, this was still the ideal in the 1940s. As reported in the previous chapter, in 1939 at the annual conference in La Paz, the "Missionary and Native Church Council" was set up, composed of four missionaries and four nationals, in an attempt to give the nationals a voice in the development of the work. This organization does not appear in the field reports after 1940.

In the annual conference of 1944, the missionaries and national believers formed a "Yearly Meeting Council," composed of members of all the organized churches, plus pastors, workers, and missionaries. Together they discussed problems, policies and plans, and sought resolution on different issues. The council formed committees to carry out their decisions during the year. This was reported in the 1944 mission field report as a significant step forward.[87]

As a new missionary, come in the midst of a time of tension and conflict, Ralph Chapman was becoming keenly aware of the need for a national organization of Friends, separate from the mission. This thought did not, of course, originate with Chapman, but he began discussing the matter with nationals and the mission board, searching for a way forward.[88] He developed a plan for the new organization, referring to it as the "Indigenous Society," and in the 1946 annual conference a committee with representatives from every church was formed to discuss and adapt the proposal during the year leading up to the 1947 conference. This plan was met with immediate approval by the nationals. Part of the challenge was responding to growing demands by certain national workers for salaries from the mission. In letters back to Oregon the name of Francisco Medrano surfaces as one fomenting the demands.[89]

In the April 1947 sessions of the annual conference, the national church and the mission together set up the *Sociedad Evangélica de Amigos Bolivianos* (SEAB, "Evangelical Society of Bolivian Friends"). With an executive committee (known in Spanish as the *mesa directiva*) composed of six national workers and two missionaries, the society was "to be responsible for the evangelistic work of the field and together with the Mission Council to work out the problems of the maintenance of this work."[90] The mission still had oversight of the farm, the Bible school, the grade schools, and the

---

87. OYM Minutes, 1944, 39, NWYM/GFU archives.

88. Roscoe Chapman, letters to OYM, August 8, 1945; November 14, 1945, NWYM/GFU archives.

89. Ralph Chapman, letters to OYM, September 2, 1946; March 11, 1947, NWYM/GFU archives.

90. OYM Minutes, 1947, p. 52, NWYM/GFU archives.

different church conferences. The president of the new *mesa directiva* was Máximo Loza, with Francisco Medrano as secretary.[91] Medrano had presented his own proposal, that the entire work be given over to the national church, with the missionaries free to go home. The representatives were not ready to go that far, and this proposal was overturned.[92]

Chapman, reporting on this development in his field report, also notes that

> visitation trips by the missionaries have been of encouragement to the nationals that they in turn carry forward the Great Commission. More and more the nationals are realizing the necessity of contributing more to the maintenance of their work. Some accept this responsibility with willingness and others are continually reminding the Mission Council of how much work they are doing. May the Lord successfully mold them in this transition period to meet the requisites of a well-founded Indigenous Church![93]

Although the new indigenous organization seemed to have the support of most of the national church, Francisco Medrano continued to stoke the fires of opposition to the mission. Medrano had grown up in the church; he was the son of Mariano Medrano, converted fisherman from the lake district and Quaker evangelist during the 1930s. The seeds of Francisco's discontent are unknown, but his attitude mirrored the social tensions of the times with indigenous peoples seeking freedom from oppression by the "white man."

Sometime after the annual conference, Francisco Medrano wrote a letter directly to the mission board in Oregon on behalf of the indigenous church, bypassing the *mesa directiva* with its missionary representation and presenting a list of twelve needs/demands, including salaries for pastors and teachers and money for the construction of church buildings. According to Chapman, the prices quoted in the letter were "exorbitant." Medrano wrote,

> As to the demands for salaries of the National pastors and workers, it is just and right that the workers receive their daily bread. It is necessary that we consider their labors for these workers and pastors are carrying more than double the load of the missionaries. These poor workers are serving the Lord willingly, suffering persecution, ridicule, and hunger in the pueblos, streets, and [in their] journeys.
>
> These faithful pastors and workers are sustaining the work of God in all the Bolivian field. Even tho we are ignorant and without teaching, we are carrying on in the name of God without fear and with more effort. Brethren

---

91. Other members were Mariano Baptista, Ismael Balboa, Baltazar Yujra, and Félix Guanca, with Ralph Chapman and Howard Pearson as missionary representatives.

92. Ralph Chapman, letter to OYM, April 10, 1947, NWYM/GFU archives.

93. Ralph Chapman, letter to OYM, April 10, 1947, NWYM/GFU archives.

of the north, the work of God grows more and more and the expenses also increase. For lack of funds and sustenance the work of God is suffering. . . .

There are a few missionaries in this city that are saying that the Bolivian believers are rich and wish to have them pay all the expenses. They are saying that the Indians do not need help and you should not help them nor pay all their wages (of the pastors). Thus the poor Indians are made to suffer and cry much. Those persons can advise you that the Indians do not need help or perhaps have already so informed you. Do not listen to these false reports that we are rich for we [with] much sacrifice are doing all that we can.

We ask for an immediate reply.[94]

The mission board acknowledged the letter but did not bend to the demands, choosing to support the mission's strategy of indigenization.

Francisco Medrano continued to stir up opposition to the mission, in spite of a time of revival in August 1947 where he publicly confessed and asked pardon.[95] Yet the disagreements continued and the situation came to a head in December when it was discovered that he had taken, without authority or permission (not being the treasurer), some money from the La Paz Church treasury to purchase property on El Alto that he hoped would become a center for gatherings of the national church. Consequently, the local church ran out of money and couldn't pay their grade school teacher. The church asked the mission to pay, and the mission told them it was the church's responsibility. Medrano responded in anger, accusing the mission of having enough money to buy a farm and a truck but letting the workers remain in their poverty. The mission called him to a meeting of the church council, and when he didn't appear, the mission dismissed him from all his roles in the work, including membership in the church. They informed the La Paz Church on the following Sunday morning.[96]

Concerning this decision, mission council chairman Ralph Chapman wrote to the board of foreign missions that

> our motive for what we have done is [to] contend against that spirit manifest by Medrano and to eliminate that contention that has defeated our work in the past few years and shall continue to hinder if we attempt to let things ride as they were. . . . It is impossible at this time to tell what shall result from it. The worst shall be the losing of some of our country stations and a large number of believers. This is the price that we here are ready to pay if need be that we may renew within our ranks that spirit of Christian love and fellowship that shall lend itself to definite establishment of believers in the Christian way. To this end, the Mission Council is standing firm before the believers here.[97]

94. Ralph Chapman, letter to OYM, June 7, 1947, translation of the letter from the SEAB, NWYM/ GFU archives.

95. Ralph Chapman, letter to OYM, August 9, 1947, NWYM/GFU archives.

96. Jack Willcuts, letter, from La Paz to OYM, December 31, 1947, NWYM/GFU archives.

97. Ralph Chapman, letter to OYM, December 29, 1947, NWYM/GFU archives.

Reaction from nationals came immediately, with a group of believers from La Paz electing to leave with Medrano. Félix Guanco threatened to leave the church and take the Achachicala (formerly Pongon Huyo) congregation with him (a threat he eventually carried out). A handful of believers from other congregations also left. But as understanding of Medrano's misdeeds grew, the rebellion slowly died down.

Another immediate result was a decision by the mission council to dissolve the SEAB, the indigenous society, and begin meeting to plan a new national organization. This was carried out during the early months of 1948, building on the original plan crafted by Ralph Chapman, with notable contributions by new missionary Jack Willcuts, as well as the insights of national leaders such as Cipriano Mamani, Máximo Loza, Feliciano Sirpa, and Mariano Baptista. Sirpa was named as president of the executive council, a council composed of both nationals and missionaries. The new organization was presented in the March annual conference as the *Sociedad Evangélica de Amigos Nacionales* (SEAN, Evangelical Society of National Friends), with the plan to try it out for a year and make any necessary adaptations.[98]

A year of meetings and discussions defined some of the policies in an attempt to clarify relations between the mission and a developing national church. Concerning the question of the construction of church facilities, the group decided that the local church would raise half the funds, with the national church contributing a quarter and the mission the final quarter. Concerning the most controversial issue, salaries for pastors, the group adopted a ten-year plan whereby each congregation would gradually assume the pastor's salary. The brethren took on the responsibilities of organizing the annual conferences, and would have a voice in the naming and assigning of pastors. The national church was given an eight-acre plot on the mission farm to raise crops as a way to make money. These were all considerable gains.[99]

In a letter home at the end of 1949, Willcuts demonstrated how the SEAN was beginning to function. At the end of the annual conference of the Amacari District, the new society set aside time where missionaries and nationals joined for "a full-fledged business and discussion meeting for the consideration of field problems." Willcuts wrote that, at one point in the meeting,

> with considerable temerity I tossed Sirpa's letter asking for a raise in salary into the meeting. We all figured probably the old refrain of their being poor and therefore the mission would have to pay it would be brought out first of all. But to our great delight that idea was not mentioned once, and instead one man suggested the new work at Pucarani [where Sirpa pastored] should give their pastor some land of his own for a garden and crops as had Amakari [*sic*]. This was excellent and decided upon. . . . Then the clerk of the Pucarani meeting protested that since they were in the process of building a new church they could not raise his salary but must concentrate their efforts on the building.

98. Jack Willcuts, letter to OYM, March 29, 1948, NWYM/GFU archives.
99. Jack Willcuts, letter to OYM, July 26, 1948, NWYM/GFU archives.

Then to our astonishment and great joy, two of the Amakari [*sic*] brethren who had been holding out against the Society each volunteered to furnish the poles for the roof of the new Pucarani church, others offered straw and offerings until the needs of the church were about all subscribed. Poor Sirpa arose to his feet weeping and said he didn't need any raise of salary after all and would postpone any further mention of the matter until the church was built. It was a real victory, and a huge step toward the goal of an indigenous Society.[100]

Throughout 1949 and 1950, the mission council discussed the necessity of incorporating the new national organization, thereby making it a legal entity under Bolivian law. These cooperative experiments show the mission actively searching for ways to encourage the church to mature and develop administratively, as well as the national church taking its own steps forward. The process was complex and progress slow.

The Dilemma of Salaries for Pastors and Teachers

The change in an indigenous strategy from the time of Tamplin in the early 1930s up to 1950 is notable. As we saw in the previous chapter, Tamplin was fanatical in his strategy of offering no foreign financial help to native workers or for church buildings. However, Tamplin himself began to offer support to selected national workers as early as 1932, when Máximo Loza received $66.70 for the year as an evangelist, and later Félix Hermosa and Juan Ayllón received workers' salaries. The mission also began in the 1930s to help support Amacari pastor Cipriano Mamani (along with contributions from the Amacari locals and the church in La Paz).

Somehow, between 1931 and 1950, the mission went from a policy of minimal financial support to generously contributing toward pastoral and teachers' salaries and local church building projects. As the decade of the 1940s came to an end, a substantial part of the annual mission budget went especially to the payment of salaries. In 1950, that amount came to $1,792, most of which was raised as a project of the Women's Missionary Union of OYM.[101]

The SEAB/SEAN financial books for 1947–1949 show the nationals making a careful accounting of monthly offerings from the different churches. The books also show the sizeable monthly offerings from the mission and their disbursement by SEAB as salary to specific pastors and schoolteachers. They also show the accounts of the tract of land on the farm that the mission had given to SEAN to be farmed as a source of income.[102]

---

100. Jack Willcuts, letter to OYM, November 4, 1949, NWYM/GFU archives.

101. OYM Minutes, 1950, 15, NWYM/GFU archives.

102. *Libro de Caja* (Treasurer's Book), 1947–1957, INELA archives.

By the end of the decade, missionaries, along with the board, were beginning to ask how the trend toward financial dependence on the mission could be reversed and local churches encouraged to care for their own needs, as a mark of maturity. In the next decade and on into the future, this tension between dependence and indigeneity would continue to be a point of contention.

Evangelistic Outreach, Discipleship, and Leadership Training

In the literature of the decade (minutes, reports, and personal letters), the resolving of conflicts and the search for a healthy design for mission/national church relationships takes priority over reports on the outreach and numerical growth of the church. Yet the church did grow during these years.

After 1947 the mission named a missionary to be secretary of evangelism. That person's task was to work with the national organization. The nationals gradually took on as their own the task of reaching into new communities. This seemed to work best through individual congregations whose pastors had a vision for evangelism. In 1947 mission secretary of evangelism Ralph Chapman reported five monthly meetings with an active outreach in evangelistic ministry: La Paz, under Chapman's leadership, along with clerk Ismael Balboa; Amacari under Pastor Cipriano Mamani; Achachicala under Pastor Félix Guanca; Corocoro under Pastor Mariano Cusicanque; and Mina Fabulosa under Pastor Rosendo Guachalla.[103] In 1948, the La Paz meeting, under clerk Ismael Balboa, was regularly involved in street evangelism and trips to new areas. Sunday school attendance was up to 170, and new churches in the district now included Mina Miluni, Chunyavi, Pucarani, Aigachi, Puerto Pérez, Laja, and Palca. The Amacari meeting under Cipriano Mamani continued strong in outreach, with a Sunday school attendance of around one hundred and continual visits to conduct services in Ojje, Isla Anapia, and Llujpaya, with other visits to new areas. A church was formed at Copajira with Máximo Loza as pastor.[104]

But by the end of the decade, in the high mining area of Corocoro where the mission had invested many years of labor, especially under Howard and Julia Pearson, the OYM mission finally turned the work over to another mission. The distance was too far and the fruit scarce. Also, by the end of the decade, the Friends work in Puerto Pérez was finally laid down.[105]

An annual Easter conference in La Paz continued to gather the believers in a time of classes, worship, celebration, and church business. In addition, annual three-day regional conferences in four or five locations drew believers together for "times of revival, doctrinal instruction and consideration of field and local problems."[106]

103. OYM Minutes, 1947, 52–53, NWYM/GFU archives.
104. OYM Minutes, 1948, 51, NWYM/GFU archives.
105. Jack Willcuts, letters to OYM, August 11, 1949; May 31, 1950, NWYM/GFU archives.
106. OYM Minutes, 1950, 55, NWYM/GFU archives.

The main vehicle for leadership training was now invested in the Bible school at Copajira, although other opportunities were sought, such as a month of special classes for all pastors and workers at Copajira in July of 1949.[107] Along with the Bible school, the grade school program continued to function during the last half of the 1940s, with schools in Amacari, Llujpaya, Achachicala, La Paz, Patapatani, Ojje, and Copajira. Roscoe Knight worked with the national church as secretary of education during these years.

In all of this, an indigenous Aymara Friends leadership was taking shape. Among the emerging leaders of the decade of the 1940s, the names of Feliciano Sirpa and Máximo Loza stand out.

FELICIANO SIRPA

A biography of Feliciano Sirpa written near the end of the 1940s[108] by one of the missionaries identifies him as being one of the oldest and among "the first of the recognized workers of the Mission."[109]

Feliciano Sirpa was born in 1885 in a small community on the railroad line between La Paz and Arica, Chile. Like most rural Aymara children, his childhood revolved around caring for the family's animals. Early on he manifested an unusual interest in learning how to read and write, and he took advantage of passing travelers to ask for help. At one point, he fashioned a pen from the tin of a discarded can and ink from a mixture of colored soil and water.

In his adolescent years, Sirpa moved to La Paz and found work as a house servant. He also found and married his wife, Raquel Cornejo, and the couple eventually had five children. After marriage he found work in a lumberyard and also began to drink in his non-working hours, as did so

Feliciano Sirpa, 1940s (NWYM)

many of his companions. Several Adventist and Methodist believers witnessed to him, and although he resisted their invitations to church, his curiosity led him to read the Bible.

107. OYM Minutes, 1950, 55, NWYM/GFU archives.

108. "Biography of Feliciano Sirpa," n.d., NWYM/GFU archives.

109. It's interesting to note that he is identified as "a worker of the Mission" and not as a Bolivian Friends leader.

One afternoon while standing in the main plaza of La Paz, he noticed a brilliant white cloud, and as he watched he claims to have heard a voice saying, "Thou hast seen that as this cloud is white and clean; so is God. Thou art in need of salvation. Thy sin is black as coal." Meanwhile, back at the lumberyard, Sirpa had come in contact with Friends believer Cipriano Mamani and his faithful witness was drawing Sirpa toward the gospel. After his cloud vision, he accepted Mamani's invitation and in his first visit to the La Paz Friends Church, he responded to the altar call and gave his life to Jesus. The year was 1930.

Sirpa's name does not come up in the literature during the 1930s. During the early 1940s, when Juan Ayllón became involved in the translation project, Sirpa apparently assumed some of the pastoral leadership of the La Paz congregation. But in 1943 he was one of the group of four leaders who accused Ayllón of sexual harassment; later that same year Sirpa himself was removed from his pastorate and membership for adultery. By 1945, he had repented and come back with his family to be reinstated, not only as a member, but as a leader among Friends. Between the years of 1945 and 1950 he served as pastor in the Palca, Ojje, Laja, and Pucarani congregations.

In the 1948 annual conference, Feliciano Sirpa was elected president of the newly formed indigenous society, the *Sociedad Evangélica de Amigos Nacionales* (SEAN),[110] a position he served in for one year. (A note from Jack Willcuts in early 1949 mentioned that a special offering of $30 from Arthur Roberts had supplied a mule for Sirpa to use in his evangelistic work.)[111]

Máximo Loza

Máximo Loza's name first comes up in the 1930s as one of the national evangelists who accompanied Carroll Tamplin on his missionary journeys to new areas, as well as serving as Tamplin's translator (chapter 3).

Loza was born in an outlying area of La Paz in 1910 and passed his childhood caring for the family's flocks. As a young man he began training as a mason, and this later became his livelihood. But one of his main activities during his growing up years was being apprenticed to his father who was a renowned animistic practitioner. (He was probably a *yatiri*, or diviner; the literature refers to him as a "witch doctor.")[112]

---

110. Jack Willcuts, letter to OYM, March 29, 1948, NWYM/GFU archives.
111. Jack Willcuts, letter to OYM, February 14, 1949, NWYM/GFU archives.
112. "Biography of Máximo Loza," n.d., NWYM/GFU archives.

Máximo Loza, 1940s (NWYM)

In 1927, Máximo first heard the gospel story through Salvation Army street meetings and the witness of two fellow-workers in the construction business, an Adventist and a member of a holiness (Westfield) Friends church, Raimundo Marca.[113] Loza resisted, claiming he "hated the gospel," and increased both his animistic practices and his attendance at Catholic mass. At the same time, he joined his comrades in regularly getting drunk.

Loza's inner struggles and his frustrated attempts to stop drinking finally convinced him that he needed to give in to the gospel message, so he went to a Salvation Army service and became a Christian. According to his testimony, the inner peace and a release from alcohol were immediate.

113. Marca later married Westfield missionary, Mattie Blount.

The reaction of his family was also immediate and violent; his father, bitter that his son would not carry on the animistic rites that were his inherited obligation, cast him out of the family. In his need, Loza turned to Juan Ayllón who was just beginning meetings in the Sopocachi area of La Paz. Ayllón discipled Loza, incorporating him into the Friends churches, and began training him for Christian service. That service began in 1931 with the arrival of the Tamplins as new OYM missionaries. From 1931 to 1933 Loza served as Tamplin's Aymara interpreter, and throughout the rest of the decade traveled with Tamplin as a national evangelist. He served a brief time as pastor of the new church in Calata, on Lake Titicaca.

For a few years in the 1940s, Loza was assistant pastor in the La Paz church, and when the Bible school at Copajira opened, he was one of the first students. He attended during the 1947 and 1948 school years, but dropped out before completing his course of studies. During 1947, as a Bible school student, he took on the task of evangelizing the *colonos* on the farm next to Copajira and saw ten of them become Christians (something that did not happen in Copajira itself).[114] On a more negative note, still during the 1947 term, he instigated a minor rebellion against the Pearsons who were teaching (and had a reputation for strictness). Student complaints included not enough pay for their labors on the farm and that the mission was keeping from them "gifts" from the North (i.e., used clothing).[115]

More and more, aspects of Loza's service began to go sour, partly from his association with Francisco Medrano and the rebellion against the mission. He was named president of the new indigenous society, SEAB, in the 1947 annual conference, with Medrano as secretary.[116] The two of them were behind the letter of demand from nationals to the OYM mission board later that year.[117] After Medrano's dismissal from the church, Loza stayed on, participating in the discussions to reorganize the indigenous society in 1948, and later he served as a member of the *mesa directiva*.

Persecution

Along with all the kinds of inner turmoil the church faced, attack from the outside also played a role. Down through the years, religious persecution tended to ebb and flow. But in 1948 it was on the rise and beginning to again affect the Friends movement; letters home mention troubles involving the believers in Ojje, Laja, Palca, Yanapata, and Copajira.[118] Jack Willcuts wrote home in 1949 that believers from Yanapata came to the annual conference in April, telling how that in the previous week, "a bad hail storm hit their community and the Catholics said the storm came because of the

114. Ralph Chapman, letter to OYM, December 17, 1947, NWYM/GFU archives.

115. Roscoe Knight, letter to OYM, January 21, 1948, NWYM/GFU archives.

116. Ralph Chapman, letter to OYM, April 10, 1947, NWYM/GFU archives.

117. Ralph Chapman, letter to OYM, June 7, 1947, NWYM/GFU archives.

118. Jack Willcuts, letters to OYM, May 31, 1948; March 15, 1949; April 19, 1949; August 11, 1949; October 13, 1949. Roscoe Knight, letter to OYM, June 28, 1949, NWYM/GFU archives.

Evangelistas and hatched up other wild ideas. The upshot was that they broke up a meeting with clubs and rocks, several women [were] badly beaten up, and 4 men were jailed."[119] This type of incident would increase in the decade of the 1950s.

In addition to persecution coming from a conservative element of the Catholic Church, opposition to Protestant movements also came from the social upheaval of clashing cultures and social classes. News of an uprising by *colonos* and the murder of the hacienda owner in the state of Sucre in 1948 set on edge all rural landowners in the country, including the Copajira missionaries.[120] And the news in 1949 of the martyrdom of a Canadian Baptist missionary along with four believers near the city of Oruro alerted the entire missionary and Protestant church community.[121] This would also become a greater part of the story in the next decade.

A VIEW FROM THE OUTSIDE

Yet, with all the challenges and the struggle to bring to maturity an indigenous Friends Church, God was working. Sometimes it takes a "view from the outside" to see this.

One view of the vitality of Aymara Friends from this period comes from none other than Frank Laubach, the reputed "Apostle to the Illiterates." At the beginning of the decade of the 1940s, Laubach was gaining fame around the world, not only as a Protestant mystic, but for his successful program of adult literacy, developed in the 1930s in the Philippine Islands. Helen Cammack had been using his methodology in the Friends schools in Bolivia, and the two had likely exchanged letters. In 1942 Laubach was touring South America to see if there was interest in the literacy program. He spent two weeks in La Paz in December 1942 and January 1943. While there he stayed with Howard and Julia Pearson in their residence behind the church on Max Paredes Street. He had the opportunity to worship in the Friends Church there, and he wrote about the impact of this experience in his journal. He shared these impressions with the mission family, and allowed Julia to make a handwritten copy. Part of that report is as follows:

> December 21, 1942—Tonight I had a spiritual experience which will echo thru the rest of my life. It was the Aymara prayer meeting in the Quaker church. There was nothing Quaker about it. After a long talk—which I did not understand—by the Aymara pastor, the congregation knelt to pray. Every one prayed aloud at the same time. It began with a murmur; then women's plaintive wails began to be heard above the rest and presently they could be heard weeping. . . .
>
> December 24—Christmas Eve! The Pearsons have a lovely Christmas tree and the house is gay with red and green decorations. They are such nice people that I am happy this evening.

119. Jack Willcuts, letter to OYM, April 19, 1949, NWYM/GFU archives.
120. Roscoe Knight, letter to OYM, July 27, 1948, NWYM/GFU archives.
121. Jack Willcuts, letter to OYM, August 11, 1949, NWYM/GFU archives.

11:00 p.m.—I am just home from the most fascinating Christmas program in my whole life. Over 300 Aymara Indians in this Quaker church gave a perfectly wonderful program. Their ordinarily poker faces were wreathed in smiles. I have never seen a more striking illustration of the power of the gospel to transform people than this evening's revelation. One could almost tell how many months or years each person present had come under the influence of the gospel. Here were women with babes over their backs wobbling Indian squaw fashion yet shaking hands like dear sisters. I think the most unforgettable number was a song by about fifteen men and 8 or 10 women. One girl, daughter of a highly educated man, formerly pastor of the church, looked like a queen. Beside her stood young women, awkward, shuffling, embarrassed to the point of pain and yet beginning to enjoy Christian life.

These Friends are working a modern miracle among the Indians of La Paz. The church is located in the center of the Indians. There are literally thousands swarming the streets so that an automobile has to creep along constantly sounding the horn. Perhaps because my heart is so much with these Indians, I feel that this Christmas Eve is the climax of my first visit to S.A.

. . . This evangelical church of the Friends, wholly controlled by the Indians themselves, is far more strict than we are at home. They allow not even lipstick. Tonight as I write, the Indians carousing in the street present a sharp contrast to these stern, puritanical Quakers!

December 25—Christmas morning. "Friend" Pearson woke me at 6:30 to enjoy their Santa Claus. It was delightful to see little Donald open the packages and hear him shriek with delight at every new surprise. He got many presents: drawing sets, a ship and torpedo boat which blows it up, a rotary printing press, puzzles, but the thing he loved most was a repeater pistol! He is out trying it on chickens now! Even being a Quaker does not take war out of the boy of nine.

January 3, 1943—This afternoon I attended the Sunday meeting in the Quaker church in front of the house where I am staying. The pastor seemed very slow, awkward & shy. He talked about Paul's doctrine of salvation thru faith. Two men came forward and knelt at the altar. Then all knelt and prayed aloud at the same time. I did as well as the rest. I think if I ever again have a mission church I shall start that custom. One fairly feels the presence of the Holy Spirit. Some of the women cried as they prayed. Then they all stopped by common consent and the two men at the altar arose and testified. One had an eye nearly gone, trachoma I suppose. As he testified to the free gift of salvation, he broke down and shook while he held his handkerchief to his face. Then everybody began to testify. . . . Here was a church full of people who did not depend upon the minister but made the meeting their own by prayer and testimony. It was marvelous to see the Spirit working in these humble people— marvelous and wholesome, a humbling experience for me. . . . I had to sink my college education and realize that in God's sight these simple people, true to their convictions, were better than I have been, were more highly esteemed than I was. . . . It was delightful to realize, here this afternoon, that God prized these dear illiterate Indians exactly as highly as he did me.[122]

Laubach's observation that "there was nothing Quaker" about the worship service probably reflects the fact that there was no silence. Actually, his description of the participatory nature of their worship and lack of dependency on the minister reflect Quaker values. The young girl in the choir who "looked like a queen" in contrast to the Aymara women was undoubtedly Dorcas Ayllón, daughter of Juan and Tomasa. It's interesting to note Laubach's observation on the strictness of conduct required, a reflection of the holiness tradition the missionaries brought with them to Bolivia. His sense that the church "is wholly controlled by the Indians themselves," while not a totally accurate reflection, does show that the locals were exercising leadership gifts and conducting their own services, in their own language and using their own Aymara styles of communication and worship. This gives a glimpse of a people gathered to offer genuine and culturally appropriate expressions of worship and praise.

Another view of what God was doing through Friends in Bolivia during these years comes from the end of the decade. Jack Willcuts arrived as a new missionary in July of 1947, prepared with information about the struggles the mission and church were facing, but also with the perspective of a fresh pair of eyes. In fact, the mission board had trusted his insightfulness enough to ask him to evaluate the work, comparing the Friends movement with other missions and efforts in the country.

After a month in the field, Willcuts commented that "the needs are so apparent and the problems many but to hear the testimony of one believer whose life has been so tangibly transformed is ample reward to any sacrifice."[123] At the end of the year Willcuts sent home his evaluation:

> It has been my privilege to visit our entire field except Puerto Perez. We attended Pongon Huyo and Amacari conferences, visited the Bible School and farm. And, as I view the other mission enterprizes, I am convinced God has given Oregon Yearly Meeting a choice and extremely needy place for service. With the strong church in La Paz, the various growing out-posts, the spiritual and enthusiastic Bible School and the farm; I'm persuaded we have a well balanced program of evangelism. Personally, I feel our present emphasis on national leadership among the churches, using Indian pastors and teachers, taught and trained personally by individual missionaries (and eventually trained in the Bible School), has gained the confidence of the rural communities and is more effective than any other method known. . . . Some wonder

122. Frank Laubach, unpublished journal entries, given to Julia Pearson and archived among the letters of Julia Pearson to OYM, NWYM/GFU archives. The complete collection of Laubach's works are found in the Frank Laubach Collection of the Special Collections Research Center, Syracuse University Libraries and in the archives of ProLiteracy.

123. Jack Willcuts, letter to OYM, August 26, 1947, NWYM/GFU archives.

at our huge program of circuit evangelism, agriculture and education while we maintain so few missionaries. Is it not more logical to invest our funds and energies in the development of national spiritual leadership when it has been proven in almost every mission field that native Christians can be more influential in witnessing and teaching than a foreigner? Yet, surprisingly to me, our policy is almost unique in Bolivia.[124]

In the same letter, Willcuts noted the strength of the field council system and the way the missionaries are getting along well with each other, despite the many differences of personality and perspective.

THE CHURCH AND MISSION AT THE END OF THE DECADE

In the title of this chapter, we observed that the 1940s were a decade of "Inner Turmoil," and so it was. The march of the church was not without its problems and challenges, some of which came from without in the social unrest of the times. But a good deal of conflict was internal. We read in this chapter of the crises of Juan Ayllón's uncertain leadership, the drama of Helen Cammack's romance and death, the interpersonal tensions between different missionaries, the threats of other Christians and denominations against the Friends churches, the loss of some of those churches, the new complexities introduced with the mission's purchase of a hacienda, and all the tensions involved in defining the changing relationships between mission and national church.

With all of this, the Bolivian Friends Church, with nineteen recognized congregations at the beginning of the 1950s, was slowly developing into an indigenous church with its own leaders and its own perspectives of the work to be done.

REFLECTIONS ON THE DECADE

In looking at the impact of culture on the development of the church, we need to consider the intercultural dynamics as three different groups came together. The potential for misunderstanding was high as the North American presence, represented by Carroll Tamplin and the other missionaries, attempted to work with a mestizo leader, Juan Ayllón, in planting a church among the Aymara peoples of Bolivia. The resulting clash between Tamplin and Ayllón should not be surprising; nor should the tension many of the emerging Aymara leaders felt with both Tamplin and Ayllón. Of course, some of the tension of the decade resulted from the difficulties different missionaries had with one another.

Juan Ayllón's case was unique, caught between two cultures, belonging neither to the missionary community nor to the fellowship of the national church. One wonders what private battles he faced as he evolved from sole missionary and founder of the INELA to a subordinate role on the mission staff under new missionary Carroll

---

124. Jack Willcuts, letter to OYM, December 11, 1947, NWYM/GFU archives.

Tamplin, was then demoted to national worker, and eventually forced to resign all relationship to the church or mission. Yet today, Ayllón, along with William Abel, is honored by the INELA as its founder.

The example of Helen Cammack shows that misunderstanding was not inevitable. She focused on coming to understand the Aymara culture, even to learning from it before entering into ministry. She loved being out with the rural believers and labored to learn their language. And she seems to have formed close bonds, earning the love of the people. She also formed a personal friendship with Juan and Tomasa Ayllón, and the three surely confided in each other, sharing their sorrows and joys. She seems to have gotten along well with her missionary peers, too, with the exception of Carroll Tamplin.

In looking at the developing relationship between mission and church, it's interesting to note the attempts of the mission to bring the church to a point of self-government. The missionaries were obviously experimenting. The different developments—the Missionary and Native Church Council (1939), the Yearly Meeting Council (1944), the Evangelical Society of Bolivian Friends (1947), and the Evangelical Society of National Friends (1948)—were all efforts of the mission to share and hand over responsibility for administering the church. Most of these lasted for only a year, with the attempts in the late 1940s, under the encouragement of Ralph Chapman and Jack Willcuts, increasing the involvement of national leaders in the planning phase. Working out the concept of indigenization was proving incredibly complex.

Added to the complexity was the reversal the mission had gradually made in its early determination not to pay national workers. Little by little, benefits, such as salaries for national workers, had crept in, and by the end of the 1940s, the mission struggled under the load of stipends to pastors and teachers, while the national church seemed to have come to a sense of entitlement to these benefits. It's almost as if progress toward the goal of an indigenous church had been reversed for a season.

Yet Jack Willcuts's comments on the development of the church at the end of the decade show that progress had, indeed, happened. Little by little, national leaders were rising up as the mission strove to take a back seat.

And in this we see the movement of the Spirit of God.

We see the Spirit in the lives of individuals. Not just the exemplary story of Helen Cammack, but people like Cipriano Mamani, Feliciano Sirpa, and Máximo Loza, with all their struggles and ups-and-downs, were stretching toward the life of Spirit, learning to administer the church.

We see the Spirit in the community gathered to worship, as witnessed by Frank Laubach and other visitors. And we see the Spirit as Aymara believers, both individually and as congregations, reached out to share the gospel message.

We see the movement of the Spirit in the hard experiences of the decade. Helen Cammack's death, like that of William Abel some twenty-five years earlier, was a seed planted for the growth of the church. It resulted in an increase of the mission staff as other couples pledged their lives in service to Bolivia. The Helen Cammack Memorial Bible School on the Copajira farm would serve to train a generation of pastors and leaders for the Bolivian Friends Church.

5

The Organization of the National Church in a Context of Revolution

INELA in the Decade of the 1950s

The 1952 revolution brought radical change to the nation of Bolivia. That same year the Bolivian Friends Church was officially organized as the *Iglesia Nacional Evangélica de Los Amigos* (INELA) and took a giant step forward. Change amid conflict characterized the rest of the decade of the 1950s for both the nation and the church.

HISTORICAL OVERVIEW

At the mid-century mark, 1950, Bolivia continued as "a predominantly rural society, the majority of whose population was only marginally integrated into the national economy."[1] Yet since 1900 significant changes had taken place: urban population had grown from 14 percent to 23 percent of the total population; the literacy rate had risen from 17 percent to 31 percent; the number of children attending school had increased.[2]

The injustices and inefficiencies of the hacienda system persisted, but although the peasant populations were still exploited, they were not unaware.

The socialist political party, *Movimiento Nacionalista Revolucionario* (MNR), whose leaders had been exiled in 1947, had been slowly gaining ground. In the 1951 national elections, it won with a clear majority on a platform of broad social reforms, putting Victor Paz Estenssoro into the presidency. But the day after the elections, before the new government could begin its program, the military intervened, handed over the presidency to General Hugo Ballivián, annulled the elections, and outlawed the MNR as a communist organization. The MNR responded over the following

1. Klein, *Concise History*, locs. 3769–72.
2. Klein, *Concise History*, locs. 3772–77.

months by consolidating its support among the workers and the peasantry, arming the people and preparing for civil war.

The war, when it finally came, was violent but mercifully short. In just three days, April 9–11, 1952, the newly armed civilians and miners overcame the military, fighting in the streets of La Paz and other cities. The widespread destruction of property and the six hundred dead seemed to pale in significance before the fact that, as Klein puts it, "in one moment the entire police power of the State was overwhelmed. . . . The arming of the popular masses and their leaders meant that a serious social revolution would be the end result."[3]

Victor Paz Estenssoro was declared president, with Hernán Siles Zuazo as his vice president. The new government immediately declared universal suffrage by removing the literacy requirement. Thousands of Indians were suddenly enfranchised. Shortly after that, the regime set up a new national labor organization, the *Central del Obreros Bolivianos* (COB, the Bolivian Workers Central) with union leader Juan Lechín at its head. In October it organized a state agency to run the mining industry, the *Corporación Minera de Bolivia* (COMIBOL), and nationalized the three largest mining companies, thus putting two-thirds of all mining industry under state control.

Under the impact of these events, the rural hacienda system began to collapse. Peasants organized themselves into unions and took over properties. Klein writes that "the period from late 1952 until early 1953 saw the destruction of work records in the rural areas, the killing and/or expulsion of overseers and landowners, and the forcible seizure of land. . . . Although the countryside had been relatively indifferent and little affected by the great conflicts of April 1952, it was the scene of tremendous violence and destruction by the end of that year."[4]

While most of the violence during this early period took place in the valleys leading down to the city of Cochabamba, *altiplano* haciendas also felt the tension.

On August 3, 1953, a radical Agrarian Reform became the law of the land, abolishing the hacienda system, requiring that the land be given to the Indians, with compensation in the form of government bonds offered to the former owners. Klein reports that "in the highland Indian areas, almost all the lands were seized."[5] Educational reforms also followed.

The birth of the Bolivian Friends Church (INELA) as an official organization took place simultaneously with the 1952 revolution. Both signified the beginning of profound change, the one in a nation, the other in the faith community known as the National Evangelical Friends Church of Bolivia.

3. Klein, *Concise History*, locs. 3820–26.
4. Klein, *Concise History*, loc. 3864.
5. Klein, *Concise History*, loc. 3875.

FROM REVOLUTION TO BIRTH

In the previous chapter, we considered the 1940s as a decade of inner turmoil, focused on inner workings of the OYM mission as this group struggled to define its goals and policies, and work out its strategies for planting a healthy Friends Church among the Aymara people of Bolivia. Struggle and conflict would continue to characterize this growing work throughout the 1950s and '60s, but the focus would take on a more intercultural aspect as the mission and the emerging Bolivian church redefined their mutual roles.

The annual report presented by the board of missions in the 1950 sessions of Oregon Yearly Meeting reiterated the purpose of the Bolivian mission as "evangelism, the preaching of the 'Gospel of Christ which is the power of God unto salvation,'" and stated strongly that "around this basic purpose all other policies and plans must gather."[6] The same report emphasized the indigenous strategy which would be the blueprint for the mission's program in the next few decades:

> It has been and is the purpose of the missionaries and the Board to develop an indigenous church, that is, a Bolivian Friends Church under national leadership and support.
>
> In the work of evangelism and development of the indigenous church, trained preachers, teachers and leaders are essential. This makes necessary the maintenance of a Bible Training School which has been established on the farm purchased for that purpose.
>
> Although the farm consisting of about three thousand acres is viewed with much interest and may have many uses, its primary purpose is the maintenance of the Bible School, supplying work for students, introducing improved farming methods and furnishing some food supplies for the missionaries.
>
> The operation of day schools is highly important in a mission program and is definitely helpful in evangelization and training of youth. For years, these schools, which are increasing in number as opportunity and finances are available, have been an integral part of our mission work.[7]

From 1950 until his first furlough in May of 1951, Jack Willcuts worked on crafting another organizational plan for the national church, drawing on the previous work of Ralph Chapman, and in consultation with both national leaders and the mission council. Several important small steps were taken, including a decision in early 1950 by the *mesa directiva* that a tithe of local church offerings be given to the national church, a practice that continues to the present time.[8]

Willcuts and the other missionaries were hoping for a decision to adopt the new plan during the 1950 annual conference in La Paz, but they were forced to table the

6. OYM Minutes, 1950, 61, NWYM/GFU archives.
7. OYM Minutes, 1950, 61, NWYM/GFU archives.
8. Jack Willcuts, letter to OYM, January 8, 1950, NWYM/GFU archives.

decision due to the reservations and questions of the mission board. Willcuts emphasized the importance of having the board's support, along with a deep concern for the fragility of the process. "Just a few mistakes could wreck the set-up or at least retard it," he wrote home to the board.[9]

In answering some of the concerns, Willcuts agreed that questions about the maturity and readiness of the national church, and the basic issues of trust underscored the risk of giving too much responsibility too soon. But he also noted that

> the Indian mind is beyond our comprehension, but not beyond God's. Perhaps if Francisco Medrano and others like him had had a place in a truly indigenous work, they would have been useful leaders instead of rebellious. In our study of indigenous works over the world we observe that this hesitancy is the major reason why many do not begin such a plan, they fear to trust the national leaders. Such distrust results in a mutual lack of confidence and eventual serious problems. Affirmatively, we do feel there are those in our work whom we could safely trust with the leadership of the organization. It is not our idea to turn great amounts of money over to the national church. It only [is] the monthly salaries of the national pastors and other *monthly* operating expenses, not the whole amount of money received by the Mission treasurer. We feel this would be good and practical experience for the new church, would assure them of our confidence in them.[10]

Perhaps if one of the national leaders had written a letter at this time, he might have stated, "The North American missionary mind is beyond our comprehension, but not beyond God's." Mutual trust was a key issue.

In the April 1951 annual conference, mission board president Walter Lee visited Bolivia and participated. At that time the new organizational plan was presented to the national church and the representatives received it with enthusiasm. The gathered representatives and missionaries provisionally adopted the plan and agreed to test it for a year. Mission council chairman Ralph Chapman described the meeting in his annual field report:

> A great step of faith has been taken this year in the reorganization of this national entity in our mission. . . . The new organization was formed with an executive committee of six national brethren and one missionary as advisor. This committee has assumed the responsibility for the leadership of the evangelistic program of the field. During this year the mission will continue the aid to pastors of the organized churches, but at the Yearly Meeting in La Paz in 1952, these funds shall be withdrawn. This is in order that more funds may be available for evangelistic work, help to new outstations, windows, benches, construction, etc., and in the educational phase of our program. Testimony

---

9. Jack Willcuts, letter to OYM, January 15, 1951, NWYM/GFU archives.
10. Jack Willcuts, letter to OYM, May 31, 1950, NWYM/GFU archives.

should be given to the fact that God has manifested Himself in a remarkable manner in the evident zeal and desire on the part of the leadership to make this work a success.[11]

Mariano Baptista was approved as president of the *mesa directiva* of the church for the 1951/52 term.

After a year of missionaries and national leaders traveling throughout the field, speaking with people in the churches, discussing the matter and fine-tuning the plan, the representatives in the 1952 annual conference officially accepted the new organizational plan and adopted the name *Iglesia Nacional Evangélica de Los Amigos* (INELA, in English, the National Evangelical Friends Church). The day was April 13, 1952, a date many consider to be the official birthdate of the Bolivian Friends Church. The different words used in the carefully chosen name are significant: the change from the more Quakerly "Society" to the more easily identifiable "Church" connected the INELA with the wider body of Protestant believers in the country. "National" was the key word of the times (as in the MNR, the *Movimiento Nacionalista Revolucionario*) and announced that this was a Bolivian church in its own right, apart from any foreign entity. "Evangelical" linked the church to its holiness roots both in doctrine and in practice. And of course, "Friends" clearly aligned the INELA with the Quaker movement. Mariano Baptista was asked to continue as president of the *mesa directiva*.

The INELA was not born in a vacuum. Easter week 1952, the week of the annual conference (now called "yearly meeting") coincided with the 1952 revolution, considered to be a turning point in Bolivian history. The city of La Paz set the scene for both events. The revolution almost cancelled out yearly meeting, but the violence was over quickly and people were again able to gather. Ralph Chapman described the events of the week:

> We had a meeting called for Tuesday to be attended by all the pastors, workers, etc. . . . only a very small group showed up. . . . Night service went off as scheduled and all looked forward to Wednesday when the Junta would get going as planned. I woke up Wed. morning with a start and realized that all about was the familiar but unwelcome sound of rifle fire. . . . We went ahead with our classes and services on Wed. but by the evening the fighting had concentrated in the Villa Victoria area just above us and on the hills as we would look out of our back windows upon the Alto. By Wed. night the troops from Guaqui, Viacha and Achacachi had lined the rim of the Alto with cannons. Planes flew over with leaflets stating that they were going to bombard the city with the cannons at 6 o'clock. . . . By that time we felt it inadvisable to try to have the night service on Wed. . . . [On Friday] word got out that the regiments had surrendered . . . that the MNR had completely gained the victory and that absolute tranquility reigned in the city so everybody was called to participate in the customary Good Friday parade. . . .

11. Ralph Chapman, OYM Minutes, 1951, 49–50, NWYM/GFU archives.

. . . Thanks again we had no casualties or difficulties from the street during the whole time even tho there was a continual whizz of bullets overhead. It seems to be the opinion on the part of all that this has been the worse revolution in the history of the country at least in the sense of time involved, ammunition shot up and the resultant dead and wounded. . . .

. . . Saturday we got all the pastors and council members of the various churches together and started in on business. . . . I sat and chewed my fingernails while the brethren hashed over innumerable things that to me weren't a particle as important as the action to be taken relative to the formation of the National Church organization. Finally it was placed before the group and without a dissenting vote the brethren adopted the recommendation that the work be nationalized.[12]

In the same letter home, Chapman expressed the desire of the mission council that this new organization be owned as theirs by the national church: "This we here feel is not to be a set of rules placed before them by the missionaries with the statement that this is the basis upon which we will carry forward. Rather we feel that we can help them with all the prayerful help and suggestions that we can offer but the final result must needs be a basis for work which they understand, which they have helped to formulate and which they will approve and support."[13]

On Sunday morning, April 13, 1952, the gathered assembly celebrated the creation of the new organization, with Mariano Baptista as president of the *mesa directiva*.

Future historians would refer to the Revolution of 1952 as one of the "best" revolutions in Bolivian history,[14] and the significance of the event as it affected not only the Friends Church, but the whole population of the country would gradually become recognized. And so two births took place that week in La Paz: a new Bolivia and a new Friends Church.

THE STRUGGLE TO MAKE IT WORK

The decade of the 1950s was not an easy one as the INELA struggled to grow into its new identity. Previous to 1952, the mission had been gradually handing over responsibilities to the national church, but now this necessarily accelerated. Finding the right rate of acceleration proved tricky. According to the new plan, the *mesa directiva* would now oversee all local church visitation and the evangelism program, as well as the planning and running of yearly meeting sessions. Local church requests, such as for help in construction or pastoral salary increases, would now all come through the *mesa directiva*, who would either take action or pass the request on to the mission. A missionary participated as a member of the *mesa*.

12. Ralph Chapman, letter to OYM, April 14, 1952, NWYM/GFU archives.

13. Ralph Chapman, letter to OYM, April 14, 1952, NWYM/GFU archives.

14. For perspectives on the 1952 Revolution, see the essays in Grindle and Domingo, *Proclaiming Revolution*.

The key players in this drama included the successive *mesa directiva* presidents (equivalent to the superintendent of OYM): Mariano Baptista (1951–1954), Pedro Guanca (1955), Vicente Yujra (1956–1958), and Antonio Mamani (1959–1960). During this same period the mission staff increased. In addition to the Chapmans, the Willcuts, the Knights, and the Cammacks, the mission council expanded to include Marshall and Catherine Cavit (1950, on loan from the NHMS), Leland and Iverna Hibbs (arriving in 1951), Mark and Wilma Roberts (1953), David and Florence Thomas (1957), Everett and Alda Clarkson (1958), and Chuck and Charlotte Scott (1958). Forest and Orpha Cammack came for a two-year term to help on the farm. Both the Chapmans and Willcuts retired from the field before the end of the decade, and the Paul Cammacks moved to open the field in Peru.

Differing Perspectives of the Struggle

Related to the continuing social unrest in the country, runaway inflation and soaring prices made the 1950s a hard time to encourage independence in the national church. Differing perspectives between the mission and the church become evident in a comparative reading of the mission council minutes and letters and the *mesa directiva* minutes of the decade. In June of 1952, shortly after the new organization was put into action, Ralph Chapman wrote home these encouraging words:

> During the last few weeks I have traveled quite extensively over the field, but now I am rather the chauffeur for the brethren that accompany me. We go to a church and Mariano Baptista, the president of the national church, or Martín Pérez, the evangelistic secretary, do the preaching or exhorting. If the church isn't toeing the line in its responsibilities, they handle the business of reaching an agreement with the church. The brethren are learning more and more that the business of the church must come through the national organization before the missionaries will attend to any needs presented to them.[15]

And yet issues of mutual trust seemed to wax and wane. The *mesa directive* began keeping official minutes in 1952. These minutes reveal some of their struggles and misgivings. In April of 1953, the minutes state the perspective that the INELA "is not a national church in truth, but only in name"[16] as long as the state of cooperation (with the mission) continues. From time to time a dispute arose over what the mission did or did not promise to give them, such as a vehicle or medical aid.

In spite of the occasional indications of conflict, the *mesa directiva* minutes from the 1950s also show the large range of tasks the national church was taking on. Items on the agenda include progress (or problem) reports from pastors, requests from churches for help with buildings and supplies, disputes over salaries for workers,

---

15. Ralph Chapman, letter to OYM, June 28, 1952, NWYM/GFU archives.

16. *Actas de la Mesa Directiva*, 1953–1956, April 2–3, 1953. See also April 26, May 10, May 24, 1953; April 16, August 3, 1954, INELA archives.

discussion of discipline problems at the day schools, ponderings over how to solve potential church splits, painful talks about the moral failures of various workers, the collection of inventories of material goods from the churches, decisions about pastoral placement, reconciliation between workers, planning for church visits and evangelistic campaigns, discussion about persecution, and, as ever, reflection on the relationship with the mission. We see the national leaders slowly taking charge of administering and growing the church.

While the problem of dependence on foreign money for pastors' salaries had not been resolved, by the end of the decade the mission was handing over to the *mesa directiva* a certain amount each month and letting the *mesa* make the decisions as to who received a salary and how much they received. The *mesa* also administered a church construction fund, receiving a set amount monthly from the mission, then deciding how to disperse it, weighing requests against resources. The mission continued to communicate its intention to eventually withdraw these funds, in favor of a healthy indigenous national church. The INELA leadership continued to resist this proposal.

Pastors' Salaries

Negotiations between the INELA and the mission centered in three areas: finances, properties, and programs. Concerning finances, the key question of mission-paid salaries for pastors and day school teachers occupied more time on the *mesa directiva* agenda than any other item. The mission's plans to gradually reduce salaries to pastors did not go well, partly due to the difficult economic situation in the country. And it seems that a certain degree of dependence and entitlement had become part of the legacy of the church. INELA leadership put constant pressure on the mission to comply with expectations.

In January 1954 Jack Willcuts referred to a letter signed by seventeen pastors during the December pastors' conference demanding a salary raise.[17] In a 1955 newsletter, Willcuts wrote that "in spite of a variety of plans and programs we are as far or farther from *complete* self-support on an indigenous basis than we were 8 years ago and there is no definite goal of attainment in sight. At times it seems hopeless."[18]

In December 1955, pastors and workers met at the Copajira farm for the pastors' conference, with between seventy and eighty in attendance.[19] At the end of the conference, a group of these pastors presented a letter of protest and demands to the mission. Willcuts reported to the mission board that "the meeting was really called because many of the pastors were discouraged (literally 'dismayed') in their work of evangelization. During the meeting each pastor presented in words of testimony his problems which resulted in a unity of opinion that most of these problems arise because of their

---

17. Jack Willcuts, letter to OYM, January 4, 1954, NWYM/GFU archives.
18. Jack Willcuts, letter to OYM, October 7, 1955, NWYM/GFU archives.
19. Jack Willcuts, letter to OYM, January 4, 1956, NWYM/GFU archives.

very low salaries."[20] The pastors then presented a list of six concrete points including their conviction that the brethren from the North (OYM) were regularly sending money, as well as used clothes, intended for pastors and that all this needed to be given to them; that the salary currently received from the mission was so low that the pastors' needs were not met and much suffering resulted; that if the mission would have the dignity to pay them a legal wage, they would then "be able to fulfill with a good conscience their service to the Lord." The last point was a request to give a 100 percent salary increase, with the promise that if this happened they would all "remain in the work." The twenty pastors that signed the letter represented all four quarterly meetings.[21] It should be pointed out that this was not the recommendation of the *mesa directiva*, but a spontaneous coming together of pastoral leaders. The mission board deferred to the field council in not responding to the demands.

In spite of setbacks, major achievements were made by the time of the April 1956 yearly meeting sessions. The *mesa directiva* created a document about financial responsibility that was approved by the representatives at yearly meeting and then sent to each local church. The document began, "Each church is to send the tithes received locally in to the treasury of the National Friends Church in order that there be sufficient funds to assist in pastoral support and the opening of new works."[22]

Salary negotiations continued through the end of the 1950s. In November of 1956, *mesa directiva* secretary Carmelo Aspi visited the mission council and formally requested that the mission do more to help pastors by giving each one a sheep and a sack of produce from the farm each year.[23] While the council did not accept this proposal, it continued to search for alternative ways to support leaders, knowing the hardships of the times. These included the large plot on the farm that the INELA cultivated for a cash crop, shipments of used clothing from the United States that the *mesa directiva* administered, a medical assistance fund to help pastors and families in emergency situations, a project that allowed pastors to buy food at half price, and even projects that supplied sewing machines, barber kits, and carpentry tools for pastors who needed to supplement their income.[24]

In their March 1960 meeting the mission council minuted its decision to discontinue pastor and worker salaries in 1961, in order to encourage pastoral support on the local level.[25] The mission presented its new plan of cooperation with the INELA

20. Jack Willcuts, letter to OYM, January 4, 1956, NWYM/GFU archives.

21. Jack Willcuts, letter to OYM, January 4, 1956, NWYM/GFU archives. Those pastors were Martín Garnica, Baltazar Yujra, Benjamín Condori, Braulio Espejo, Pascual Quispe, Francisco Avalos, Antonio Mamani, Venancio Cortez, Emilio López, Jacinto Mendoza, Eugenio Espinoza, Santiago Illaluqui, Santiago Mamani, Anastacio Mamani, Carmelo Aspi, Pablo Coloma, Domingo Espinoza, Vicente Mamani, and José Flores.

22. In Jack Willcuts, letter to OYM, April 4, 1956, NWYM/GFU archives.

23. BMC Minutes, November 7, 1956, NWYM/GFU archives.

24. BMC Minutes, November 4, 1955, NWYM/GFU archives.

25. BMC Minutes, March 18, 1960, NWYM/GFU archives.

in the April representatives gathering. As minuted by the mission council later, "The new plan of the mission was presented, but some parts were not accepted at first, especially that of pastoral support. Many hard words were spoken, but when it seemed a walk-out was imminent, God undertook, and a new spirit came upon the group."[26] The overall sessions seemed to be a time of spiritual blessing, with over 1620 present in the Sunday morning worship service."[27]

GROWTH AMID THE STRUGGLE

The INELA grew in many ways during the 1950s, all against a dual background of struggle and the sometimes hidden movements of the Holy Spirit.

Administrative Growth

Through the years since the 1920s and 1930s, the annual gathering to celebrate Easter had incorporated church business as well, according to Quaker ways of doing business in a participatory and representative manner. By the 1950s these gatherings were known as "yearly meetings," and continued to combine decision-making with Easter Sunday celebration.

In the 1955 yearly meeting, the INELA was divided into four quarterly meetings, according to geography: La Paz (the city and surrounding region), Cordillera (*altiplano* and mountain areas), Frontera (another area of the *altiplano*), and Península (the area around the lake). Churches in these regions had been gathering in their own annual conferences for years, but this decision made the organization official. Gathered meetings at this area level would take place every three months, and each area, called a quarterly meeting after the custom of meeting four times a year, would have its own executive board. This served to broaden the administrative and leadership base of the church. The INELA *mesa directiva* would continue to administer on a national level. Willcuts considered this a step not only toward greater efficiency of administration, but also toward a more participatory, horizontal, "Quakerly" way of carrying out the business of the church.[28]

Another important step forward was obtaining official recognition from the Bolivian government for the INELA. While the Bolivian Friends Church's acceptance of its new name and organizational plan in April of 1952 indicated a significant change for both the church and the mission, the church was not yet a legal entity according to Bolivian law. The church and the mission joined in seeing this as the next step. Part of the process was the crafting of a constitution and discipline, known in Spanish as the *Estatutos* ("statutes") of the church, then having this document accepted and legalized

26. BMC Minutes, April 19, 1960, NWYM/GFU archives.

27. BMC Minutes, April 19, 1960, NWYM/GFU archives.

28. Jack Willcuts, letter to OYM, January 22, 1955, NWYM/GFU archives.

by the appropriate government agency. It was an arduous process, and the two entities worked together, with the help of a lawyer employed by the mission.

The mission took the lead in writing the new *Estatutos*, in frequent conversation with the *mesa directiva*, using the *Faith and Practice* documents from Oregon Yearly Meeting, Kansas Yearly Meeting, and Central America Yearly Meeting as guidelines, and constantly exploring Bolivian law for requirements.[29] It was arduous work, but Jack Willcuts especially felt called to this type of organizational ministry.[30] In recognition of Willcuts's contribution, historian Ron Stansell notes that "Jack, with the approval of the council, had essentially written the first Constitution and Discipline (*Estatutos* in Spanish) for the Bolivian Friends National Church . . . gifting it with a Friends statement of faith, Friends terminology, and outline of a basic organization structure that persists nearly sixty years later. Jack Willcuts just happened to be the most articulate spokesperson for the national church and helped focus the attention of the Northwest home base, the missionaries, and the Bolivian leaders upon this crucial step."[31]

Jack Willcuts and family, 1940s–1950s (NWYM)

29. Jack Willcuts, letter to OYM, November 4, 1955, NWYM/GFU archives.

30. Jack Willcuts, letter to OYM, October 10, 1957, NWYM/GFU archives.

31. Stansell, *Missions by the Spirit*, 233.

Willcuts and others on the mission council staff worked to draft the document, then had the *mesa directiva* read and revise, until they felt clear to submit it to the government. The document of official acceptance was signed by the president of Bolivia on March 16, 1956,[32] and later that month copies were passed out to the representatives gathered for their annual meeting in La Paz. Everyone involved considered this a major step forward and cause for great rejoicing.

The representatives in the annual meeting of 1958 took another step forward on the national level in setting up four boards to fulfill functions that previously were under individual "secretaries," all members of the *mesa directiva*. The secretaries continued, but now as chairmen of a board or committee. These were the committees of evangelism, literature and publication, Christian education (over day schools and Sunday schools), and construction (to oversee day school and church building projects).[33]

Property Titles

One of the implications of the INELA's new legal status was that the national church could now own properties. In May 1956, OYM superintendent Dean Gregory on a visit to the field participated in a meeting of the *mesa directiva* and officially informed them of the mission board's decision to turn over to the INELA all lands, church buildings, and schools, except the missionary residence in La Paz and the farm at Copajira.[34] The INELA was anxious that the title transfers happen, and the subject comes up from time to time in the *mesa directiva* minutes. The brethren were not in accord with the decision not to hand over the farm, and that thorn would continue to prick.[35]

In 1956, the mission made a significant property purchase on El Alto, the upper section of La Paz. It had been acknowledged for several years that the La Paz property on Max Paredes Street had outgrown its capacity to host the crowds of Friends coming in for the yearly meeting sessions and other large gatherings. So after searching, the mission and the INELA agreed on a large tract of land on El Alto, and the mission purchased it for $1,757.20. This purchase was made feasible largely because of an offering by Marshall Cavit, still on loan from the NHMS to the OYM mission.[36]

The project was swiftly financed and completed, and Bolivian Friends gathered for their 1957 yearly meeting sessions in the new Charles R. Cavit Memorial Tabernacle, dedicated to Marshal Cavit's father. In a newsletter, Jack Willcuts wrote, "Meeting for the first time in the new Alto La Paz tabernacle (105 x 85 ft. on a lot 200 x 400 ft.)

---

32. Jack Willcuts, letter to OYM, April 5, 1956, NWYM/GFU archives. The official incorporation is known as the *personería jurídica*, and the INELA's presidential recognition number is *Resolución Suprema # 70353*.

33. Jack Willcuts, letter to OYM, April 7, 1958, NWYM/GFU archives.

34. *Actas de la Mesa Directiva*, 1953–1956, May 1, 1956, INELA archives.

35. OYM Minutes, 1959, 58, NWYM/GFU archives.

36. BMC Minutes, June 6, 1956, NWYM/GFU archives.

found an unprecedented attendance with 1,300 persons actual count and a probable 1,500 people on Sunday afternoon."[37] Early in 1958 the mission was able to turn the El Alto property and tabernacle over to the INELA, legal titles and all.[38]

The Copajira Farm

The farm property was a more complex issue. As mentioned above, on August 3, 1953, the agrarian reform laws did away with the haciendas, requiring landowners to give their properties to the *colonos*. The Friends Mission farm at Copajira found itself in a unique situation. The mission had already freed the *colonos* that were living there when the farm had been purchased in 1947,[39] and large sections had already been subdivided and legally turned over. The mission had kept the land that remained for the Bible school, and some farmland as a way of maintaining the programs of the church. In addition, experimentation with agricultural methods and the purchase of modern machinery had turned the farm into a community service. Reports home frequently noted bumper crops, sometimes in contrast to the surrounding farms.[40]

And yet the restlessness of the indigenous peoples, feeling a new sense of power, touched Copajira to a certain extent, and the mission's possession of the farm seemed precarious for most of the 1950s.

In February 1955, Jack Willcuts wrote from Copajira this frightening description:

> Today . . . Paul [Cammack] went up to plow with the Cat in an area the peons had hopefully assumed would be theirs in the land reform. Hence they quickly gathered about 34 strong and Paul came down at lunchtime uncertain whether he would return for fear of being stoned or worse. We talked it over and advised him against it. . . . There is a tenseness in the air this evening which is rather uncomfortable. The peons around are certainly of a different, hateful spirit than when I visited here last. Did you ever look a man in the eye whom you know wanted to kill you if he dared?[41]

In a more positive note, in his annual report to the mission board in 1956, Paul Cammack wrote,

> The agricultural reform to date has not taken any land from us and we have reasonable assurance that we will not be affected by the reform because of our philanthropic work and mechanization. However, in a voluntary manner we have carried out the reform by increasing the amount of land for the use of our Indians. We have given them liberty to use various plots of land unusable for

37. Jack Willcuts, letter to OYM, April 27, 1957, NWYM/GFU archives.

38. BMC Minutes, February 5, 1958, NWYM/GFU archives.

39. They freed all who wanted to be freed. Those who preferred to remain as *colonos* were paid a fair wage for their work.

40. For example, OYM Minutes, 1951, 54, NWYM/GFU archives.

41. Jack Willcuts, letter to OYM, February 15, 1955, NWYM/GFU archives.

tractor farming near the mountains and 100 acres of flat land which they had used on a rental basis previously.... The Indians probably will receive titles for these additional lands in the future.[42]

The good news continued to alternate with hard news. A praise note in the March 1960 minutes reads, "Seizure by farm Indians of the upper valley of the farm thwarted."[43]

Paul Cammack oversaw the agricultural aspect of the farm for most of the decade. He was joined in 1956 by Forest and Orpha Cammack who came as short termers to help in this work. In addition to the Bible school, the farm hosted pastors' conferences, classes for young women, and Aymara classes for missionaries of all denominations. Yet council members expressed concerned that the hard work of running the farm might detract from the more fundamental evangelistic purposes of the mission.

Discipleship and Leadership Training

The presence of the farm facilitated fulfillment of the mission's goals in leadership training.

The Bible School

One of the fundamental purposes of the mission was fulfilled in the Helen Cammack Memorial Bible Training School, an institution for leadership training that actually depended on the functioning of the farm for its feasibility. During the 1950s, the Bible school flourished, with most of INELA's leadership graduating or at least having attended. As its usefulness was demonstrated in the product of the leaders it formed, its prestige among INELA members also rose.

Copajira Bible school boys, 1950s (NWYM)

42. OYM Minutes, 1956, 39, NWYM/GFU archives.
43. BMC Minutes, March 7, 1960, NWYM/GFU archives.

The basic plan of the school continued as in previous years, with morning classes in Bible and pastoral ministry, afternoon work assignments on the farm, weekend evangelistic trips or church visits, and special holiness revival weeks once or twice a year. Before the end of the decade a year of practical ministry service before graduation was added to the program.[44] In 1950 the school graduated its first four students: Casimiro Quaquera, Pedro Guanca, Pablo Mendoza, and Braulio Espejo; they were all given pastoral assignments. Missionaries continued as teachers, taking turns as school director, and living on the farm.

Enrollment grew with the passing years, from twenty-three students in 1950[45] to a high of eighty-five in 1958.[46] Students contributed to the work of the INELA through their weekend activities. Some of the second- and third-year students actually pastored churches. Mission council minutes observed in 1954 that "approximately 200 people are being reached by boys from school over each week end."[47] In a report home in 1955, Ralph Chapman summarized these activities: "The boys are very active in evangelism with as many as 15 or 20 going out each week-end to minister in churches or for evangelization in homes or out on the highway. We have a student evangelization committee named which works out the appointments and then gets the director's approval. . . . We have a Thursday night prayer meeting for students and a separate one for faculty at the same hour. An 8:00 AM Sunday prayer meeting and the first Thursday of each month for prayer and fasting are in the schedule."[48]

In 1957 the mission council minuted its intention to develop a program for the formation of national teachers for the Bible school, and a decision to approach Carmelo Aspi about teaching in the near future.[49] Aspi, a third-year student himself at that time, was also a member of the *mesa directiva* and an up-and-coming young leader in the national church. The council later invited Aspi to teach full time in the Bible school for the 1959 year, with the mission paying half his salary and the *mesa directiva* the other half.[50]

The 1959 school year demonstrated the tension that existed between the mission and the national church. In May the student body (which at that time consisted of forty-eight men) presented to the director and teachers its demand that the school expand beyond its Bible school status, offer pedagogy and other secular courses, and become a legal, degree-offering educational institution within the country's system.

44. Ralph Chapman, letter to OYM, August 1, 1956, NWYM/GFU archives.

45. OYM Minutes 1951, 50, NWYM/GFU archives.

46. BMC Minutes, January 9, 1958, NWYM/GFU archives.

47. BMC Minutes, February 9, 1954, NWYM/GFU archives.

48. Ralph Chapman, letter to OYM, April 6, 1955, NWYM/GFU archives.

49. BMC Minutes, March 6, 1957, NWYM/GFU archives.

50. BMC Minutes, June 5, 1958, NWYM/GFU archives.

This was in line with national education reforms going on all around, but it was clearly not in sync with the mission's focused purpose of pastoral formation."[51]

The student organization then presented to the mission council a list of demands that included both the trivial (e.g., better food at breakfast) and the more substantial. In addition to the demands that the school be legalized and offer training in various trades, with legally recognized credit, they also protested that the courses were too hard, and specifically named the missionaries that needed to leave, including the director. They asked for higher wages for the wives who were working at the farm. They also demanded that the mission turn over both the school and the farm to the *mesa directiva*. The students ended the interview by stating that if the mission did not attend to these criticisms and demands, they would go on strike, then leave the school.[52]

The mission's response was equally hard-line: "The council stood fast on its purpose to have the Bible school only for spiritual advancement of those who wish to study the Bible and follow the Lord's will."[53] In a separate session, the missionaries also decided to disband the student organization and "to suspend the school indefinitely 'til we have time to study the problem and hear from the north."[54] Actually, classes were suspended for only two weeks, reopened "without compromise on curriculum," and two-thirds of the student body returned. The mission reported that these returning students "were, with very few exceptions, the young men most interested in spiritual values, and doing the will of God."[55] The year ended with ten graduates.

The missionaries reorganized what remained of the 1959 school year to end in July and then offered four months of "upper grade school" to those Bible school students who desired it. The students were then able to be accredited in the national educational system, at great advantage to them. Ten students participated in the program. In addition, at the end of the 1960 school year, the mission offered all graduates one month of instruction with a master in a trade of their choice, recognizing that future pastors would need a means of livelihood in addition to the ministry.[56] It seems that the mission was, after all, sensitive to the times and to the economic needs of the students.

The Bible school had only twenty students in 1960, and the mission council decided to suspend the school for the entire 1961 year because of lack of mission staff and "other considerations."[57]

---

51. OYM Minutes, 1959, 60, NWYM/GFU archives. The INELA president at that time was José Acero.

52. BMC Minutes, May 7, 1959; July 1, 1959. OYM Minutes, 1959, 60, NWYM/GFU archives.

53. BMC Minutes, May 7, 1959, NWYM/GFU archives.

54. BMC Minutes, May 10, 1959, NWYM/GFU archives.

55. OYM Minutes, 1959, 60, NWYM/GFU archives.

56. OYM Minutes, 1960, 36–37, NWYM/GFU archives.

57. OYM Minutes, 1960, 37, NWYM/GFU archives.

DISCIPLESHIP AND LEADERSHIP TRAINING FOR WOMEN

In addition to the Bible school, the mission also added programs for the encouragement of women in discipleship and ministry. This corresponded to the Friends value of gender equality. The mission council observed in 1954, "We feel sure that as yet there is a barrier to the education of the girls among the Aymara believers in our churches. But we are encouraged that so many came this year and feel that as time goes on and as the school proves itself that this reluctance on the part of some of the parents will disappear."[58] This statement referenced a new two-week intensive Bible school program for young single women.

The day school program for children included girls as well as boys, although the 1950 field report notes that "many of the believers do not send their daughters to school as they are too useful at home."[59] The Bible school did not stipulate men only, and in the beginning a few young women attended. But the educational level of Aymara women in the country as a whole was lower than that of men, and as the Bible school found it necessary to raise its entrance requirements, fewer women were eligible.

In an attempt to address these challenges and encourage the leadership development of women in the INELA, the mission inaugurated the intensive Bible school program for *señoritas*. Phyllis Cammack directed the program, and between September 28 and October 13, 1954, thirty-six young women met on the Copajira farm for lessons in Bible, ministry and, literacy.[60] Forty-five attended the next year, with three weeks of classes in the morning, working on the farm in the afternoons, and evangelistic services in the evenings; enthusiasm among the women was growing. Classes taught by the missionary women included "memory texts, Bible study, reading and writing, music, and a general class which included hygiene, gymnastics, games and practical aspects of living." Phyllis Cammack's report of the event concluded with the expression of its goal, "that these young women will be real workers throughout the field in their own communities and churches."[61] By 1957 enrollment was up to seventy-one women in the special classes. In addition, eighteen pastors' wives accompanied their husbands that year for their own classes during pastors' conference in December.[62] The 1959 annual field report of the women's classes observed that "many of the girls not only found the Lord but also learned to read the Scriptures in their Aymara tongue which is a tricky art even for the more educated. These girls going out from these short period Bible Schools are taking their places in kingdom work in their communities. The women's work in the Gospel is beginning to move ahead."[63]

58. BMC Minutes, November 11, 1954, NWYM/GFU archives.

59. OYM Minutes, 1950, 56, NWYM/GFU archives.

60. OYM Minutes, 1955, 33, NWYM/GFU archives.

61. OYM Minutes, 1956, 37, NWYM/GFU archives.

62. OYM Minutes, 1958, 17, NWYM/GFU archives.

63. OYM Minutes, 1959, 60, NWYM/GFU archives.

Marie Chapman teaching women on the altiplano, 1950s (NWYM)

In addition to these training programs, several local churches had begun to set up women's organizations, and 1953 saw the beginnings of a district wide women's organization in Amacari.[64] In 1955 the mission council decided to encourage the *mesa directiva* to give workers' cards "to women who feel the call of God to evangelize among the women in our field" (men already having these), and mentioned the names of Francisca Quispe, Petrona de Mamani, and Petrona Ott.[65]

DAY SCHOOLS

We have seen how the INELA primary day schools had developed during the 1940s. Following the revolution of 1952, educational reform was an important part of the many changes sweeping the country. And while it took years to flesh out, the education of indigenous children was slowly becoming a government priority. Soon many of the communities where Friends churches were being planted also had a government school for local children.

64. BMC Minutes, November 13, 1953, NWYM/GFU archives.
65. BMC Minutes, August 30, 1953, NWYM/GFU archives.

Even so, the decade of the 1950s saw a boom in the Friends schools, with an expansion of five schools and 184 students in 1950[66] to a high of twenty-five schools serving 644 children in 1958.[67]

In 1950 the mission paid the salaries of the six teachers working in the five different Friends schools and also helped in the construction of classrooms and the provision of supplies. A missionary served as director of schools.

One of the tasks of the mission after the revolution of 1952 was to legalize the existing schools, getting government approval and putting each school into the developing government system. As early as August 1953, the mission council reported that all eleven schools running that year had been "officially recognized by the government."[68] Any new schools in the coming years followed the procedures for recognition.

Children in an altiplano Friends school, 1950s (NWYM)

Another task was assuring that the schools continued being Christian in character and that the teachers were morally upright and responsible. Mission council minutes from August of 1953 noted that "the subject of the day schools was thoroughly discussed. The consensus of opinion was that the teachers have not been teaching the gospel, that for the amount of time and money put out very few students come out who are helpers in the work. All favored curtailment until the entire program can be revised. From the

66. OYM Minutes, 1950, 56, NWYM/GFU archives.
67. OYM Minutes, 1958, 17, NWYM/GFU archives.
68. OYM Minutes, 1953, 49, NWYM/GFU archives.

eleven schools for this year the list was cut to seven, with the idea of having as many schools as good teachers are available."[69]

OYM superintendent Dean Gregory visited the field in 1960 and joined the mission council in deciding that beginning in January 1961 the schools would be completely under the direction of the national church, with the mission helping new schools with some supplies such as chalk and a blackboard, a flag, and patriotic pictures. They would generously give a soccer ball to both new and established schools. The national church approved of this change at the annual representatives meeting.[70]

Evangelism and the Growth of the Church

The mission's annual field report of 1951 reported nineteen congregations with regular services, plus several outposts.[71] Quentin Nordyke's church growth research gives the church roughly five hundred believers at that time.[72] By 1958, some three thousand believers were attending Sunday school in the eighty-five churches and preaching points.[73] Several reasons are given for this high growth rate,[74] but one factor must surely be the gradual transfer of evangelistic responsibility from the mission to the national church.

The 1950s saw development in the evangelistic ministry of the INELA with the adoption of an evangelism committee under the *mesa*, and the naming of secretaries of evangelism in each district. Local churches also assumed responsibility for planting new churches in their areas. The mission cooperated, naming one mission council member to work with the national secretary of evangelism, offering $100 a month for evangelistic travel,[75] transporting the evangelists in a mission vehicle, and providing large tents for the meetings. People flocked to this novelty, enjoyed the music, and stayed for the message.

69. BMC Minutes, August 25, 1953, NWYM/GFU archives.

70. OYM Minutes, 1960, 38, NWYM/GFU archives.

71. OYM Minutes, 1951, 60, NWYM/GFU archives.

72. Nordyke, *Animistic Aymaras*, 137–39. Accurate statistics for the first four decades of the church were not kept, so figures are based on letters, occasional reports, and the guestimates of the missionaries on the field.

73. OYM Minutes, 1958, 17, NWYM/GFU archives.

74. For example, see Nordyke, *Animistic Aymaras*, 131–44.

75. OYM Mission Council Minute, January 21, 1955, NWYM/GFU archives.

Altiplano tent evangelism, 1950s (NWYM)

Methodologies focused on evangelistic meetings in established churches or quarterly meeting sessions, open to the public, with national evangelists giving the message. Open-air meetings in receptive communities were also a way many Aymaras came to faith, often in family units.

In a letter to the mission board in 1955, Willcuts wrote of "95 open-air meetings held in the past 3 months," contacting, according to his estimates, some 3,650 people, making 272 converts, and resulting in five new congregations. The La Paz congregation saw over seventy new believers added to its community in that same three-month period.[76] The following month Willcuts reported 120 new converts at a revival in Chirapaca.[77] From time to time mission council minutes reported, as a regular part of their business, how many new congregations had recently been planted.[78]

In reference to the challenge of how to disciple and incorporate into the church so many new believers, in 1957 the mission council reported to the board the *mesa's* plan:

76. Jack Willcuts, letter to OYM, September 5, 1955, NWYM/GFU archives.

77. Jack Willcuts, letter to OYM, October 4, 1955, NWYM/GFU archives.

78. For example, see BMC Minutes December 23, 1955; March 6, 1957; September 4, 1957; October 2, 1957, NWYM/GFU archives.

In view of rapid growth of new points, it is recognized many new believers lack understanding about the National Church and denominational program. A major problem before the Mesa Directiva is absorption of new churches into a systematic and uniform organization. To meet this need the following plan was adopted: Name 5 secretaries of visitation for two months, Nov. and Dec., to cover the field with charts illustrating church organization, tithing program, etc. plus doctrinal teaching. These five men, Angel Tintaya for Cordillera, Antonio Mamani for Peninsula, Eugenio Espinoza for La Paz, Cipriano Copa for Yungas, Carmelo Aspi for Frontera, will all be trained in a special class during pastors' conference this month. They will receive pay and passage money from the Mesa Directiva. The enthusiasm displayed by national leaders for this idea is gratifying and promising.[79]

The church evangelized and grew during this period against a backdrop of persecution. Much of this emerged from the revolutionary spirit of the times, with the radical extremes of the MNR movement against anything to do with the United States, including missions and their resulting churches.

In a report home to the mission board in 1956, Jack Willcuts referred to persecution against believers in the communities of Karhuisa, Pucarani, and Tambillo and efforts by the mission to secure legal protection under the laws of the land. He wrote that

four witch doctors live in the same community and they with the priests are leading the drive to rid the area of all evangelicals. Tomorrow I am to appear before the officials in Pucarani to report our side of the incidents which have been taking place. . . .

Our believers have been attacked again too in Tambillo. I am going out there on Sunday morning with a government order to try to gain legal protection so far as possible. Frankly, it is obvious that a general tightening down by Catholic leadership is being attempted. . . . Undoubtedly a concerted effort is being launched to halt evangelical inroads in the relatively open country of Bolivia.[80]

In the December 1958 mission council minutes, the mission asked special prayer for believers in a church near Copajira, under persecution headed up by an Italian priest against the new Friends school in the village. The minute says that

authorities in Guaqui refused to exert any effort in the cause of justice. This week has been a series of new outrages—four believers on way to Copajira pastors-teachers conference attacked on road and three bicycles taken. Three of the four were able to escape, one was held for a time. Next the new church, up 6 feet or so, was leveled, rocks stolen, adobes broken. Then followed beatings

---

79. BMC Minutes, October 2, 1957, NWYM/GFU archives.
80. Jack Willcuts, letter to OYM, August 15, 1956, NWYM/GFU archives.

of the believers, theft of sheep. The latest was an attack on the neighboring community of San Pedro Tana. Believers were beaten with whips, animals driven off, windows and doors of church stolen. The belief is that the enraged gang is on its way to other communities close by.[81]

These types of incidents were repeated at various times and in different areas throughout the decade.

YUNGAS

A special chapter in the INELA's story needs to be dedicated to the ministry begun in the Yungas valleys to the east of La Paz through the work of Roscoe and Tina Knight and a core of national workers who both preceded them and accompanied them.

The Yungas valleys follow the rivers to the east down from the *altiplano* in a series of steep canyons that grow more tropical the further down they wind. For many years Aymaras had been colonizing these lush mountain valleys, forming communities and raising tropical crops. In 1954 Marshall Cavit described the area as "thickly populated with literally thousands of people without the gospel."[82]

Friends interest in beginning ministry in the Yungas goes back to Juan Ayllón who made exploratory trips in the 1920s, but it was not until the 1950s that INELA and the Oregon Friends Mission sensed the time was ripe for them to enter.

The mission's first foray in the 1950s into the area was not for ministry but to prepare a lower-altitude place where missionaries could go to rest. In 1951 the mission obtained a fifty-year lease to part of a hacienda property in the village of Pichu, a small clearing overlooking the river. Rent was $25 a year, and money raised by the OYM women's organization provided the means to build a small rustic cabin that the missionaries could use for brief vacations.[83]

INELA leader Mariano Baptista made short evangelistic trips in the area in or shortly before 1953.[84] By mid-1953, both the INELA minutes and the mission council annual field report refer to a small group of new believers in Chojlla.[85] The *mesa directiva* named Baptista to pastor the group.[86] In 1954 Marshal Cavit made several exploratory trips to the Yungas, accompanied by national evangelist Baltazar Yujra,

81. BMC Minutes, December 4, 1958, NWYM/GFU archives.

82. OYM Minutes, 1954, 70, NWYM/GFU archives.

83. Tina Knight describes it as "nothing fancy, a rustic 33 by 24-foot room with no ceiling, a red tile roof, and no plumbing. No one would call it beautiful, but it provided restful vacations" (*On Down the Trail*, 3).

84. Ralph Chapman, letter to OYM, May 26, 1953, NWYM/GFU archives.

85. *Actas de la Mesa Directiva*, 1953–1956, April 31, 1953, INELA archives; OYM Minutes, 1953, 50, NWYM/GFU archives.

86. *Actas de la Mesa Directiva*, 1953–1956, June 20, 1953, INELA archives.

and in the 1954 annual field report, he noted that there were now five places where a few believers were meeting, one of which was already constructing its meeting place.[87]

National evangelistic team in the Yungas (NWYM)

The mission council agreed that God was opening this work,[88] and the mission board concurred and appointed Roscoe and Tina Knight, on furlough in the United States, as missionaries to the Yungas when they returned to the field in 1955.

In May 1955, a month after their return to Bolivia, Roscoe and Tina Knight, with their three young children, moved to the Yungas. While their first task was to fix up the Pichu cabin, turning it from a rustic vacation spot into a viable home, Roscoe wasted no time getting into the work of evangelization. Accompanied by Francisco Ávalos, a young Bible school graduate, his first strategy was extensive house-to-house visitation. Tina Knight describes this phase in her book about the beginnings of the Yungas work, *On Down the Trail*: "Many mornings after packing a back-pack with tracts and Bible portions, Roscoe and Francisco set off to spend the day evangelizing from house to house. They would drive along the main road from one community to another but always had to hike up or down the mountain to find homes hidden

---

87. BMC Minutes, June 15, 1954; OYM Minutes, 1954, 70, NWYM/GFU archives.
88. BMC Minutes, December 27, 1954, NWYM/GFU archives.

among the banana, orange, coffee or jungle trees."[89] They also visited the small groups already meeting. This phase of the ministry lasted two months, at which time Knight felt ready to begin a tent ministry, drawing people in to hear the gospel message.

The tent meeting strategy was successful in drawing large numbers of people in to hear the gospel. Soccer fields provided the only flat place in hilly villages, and their central location proved advantageous. Tina Knight's description of one of the early meetings in the village of Sacahuaya gives some of the flavor of the experience:

> A public truck unloaded the tent, poles, and stakes, plus four evangelists—Martín, two Marianos and Baltazar with their Bibles, projector, Bible slides and pump organ—at Sacahuaya. Roscoe drove up and down the road announcing the meeting from a loudspeaker. It frightened some. They had never heard a loudspeaker before. The announcement echoed up and down the canyon, even reaching up into a logging camp across the river.
> *Maybe it's the judgement,* the rumor spread.[90]

Knight went on to describe how some two hundred people crowded into the tent that first night, drawn by curiosity and excitement. They sang along with the songs played on the pump organ, listened to the gospel stories, and were especially fascinated by the slide show of the creation story. Services went on for four days, ending at midnight each day. At the end of the campaign, some sixty Aymaras had decided to become Christian.

The Knights, along with the rest of the mission council, also felt the necessity of the development of national leadership in the Yungas, and always ministered in the company of national pastors and evangelists. This proved to be a challenge since the work was so new and required that established workers from other areas of work spend time in the Yungas. The turnover in national workers was notable, as many found the lower altitude difficult. Another obstacle was persecution of new believers. Yet the work prospered and people were added to the churches. In Knight's 1956 annual field report, he informs of twelve places with regular church services and people coming from over twenty-two communities; an estimated 250 believers; one completed church building and four under construction; and four grade schools, all locally supported. Methods continued to focus on house evangelism, tent meetings, and constant visitation and vigilance of the new church groups. He summed up the challenges in the following words:

> We have had a ready response in all places with many professing conversion. However . . . friends, superstitions and worldly habits work hard to drag these new converts back to their former ways of life. Many have fallen, usually within the first month but in every place where we have had meetings there have arisen those who have resisted strong persecution and have become strong

89. Knight, *On Down the Trail*, 24.
90. Knight, *On Down the Trail*, 27–28.

unshakable Christians. As we cannot by any means supply pastors to all these new places, most of these people have had only occasional visits and help by missionaries and native pastors. The Holy Spirit has been a faithful pastor, and on this assurance of His continued workings, we are continuing to enter new communities with the Gospel though we cannot give them pastors.[91]

In 1958 when the INELA representatives in their annual meeting approved making the Yungas their fifth quarterly meeting,[92] fifteen churches had been established. The *mesa* named Cipriano Copa as the first president of Yungas Quarterly Meeting. By the end of that year the number of groups meeting regularly had risen to at least twenty-five,[93] and the number would continue to rise.

In facing the problem of so many new believers with the limited number of trained national leaders and pastors, the Knights instituted a Yungas Bible School in a tent on their property. The school opened in 1957 for two weeks, with thirty-five male students. By this time Roscoe was able to teach in the Aymara language, and classes included biblical and doctrinal materials, practical ministry skills, and reading, for those who needed it.[94] By popular demand the school soon grew to a twice-a-year event, and by 1959, seventy-three men from twenty churches were attending.[95] In addition, the Knights began a separate Bible school for women, and by 1959, seventy women were also being discipled and formed into leaders.[96]

When Knights returned to Oregon on furlough in 1959, David and Florence Thomas took their place for a year in the Yungas. Within a few years after their return to Bolivia, the mission board transferred the Knights to the new work in Peru. But the work in the Yungas had been firmly established and would now move forward under national leadership.

EMERGING LEADERS

In the literature of the decade, several names emerge of men who were becoming leaders in the INELA. One of the foremost of these was Mariano Baptista, the first president of the INELA in 1952.

91. OYM Minutes, 1956, 32, NWYM/GFU archives.

92. *Actas de la Mesa Directiva*, 1957–1962, April 2, 1958, INELA archives.

93. BMC Minutes, October 8, 1958, NWYM/GFU archives.

94. Knight, *On Down the Trail*, 174–75.

95. Knight, *On Down the Trail*, 177.

96. Knight, *On Down the Trail*, 177.

Mariano Baptista

Mariano Baptista (also referred to as Mariano Bautista)[97] was born in 1912 in the small *altiplano* community of Caquingera, near the mining center of Corocoro.[98] His family was traditional Aymara, with animistic roots and a nominal connection to the Catholic Church. His father, Antonio Baptista, worked in the mines. Mariano's childhood was typical, spent helping in the family's fields, with the animals, and, as he grew older, helping his father in the mines.

At the age of eighteen, Mariano put in his obligatory two years in military training, then came home again to help his father in the mines. This lasted for a year, and in 1932, when the Chaco War with Paraguay broke out, Mariano was conscripted with the first group of indigenous soldiers and sent to the front lines of the war. After two years as a soldier, he was captured and spent one year as a prisoner of war in Paraguay. Upon his release at the end of the war, he returned home.

Mariano's war years in the lowlands made difficult his acclimation to the high altitude, and he soon moved down to La Paz where he found work, first as a police officer and later in construction. It was during these years as a worker in La Paz that Mariano came in contact with the gospel message through the faithful witness of two companions at work. The first, a Methodist believer, persuaded Mariano to attend services at his church, which he consented to do only at night, for fear of being seen by family members or friends. The gospel message had an impact, but Mariano resisted, not ready to give up the drinking habits he had acquired in the city.

In 1939, another work companion, Francisco Flores, a believer in the La Paz Friends Church on Max Paredes Street, faithfully shared the gospel with him and finally persuaded him to attend church services. Mariano's sense of conviction grew until finally, under the ministry of Pastor Juan Ayllón, he decided to become a Christian.

He publicly testified to his conversion and endured a time of ridicule and testing by his fellow construction workers, but this seemed to only strengthen him in his new life. By this time he had married, and Paula followed him in Christian conversion. They began to build their family on a Christian foundation. A brief biography written about him in 1953 states that "since his conversion, Mariano has helped in the church work in about every office open to any individual member."[99] Under the guidance of Carroll Tamplin, he led in open-air evangelistic services, served on the local church council, and taught Sunday school. Doris Tamplin taught him to play the organ. During the 1940s he served for a while as the visiting Sunday preacher at the Puerto Pérez

97. Baptista/Bautista's granddaughter, Elizabeth Bautista de Choque, says that his original surname was Baptista (from father Antonio Baptista), but that during his inscription into the Bolivian army, an official mistakenly wrote Bautista. Mariano seemed to use both surnames for a time, but eventually settled on Bautista. Future generations of the family now go by Bautista. From an interview with Elizabeth Bautista de Choque, by Nancy Thomas, July 15, 2015, Tillamook, Oregon.

98. Much of the information for this section comes from a biography of Baptista written by an unnamed missionary in 1953, "Biography of Mariano Baptista," n.d., NWYM/GFU archives.

99. "Biography of Mariano Baptista," 1953, NWYM/GFU archives.

meeting.[100] In 1946 and 1947, he was president of the La Paz Church council; this was during the controversy with Francisco Medrano. During the time in the late 1940s when Jack Willcuts served as pastor of the La Paz church, Mariano was his associate pastor,[101] and much of his pastoral and leadership formation came from this time. When Jack stepped down from the pastorate (the last missionary to pastor a church in Bolivia) in 1951, Mariano became lead pastor of this church. For a brief time in the early 1950s he pastored the Ojje Friends Church on the lake.[102]

Mariano Baptista (NWYM)

In addition to his leadership in the local La Paz church, Mariano also was becoming a leader on the national level. In both 1947 and 1948 he was named to the executive council of the new organizations (SEAB and SEAN) that were the forerunners to the INELA.[103] And as we have already seen, Mariano Baptista was named first president of the INELA in 1952 and served three years leading the *mesa directiva*. Part of his role after 1952 was to serve as go-between between the mission council and the *mesa directiva*.[104] It's significant that his name consistently appears as a leader in the different developmental stages of the national church organization.

As we have seen above, Mariano Baptista led the effort to plant INELA Friends churches in the Yungas, and the *mesa directiva* named him to pastor the first Yungas church in Mina Chojjla in 1953; he continued in that capacity for several years. In 1957 he was named pastor of the new church meeting in Alto La Paz and caretaker of the tabernacle property.[105] During 1957 and beyond his interest in the Yungas work continued, and he traveled from time to time with Roscoe Knight to encourage the new churches.[106]

---

100. Ralph Chapman, letter to OYM, August 27, 1945, NWYM/GFU archives.

101. Jack Willcuts, letter to OYM, March 29, 1948, NWYM/GFU archives.

102. Jack Willcuts, letter to OYM, April 12, 1950, NWYM/GFU archives.

103. Ralph Chapman, letter to OYM, April 10, 1947; Jack Willcuts, letter to OYM, March 29, 1948, NWYM/GFU archives.

104. BMC Minutes, May 7, 1952, NWYM/GFU archives.

105. BMC Minutes, May 9, 1957, NWYM/GFU archives.

106. *Actas de la Mesa Directiva*, 1957–1962, May 2, 1957, INELA archives.

Jack and Geraldine Willcuts returned to the field in 1954, after an extended medical leave. In their absence the INELA had been formed and the church had grown. In noting the growing maturity of the national church, Willcuts especially expressed his appreciation for Mariano Baptista, remembering the times of discipleship when they co-pastored the La Paz church:

> One thing for which I rejoice is the character of Mariano Baptista. So far as I know, he is the first leader of our work who was ever ousted from the pastorship of the La Paz church and the presidency of the national church at the same time who didn't either sue us or leave the work. But Mariano instead went into outpost work in the Yungas and now tells me he has 4 churches started. It is largely thru his vision and work that the Yungas work has opened up to us. He has his faults as do we all, but it is wonderful to find those who have caught the vision of stability. I do not take the credit personally for his progress at all, but I do feel that our effort to spend hour on hour with him in counsel, prayer, instruction and personal interest has gone a long way toward bolstering his loyalty to the Mission and to the Lord. To me this is the most valuable work of the missionary today, even in the Bible School.[107]

In a 2015 interview with Geraldine Willcuts, she remembers Mariano Baptista as being both a close friend and trusted national leader in the church, someone who had the respect of both missionaries and nationals. She remarked that he was a mature Christian disciple in all senses of the term.[108]

His leadership would continue to develop into the decade of the 1960s.

Silas Casas

Silas Casas is another name that comes up in the literature of the decade. His story highlights an issue that would only grow more important in the coming years, that of the contrast between traditional rural Aymara populations in the church and the second generation of young believers raised in the city and with a higher level of education.

Silas Casas was the son of Calixto Casas, one of the early believers from a rural community. Calixto's name comes up occasionally in the 1950s and on through the early 1960s[109] when he served as a member of INELA's *mesa directiva*. Casas, the son, was apparently raised in the city of La Paz where his education and own natural abilities would cause Ralph Chapman to note that "he is a class higher than our other

---

107. Jack Willcuts, letter to OYM, October 9, 1954, NWYM/GFU archives.

108. Geraldine Willcuts, interview with Nancy Thomas, June 26, 2015, Newberg, Oregon.

109. *Actas de la Mesa Directiva*, 1953–1956, April 2, 1953; May 24, 1953; April 14, 1954; *Actas de la Mesa Directiva*, 1957–1962, January 8, 1962, INELA archives.

boys"[110] and inspire both the *mesa directiva* and the mission council to struggle to find a place of service for him.

In 1950 while still a young man, Casas was named the worker to minister at a new church plant in the section of Miraflores in La Paz, a work that apparently was short-lived. That same year in a letter home, Chapman notes that "Silas Casas has married and settled down, and now can be a real help to the work."[111] That would prove to be wishful thinking.

In recognition of his potential, the national church and mission appointed the young Casas to be on the *mesa directiva* of the national church in the 1951 yearly meeting sessions where he occupied the role of treasurer.[112] When the SEAN became the INELA, Casas continued as treasurer of the *mesa directiva*, but left midyear to travel to Buenos Aires.[113]

Silas Casas also served as teacher in the La Paz day school and was, off and on, a source of conflict over salary, sometimes complaining that he wasn't receiving his just dues from the mission or the local church,[114] another time attempting to organize the teachers to request salary raises. In the meantime, he was probably an excellent teacher for young urban Quakers.

While his secular education was apparently strong, mission and church leaders saw the need for him to become theologically and biblically prepared also, in order to serve the INELA in leadership positions. Yet it was obvious that he would not fit in with the other Quaker young men in the Bible school at Copajira; Chapman noted, "Our Bible School is entirely country lads, and Silas would be in a class by himself."[115] So, with their blessing, the members of the *mesa directiva* sent him on his way in early 1953 to a Baptist Bible school in Buenos Aires with hope that he would return to give leadership to the national church.[116]

Casas's stay in the Baptist Bible school was short-lived, and by January of 1954 he was back in La Paz. The *mesa directiva* minutes record receiving him home joyfully but also great concern that he find an adequate place of service in the church. He met with the *mesa* and expressed his desire "to do any assignment whatsoever in the work of the Lord." In some bafflement as to what that service might be, the *mesa* asked the mission to step in and meet with Casas.[117] The results of that particular meeting are

---

110. Ralph Chapman, letter to OYM, January 5, 1953, NWYM/GFU archives.

111. Ralph Chapman, letter to OYM, July 23, 1953, NWYM/GFU archives.

112. BMC Minutes, March 17, 1951; OYM Minutes, 1951, 4, NWYM/GFU archives.

113. Ralph Chapman, letter to OYM, January 5, 1953, NWYM/GFU archives.

114. BMC Minutes, August 17, 1951; January 21–22, 1955, NWYM/GFU archives.

115. Ralph Chapman, letter to OYM, February 7, 1953, NWYM/GFU archives.

116. BMC Minutes, February 4, 1953; Ralph Chapman, letter to OYM, February 7, 1953, NWYM/GFU archives.

117. *Actas de la Mesa Directive*, 1953–1956, November 17, 1953; January 14, 1954, INELA archives.

unknown, but what is obvious is the effort both the mission and the national church put forth to find a place for him.

Casas's own restlessness manifested itself before the end of the year, and the mission council minutes of December 1954 recorded the following: "A report and request for prayer was given about the situation of the young people in La Paz, led by Silas Casas in an effort to make extensive changes in the church. This group of 20 or so young people (married) feel dissatisfied with caliber of leadership in the church. It was decided our only course at present is to wait and pray, asking the Lord for special leadership and wisdom in dealing with this."[118]

In a letter home to the mission board, Jack Willcuts commented at length on the significance of this particular case:

> Silas has done a great job in lifting himself above the educational, social, cultural level of his family and people. How he did it, I don't know, he just has a higher mentality and vision than most. But genius is not always congenial and he has been eager to reorganize our La Paz church, the Sunday school, the young people's work, the children's work . . . in fact, he has a radical reorganization plan for everything. Naturally, the La Paz church council has taken an apprehensive view of some of these proposals, particularly in view of the fact that the church is growing at an unprecedented rate and is filled every Sunday. They hate to upset the present schedule and so do we. Silas considers this utter stupidity, obsolete and all but evil. He has gathered about him a group of young married fellows, formerly of the young people's society and they have written a letter to the [church] council and to me demanding a voice in some of these departments of the work or they will do something drastic. I met once with Silas and the [church] council together trying to arrive at an understanding and felt the meeting worthwhile but inconclusive. . . . Silas feels frustrated, abused and "above" the others. They resent this and criticize him for his pride.[119]

Willcuts concluded that "this is more a social problem than a spiritual problem. I am willing to believe that Silas and his group really want to serve the Lord and see things move. But you can't push a church full of old tatas and mamas too fast and he isn't able to see this."[120]

In 1955, Willcuts and Casas joined in a series of classes in the La Paz church, Jack teaching doctrine and church administration, and Casas giving adult literacy classes and teaching on leadership. Young people in the congregation formed a new society with Casas as president and were having their own Sunday evening worship services.

---

118. BMC Minutes, December 27–28, 1954, NWYM/GFU archives.
119. Jack Willcuts, letter to OYM, December 29, 1954, NWYM/GFU archives.
120. Jack Willcuts, letter to OYM, December 29, 1954, NWYM/GFU archives.

Willcuts affirmed some of Casas's progressive ideas on administration and managed to insert them into the new INELA *Estatutos*.[121]

Yet problems continued to surface. In 1956 the new young adults society tried to depose the pastor of the La Paz church and put Casas in his place. The mission council minuted its disapproval of this rebellion,[122] which did not succeed. Willcuts reported that Silas was giving a weekly Aymara gospel radio program, writing, "I think this will be a fine thing for him and he will do a good job. He is a talented boy and I have racked my brain trying to find a place where he could serve yet not harm the national church program. . . . I believe this is it. He is original and so individualistic that this sort of thing will be his meat."[123]

This is the last we hear of Silas Casas in the story of the INELA. He eventually migrated to Buenos Aires with his family. While his attempted leadership did not make much of an impact on the overall development of the church, it highlights a social problem that would continue to characterize the Friends Church in the years ahead.[124]

CHURCH AND MISSION AT THE END OF THE DECADE

The 1950s saw some remarkable advances in the development of the national church, including the organization of the INELA, the forming of the document of discipline and practices (the *Estatutos*), official government recognition, and the division into quarterly meetings. Leaders continued to emerge from local churches, the Bible school, and other discipleship programs of the mission and the INELA. Growth statistics reflect this development.

From a national church of twenty-one congregations in 1950[125] with a constituency of approximately 500 believers, statistics in 1958 (the last reliable source of the decade) show eighty-one congregations (of which fifteen were organized monthly meetings), an average Sunday school attendance of 2,713 persons, 457 converts in 1958 alone, twenty-five day schools with an enrollment of 669 students, thirty-five completed church buildings, and a total offering of $3,712.11 for the year from Bolivian believers to the national church programs.[126] The incredibly responsive nature of the new work in the Yungas sparked enthusiasm and hope in the hearts of missionary and national alike.

---

121. BMC Minutes, January 21–22; Jack Willcuts, letter to OYM, January 22, 1955, NWYM/GFU archives.

122. BMC Minutes, March 6, 1956, NWYM/GFU archives.

123. Jack Willcuts, cover letter to Board of Foreign Missions, OYM, July 30, 1956, NWYM/GFU archives.

124. As of the writing of this book, it appears that Silas Casas is alive and well, living in Buenos Aires. Other than that, not much is known of him.

125. Jack Willcuts (letter to OYM, April 17, 1958) records twenty-one churches in 1950, while Nordyke records nineteen churches in 1951 (*Animistic Aymaras*, 137–39); the difference may reflect new church plants that did not develop.

126. Jack Willcuts, letter to OYM, April 7, 1958, NWYM/GFU archives.

In the 1958 OYM yearly meeting sessions, mission board president Walter Lee informed the assembly that *Moody Monthly* magazine was planning on featuring the INELA in their fall issue, "as one of the outstandingly successful indigenous church programs on today's mission fields."[127]

Yet, with all this good growth, it was clear that troubled waters lay ahead. Student walkouts in the Bible school, persecution of believers in all areas of the field, the still uncertain position of the mission farm in the midst of radical agrarian reform, growing distance between urban youth and the rural churches, and the continuing tension between missionaries and nationals over salaries and the management of programs highlighted a strange mix of conflict and hope as the church entered the decade of the 1960s.

REFLECTIONS ON THE DECADE

The coincidence of the birth of modern Bolivia in April 1952 and the organizational birth of the INELA at the same time in the same city may be just that: coincidence, at least in terms of the date and place. On the other hand, passions in the country for the right of the people to govern themselves were running high. It's not surprising that a church made up primarily of indigenous people would be ripe to take this step forward.

In terms of the relationship of the mission and the national church during this era, a key question was that of trust. The difficulty, yet the importance, of building mutual trust between two culturally different entities was underscored by the conflicts and tensions of their changing relationship. Jack Willcuts observed that "the Indian mind is beyond our comprehension"; the confusion was mutual. Yet the mission was behind gradually turning the administration of the church over to the nationals. The process and its timing were fragile. The mission was willing to lay aside the question of whether the church was mature enough, perhaps sensing that maturity would grow in the actual exercise of authority.

The risk was certainly demonstrated in the transfer of property titles, in a national context of corruption in these kinds of legal processes. It was like handing over to the church a perpetual headache, but it was a necessary step forward. On the other hand, the mission was not ready to accede to the church's demand for ownership of the Copajira farm, and this reluctance rankled many of the national leaders for years to come. Was it mistrust of the national church's ability to manage such a large enterprise, or a realistic assessment that the time was not right? Perhaps it was a combination of the two. Under all the uncertainty of the transfer of responsibility, one senses a trust on the part of the mission that, in the words of the Apostle Paul, "He who began a good work in you will carry it on to completion until the day of Christ Jesus" (Phil 1:6).

127. OYM Minutes, 1958, 17–18, NWYM/GFU archives.

We noted that a few years after the official organization of the INELA in 1952, the national church was divided into four quarterly meetings. This followed the organizational structure of Friends around the world. The annual "yearly meetings" for business and worship, the quarterly meeting structure, the decentralization of leadership even on the *mesa directiva* with its divisions into committees according to ministry area—all of these were adoptions of Quaker practices, following the highly participatory, horizontal Quaker style of leadership.

What is noteworthy about all this Quaker practice is how closely it reflects Aymara cultural styles of leadership. We don't know if the earliest missionaries were aware of this when they first set up the organizational practices of the INELA, but Aymara community meetings are highly participatory and leadership is horizontal and shared.

The only strange note is that the early missionaries instituted voting in the meetings as the way to make decisions, similar to the way the Spanish and mestizo people decide. Yet this is not only singularly un-Quaker, it is not Aymara either. Aymara community meetings make their decisions by consensus. Why this was not incorporated into the national church's early practice is both ironic and mysterious.

We see the movement of the Spirit in this decade in the gracious affinity of many Quaker governing processes and Aymara leadership styles. It seemed that aspects of the Quaker way fit this church that was developing in the Bolivian Andes. The quarterly meeting gatherings soon became expressions of joyful celebration where everyone dressed up in their brightest colors and every congregation had its chance to present a special musical number. People entered into the times of worship, prayer, fellowship, singing, and, of course, the times of eating together. The three- to four-day celebrations effectively took the place of the old community fiestas, but without the inevitable drinking and fighting. People sensed the Spirit as they gathered and celebrated their life together.

We also see the movement of God's Spirit in the receptivity of people to the gospel message as presented by both nationals and missionaries serving in partnership. The growth of the church in the Yungas Valleys illustrates this. Begun by national evangelists, later joined by Roscoe and Tina Knight, this pioneer work flourished as twenty-five small churches rose up in a five-year period. In one of his reports home, Roscoe Knight wrote, "It is extremely gratifying to see how the Holy Spirit has been preparing the hearts of these people."[128] Concerning the lack of qualified pastors to meet the needs of so many new churches, he wrote in another letter, "The Holy Spirit has been a faithful pastor, and on this assurance of His continued workings, we are continuing to enter new communities with the Gospel though we cannot give them pastors."[129]

128. OYM Minutes, 1955, 30, NWYM/GFU archives.
129. OYM Minutes, 1956, 32.

All over the field, the Holy Spirit was growing the church, by new converts as well as better ways of administration.

6

Struggle for Stability

INELA in the Decade of the 1960s

The decade of the 1960s saw a strange balance between violent change and the ongoing struggle for survival and stability, both on the national level and in the Friends Church (INELA). Relations with the United States played a part in both scenarios. The US government had its hand firmly in the internal politics of the nation, leading to protest from both the left and the right. On the level of the church, relations between the INELA and the mission, with its intention to promote indigenization, both reflected and contrasted with the scene played out on the national level.

HISTORICAL OVERVIEW

The beginning of the 1960s saw the *Movimiento Nationalista Revolucionario* (MNR) still in control of the government, but the spirit of the revolution had been gradually shifting from the original vision of 1952. Under the presidencies of Victor Paz Estensoro and Hernán Siles Suazo, and in light of the economic hardships, the government had increasingly strengthened the military and opposed the labor movement, all while seemingly supporting the peasantry of the nation.

In the elections of 1960, Victor Paz Estensoro won his second term as president of the nation, and the policies initiated in the mid-1950s continued. He "showed himself implacably opposed to the continued power of the COB [labor union] and the mineworkers. He rearmed the army, justifying this constantly to the United States as a means of preventing communist subversion. He allowed the United States army to infiltrate the Bolivian command structure, and to push its ideas of 'internal subversion' and counterinsurgency in its training of the local army."[1] Those policies would prove the undoing of the MNR.

Paz won reelection in 1964, but months after his inauguration, the army ousted him in a violent but relatively bloodless coup and put the government under his

1. Klein, *Concise History*, locs. 3989–95.

former vice president, army General René Barrientos. This effectively put an end to the revolution and ushered in an eighteen-year era of military dictatorship. Actually, the military regimes were considered "semipopulist"[2] as they continued, for the most part, to support the rights of the peasantry won during the revolution. Yet the next eighteen years would see many violent changes of government and be characterized as an era of "radical shifts of viewpoint, abrupt changes of regime, and constant emergence of new and unexpected personalities."[3] On an official level, the government was committed to serving the interests of the United States in order to keep the needed investments flowing into the country; these included an anti-communist stance that forced opposition to the labor unions. Leftist, anti-US groups continued to flourish, resist, and march the streets.

It is not to be wondered at that the growth and development of the INELA in this context would show its own ups and downs. Outgoing mission board president Walter Lee observed at the beginning of the decade, "The unrest that has gripped the nations of the world has not overlooked the Aymara Indian and strong national aspirations have been evident among the leaders of the church."[4]

INELA AND THE MISSION DURING THE 1960S

As the new decade opened and the Bible school at Copajira again received students, an atmosphere of uncertainty recalled the student rebellion of the previous year. Unrest among the ex-*colonos* on the farm added to the tension, and the mission council decided to cancel the 1961 school year.

INELA leadership through the 1960s included the following presidents: Antonio Mamani (1959–1960), José Acero (1960–1961), Timoteo Condori (1962–1963), Carmelo Aspi (1964–1965), Antonio Mamani (1966–1967), Felipe Apaza (1967–1968), and Antonio Mamani for a third term (1969–1970).[5]

The mission staff had an unprecedented number of eleven families on the field spread out over different times during the 1960s. These included those who were continuing in service: the Knights, the Cammacks, the Roberts, the Hibbs, the Thomases, and the Clarksons. Those welcomed as new missionaries included Oscar and Ruth Brown (1960–1963), Gene and Betty Comfort (1961–1972), Quentin and Florene Nordyke (1962–1963), Paul and Martha Puckett (1963–1965), and Ron and Carolyn Stansell (1968–). Marshall and Catherine Cavit, as well as Ralph and Marie Chapman, also offered short terms of service during this decade.

This missionary presence wasn't as overwhelming as it looks. Several families moved from Bolivia to the new field in Peru (Cammacks in 1961 to start the new work, Knights in 1962, Nordykes in 1963, Clarksons in 1964, and Puckets in 1965). Illness

2. Klein, *Concise History*, loc. 4016.

3. Klein, *Concise History*, loc. 4016.

4. OYM Minutes, 1960, 34, report by Walter Lee, NWYM/GFU archives.

5. Chapman, *Los Amigos de Bolivia*, 37.

afflicted several families who either retired early or took leaves of absence stateside. In his 1960 annual report, David Thomas noted, tongue in cheek, that "aside from three major operations, one minor operation, two severe cases of infectious hepatitis and one family forced home because of failure to adjust to the altitude, the health of the missionaries has been good."[6]

Concerning the growth of the church, in a December 1960 cover letter accompanying mission council minutes, David Thomas estimated some 3,000 believers;[7] Nordyke puts the number closer to 2,000,[8] while Chapman lists 2,500 members and 3,750 adherents for the same date.[9] The most reliable mid-decade statistics for numbers of congregations are from 1966; these record a total of ninety-one regularly meeting congregations, including twenty-six monthly meetings.[10] By 1970 Nordyke puts membership figures at 7,112 people.[11] At that time the six quarterly meetings reported 114 congregations (combining twenty-nine monthly meetings and eighty-five dependent congregations).[12]

GROWTH AND DEVELOPMENT THROUGH CRISIS

During the first part of the decade, two major crises would rock the church and mission. In both cases the threat they posed would also provide opportunity for growth and development.

Crisis on the Farm

The first major crisis concerned the farm at Copajira. We saw in the decade of the 1950s the struggles in light of the Agrarian Reform of 1953. These never let up; the ex-colonos of Copajira were prodded by neighboring communities and their peasant unions to demand more land and other rights from the mission. Threats broke into outright attacks from time to time. After an especially frightening attack by the ex-colonos in September of 1960, when Paul Cammack escaped a stoning, the mission council decided that no mission family should live on the farm and recommended that the mission consider disposing of machinery and other goods little by little, but

6. OYM Minutes, 1960, 36, report by David Thomas. In another "medical report" to the mission board, Thomas wrote in 1965 that his wife Florence had needed a biopsy, and that "the doctor turned out to be a bit of a cut-up, and left her in stitches" (letter, October 1, 1965, NWYM/GFU archives).

7. David Thomas, letter to OYM, December 29, 1960, NWYM/GFU archives.

8. David Thomas, letter to OYM, December 29, 1960, NWYM/GFU archives.

9. Chapman, *Los Amigos en Bolivia*, 29.

10. David Thomas, statistical report to OYM, 1966, NWYM/GFU archives.

11. Nordyke, *Animistic Aymaras*, 133–35.

12. *Actas de la Junta Anual*, 1966–1977, January 1970, INELA archives. Since Caranavi Quarterly Meeting did not report numbers of churches, this figure may be low. The number of congregations Caranavi had in 1966 was added to the amount.

as soon as possible.[13] Council president David Thomas wrote home that "it is our recommendation that we dispose of the farm."[14]

In May 1961, Paul and Phyllis Cammack left Copajia and moved to Juli, Peru to begin OYM's new missionary work in this field, and Mark Roberts took over as director of the farm. The plan was to continue with the regular cycle of the sowing and harvesting of the crops, even though Bible school had been cancelled for the year. New missionaries Oscar and Ruth Brown and Gene and Betty Comfort, stationed in La Paz, temporarily moved out to the farm to help with the harvest. The mission secretly planned to vacate the premises as soon as the harvest had been gathered in.

This determination to leave was affirmed when one of the trusted farm workers confided some information to Mark Roberts that he had received of the peasant organizations of Copajira and the neighboring towns of Locoyo and Sulcata. Roberts immediately wrote home that "the three communities had agreed to cooperate in seeing that none of the machinery or goods was taken from the farm. Also it seems to have been agreed that everyone would conduct themselves in a normal manner for some time and then launch a surprise attack at night in which they would confiscate everything in the patio and put the missionaries off the place."[15] Roberts concluded his letter with a note of faith: "I am sure we will be here till God wants us to be elsewhere. . . . But if God says this is the time to depart from this place we do not wish to stay. . . . I feel we must have a Bible School and if not here the Lord will provide a place."[16] This reflected the consensus of the mission staff.

The families living at Copajira informed Roscoe Knight, still living in the Yungas, that the crisis was accelerating and that his presence would be helpful. Knight and Everett Clarkson joined the families on the farm to help bring in the harvest. They planned to then sell the machinery and give most of the rest of the land to the peasants, keeping only the Bible school buildings, and some small plots for crops.

During the first week of June, as the last of the harvest was gathered in, the missionary women and children still on the farm moved back to La Paz, as discretely as they could. Tina Knight reported home on the exciting events that followed, beginning at 4:00 a.m. on June 3.

> At last they were ready. They tried to start the John Deere and it wouldn't start. All held their breath! What was wrong? The starting motor was out of fuel. When that was remedied the machines began to roar. They made more noise than usual. At least it seemed that way as the roar sounded across the morning air and echoed back from the cliff below. Roscoe opened the gate and waved them out, banging and locking the gate after them. They were off!! Oscar led the way on the combine. Then came Gene with the John Deere pulling the

13. BMC Minutes, September 1960, NWYM/GFU archives.

14. David Thomas, letter to OYM, October 10, 1960, NWYM/GFU archives.

15. Mark Roberts, letter to OYM, May, 24, 1961, NWYM/GFU archives.

16. Mark Roberts, letter to OYM, May 24, 1961, NWYM/GFU archives.

disc. After that was the farm truck and then the blue pick-up. Off across the field east of the river to the main road!! They felt no rocks nor heard any shots! They had made it!! Oscar looked back to see a parade of machinery glistening in the early morning moonlight. The sight made little chills run up and down the spine. As they pulled out into the main road they could look back on a quiet Copajira, still sleeping in the early dawn, unconscious of the fact that "their" machinery was on its way to La Paz.[17]

More than four hours later, after parking the machinery in the tabernacle lot in El Alto (upper La Paz), the missionaries arrived at the mission house in La Paz. The next day, a Sunday, the men decided to go back to assess the situation and see about their personal belongings. Knight continues her report:

> On Sunday the fellows decided to go back. Cipriano had said that all was calm, so they went back fearlessly. As they approached the gate, it swung open disclosing a drunken mob brandishing rifles. They forced the fellows out of the car, roughly pushed and pulled, pinched and knocked them about. They frisked each man thoroughly, taking their keys but leaving their billfolds. Through the compound and out back to the warehouse patio they were marched. "What did you mean sneaking off at night?" "Where's the machinery?" "Why didn't you ask us if you could take it?" "Don't you have confidence in us?" "Don't you trust us?" All these questions tumbled out as they brandished rifles in their faces. Those without guns were carrying clubs and whips.
>
> For about an hour they talked with the alcohol being passed around in the background. Frequently someone would shout, "Kill them!! Kill those foreign devils!" Roscoe, as spokesman, found his mouth dry and it was almost too dry to speak the difficult Aymara language. No one was allowed to leave or move until some agreement was reached. . . . Finally, they agreed to let us take out our personal belongings and half the potatoes, barley and sheep."[18]

The missionaries, glad to be alive, left the farm and returned to La Paz. Bargaining with the ex-*colonos* of Copajira continued, with them agreeing that the missionaries could return for the rest of their personal belongings, if the mission would turn over the property titles. Legal papers of agreement were written up, but the processes would continue for several years.

Roscoe Knight summed up the whole fourteen-year Copajira experience:

> We are still convinced that Copajira was purchased under God's direction, that it has well served its purpose as a home for the Bible School and has been the means of training many men for God's work as well as a base for the establishment of many churches in that area. But due to the rapidly changing conditions in Bolivia, these days are past, as well as many of our systems and

---

17. Tina Knight, letter to OYM, June 6, 1961, NWYM/GFU archives.
18. Tina Knight, letter to OYM, June 6, 1961, NWYM/GFU archives.

ways of doing missionary work. Our missionary approach needs [to] be highly flexible to be able to change with conditions in the country. Only in this way can we continue our service for Him here. May God give us wisdom![19]

Crisis of Relationship

The second crisis had to do with the relationship between the INELA and the mission. Always in the background was the uneasy relationship between Bolivia and the United States in general, acerbated by economic hardship. Although the yearly meeting representatives in 1960 apparently accepted the cessation of salaries for pastors and teachers, confusion about the relationship with the mission and a sense of entitlement to benefits continued. Shortly after the loss of the Copajira farm, the Peninsula and Cordillera Quarterly Meetings sent a letter to the *mesa directiva*, accusing the mission of not handling the situation well. The letter states, "It appears that the Mission does not have any love for us anymore. The fact that the Mission gave so many millions of Bolivianos to the wicked people of Copajira and nothing to us certainly illustrates this thought. The pastors have labored for some 15 years without compensation of any kind. If you the Mesa Directiva do not call an extraordinary Meeting of the pastors and the representatives, it will probably result in a split in the Church."[20]

During 1962, the *mesa directiva* and its president, Timoteo Condori, continued to make demands of the mission council for benefits that included more used clothing, Bibles and literature, a pick-up truck, evangelistic equipment such as a projector and loud speaker, medicine, accordions, and the list goes on. Missionaries continued to present the indigenous principle, but with seemingly little understanding on the part of the nationals.[21] In December the *mesa directiva* wrote directly to the mission board of OYM with an explanation of their spiritual needs, a list of desired gifts for use in ministry, culminating in the request that the OYM buy them a pick-up that would help them "meet the needs and solve the problems of the church." They suggest that funds from the truck come from all the equipment that the missionaries rescued from Copajira and later sold.[22] The mission board graciously refused the request.

Things came to a head in the April 1963 annual representatives meeting, when, in a surprise move, Timoteo Condori resigned as president, and advised all the other *mesa directiva* members to do likewise. The Minute of Suspension concludes with the demand that the mission again take charge of the work of the church, stating that they as nationals will offer their help. The 130 representatives (all but four) approved the minute, thus making it official.[23]

19. Roscoe Knight, "Analytical Report of the Copajira Situation," 1961, NWYM/GFU archives.

20. Peninsula and Cordillera Quarterly Meetings, letter to the INELA, June 21, 1961, INELA archives.

21. BMC Minutes, March 13, September 5, October 3, October 29, 1962, NWYM/GFU archives.

22. *Actas de la Mesa Directiva*, 1957–1962, December 4, 1962, INELA archives.

23. *Acta* of Suspension, April 13, 1964, INELA archives.

Mission council minutes state that 2,500 people attended the worship services in the tabernacle, but that the representatives meetings were conflictive. After describing the resignations and the acceptance of the representatives, the council affirmed that "the church in general will not suffer immediately. The Quarterly Meeting organizations are functioning as always. The [Mission] Council does not intend to dispense any extra funds, but to resolve this situation in the Lord's leading for the best for the Nat'l Church. We appreciate the fact that there is no animosity toward the missionaries, and feel that by working with the Nat'ls in a good spirit, this situation will be righted in God's own way."[24]

And the life of the church did go on, without the participation of an active executive council (*mesa directiva*), and key national leaders continued talking with the missionaries, exploring ways to move forward. INELA leaders decided to draw people together in October to discuss a reorganization of the national church and redefine relationships with the mission. The mission invited Ralph and Marie Chapman to return for a two-year term, mainly to help with the development of a new Bible school, but also for their contribution to solving the impasse between mission and church. The mission also invited OYM superintendent Dean Gregory and mission board president Clare Willcuts for the October meeting.

Missionaries and visitors from OYM were present for part of the deliberations. The mission had prepared a proposal, an eight-point plan for ways they could continue to cooperate with the INELA, while promoting indigenous development. The eight points included (1) continued assistance with medical help for pastors, (2) help in obtaining hymnals, records, record players (Gospel Recordings), and accordions; (3) literature; (4) assistance in area Bible schools and classes; (5) assistance in evangelistic tent campaigns; (6) visitation in churches; (7) assistance in pastors' conferences and classes; and (8) help in quarterly meeting conferences. This was basically a continuation of benefits already in place, with some items conspicuous by their absence (e.g., salaries).

Prior to the gathering, the Cordillera Quarterly Meeting once again wrote a letter of protest and demand to the church leaders, and this became part of the agenda for the meetings, held in La Paz on October 16–17, 1963.

Some seventy-five nationals[25] met alone on the 16th and crafted the following letter, addressed specifically to the representatives of OYM, Gregory and Willcuts:

> Beloved Spiritual Brethren,
>
> We address you by way of this official letter, informing you that just this afternoon we unanimously approved the letter submitted to us by the Cordillera Quarterly Meeting, adding a few points. Here are [our requests]:
>
> 1. Transfer of legally cleared property titles, with freedom from taxation;

24. BMC Minutes, April 16, 1963, NWYM/GFU archives.
25. OYM Minutes, 1964, 24, NWYM/GFU archives.

2. Medicines, including first aid kits for the pastors;

3. Clothes for pastors and teachers;

4. Help with church construction, as usual;

5. A pick-up truck to help us oversee the national work;

6. A Bible School, completely under the supervision of the Mission;

7. Complete evangelistic equipment, including a tent, a generator and a projector;

8. That the Mission pay the salaries of the Secretary of Evangelization and the Director of the primary schools.

9. That the Mission pay the salaries of pastors and teachers.

10. That the Mission obtain for us the benefits given to pastors and teachers through Caritas [the Catholic charity].

If you accept these listed points, we will work arm in arm with the missionaries in the work of the national church.

In the case that you do not accept them, we will consider ourselves independent of the Oregon Yearly Meeting of Friends.

We conclude, again greeting you attentively as we await your response.[26]

Gregory and Willcuts met with the mission council and responded immediately with a letter dated October 17. In it they explain their reasons for not accepting the list of demands, stating that some of these "are contrary to our concept of the growth of the National Church." They conclude the letter on a note of sorrow, with an attempt to leave the door open for future discussion:

> No other recourse remains for us but to accept your decision to function as a church independent of Oregon Yearly Meeting. We love all the brethren in the love of Christ. Our hearts are broken to learn of your desire to sever relations between the Mission and the National Church when there are so many ways in which the Mission can provide spiritual help for you. In case you reconsider a cooperative plan between the Mission and the National Church on the basis of our proposals presented in our last meeting, we will be receptive to negotiation.[27]

By the end of 1963, three missionary families—the Eugene Comfort, Oscar Brown, and Mark Roberts families—went home to Oregon, leaving Ralph and Marie Chapman and new missionaries Paul and Martha Puckett in Bolivia to take care of legal matters and consult with the national brethren as needed. The work of the mission was, in effect, suspended. The nationals called a meeting of representatives for January 1964, and hopes on all sides were aimed at the reorganization of the INELA and a possible reconciliation with the mission.

26. Letter from INELA leaders to OYM leaders, October 16, 1963, translated by Nancy Thomas, NWYM/GFU archives. The letter was signed "for the Friends Church" by all the nationals present in the meeting. Unfortunately, the page with signatures has been lost.

27. Clare Willcuts and Dean Gregory, letter to INELA, October 17, 1963, NWYM/GFU archives.

Reactions from the national church ranged from complete surprise on the part of almost everyone, to anger at either the mission or national leaders, sorrow, backtracking on the part of some leaders, and, eventually, a plan to move forward with the reorganization. Four leaders—Carmelo Aspi, Timoteo Condori, Eduardo Mamani, and Vicente Yujra—wrote to Chapman in early November, distancing themselves from the list of demands, and asking the missionaries to take over the January meeting and choose the new leaders.[28] This, of course, Chapman would not agree to; he continued to encourage the leaders to carry out their own planning.

Carmelo Aspi wrote another letter that same month to Clare Willcuts, informing that

> the fact that some of us stated that the INELA should be completely national has been a demoralizing action for the majority of the churches. Furthermore, many have come to me stating that the missionaries should continue to work as always as long as the Lord permits them to be here. I am also one hundred percent in favor of this, for I have not said that the missionaries should leave, nor have I said that they should be here forever. However, I did say that while the missionaries are present, the Mesa Directiva cannot function. When the time should arrive for various reasons that the missionaries should all leave, then we can reorganize the Mesa Directiva.[29]

Aspi was diplomatically keeping the door open for the return of the mission, yet stating his position that inappropriate missionary presence could hinder the development of the national church. He was carefully treading a difficult path, seeming submissive and conciliatory, yet trying to maintain a position of dignity for the national church.

Carmelo Aspi and family (NWYM)

As the time for the January meetings approached, Chapman wrote home about the positive approaches INELA leaders were taking, focusing both on a reorganization of the INELA's administration and relations with the mission. He mentions Carmelo Aspi in particular:

28. Carmelo Aspi, letter to Clare Willcuts, possibly translated by Ralph Chapman, November 8, 1963, NWYM/GFU archives.

29. Carmelo Aspi, letter to Clare Willcuts, translated by Ralph Chapman, November 19, 1963, NWYM/GFU archives.

Carmelo Aspi seems to be the one who the other leaders are accepting as one capable to head up the plans for the meeting. . . . I believe he is very seriously considering accepting the presidency of the Mesa Directiva if the brethren ask him to take the job. We have been praying that God will bring His man to the foreground, and as we can see it, I know of no one more capable to take over, and one who is more spiritually qualified. . . . I appreciate the positiveness that Carmelo has evidenced in his whole attitude of late.[30]

Under Aspi's leadership, INELA leaders and representatives met in La Paz, January 17–19, 1964. Chapman and Puckett made themselves available, but they did not attend the meetings as people considered, and approved, the administrative "suggestions" Aspi presented. The group also accepted the mission's eight-point plan of cooperation and, in essence, invited Oregon Yearly Meeting to renew its relationship with the INELA. The Chapmans and Pucketts were invited to attend the Sunday services on the last day and Ralph Chapman installed the newly elected *mesa directiva*, with Carmelo Aspi as president.

The administrative details[31] worked out in the meeting included "financial maintenance of the work of the INELA . . . based on a system of tithing and not looking to other outside means. It handled salaries and church construction among similar items. These were all apparently joyously adopted, a miracle that would never have come to pass under mission supervision."[32] In the future, the activities of the missionaries would first be approved by the *mesa*, and any new requests from the *mesa* would be presented directly to the mission board of OYM.

At the end of the meetings, the new *mesa directiva* wrote a letter to Dean Gregory, superintendent of Oregon Yearly Meeting, summarizing the decisions, asking pardon, and opening the way for a new relationship. The letter ends on a note of contrition:

Upon closing the sessions of the annual sessions of the National Church, the representatives group invited the missionaries to unite with them during a service of worship, and the Chapman and Puckett families were present. Of these, some personally asked pardon, and the rest raised their hands, begging pardon of the missionaries present, with the same sign asked pardon of the missionaries who are now in the United States, and of all the leaders of Oregon Yearly Meeting for the wrongs committed with which we have offended.

We are grateful to remain anew at your complete direction in the noble cause of the Gospel of Christ.

30. Ralph Chapman, letter to OYM, January 2, 1964, NWYM/GFU archives.

31. A thirteen-point plan proposed by Aspi and accepted by the representatives contained the following categories: (1) organization of the *mesa directiva*, (2) relation between mission and INELA, (3) aids offered by the mission (the eight-point plan), (4) funding for transportation and construction, (5) classification of pastors, (6) marriages and dedication of children, (7) schools, (8) old and new teachers, (9) fathers of families, (10) construction of churches and schools, (11) membership requirements, (12) tithing, and (13) youth and women's societies (January 19, 1964), NWYM/GFU archives.

32. Ralph Chapman, letter to OYM, January 20, 1964, NWYM/GFU archives.

The Mesa Directiva of the National Friends Church.[33]

The phrase "remain anew at your complete direction" followed the dictates of formal style and in no sense promised the future submission of the church to the mission.

Chapman evaluated the importance of the steps taken as he observed that the nationals "were able to gather at this meeting . . . and with oneness of heart accept the responsibilities before them to the end that the Friends National Church has either been born or 'born-again' depending whether you want to stick to technicalities of when the work was really done in their hearts and minds."[34] In other words, he saw in this reorganization the psychological birth of the INELA as an independent entity.

Ralph and Marie Chapman family (NWYM)

33. INELA *mesa directiva*, letter to OYM, January 19, 1964, translated by Ralph Chapman, NWYM/ GFU archives.

34. Ralph Chapman, letter to OYM, January 20, 1964, NWYM/GFU archives.

The mission board accepted the INELA's invitation to renew ministry alongside the national church but during the rest of 1964 maintained a low profile, with only the Chapman and Puckett families on the field. The *mesa directiva* was careful to emphasize its leadership, inviting the mission to help out with some of the material needs of hosting the annual Easter conference (e.g., supplying loud speakers and kerosene for cooking), but asking the missionaries not to visit local churches or to participate in quarterly meeting conferences. Chapman, although concerned about the need to encourage the churches, determined to respect the wishes of the *mesa*, and of its president, Carmelo Aspi. Relationships moved forward carefully, continuing in negotiations about mission benefits, with both sides trying hard not to give offense.[35]

In July 1964, INELA president Carmelo Aspi wrote a letter directly to Clare Willcuts, president of the OYM mission board. He expressed gratitude that the missionaries present in La Paz "have been generous in cooperating with us in every way." He then invited the OYM to maintain two missionary families in La Paz, sending David Thomas to take Chapman's place when he went home as planned, and sending the Comforts back for the Caranavi area. He concluded by asking that the board reinstate the used clothing benefit for pastors and teachers, offering a plan to make it feasible. The letter was friendly and very specific.[36]

In Chapman's accompanying letter, he summed up advances to that point:

> It is with joy that I can report that INELA has not proven to be just an upstart born on the spur of the moment to fade away when the way got rough. Without question the altiplano churches are 100% behind the Mesa Directiva and any sense of transition from the Mission to the National Church has been accomplished. There appears to be a slower transition in the Yungas-Caranavi area. . . .
>
> Carmelo Aspi's sincerity in seeking counsel in areas where he needs help to more effectively attend to the duties of his office characterizes the feeling of harmony that now exists between the missionaries and the church leaders. The major area of problem yet for the Mesa Directiva is for transportation and thus they immediately turn to us. There hasn't been any abuse of requests made to the missionaries for use of the vehicles altho we have found our schedules quite full. . . . Of the 8-point program accepted by the INELA, the only area as yet with thumbs down is that of missionary visitation in the churches as an activity entirely on their own.[37]

Missionaries began returning to Bolivia in 1965, but some moved on to Peru within a few years. The missionary profile for the rest of the 1960s was kept low, usually with two families, at the most three, on the field at once. Relationships between

35. Ralph Chapman, letters to OYM, February 26, April 12, May 7, May 23, July 17, August 21, 1964, NWYM/GFU archives.

36. Carmelo Aspi, letter to OYM, translated by David Thomas, July 13, 1964, NWYM/GFU archives.

37. Ralph Chapman, letter to OYM, July 17, 1964, NWYM/GFU archives.

mission and church continued to develop, with church leadership increasing, and missionaries more and more taking a back seat.

GROWTH AND DEVELOPMENT THROUGH THE PROGRAMS OF THE CHURCH

In spite of the crises of the early part of the 1960s and in the context of the revolutionary politics of the decade, the ordinary life of the church went forward. Leaders planned and carried out those plans; evangelists spread the word; teachers discipled, both formally and informally; children attended Friends schools; and the INELA and the mission continued to negotiate their relationship for the overall good of the work.

Administrative Development

The high point of the church's administrative development was the 1964 reorganization with its refining of the respective roles of church and mission. But other, less dramatic, changes also took place.

In 1960 and 1961, the *mesa directiva* decided to reorganize and divide the functions of the annual gathering, referred to simply as the *junta anual*, or "yearly meeting." Previously representatives and pastors from all the churches had gathered in the week preceding Easter to carry out the business of the national church; this was followed by several days of worship, open to all the constituency of the church. Beginning in 1961, representative and pastors gathered in a different month for the administrative business of the INELA, and they reserved the Easter week celebrations for worship and classes, open to all.

The meetings for celebration continued to be a highlight of the church year, and these included the quarterly meeting sessions, held four times a year in each district, combining church business and celebratory worship. These were highly participatory in nature and corresponded to the Aymara style of celebration with lots of music, color, and participation. They reflected Quaker roots in the focus on equality, with everyone's voice encouraged (although Quaker silence was notably absent). In late 1967, the Caranavi area became the sixth quarterly meeting.

The decade finally saw solid beginnings for national youth and women's organizations as part of the INELA.[38] These came about partly through cooperation with Oregon Yearly Meeting. OYM sent youth leaders Chuck Mylander (1964) and Ron Stansell (1965) to visit the youth in the different quarterly meetings, sharing about youth organization and activities in the Northwest and encouraging these kinds of activities in the INELA. Both the Bolivian youth and INELA leaders responded positively. In 1968, the first national youth conference of Friends took place in La Paz, and the INELA's official youth organization was born: UJELAB (*Unión de Jóvenes*

---

38. An attempt to begin a youth organization in 1953, with Benjamín Balboa as president, proved to be short-lived.

Evangélicos de Los Amigos de Bolivia, Union of Evangelical Friends Youth of Bolivia). The first president, Severino Bartalama, was a young man from the new Caranavi Quarterly Meeting.[39] Mission council reported that attendance at the second annual youth conference in 1969 had grown to 150.[40]

First UJELAB leaders, 1968 (NWYM)

Another visitor in 1965, May Nordyke, represented the Women's Missionary Union of OYM and spoke in the different quarterly meeting gatherings about the importance of women organizing for the work of the church. As in the case with the youth, various attempts had been made previously to organize, but with Nordyke's visit, the time seemed right. As a result of her visit, women's groups were officially organized on the quarterly meeting level in all five districts.[41] In that same year, 1965, the national UFINELA (*Unión Femenil de INELA*, Women's Union of INELA) was organized under the leadership of Florentina de Sillerico, Gregoria de Tito, and Francisca de Tintaya.[42]

39. David Tintaya, "Presentación," n.d., INELA archives.

40. BMC Minutes, November 19, 1969, NWYM/GFU archives.

41. Ralph Chapman, letter to OYM, March 12, 1965, NWYM/GFU archives.

42. Aspi, *Los Amigos en marcha*, 13.

UFINELA leaders, 1960s (NWYM)

The mission and the church continued to balance their relationship and lean into the changes. The greatest challenge, perhaps, for the mission was submitting its activities to the guidance of the *mesa directiva*. Churches and individuals continued to make requests of the missionaries, and the mission staff in turn was learning to redirect requests to the *mesa*. A mission council minute at the end of 1969 noted that mission board president Gerald Dillon "reported that the Board at home is happy with the 'silent partner' approach on the part of the missionaries. It was noted that the growth of the church has continued and accelerated under this policy. We all feel that there are still ways in which the missionary can counsel in the background."[43]

Evangelism and Growth of the Church

The church indeed did grow during the 1960s, going from eighty-five regular meetings (monthly meetings and dependent congregations) in 1960 to 106 in 1968 (thirty-one monthly meetings and seventy-five dependent congregations),[44] and possibly more

43. BMC Minutes, December 3, 1969, NWYM/GFU archives.
44. OYM Minutes, 1968, 8, NWYM/GFU archives.

than 114 regular meetings in 1970.[45] Most of this growth came from the evangelistic efforts of national men and women, and as local congregations reached out to neighboring villages, gathering converts into dependent congregations.

The most helpful statistics come from a 1966 report David Thomas sent to Jack Willcuts.[46] It gives names of each congregation according to quarterly meeting, with the name of the pastor or worker; numbers of believers are not included. The quarterly meetings with the numbers of their monthly meetings and dependent congregations are listed as follows:

Quarterly Meeting	Monthly Meetings	Dependents	Total Congregations
Yungas	10	23	33
La Paz	6	12	18
Cordillera	5	12	17
Frontera	2	11	13
Peninsula	3	7	10
TOTALS	26	65	91

Thomas noted that the list was not complete, that several new congregations had not yet been reported. It's interesting to note that one of the youngest quarterly meetings, Yungas, was the largest and fastest growing.

The mission made the decision to decentralize its staff, and for a brief time in 1961, David and Florence Thomas lived in Amacari, on Lake Titicaca. The Gene and Betty Comfort family lived in Amacari for a year, from 1961 to 1962, until the rising of the level of the lake forced them back to La Paz. In 1963 the Comforts were relocated in the newest area to the north of the Yungas, centering around the town of Caranavi. The Mark Roberts family took the place of the Knights in the Yungas when Roscoe and Tina moved to Peru. The mission council stated its goal as having missionaries living in the different areas to give oversight and promote indigenization. They were not to specialize in evangelization or education, but rather to promote the work of nationals in these areas.[47]

The new work in the Caranavi area was an outreach of the Yungas Quarterly Meeting. Early in the decade, Pascual Quispe, another Copajira Bible school graduate, expressed his concern for this region, and the Yungas brethren, also with a vision for

45. *Actas de la Junta Anual,* 1966–1977, January 1970, possibly a low number, as not all districts reported, INELA archives.

46. David Thomas, statistical report, 1966, NWYM/GFU archives.

47. BMC Minutes, July 4, 1963, NWYM/GFU archives.

planting churches there, declared him their national missionary and began actively supporting him.[48] The Yungas brethren also sent and supported Mario Surco as a national missionary; he worked there from 1960 to 1962. Both Quispe and Surco moved with their families into the Caranavi area.[49]

By the time the Comforts came to live in Caranavi in 1963, there were already five congregations, with Quispe pastoring the main church in the town of Caranavi. Comforts returned home to the United States with the other missionaries at the time of the 1963 crisis between the mission and the INELA, and when they returned to the field in 1965, they were assigned to the same area, and served in Caranavi until the end of 1967. They worked with Quispe and other national leaders, visiting the young congregations, evangelizing in new areas, and hosting Bible classes for men and women in the town. The *mesa directiva* had specifically invited the Comforts to live in Caranavi and help with that work, but they had also made it clear that it was to be for only one term and that the work would then be entirely under the national church.[50] This type of mutual relationship was in line with the thinking of both the mission and the church, and the cooperative effort bore fruit as new churches sprung up in the area.

At the end of 1967 when the Caranavi Quarterly Meeting was organized, the area had one monthly meeting (in the town of Caranavi), nine dependent congregations and other outposts. Quarterly meeting gatherings throughout the field continued to have an evangelistic thrust, with new converts routinely reported.

Mission council minutes at the end of 1969 record that, in terms of evangelistic activity, "we all agree that it seems best for the nationals to be in the forefront, with the missionaries cooperating and counseling in the background."[51]

Leadership Training and General Education

The formation of the Patmos Bible Institute in 1966 was one of the highlights of the decade. Ever since the loss of the Copajira farm with its Bible school, both the national church and the mission were giving priority to the formation of a new school for pastoral and leadership training.

Carmelo Aspi gave leadership to exploring how this might happen, and in 1964 and 1965 the church and the mission cooperated in a series of short-term Bible classes held in each quarterly meeting. These were organized and directed by the *mesa directiva* and taught by national/missionary teams. But it was obvious that something more stable was required. Ralph Chapman especially worked with Aspi to come up with a long-term plan. Knowing the importance of consensus among the whole

---

48. BMC Minutes. August 1962, NWYM/GFU archives.

49. Mario Surco, interview with Félix Huarina, 2013, Caranavi.

50. Betty Comfort, letter to OYM, February 7, 1967, NWYM/GFU archives.

51. BMC Minutes, December 3, 1969, NWYM/GFU archives.

constituency of the INELA, in 1965 the *mesa directiva* sent the proposed plan to each quarterly meeting, asking them to take time in their June sessions to evaluate and send back concrete suggestions. They considered location, name, length of time each year, curriculum, entrance requirements, graduation requirements, and other details. The quarterly meetings responded in writing. The *mesa* took their suggestions seriously and changed the plan accordingly in what turned out to be a healthy and highly participatory process that paved the way for approval in the annual representatives meeting.

After some negotiation and many changes to the plan, the Patmos Bible Institute, under the directorship of Carmelo Aspi, opened its door to some forty-two students in March 1966. Following the same basic curriculum as the school at Copajira, the institute would run for two three-month terms, with a month of vacation between, and students would be housed on campus. Located in the old mission house behind the La Paz Friends Church on Max Paredes Street, students gathered for the first of the three years of school required for graduation. Missionaries and nationals both taught under Aspi's direction. While the mission provided the accommodations, all other expenses were to be met from student fees.

David Thomas wrote home with a report during Patmos' second term in 1966, showing the variety of activities, as well the encouragement the institute was giving the church: "Florence is engaged in music classes and playing for the Bible Institute Choir among other things. Marshal Cavit is Choir director. Last Sunday the Choir presented their first full concert at the Max Paredes Church here in La Paz. They did very well. In the afternoon they sang for another Mission, and did equally well. The Bible Institute, under National direction has been forging ahead with good success. The psychological uplift to the brethren has been a joy to see."[52]

David and Florence Thomas and Marshall Cavit (again on loan to the Friends to help get Patmos started), joined national teachers Carmelo Aspi and Mateo Mamani for that first year.[53] Later years would see continuing cooperation between national and missionary teachers, under national direction. In 1969 the *mesa directiva* gave the Patmos directorship to Francisco Mamani, an up and coming young leader and son of Antonio Mamani, former INELA president. Aspi would continue as a teacher and a strong influence for the institute. The students' evangelistic trips on weekends and between semesters provided an appreciated boost to the INELA's outreach program, as well as good ministry training for the students themselves.

The other major educational program of the INELA was its system of Friends day schools, and these continued throughout the decade under the direction of the national church. Although the number of schools did not grow dramatically, the school program continued strong, ranging in number from twenty in 1960[54] to a high

52. David Thomas, letter to OYM, August 1966, NWYM/GFU archives.

53. Patmos report to INELA, August 1966, INELA archives.

54. OYM Minutes, 1960, 37, NWYM/GFU archives.

of twenty-six schools in 1969.[55] The director of the school program also served as a member of the *mesa directiva*. An outstanding leader of the decade in the school program was Melitón Mollesaca. Mollesaca had received his training in Warisata, site of Bolivia's most innovative pedagogical institute, and he brought his expertise to bear on the development of the Friends schools. This included the standardization of Bible training for all the schools, as part of the Friends contribution. The schools continued open to both boys and girls and were available to all the children of an area, not just Friends.

Mollesaca enjoyed a good reputation as an educational leader, with one exception. He happened to win $160 in the 1966 national Christmas lottery, and his photo appeared in the newspaper, giving his address at the Friends Church on Max Paredes Street. This stirred up a scandal, and the *mesa directiva* disciplined him. He had been serving on the *mesa* and in Patmos, as well as in the day school system, and he was forced to resign all positions. For a time, before he was reinstated as a leader, the INELA lost his valuable input. (The bylaws of the Patmos Bible Institute required that students be expelled for such acts as playing the lottery or going to the movies. The same standards held for all church leaders.)[56]

A significant development in the day school program was the formation of the George Fox Friends School in the village of Batallas. This boarding school was the first school that offered the fifth and sixth grades and was developed by the INELA under the leadership of Mollesaca. When the school opened its doors in April 1965, on land leased by the mission to the church, forty-three boys and girls between the ages of thirteen and seventeen showed up. Mollesaca reflected on the importance of the school and of the INELA's education program in general:

> We believe the religious education is the most important aspect of the work of the National Church because it is upon this that the future of the Friends Church in Bolivia depends as well as the stability of our nation and all humanity. . . . This school (George Fox) is recognized by the Bolivian government and with their approval it exists to offer religious education with specific training given in accord with the doctrines of our church as well as the regular normal courses. The purpose of the school as defined on the opening day is to educate boys and girls as Christian ladies and gentlemen; to give them balanced instruction in religion, morality, intellectual development; and to benefit the physical and social development of character, and whatever capacities they may have. This school is important to the future of the Friends Church which greatly needs men who are spiritual and whose lives reflect Christ within.[57]

---

55. David Thomas, letter to OYM, January 30, 1969, NWYM/GFU archives.
56. Betty Comfort, letter to OYM, January 5, 1967, NWYM/GFU archives.
57. OYM Minutes, 1965, 24–25, NWYM/GFU archives.

In the development of the school in Batallas, we see the INELA attempting to meet the social and educational needs of its children. The end of the decade saw the George Fox School flourishing; Melitón Mollesaca, back in the good graces of the leadership, was again serving as secretary of education on the *mesa directiva*.

GROWTH AND DEVELOPMENT THROUGH OTHER CHALLENGES

Among the other challenges the INELA faced during the 1960s were persecution of its believers, legal hassles over properties, and the balance of power in the internal governing of the church.

Persecution

During the decade of the 1960s, much of the persecution of Protestant Christians came from growing radical communist/socialist influences. The Catholic Church itself experienced internal changes following Vatican II and the development of a radical leftist branch.[58]

Whatever its sources, persecution of Friends believers and congregations continued to a certain degree into the 1960s. In 1966 community members attacked a Friends church and school in the village of Kollucachi, with motives that seemed more connected with animistic antagonism than a political viewpoint. David Thomas sent this description home:

> Toward the end of the week, a heavy hail passed through this region, damaging many of the fields of grain and potatoes, which were nearing maturity. The community gathered together to fix the guilt for this visitation of judgement on them. They quickly blamed the new group of Evangelicals [Friends] who had recently erected a new chapel on the ex-hacienda. It was rumored that one of the women had had a new baby which died without being baptized. In anger, and under the influence of alcohol they directed themselves to the area where the new church and school were located. There they tore off the new sheet-iron roof, burned the roof framing lumber, and broke down the adobe walls to the foundation. They then directed themselves to the school nearby, broke in the door and windows, destroyed the school records and materials, and tore down the flag pole, tearing up and burning the Bolivian flag in the process. Several of the believers were severely beaten. . . . A group from the CID (Criminal Investigation Department) were sent to the area to capture the leaders of the violence, but were unable to complete their orders because of the mob that assembled and threatened them with stoning.[59]

58. Frances Payne's memoir, *They Make Us Dangerous*, details the Catholic experience during the 1960s and 1970s. Payne, herself a nun in Bolivia during those years, became part of the radical Catholic movement.

59. David Thomas, letter to OYM, March 3, 1966, NWYM/GFU archives.

The church building had been constructed the previous year, using local resources. The case woke the sympathy of the church at large, and in the 1966 Easter conference, churches from all areas of the field gave special offerings for rebuilding.[60] Mission council minutes informed that those responsible in the community were finally held accountable by local authorities, and that, plus the offering from the churches, allowed believers in the community to reconstruct. The church was rebuilt and publicly dedicated the following year.[61] It's important to note the active advocacy on the part of the national church working through local government channels to see justice done in this case. Among the results attendance increased to about one hundred people coming to worship; these included "many" of their former persecutors.[62]

Another incident in 1967 gives insight into new ways the believers were handling persecution. Canuta Choque was the Friends worker in the church in Patarani, an ex-hacienda community in the Frontera Quarterly Meeting. In March of that year Choque wrote a letter to local officers of the workers syndicate, telling them about his conversion along with others in the community who now formed the Friends Church. He refers to the constitutional right of freedom of religion and then informs them of threats and actual attacks of armed violence against the believers, naming specific people from the community and asking for intervention. He ends the letter by saying that if they, as representatives of rural working people, don't do something, he will have to go to the law.[63]

The very next day, the syndicate officials responded by writing another letter to the secretary general of the Patarani branch of the syndicate, telling him to restrain those who were attacking the Protestant Christians, and repeating the threat to go to the law if that didn't happen. Again, the appeal was to the constitutionality of freedom of religion. The letter states that the Friends believers have exactly the same rights as Catholic believers.[64]

Later that same month of March, Friends believers in the neighboring community of Sullcata wrote to the *mesa directiva* and to all five quarterly meetings, informing them of the problems in Patarani, stating that nonbelievers are making it difficult for Friends to attend worship, to construct their church building and even to preach. The letter asks for support in facing the attacks. It was to be read in the Easter conference and a special offering taken to help in the legal work of the case.[65]

Apparently the abuses continued, and in May three men from the community broke into the home of Canuta Choque and beat him, causing severe injuries. In

60. BMC Minutes, March 1966, NWYM/GFU archives.

61. BMC Minutes, August 1967, NWYM/GFU archives.

62. OYM Minutes, 1967, 32, NWYM/GFU archives.

63. Canuta Choque Quispe, letter to the rural workers federation, March 2, 1967, INELA archives.

64. Gutiérrez Flores et al., letter to the secretary general of the workers union in Patarani, March 3, 1967, INELA archives.

65. Timoteo Condori et al., letter to INELA, May 22, 1967, INELA archives.

response, Felipe Apaza, the president of the INELA, wrote directly to the head of the Ministry of Justice of the Bolivian government. Apaza gave details of the attack, named the attackers, but he didn't ask for punishment, only protection of the believers, according to their rights:

> Señor Minister, we are asking with this denouncement for your collaboration, through the corresponding officials, in bringing a halt to these acts, that these people stop their mistreatment and persecution of others merely because they believe in a healthy religion, having logically and honorably accepted and put their faith in Christ. We don't ask for sanctions or punishment. We ask that, through your Ministry, that we have justice, support and the guarantee of our rights so that we can continue to live, worshiping and honoring our Almighty God.
>
> Señor Minister, we evangelicals in Bolivia are in a stage of overcoming, spiritually and morally, and we trust that we now live under a government of justice and order. As citizens we have confidence in our government officials.[66]

Apaza wrote at least three other letters in 1967 to officials in the communities of Tonkopugio, Calteca, and Huacallani, informing of the persecution of believers and asking for intervention on the basis of the constitutionally guaranteed right of freedom of religion.[67] Down through the years, the incidents of persecution seemed to wax and wane, and it isn't clear how widespread it was in the 1960s. What is interesting is the response of the national church. Quite in line with the reforms that began in 1952 and continued to be carried out in the 1960s, indigenous people were learning to claim their rights. The response on the part of the INELA was now not one of victimization, but a proactive claiming of their rights and a trust—or at least a hope—that the government would support those rights.

Problems with Properties and Titles

The mission continued through the 1960s to try and clear up church property titles and turn these over to the INELA. Because of irregularities and a certain amount of corruption in the legal system, this was not an easy task.

We read in the previous chapter how in 1958 the mission had turned over to the INELA the titles for the new tabernacle property on El Alto (upper La Paz). In 1966, it was discovered that these titles were not completely clear after all, that a party other than the one that had sold the property to the mission was also claiming ownership.[68] The case was headed for the courts when the INELA in its 1967 representatives meeting decided to avoid a court case which experience told them they would probably

66. Felipa Apaza, letter to the Bolivian Minister of Justice, May 23, 1967, INELA archives.

67. Felipe Apaza, letters to Bolivian government officials, May 8, June 14, July 3, 1967, INELA archives.

68. For background details on the legalities of the case, read David Thomas, letter to OYM, December 15, 1966, NWYM/GFU archives.

lose. They approved relocating the tabernacle and negotiating a settlement with the party claiming ownership.[69] This decision to "relocate" meant giving up the tabernacle built with the funds Marshal Cavit had raised, the place where the church had celebrated the yearly Easter conference, and other large events, between 1957 and 1967.

The INELA requested help from the mission board, and in light of the circumstances the board decided against their current no-help policy on constructions and agreed to help purchase new property with funds from the sale of the farm equipment;[70] the need for a large gathering place was obvious to all. The party claiming ownership gave $2,000 to the INELA as part of the settlement, and the *mesa* inverted this into construction costs.[71]

The *mesa directiva* went on a search to find another piece of land on El Alto. Before the end of 1967, they had purchased property for $2,000 and begun a campaign to raise funds locally to build a new tabernacle.[72] They dismantled the old tabernacle and transferred all usable materials to the new site. In August 1968, the cornerstone was laid and construction went forward, all on national church initiative.[73] Each church was to give one day's labor, plus fifty adobes;[74] believers in all areas sacrificed to see the project completed. The INELA held its 1969 Easter conference in the new tabernacle, even though it was not yet completely roofed. Although OYM took an additional offering to help with the cost of roofing, the project was carried out mainly through INELA initiative and sacrifice.

Patmos graduates in front of tabernacle, 1972 (H. Thomas)

69. BMC Minutes, February 7, 1967, NWYM/GFU archives.

70. OYM Yearly Meeting Minutes, 1967, 32. These funds from the mission amounted to $2,085, NWYM/GFU archives.

71. BMC Minutes, May 31, July 4, 1967, NWYM/GFU archives.

72. Ralph Chapman, letter to OYM, July 29, 1968, NWYM/GFU archives.

73. BMC Minutes, August 27, 1968, NWYM/GFU archives.

74. BMC Minutes, August 1967, NWYM/GFU archives.

At the 1970 representatives meeting, the mission was finally able to hand over to the national church the titles to the property on Max Paredes Street in La Paz, home of the La Paz church, the *mesa directiva* office, and the former mission residency (Hadley Hall), now home to the Patmos Bible Institute.[75]

Internal Power Struggles

While the beginning of the 1960s saw struggle between the mission and the national church, at the end of the decade the power struggles were more internal to the INELA as a developing organization where lines of authority were not always clear. The final decision-making body continued to be the gathered representatives in their annual business meeting. But a certain degree of confusion existed between the executive council (the *mesa directiva*), and the quarterly meetings executive councils, local churches, and other organizations like the Patmos Bible Institute.

In 1965, the La Paz Quarterly Meeting, in protest against the strong leadership style of INELA president Carmelo Aspi, decided to withdraw from the national church and requested to come under the care of the mission as an independent body, a request that the mission council naturally refused.[76] The *mesa directiva* met with quarterly meeting leaders along with leaders of the La Paz church and temporarily worked out their misunderstandings, but the struggles would surface again.[77] At the same time a pastor in the Cordillera Quarterly Meeting, Pablo Mendoza, troubled about authority issues over management of the properties at Batallas, left the INELA and established his own small independent church.[78] (Mendoza would later return and minister in the INELA for many years, until his death.)

In 1967 a case of disputed authority and discipline arose that illustrates the levels of conflict between strong leaders. In this case Patmos Bible Institute director Carmelo Aspi (no longer INELA president) expelled a number of students for some infraction of the rules. The La Paz church youth group got up in arms on behalf of the expelled students, claiming that the action was unjust, with the result that the local church council met with Aspi to question and challenge him. Aspi told the council to send their request that the students be pardoned and reinstated directly to the *mesa directiva* of the national church.[79]

---

75. *Actas de la Junta Anual*, 1966–1981, January 1970, INELA archives.

76. BMC Minutes, March 27, 1965, NWYM/GFU archives.

77. In a letter home in 1968, Gene Comfort spoke of "discipline problems" between the *mesa directiva* and the La Paz church. He noted, "Especially the Max Paredes church feels the Mesa Directiva doesn't have the right to control them as the MD doesn't hold title to the property. It is in the name of the mission until the INELA gets its own liberation of taxes." He adds that "it isn't the entire Max Paredes membership, only a very few men that keep a hornet's nest stirred up" (Eugene Comfort, letter to OYM, May 14, 1968, NWYM/GFU archives).

78. BMC Minutes, May 14, 1965, NWYM/GFU archives.

79. Unión Juventud Cristiana, letter to La Paz Friends Church, July 2, 1967, INELA archives.

INELA president Felipe Apaza sent a memo to Aspi telling him to receive back the expelled students. He claimed they had admitted their errors and wished forgiveness. He underscored the importance of his "orders" in favor of "the sinners" being followed or he would have to take the case before the whole representatives meeting to let the gathered body "judge me according to my crimes."[80]

Aspi was forced to reinstate the students, but a group of students flunked out of school at the end of the year, causing more protests from the church at large. Continued protests caused the matter to come before a special meeting of the representatives in November 1967. Aspi defended failing the students and cast the blame back on local pastors, noting the inadequate educational preparation of many students. The representatives approved his report.[81]

In 1968 the *mesa* met several times with Aspi and were able to find ways to begin to resolve the authority issues. They named a committee of quarterly meeting presidents, *mesa* members and others charged with developing a set of bylaws for Patmos that would later be approved by the representatives.[82] This was partly to ensure that no single leader would be able to usurp control of the institute. The *mesa*, for its part, struggled with the temptation to micromanage.[83]

In 1969 the national church was caught up in another power struggle, this time involving the *mesa directiva* and the La Paz Friends Church. Eugenio Nogales was president of the church council, and also served, under the local church, as director of the La Paz day school. His mismanagement of the day school funds came to the attention of the INELA *mesa directiva*, and unraveling the conflict consumed most of the national church's year.[84]

Following failure to resolve the matter in called meetings of the church, INELA leaders instigated a flurry of letters, meetings, and denunciations before the Ministry of Justice and Immigration, the Ministry of Education, and the Ministry of Religion.[85]

In one especially conflictive meeting involving representatives of the whole national church, the La Paz church unanimously voted to relieve Nogales of his position as president of the church council. A new church council was then named. In a subsequent church meeting, Nogales and his followers tried to take over the church again.[86] As a result of Nogales's attempted takeover, the *mesa directiva* assumed control of the church through the end of the year. They locked the church doors on Sunday, September 7, to prevent a meeting of La Paz Quarterly Meeting officers that Nogales had called. Church members celebrated Sunday worship in a tent erected in the back

---

80. Felipe Apaza, memo to Carmelo Aspi, June 30, 1967, INELA archives.

81. *Actas de la Junta Anual*, 1966–1977, November 1967, INELA archives.

82. David Thomas, letter to OYM, July 29, 1968, NWYM/GFU archives.

83. *Actas de la Junta Anual*, 1966–1977, January 1969, INELA archives.

84. INELA *mesa directiva*, memo to Eugenio Nogales, May 3, 1969, INELA archives.

85. These are all on file in the INELA archives in La Paz.

86. Callejas Q., letter to INELA, September 9, 1969, INELA archives.

patio, and many reported feeling the presence of God. Eugene Comfort, in the name of the mission council, encouraged the church constituency to recognize and honor "those whom [God] has placed as leaders and pastors of his people."[87]

In December the *mesa*, in a meeting with the quarterly meeting presidents and the missionaries, expelled Nogales from the INELA for "rebellious and divisionist activities."[88]

The Nogales rebellion garnered support from members of several other Friends churches, and early in the 1970s they formed a new Friends denomination in El Alto, which they called the Sardis Evangelical Friends Church of Prophecy. The Prophecy group claimed to be seeking a greater level of holiness than the rest of the Friends. They accused INELA Friends of being "carnal Christians," and condemned such practices as using the newer version of the INELA hymnal, applauding in worship, and even tithing, on the basis that salvation is free. The sect caused confusion among other Friends churches for several decades, but never flourished as a movement and gradually died out. Nogales himself claimed to have inverted some of the funds he had taken into resolving the legal matters of the Friends school. He turned the property of his Prophecy church over to the INELA in 2016, through the mediation of the Tabernacle Friends Church, and has attempted to make things right and clear his name, some forty-seven years after the original conflict.[89]

THE STORY OF CARMELO ASPI

The decade of the 1960s saw the continued development of the leadership of the INELA, in the midst of turmoil. Of the different believers who came to the forefront during these years, Carmelo Aspi stands out. As we have seen in this chapter, Aspi was the first indigenous teacher in the Bible school on the Copajira farm, the leader of the reorganization of the INELA (its "psychological rebirth"), a key player in the restoration of relationships between the church and the mission, and the organizer and first director of the Patmos Bible Institute.

Carmelo Aspi was born in Parina Arriba, a village on the *altiplano*, sometime in the 1930s. His parents, Manuel Aspi and his wife, Remedios, had just two children, Carmelo and his sister, Gregoria. Manuel had served in the Chaco War of the 1930s. Remedios apparently came from another community because she was a Christian, but there was no church in Parina Arriba. There was, however, a small grade school in or near the village, and Carmelo received a basic primary education.[90]

---

87. Eugene Comfort, letter to OYM, September 10, 1969, NWYM/GFU archives.

88. *Mesa directiva*, Resolution #2/69, December 8, 1969, INELA archives.

89. Eugenio Nogales, interview with Humberto Gutiérrez, June 19, 2016, La Paz.

90. Information about Aspi's childhood and youth come from interviews with his adult children: Dionisio Aspi, interview with Harold Thomas and Nancy Thomas, February 22, 2016, La Paz; Paulina Aspi de Tórrez, interview with Harold Thomas and Nancy Thomas, February 23, 2016, La Paz.

As a child Carmelo had occasional dreams about people praying in a church. While he did not understand those dreams, they impacted him and created longings for something he could not quite grasp. In spite of those dreams and longings, "he was a real pagan in his village," someone who loved to play pranks on people, claims his daughter Paulina. He also loved soccer and apparently was quite good at the sport.

As a young man Carmelo spent his obligatory year of military service, then returned to Parina Arriba where he married a local girl, Maria Cosme. At that time a friend who had become an Adventist Christian shared the gospel story with Carmelo and gave him a Bible. Through his own reading of the Scriptures, Carmelo became convinced of the truth of the Christian way, but he wasn't convinced that Saturday worship was right, so he held back from joining his friend's church.

In the beginning of the decade of the 1950s, Carmelo decided to go to the Friends Bible school at Copajira. It's uncertain how he came into contact with the Friends; perhaps that was part of his mother's background. At any rate, this was the group he chose to become affiliated with.

While a student at the Bible school, his faith was confirmed and built up. And it was there that Maria also became a Christian. On one of his school breaks, he returned to his community determined to begin a Friends Church, which he did. At that time, he took the radical steps of throwing out all his old animistic paraphernalia (including coca leaves for divination), all his soccer equipment, and his military certificates. He had become convinced that as a Christian he needed to make a break with absolutely everything connected with the world.

Carmelo and Maria's five children would all be born in Parina Arriba.

In December of 1952 Carmelo wrote a letter to the *mesa directiva* representing the new church at Parina Arriba, informing that the group now had fourteen believers and that they had gathered enough adobe bricks to construct a chapel. They asked the *mesa* to help supply them with a roof, a door and some windows. They informed the *mesa* that they had been giving offerings and tithes to the "Evangelical Friends Mission" and would continue to do so. The signers included Carmelo Aspi (identified as the Sunday teacher), Manuel Aspi (Carmelo's father), and Isidro Cosme (probably from his wife's family). There is no pastoral signature.[91] This shows conversions happening in the extended family and a serious intent to form a church.

Another letter written in December 1952 shows Carmelo in relationship with the leadership of the national church, representing his community in a common concern. Eighteen leaders, representing eighteen different churches, including Carmelo Aspi of Parina Arriba and Mariano Baptista as president of the newly organized INELA, wrote to the government Ministry of Indigenous Affairs to protest the fact that the provincial officials had been trying to force them to join the new syndicates (unions and cooperatives) that required Sunday meetings and a certain amount of obligatory drinking. The letter stated that as Christians, they dedicated Sunday to worship in

91. Carmelo Aspi et al., letter to INELA, December 17, 1952, INELA archives.

their churches and that they had all given up alcohol. It also stated that as believers they wished to have nothing to do with politics.[92]

In 1954 Carmelo was a third-year student in the Bible school and also pastoring the church in Pucarani, perhaps as his practical ministry assignment.[93] He apparently graduated in 1955, and in 1956 he was elected secretary of the INELA and a member of the *mesa directiva*.[94] During the next several years he also served as secretary of evangelism, secretary of literature, president of the Frontera Quarterly Meeting, and first national teacher in the Copajira Bible School. He continued to live with his family in Parina Arriba, but spent a lot of time traveling.

He was pastoring the Parina Arriba church in 1960, and the end-of-the-year report he sent to the *mesa directiva* of the INELA reveals much about him and about the life of a local Friends church in this era. The church actively participated in the meetings of the Frontera Quarterly Meeting, as well as the INELA yearly meeting sessions. Members tithed of their products, organized a youth group, had an active Sunday school for all ages, and even organized a choir. Carmelo's musical gifts would come to benefit the whole national church in the future. Carmelo emphasized Bible study and memorization for all ages in the church; his teaching included how to sing the INELA hymns. The church visited another Friends church in the area in order to encourage them. They began construction of a new meetinghouse on property donated by Carmelo, and they reroofed the house of one of the church members who had fallen on hard times.[95]

The disciplinary matters the report dealt with reveal the impact of the holiness doctrine and the strict standards for behavior that Carmelo Aspi adopted wholeheartedly. One matter dealt with the worker who had been named by the *mesa directiva* to assist Carmelo. This man had "committed the sin" of getting into a fight with a nonbeliever over property (not an uncommon situation). The church leaders took away his right to minister as an official worker. The report noted that he eventually repented publicly, asking pardon of the whole church.[96]

The report also noted that four of the believers had participated in one of the community's fiestas, one selling drinks, and three in food preparation. Carmelo wrote that "these believers strayed from the way of God and caused great spiritual pain to the church because to participate in worldly activities is sin."[97] He informed that the four repented and asked forgiveness of the church, which was granted.

---

92. Mariano Baptista et al., letter to Ministry of Indigenous Affairs, La Paz, December 18, 1952, INELA archives.

93. BMC Minutes, September 24, 1954, NWYM/GFU archives.

94. *Actas de la Mesa Directiva*, 1953–1956, March 30, 1956, NWYM/GFU archives.

95. Carmelo Aspi, report to INELA, December 1960, INELA archives.

96. Carmelo Aspi, report to INELA, December 1960, INELA archives.

97. Carmelo Aspi, report to INELA, December 1960, INELA archives.

In this present chapter on the decade of the 1960s, we have seen Carmelo Aspi rise to the forefront of leadership in the INELA, especially in the events following the exodus of OYM missionaries in 1963. Carmelo was the protagonist in the drama involved in the reorganization of the INELA and the slow reintegration of the national church and the mission. As part of the reorganization, he was elected INELA president in 1964 and served in that role until mid-1965.

His strong gifts in administration manifested in the new organization of the INELA and in the set-up of the Patmos Bible Institute. On into the 1970s and 1980s, Carmelo would give leadership to many INELA programs, including another term as president from 1974 to 1975. His main contributions were in the areas of administration, theological education, literature development, and music.

Carmelo Aspi leading Friends choir (H. Thomas)

But none of this was without conflict, both internally among leaders, and with the mission. We get hints of misunderstandings with the mission in various remarks in the correspondence. In 1958, Marshal Cavit, who developed a close relationship with Carmelo and his family, noted a positive change in that Carmelo was now "with a new testimony of full salvation in his life,"[98] yet a year later the mission council asked the churches of the north to pray for the sanctification of Carmelo Aspi.[99] This would have been at the time of the Copajira Bible school student rebellion, during the year when Carmelo was serving as the first national teacher. In that same year the mission council

98. BMC Minutes, December 4, 1958, NWYM/GFU archives.
99. BMC Minutes, August 2, 1959, NWYM/GFU archives.

reported that *mesa directiva* members José Acero and Carmelo Aspi had resigned over money issues, with demands for higher level of support from the mission. In a mission council report from 1962, it was noted that "Carmelo has asked pardon for talking so hard against the missionaries and had made restitution for stolen things." It also reported that he "recently returned to the Lord."[100]

Embedded in these assessments of Carmelo Asp's spiritual condition are the possibilities of cultural misunderstanding. Parina Arriba was a free indigenous community, while the Bible school at Copajira was on a former hacienda, a community of *colonos*, and all this in a context of indigenous protest of centuries of past injustices. That Carmelo, or any of the Friends brethren, might view the foreign missionaries with suspicion seems only natural. And a judgment of unsanctified, rebellious behavior by foreigners coming from a holiness background might actually have been misinterpretation of something far more complex. That national believers and missionaries actually managed to reunite after 1964 seems a minor miracle.

Carmelo's story provides a fascinating case study of national/mission relationships. Carmelo did form close ties with several missionaries. We've seen a cautious but respectful friendship between Carmelo and Ralph Chapman following the traumatic split between the mission and the church. Chapman's natural reticence and patient respect elicited a response in kind from Carmelo, and this certainly paved the way for a broader reconciliation between church and mission, even while the mission continued to insist on an indigenous policy. He also developed a close relationship with Marshal Cavit. While Cavit respected the indigenous goals of the mission, by nature he conformed more to an image of the open-handed generous patron. Being on loan to the mission, he didn't always feel constrained to follow its strict policies, and his offerings occasionally irritated the other missionaries, while they delighted the brethren who benefited from them. The Aspi family graciously received from Cavit both material benefit and a friendship that was genuine.

The conflict that characterized Carmelo Aspi's ministry was also internal, with other leaders of the INELA. During Carmelo's brief term as president of the newly organized INELA (1964–1965), leaders in different parts of the yearly meeting were beginning to complain about his dictatorial style of leadership.[101] In mid-1965, half way through his term of service, Carmelo resigned, letting Antonio Mamani take his place.[102] We've seen the conflict between Carmelo as director of the new Patmos Bible Institute and the *mesa directiva*, a conflict that dominated the church's attention for several years at the end of the 1960s.

In the 1970s Carmelo served the church as director of the extension Bible school for several years. He also inverted time into a major revision of the popular INELA

---

100. BMC Minutes, March 14, 1962, NWYM/GFU archives.

101. Ralph Chapman, letter to OYM, April 12, 1964; BMC Minutes, March 23, 1965, NWYM/GFU archives.

102. Ralph Chapman, letter to OYM, June 3, 1965, NWYM/GFU archives.

hymnal that was used and venerated in all the churches. Carmelo brought to the project his own expertise in music and writing, revising the words of some hymns that went back to the INELA's beginnings in the 1920s and 1930s. This included hymns translated from Spanish to Aymara by Juan Ayllón, the church's founder. While the revisions were possibly aesthetically superior, the resulting uproar in the national church lasted for years.[103] Conservative rural brethren, including many adults who were functionally illiterate and sang the old songs from memory, protested, going as far to state that, next to the Bible, the original version of the hymnal was sacred.

In 1974 Carmelo was again elected INELA president, but several times during his two years of service, he resigned under the criticism coming from the hymnal controversy. His resignations were not accepted, and he continued as president until another opportunity presented itself.[104]

Marshal Cavit, no longer associated with the OYM mission, was opening a new mission work in Ecuador and he invited Carmelo to come for several years to teach in his new Bible school. The invitation came in the middle of Carmelo's three-year term as INELA president, so he presented it to both the *mesa directiva* and the mission, asking for prayers of discernment.[105] The *mesa directiva* gave its blessing, so Carmelo finished the 1975 year as president, and the gathered brethren saw him, his wife, and one of his sons off, in March 1976, on the bus ride to Ecuador,[106] where he would serve for the next three years.

Back home in 1979, Carmelo was again made director of the Patmos Bible Institute. He also served on the *mesa directiva* in the 1980s as secretary of literature and secretary of social action. He was especially appreciated for his contributions as a choir director and for his literature work in writing pamphlets and booklets. But at the end of the 1980s another adventure would take him out of commission as a leader in the INELA.

Sometime in the 1980s, Carmelo's son Dionisio had been invited by Korean Presbyterian missionaries to teach music in their seminary, located in the barrio of Llojeta near to where the extended Aspi family now lived. At the time Dionisio was also teaching in the Patmos Bible Institute and the San Pablo Seminary. The Koreans offered Dionisio a full scholarship to attend their seminary, an offer he could not refuse. Soon he accepted the pastorate of a small Presbyterian church and switched his denominational allegiance.[107] Carmelo followed the footprints of his son and was soon totally involved as a worker under the Korean Presbyterian Mission, a work he carried on through most of the 1990s.

103. *Actas de la Mesa Directiva*, 1974–1977, January 6, 1975, INELA archives.

104. *Actas de la Mesa Directiva*, 1974–1977, January 6, 1975, INELA archives.

105. BMC Minutes, December 8, 1975, NWYM/GFU archives.

106. BMC Minutes, March 21, 1975, NWYM/GFU archives.

107. Dionisio Aspi, interview with Harold Thomas and Nancy Thomas, February 22, 2016, La Paz.

In 1998, Carmelo Aspi was formally reincorporated into the INELA, along with several other Friends who had "strayed."[108] By then he was older and very tired. He remained a faithful Christian and a part of the Llojeta Friends Church and continued to contribute through his writing until his death in 2013.

CHURCH AND MISSION AT THE END OF THE DECADE

The decade of the 1960s was turbulent, within the national church, in relationship to the Friends Mission, and in the surrounding context. Yet an overview view shows growth and development in the midst of all the conflict. A reorganized church structure facilitated a stronger indigenous leadership, while maintaining a relationship with the Friends Mission. The mission footprint was considerably reduced, although issues of dependency would continue to plague the church in the years ahead.

The new Patmos Bible Institute, organized and directed by the INELA, put leadership training clearly into national hands, with the mission now playing more of a background role.

The dawn of the new decade saw the church organized into six quarterly meeting districts and with approximately 114 congregations.

REFLECTIONS ON THE DECADE

Throughout this chapter on the decade of the 1960s, we have observed the parallel situation of instability and chaos on the national level and in the development of the INELA. The question of how much the national situation influenced the events that took place in the church is open to debate. Some have noted that the church's constituency at this time was fairly indifferent to national politics; indeed, the *Estatutos* discouraged involvement on the part of believers in politics, even on the local level. And yet it seems unlikely that the frequent changes, the confusion, and even the violent leftist reaction to the influence of the United States would not in some way affect the reactions of the national believers to the presence of foreign missionaries. That the differences were resolved and the church and mission able to move forward together is certainly noteworthy.

The mission's response to the crisis on the Copajira farm is also difficult to evaluate. Many national believers at the time deeply resented the actions of the mission in giving the farm back to local *campesinos*, rather than legally turning it over to the church. Some believers today, looking back, carry that resentment. When Ramiro Carrillo wrote the history of the INELA for its seventy-fifth anniversary, he referred to what he judged as the mission's "stubbornness and arrogance" in not giving the farm to the church.[109] The mission actually never considered the option of turning over the property to the church, judging that the church was not yet mature enough to manage

---

108. Remigio Condori, annual INELA president's report, January 1998, INELA archives.

109. Carrillo, *Los Amigos en la historia*, 38.

such a huge project. National leadership was still too fragile, and such responsibility could have destroyed the young church; such was the "sense of the meeting." The mission never communicated this to the church, and perhaps that would not have even been possible. Hindsight seems to say that the mission was correct in this assessment. Yet it led to much misunderstanding.

On the other hand, one has to ask if the mission or the OYM, back in the 1940s and 1950s, had any sense of the gravity of owning an ex-hacienda in such revolutionary times. Again, in hindsight, it seems a blessing that the whole situation did not turn out worse than it did.

In considering the crisis between the mission and the church that came to a head in 1963 and 1964, one thing that stands out is the role of two of the protagonists, Carmelo Aspi and Ralph Chapman. Many believers today have the mistaken perception that Aspi was the one who "kicked out the missionaries." Actually, no one "kicked out" anyone; the missionaries left voluntarily in response to the demands of the church. And Carmelo Aspi played the role of smoothing the waters. He was somehow able to rally the majority of the believers into considering a reorganization of the church that would allow a better relationship with the mission, while enabling the church to take on its own primary leadership role.

And Ralph Chapman was perhaps the one member of the missionary team who was diplomatic, low-key, patient, and respectful enough to work with Aspi to enable all of this to happen. When one asks the question, "How was the Holy Spirit moving in this crisis?" one answer is certainly in the raising up of two such men "for such a time as this."

We can also see the Spirit's movement in the very fact that the reorganization of the INELA and the reconciliation of the church and mission did, indeed, take place. From that time the work of the INELA went forward on a new level of independent leadership (though not without problems), and the church grew in both administrative ability and in numbers of congregations.

7

New Initiatives of Church and Mission

INELA in the Decade of the 1970s

The death of Bolivian president René Barrientos in a helicopter crash in 1969 led to a series of military governments than ran the course of the 1970s, not to end until 1982 with the beginning of the country's experiments with democracy. These military governments shifted from leftist to the extreme right in terms of political stance, with the dictatorship of Hugo Bánzer Suárez dominating the decade. Concurrent with this political reality, the winds of Pentecostal/charismatic revival added their own dynamic, affecting not only the Protestant and Catholic expressions of Christianity, but influencing the country as a whole. In the midst of these changes, the INELA continued its struggle to grow into its own identity, and the Friends Mission continued its efforts to help that happen, in a series of setbacks and advances.

HISTORICAL OVERVIEW

A few months after the death of Barrientos, his chief of staff, leftist-leaning General Alfredo Ovando, took control of the government, and in short order nationalized the Gulf Oil Company, legalized the labor union (COB), invited labor leader Juan Lechín to return to power, and recalled the troops from the mines. His government lasted barely a year when during one violent weekend in October 1970, different branches of the military staged "a coup followed by a counter-coup, followed by a counter counter-coup. In one weekend Bolivia had six presidents."[1] General Juan José Torres emerged as the new leader. Klein observes, "Thus began one of the most extraordinary governments in Bolivian history. From October 1970 to August 1971, when he was overthrown, Torres would prove to be the most radical and left-leaning general ever to have governed Bolivia."[2]

---

1. Payne, *They Make Us Dangerous*, loc. 2041.
2. Klein, *Concise History*, loc. 4076.

Torres mobilized the workers and leftist politicians, accepted Russian financial aid for the miners' union (COMIBOL), annulled several agreements with the United States, and expelled the Peace Corps. Anti-US sentiment was running high.

Torres's government also lasted just under a year, when in August of 1971 right-wing military forces under General Hugo Bánzer Suárez led the bloodiest revolution since 1952 and ushered in a dictatorship that lasted an unprecedented seven years. This dictatorship set the tone for most of the decade of the 1970s.

On the social scene, some of the forces unleashed in 1952 were bearing fruit. Literacy rates rose from 31 percent of the population in 1950 to 67 percent in 1976, with about 80 percent of children between the ages of ten and fourteen in school. Spanish was acknowledged as the majority language in 1976 (with many speakers being bilingual), a direct result of universal education. By that same year, 50 percent of the population was living in cities, up from 34 percent in 1950.[3] This was accompanied by a massive construction boom, as high-rise buildings began changing the landscape of La Paz and Santa Cruz.

The agrarian reform was also bearing fruit in an economic boom, especially between 1970 and 1974. This was accompanied by the rising price of tin and other minerals on the world market. Another aspect of this boom had to do with the emergence of the Santa Cruz lowlands as a force in agriculture. For the first time, Bolivia began exporting agricultural products, mainly sugar and cotton. To these exports, the country soon added natural gas, also from the lowlands. An improved network of roads linked one end of the country to the other, aiding this prosperity. One particular aspect of this was the road in the Chapare coca-growing region that opened up the illegal drug market.

This boom gave a certain popularity to Bánzer's government at first, in spite of harsh repressive measures. But as the boom faded, Bánzer found he could not control the newly mobilized Bolivian society. Overspending and corruption added to the complexities, and after 1974 social unrest increased. Bánzer sent troops to again control the mines, but labor strikes, hunger strikes, and protest marches dominated local news. Bánzer's attempts to control his opponents, including deliberate use of assassination and torture, only made the situation worse.

Following Bánzer in 1979, a series of short-lived presidencies added to the political chaos.

Changes were also happening on the spiritual level. The Catholic Church was experiencing the changes instituted by Vatican II in 1964, including the movement known as liberation theology. In 1971 Peruvian priest Gustavo Gutiérrez published *La teología de la liberación*, further mobilizing the more radical side of the Latin American Church to work for social justice. This was certainly felt in Bolivia, as parts of the Catholic Church aligned with the workers, students, and the poor in their marches and strikes.

3. Klein, *Concise History*, loc. 4233.

The Latin American Protestant church as a whole was also experiencing an awakening to its social responsibilities. This was especially evident in the worldwide Lausanne Conference in 1974, where Latin American theologians Samuel Escobar and René Padilla were influential in promoting the concept of holistic mission. Many evangelical thinkers were bringing together the evangelistic and social activities of the church in a broader movement that reached out to the poor and disenfranchised.

The Pentecostal/charismatic movements also entered the scene, affecting both the Catholic and Protestant branches of Christianity. Of special note was the ministry of Julio César Ruibal, a young member of an elite Bolivian family who had experienced a radical conversion to Christianity and an introduction to the healing ministry of Katherine Kuhlman in Los Angeles, California, where he was a medical student. After receiving a gift of healing, Ruibal returned to his native Bolivia, and in 1972 his evangelistic/healing campaigns filled the national stadium in La Paz and made front-page headline news for weeks on end. His influence continued for years afterward in the rise of Pentecostal denominations and mega-congregations.

It's hard to juxtapose the religious revival with the political chaos that was taking place. This was the context in which the Bolivian Friends Church continued to grow and develop during the 1970s.

INELA AND THE MISSION DURING THE 1970S

The 1970s would prove to be a decade of growth for the INELA on several different levels. Numerical growth was certainly one measure with the six different districts reporting over one hundred churches in 1970,[4] and ending the decade with a reported 165 congregations[5] from eight districts, along with new areas under evangelization. In addition to numerical growth, the church experienced administrative growth, as well as development in its strategies of ministry and leadership training. The different *mesa directiva* presidents during these years included Antonio Mamani (1970), Pascual Quispe (1971–1973), Carmelo Aspi (1974–1975), and Francisco Tintaya (1976–1981).

Changing relations between the INELA and the mission would continue to play a part in the story. Missionary presence was generally smaller at any given time than in previous decades, as different families came and went. These included David and Florence Thomas (–1971), Gene and Betty Comfort (–1972), Ron and Carolyn Stansell (1968–), MaryBel Cammack (1970–), Harold and Nancy Thomas (1972–), Quentin and Florene Nordyke (1972–1974), Mark and Wilma Roberts (1974–1978),

---

4. Five districts reported twenty-eight monthly meetings and sixty-one dependent congregations in the January 1970 representatives meeting, with the Caranavi-Alto Beni District not reporting. A low estimate for Caranavi-Alto Beni of one monthly meeting and nine dependent meetings (1967) brings the estimated number of churches up to 101. *Actas de la Junta Anual*, 1966–1981, January 1970, INELA archives.

5. *Actas de la Junta Anual*, 1966–1981, January 1980, INELA archives.

Gil and Louise George (1976–1978), Roscoe and Tina Knight (1978–), and James and Gail Roberts (1978–).[6] During much of the decade, two families in La Paz handled the workload, which helped in keeping a low profile. Constantly changing personnel also helped prevent dependency on any personality.

A pattern of the decade was the tension between the INELA and the mission. The mission continued firm in its policy of promoting an indigenous and independent national church, and the INELA continued to push against this. The mission juggled the dangers of dependence (financial and otherwise) against the actual material and educational needs of the church. The ideal of following two steps behind the church in order to let national leadership develop sometimes clashed with the need to step out, hopefully under the guidance of God, in support of policies or programs that differed from the expressed wishes of the INELA. The potential for misunderstanding was ever present.

Another pattern that comes out in the stories of the 1970s is the tension within the INELA between the desire for a high level of participation, according to Aymara cultural norms, and the need to control. The difficulties of determining authority played their part in the drama, as new churches and new church structures arose.

SETTING THE STAGE

Political revolution set the stage for the decade. In January 1971, with the country under the leftist military control of Torres, David Thomas wrote this report, printed in the OYM's Aymaragram:

> Only ten days into the new year, and another attempted coup. We arrived from three days in the country with a Quarterly Meeting. On retiring, we noticed a small plane flying over the city. A little after midnight in the light of the moon, the old Mustang fighters of the Bolivian Air Force in support of the present government opened up on the Military Headquarters across the river from our home. Later, as clouds and fog moved up the valley, flares were dropped and more strafing was carried out.
>
> We turned on the radio, and heard calls for the Workers' Unions, University students, and citizens to take to the streets in defense of the present Revolutionary Government....
>
> Against this background of unrest, and with the pressures from right and left, the Bolivian Friends Church is scheduled to meet next week for their Yearly Meeting of Representatives. They will be naming new officers, reviewing present policies and seeking to chart a course according to God's will for representing the kingdom, not of this world, but of peace and righteousness.[7]

---

6. The David Thomas and Gene Comfort families retired from the field during the decade, while the Mark Roberts and Roscoe Knight families served in Santa Cruz, and several families moved from the Bolivian to the Peruvian field for service (Mark Roberts and Gil George families).

7. David Thomas, *Aymaragram*, February 1971, NWYM/GFU archives.

The annual representatives meeting did go forward as usual, along with most of the other church activities in the following months.

In August of that same year, another coup against Torres successfully, and violently, ousted the leftist leader, replacing him with another general, right-wing Hugo Bánzer. The contrast between the two military politicians couldn't have been more drastic. Betty Comfort wrote home a harrowing report of how the coup affected the missionaries. The mission home, situated on the side of a hill, directly faced one of the city's military compounds, putting them in the line of fire. During the heaviest part of the fighting in La Paz, the Comfort and Stansell families huddled on the kitchen floor. Machine gun–toting soldiers broke in, robbed them of a few items, the largest of which was one of the mission vehicles, and left with an apology for frightening them.[8]

Another story of the events in August 1971 comes from emerging INELA leader, Arturo Tito, who had become involved in the coup on the side of Bánzer, although political involvement was frowned on by the church. He was critically wounded in the fighting and ended up in the city morgue, presumed dead. When family members went to the morgue to identify him, he was discovered to be alive and reclaimed. The whole adventure caused Tito to do some deep repenting, and he subsequently gave good service to the INELA during much of the remainder of the decade.[9]

DEVELOPMENT OF LEADERSHIP TRAINING AND PASTORAL FORMATION

With the church continuing to grow numerically, both the INELA and the mission concurred on giving priority to leadership training. But the strategies for carrying out this priority would differ between the two groups throughout the decade.

The Extension Bible School

The mission continued to support the indigenous principle that would lead to an independent national church, but, no longer content to follow the lead of the INELA in every area (an attitude that had been necessary following the 1964 reorganization), it began to take the initiative in some innovative programs. The first of these was the development of a theological education by extension program for pastoral formation. The TEE movement rose out of another Latin American context in the late 1960s: the Presbyterian Church in Guatemala. During the 1970s the movement began to spread around the world, partly fueled by seminaries such as Fuller Theological Seminary's School of World Mission in California.

Quentin Nordyke studied in Fuller and brought the concept of TEE back with him to Peru. In 1969 Nordyke, representing Peruvian Friends, and Ron Stansell from

---

8. Betty Comfort, letters to OYM, August 23, August 24, 1971, NWYM/GFU archives.

9. Arturo Tito told this story to Hal Thomas, and later his wife, Gregoria, and son, Javier, corroborated, n.d.

the Bolivian field, attended a six-day TEE workshop in Cochabamba, Bolivia, and moved forward with plans to implement the program in both fields. The program actually began functioning among Peruvian Friends in 1969; the Bolivian program would follow within a year.

The mission saw the advantage of TEE in that it would allow the church's natural adult leaders to remain in their communities and places of service during their time of preparation, in contrast to a residency Bible school education that required people to temporarily move to the city and thus attracted mainly young unmarried people (future, rather than actual, leaders). Students would study at home specially prepared semi-programmed textbooks, then gather as a group once every one or two weeks with a teacher who would travel out to the community. This thinking was accompanied by the mission's perception that neither the Copajira Bible institute nor the Patmos residency program had been able to adequately meet the need of pastoral supply for the growing number of churches.[10]

During 1969 Stansell met with other missions in La Paz interested in beginning TEE, focusing especially on the challenges of developing an appropriate curriculum. The group sensed that materials developed for Aymara leaders in a rural setting would need to begin at the level of a third-grade education and be bilingual: Spanish and Aymara. They recognized that coming up with the materials would be difficult and costly. That year Stansell began writing the text on the book of Acts. A text on the book of Mark had previously been prepared by the Peruvian missionaries. These were tested in Peru in 1969, with "reasonably good results."[11]

In the 1970 representatives meeting, the INELA approved giving the program a trial run in the Frontera District.[12] Mateo Mamani served as national director and teacher, assisted by Ron Stansell. Twelve students participated. In 1971 INELA representatives in their annual meeting approved that the program continue functioning.[13]

In October 1971, Stansell reported home: "We're really excited about the beginning of extension classes this past week in [two] districts . . . with three national teachers. There are 9 or so local meeting classes with maybe up to 75 students. Five more teachers desire to start classes in February in 4 more districts, so it looks like the sky is the limit on the interest. We'll have our hands full as missionaries keeping up with them on materials, books, and encouragement for the director and teachers, but those are the sort of problems that make us happy."[14]

Mission council minutes for January 1972 reported over 120 students, six national teachers and centers in six districts. The extension Bible school program was off

10. Ron Stansell, letter to OYM, October 7, 1971, NWYM/GFU archives.

11. Ron Stansell, Annual Report, July 1969, NWYM/GFU archives.

12. *Actas de la Junta Anual*, 1966–1981, January 1970, INELA archives.

13. *Actas de la Junta Anual*, 1966–1981, January 1971, INELA archives.

14. Ron Stansell, letter to OYM, November 24, 1971, NWYM/GFU archives.

and running.[15] Numbers of students through the decade would wax and wane, but the program remained strong, reaching a peak in 1974 with 170 students.[16] Numbers of students had leveled out to just under one hundred in 1979, but with centers in all seven of the church's districts.[17]

Clearly still an initiative of the mission, a main task of the mission throughout the decade was encouraging the national church to "own" it.

In addition to advocating the program with the national church, the mission's main roles were curriculum development and production (subsidizing the costs in the sale of the texts), teacher training, and transporting teachers to the centers. Writing and producing the textbooks became a daunting task, and the missionary writers managed to barely keep ahead of the students.[18] Different nationals contributed as consultants, proofreaders, and translators to Aymara. Nancy Thomas finished the last of the textbooks for the thirty-six-course program in 1979,[19] and the focus shifted to revising and updating the books, partly to meet rising educational levels. Cooperation with several other mission groups facilitated completion of the tasks, and the teacher training workshops increasingly became interdenominational.[20]

The INELA participated by providing a national director to administer the centers, promoting the program in the churches, teaching in the centers, serving as consultants in curriculum development, and officially recognizing the graduates as pastors.

In 1978 the first group of twenty-three students finished the program, even though the last textbooks had not been completed. The mission council appointed Hal and Nancy Thomas as teachers (an exception to the practice of having only national teachers) to make it possible for this group to finish on time. So midyear, the Thomases and a group of extension students from the Caranavi, Frontera and Cordillera Districts gathered in the Alto Lima church (Caranavi District) for a week's intensive retreat. The following gives a view of the TEE experience, showing the mission's focus on the Aymara culture:

> This week Hal and I are teaching the last three courses required for graduation. It's an intensive but exciting experience. Take last night's class in Friends History. The students had previously studied and filled out their textbook, so I concentrated on an overview of the whole Friends' movement. The class was fascinated by the *National Geographic* photos of England, brought to give

---

15. BMC Minutes, January 28, 1971, NWYM/GFU archives.

16. Hal Thomas, letter to OYM, June 16, 1974, NWYM/GFU archives.

17. *Actas de la Junta Anual,* 1966–1981, January 1979, NWYM/GFU archives.

18. Writers included current and former missionaries: Ron Stansell, Phyllis Cammack, Betty Comfort, Ralph Chapman, Nancy Thomas, and Mary Bel Cammack.

19. BMC Minutes, May 9, 1979, NWYM/GFU archives.

20. Those cooperating with the NWYM Mission were the Bolivian Holiness Mission, the Church of God Holiness Mission, and the Central Friends Mission.

flavor to the story of Friends' beginnings. And the story certainly is interesting, covering the dynamic early years, the periods of quietism and then revival, and ending with God's moving in Latin America through Friends.

But, even more than the story, the class enthusiastically noted all the applications. The fervor of the "valiant sixty" as they spread out two by two to evangelize England, their consistency in the face of persecution—these struck responsive chords. Many of these students have faced similar persecution in their own communities.

We talked also of the work of Friends for social justice, noting the many similarities between conditions in Bolivia today and in the England and US of the 17th through 19th centuries. How would God have Bolivian Friends respond to the social injustices, poor prison conditions, and ignorance that exist in some sectors? We then discussed at length the different divisions and historical squabbles over the authority of Scripture versus the Holy Spirit.

Thinking of the current nativistic prophet movements in Bolivia, Alejandro asked, "Well, how *do* we know when the Holy Spirit is speaking?" That question was good for another hour. We concluded the class with a resolve to further reflect on the triumphs and mistakes of the past, to learn what we can, and to go on from there.

That was last night.

This morning Hal got through only the first point on his outline on the theology of God: "God is spirit." The Aymara word for spirit, *ajayu*, had connotations vastly different from the "same" word in either Spanish, English, or Greek. To say, "God is *ajayu*," and just leave it at that, would simply add God to the list of existing Aymara spirits and gods. What does the Aymara person understand when he or she hears the word *ajayu*? What are the characteristics of God as "spirit" that would differentiate Him from the Aymara *ajayu*? And, having figured out all that, how then do we "worship Him in spirit and in truth"? . . .

The class spent the morning on "God is spirit," slowly grasping it and becoming able to express the concept in their own language and thought patterns.[21]

21. Nancy Thomas, "Alto Lima," 8–9.

First TEE graduates, Alto Lima (H. Thomas)

In the January 1979 annual representatives' meeting, the first seventeen INELA graduates from the extension Bible school were officially recognized as pastors. By the end of that year, nine more INELA graduates were ready to be recognized. The program was clearly doing what it was created to do.

In spite of the success of TEE in pastoral formation, the problem of finances continued to baffle. While production expenses of the textbooks were shared among the participating missions, it was still necessary to heavily subsidize the books in order for rural students to afford them. The total costs, in time and finances, added up to a program that would be extremely difficult for the national church to administer on its own, an indigenous goal that might not be attainable. Added to this dilemma was the recurring question as to whether the INELA really "owned" this program or was merely content, for a time, to let the mission "do its thing."

San Pablo Seminary

As early as 1970, Ron Stansell began asking the mission council, "After Bible school, what?" The council acknowledged that some kind of higher level of education was becoming necessary, especially in light of the increasing educational levels of young people in the churches. In the April 1972 mission council meeting, Stansell reported that an interdenominational cooperative effort was underway to plan for a new seminary. The Church of God Holiness and the Bolivian Holiness Missions had joined with the Northwest Friends (formerly known as the Oregon Friends), and were inviting one representative from each national church to move forward with this initiative.[22]

The San Pablo Seminary officially opened in the fall of 1972 with twenty students, eight of whom were from the INELA. Stansell served as director, and all the teachers were missionaries from the three cooperating missions.[23] Classes were held on the INELA property on Max Paredes Street at night to accommodate the schedules of adult students.

Ron Stansell teaching in San Pablo (H. Thomas)

Administering and teaching in the seminary and promoting it in the national church became mission priorities through the rest of the decade of the 1970s. The mission gave scholarships to INELA students. The program slowly grew with twenty-eight students (eighteen of them INELA) in 1975,[24] and its first two graduates in 1977.[25]

While the San Pablo Seminary was clearly a mission-sponsored program, gradually national teachers were being incorporated. In the 1980 INELA annual meeting, the representatives decided that graduates of the Patmos residency and extension programs be encouraged to attend San Pablo Seminary for further training in ministry.[26]

22. BMC Minutes, March 23, 1972, NWYM/GFU archives.

23. NWYM mission teachers that year were Ron Stansell, Quentin Nordyke, and Hal Thomas.

24. BMC Minutes, November 18, 1975, NWYM/GFU archives.

25. BMC Minutes, February 22, 1977, NWYM/GFU archives.

26. *Actas de la Junta Anual*, 1966–1981, January 1980, INELA archives.

Patmos Bible Institute, Residency Program

While the mission perceived that the Patmos residency program was not as effective as it needed to be in forming pastors for the INELA, the leadership of the INELA continued to give priority to this more traditional style of Bible school. This may have been in part because the Patmos Bible Institute had been planned and instituted by the INELA itself, although based on the mission's original institute at Copajira. At any rate, during the decade of the 1970s a certain amount of tension existed between the Patmos Bible Institute residency program (considered an INELA program) and the newer extension Bible school and San Pablo Seminary (both initiatives of the mission).

In 1972, when the extension program and the San Pablo Seminary were just getting started, the mission council decided to assign new missionary Hal Thomas to join Betty Comfort in teaching a limited number of classes in the residency program. This was partly to support the *mesa directiva's* priorities and partly because it seemed a good introductory assignment for a new missionary. When the Comforts retired from the field in mid-1972, that left only one missionary serving in Patmos, freeing Ron Stansell and Quentin Nordyke (who returned to Bolivia in 1972) to focus on the newer extension and seminary programs.

In 1973 the representatives in their annual meeting suspended Patmos classes for the year and appointed a commission of leaders to work on a plan for restructuring the institute. The six-member commission included secretary of education Salustiano Aspi, Carmelo Aspi, and Hal Thomas.[27] In August of 1973 the commission presented a balanced and complete plan that would combine the residency and extension Bible school programs into one institute. Goals, requirements, curriculum, and administration were carefully developed, along with an ambitious proposal to build a center on the tabernacle property in El Alto with space for classrooms, dorms, and administrative offices.[28]

Francisco Ucharico, one of the commission members, gave an emotional report of the results of the commission's work in the 1974 annual representatives meeting, calling the whole effort a failure because of the mission's refusal to agree to support the construction of a new building in El Alto. He accused the mission of once again causing the national church to pass through hard trials by "strangling the forward march of the Institute," in contrast to other foreign missions who, he claimed, financed their churches' educational institutions 100 percent.[29] While Ucharico's response was extreme, it reflects the tension between national church and mission.

The residency Bible institute continued to function during the 1970s, although several years classes were cancelled due largely to financial difficulties (including the inability to collect fees from students). It was noted that some years over half of the

---

27. Other members were Daniel Ticona, Francisco Ucharico, and Hipólito Llanqui.

28. "Instituto Bíblico 'Patmos,' Resoluciones," August 4, 1973, INELA archives.

29. Francisco Ucharico, report, January 24, 1974, INELA archives.

students came from other denominations.[30] In a report presented to the representatives in their 1980 annual meeting, the committee in charge of pastoral oversight presented pastoral recognition for seventeen graduates from the extension Bible school and five from the Patmos residency program.[31]

ORGANIZATIONAL DEVELOPMENTS

The January representatives meeting continued as the main decision-making body of the church, with authority given to the executive council, the *mesa directiva*, to oversee and carry out the ongoing work of the church. *Mesa directiva* officers began to be elected for regular three-year terms, with a third of its members being new every year. This added to the stability of the church. Although the national church continued to wrestle with and negotiate issues of authority, the decade also saw more administrative delegation of authority and greater participation from a broader leadership base.

Among the new roles and structures, the representatives added a pastoral oversight committee (*comité jurado*) in 1971, originally comprised of the *mesa* president and secretary of evangelism.[32] Its role was to oversee disciplinary matters and to give general supervision to the growing numbers of pastors, workers (*obreros* and *encargados*),[33] and teachers. This committee reported directly to the *mesa*.

The representatives also expanded membership of the *mesa* to include two secretaries of evangelism to handle the growing workload (1973), and a secretary of health (1976) to administer the mission's fund for the medical needs of pastors, workers, and teachers and to develop the INELA's own program to promote health among its greater constituency.

The *mesa directiva* met monthly, and in special sessions when necessary, to oversee the different committees and ministries of the church, administer the ongoing processes of the legalization of property documents, problem solve both on the micro and macro levels, and respond to petitions from districts, local churches, and individuals. The president and other *mesa* members now kept regular hours in their office on the Max Paredes Street property in La Paz. They traveled extensively on weekends, participating in quarterly meetings, conferences of all types, evangelistic campaigns, and local church visits. It was expected that leaders in the church, along with pastors, would work hard and suffer much for the Lord.

The need for wide participation of leadership on many levels frequently clashed with the other felt need to control. For example, in the 1976 representatives meeting, the *mesa* was criticized for its lack of control over which people got to rent rooms on church property on Max Paredes Street and for allowing the unauthorized sale

---

30. BMC Minutes, February 11, 1975, NWYM/GFU archives.

31. Report of the pastoral oversight committee, January 9, 1980, INELA archives.

32. *Actas de la Junta Anual*, 1966–1981, January 1971., INELA archives.

33. *Obrero* ("worker") was the term given to a local leader in training to become a pastor; *encarcado* ("one in charge") was the term given to a local leader temporarily appointed to serve in a pastoral way.

of agricultural products on the tabernacle property on El Alto; it was minuted that the *mesa* needed to exercise "stricter control." At the end of the same meeting the presiding clerk "recommended to the quarterly meeting presidents that they control the members of the *mesa directiva* in order to promote the forward march of the National Evangelical Friends Church. And in opportune moments they should let [*mesa* members] know the errors they may be committing, so that these may be promptly rectified."[34]

Financial troubles continued to plague the national church and much of the tug-of-war with the mission centered on money. But financial accountability was growing, with the treasurer of the *mesa directiva* giving annual reports, along with separate reports from the different committees that handled their own budgets (education, evangelism, and construction, for example). While the mission continued to contribute toward certain funds, the church was gradually becoming financially independent in some areas, in spite of it being a period of national economic inflation.

Recognition of the INELA as a Yearly Meeting

From the perspective of someone from the outside looking in, the official recognition of the INELA as a yearly meeting in 1973/74 would likely be counted as the organizational high point of the decade. From the perspective of the INELA itself, however, this event passed as a curious blip on their radar screen.

As is customary among Quakers worldwide, at an appropriate point in time a newer regional group of Friends churches is officially recognized as an independent "yearly meeting" in its own right by the founding yearly meeting. The recognition is on the level of yearly meeting to yearly meeting, and it puts the newer group on the same level as other yearly meetings around the world.

The mission council, in its July 1972 meeting, considered a letter from Northwest Yearly Meeting (NWYM, formerly OYM, Oregon Yearly Meeting) superintendent Norval Hadley encouraging them to think about giving official recognition as a yearly meeting to the INELA. The council responded initially in surprise at the realization that this had never happened, and secondly in concern at the effect such a recognition might have on the INELA. They wondered if it was even necessary: "The council's feeling was that the INELA is already an autonomous national church, and, therefore, probably a Yearly Meeting."[35]

The discussion continued, and the council sent this recommendation to the mission board in early 1973: "Council recommends that the Northwest Yearly Meeting recognize the INELA as a yearly meeting (retroactive to January 1964 if possible), but that this decision not be played up to the INELA. It is not advised to send delegates to Bolivia. The brethren believe themselves to be a yearly meeting (or the equivalent)

---

34. *Actas de la Junta Anual*, 1966–1981, January 1976, INELA archives.
35. BMC Minutes, July 17, 1972, NWYM/GFU archives.

and would be offended at any fanfare."[36] In his accompanying cover letter, Ron Stansell wrote that "the official action by Northwest Yearly Meeting of Friends is long overdue, it appears to me, and should be done in a quiet and unobtrusive manner. The only issue that council feels might arise is what relationships should the INELA establish, if any, with other independent yearly meetings of Friends?"[37]

In their 1973 yearly meeting sessions, the Northwest Yearly Meeting of Friends extended official recognition to the *Iglesia Nacional Evangélica de Los Amigos* (INELA) as a yearly meeting. In the INELA's January 1974 annual representatives meeting, a certificate of recognition was read on the floor of the meeting and presented to the delegates. It happened on a Friday morning as a regular agenda item, tucked in between a report of the Patmos Bible Institute and the discussion of a possible parsonage on the Max Paredes property. Missionary Ron Stansell commented briefly on the meaning of this recognition and the group passed on to the next item.[38] No fanfare or even celebration accompanied this announcement. (Years later, in 2013, Hal Thomas discovered the damp but otherwise undamaged certificate of recognition in a cardboard box in a basement room, part of the INELA's as yet unsorted archival documents.)

INELA president Pascual Quispe receiving yearly meeting recognition (H. Thomas)

This recognition did, of course, have an impact on the INELA's relationship with worldwide Quakerism, as would soon become obvious. Actually, contacts with other Quakers had begun earlier. In 1973 William Barton, president of the Friends World Committee on Consultation (FWCC), visited the field. Barton spent time with the missionaries and through their facilitation was also able to be with the *mesa directiva* and visit various churches.[39] He expressed his desire to develop a relationship with the INELA.

In 1974 the FWCC sent an invitation to the INELA, by way of the mission, not only to send delegates to a worldwide gathering of Quakers that would take place in Wichita, Kansas in 1977, but also to participate on the planning committee for the event. This invitation caused

36. BMC Minutes, January 22, 1973, NWYM/GFU archives.

37. Ron Stansell, letter to NWYM, January 25, 1973, NWYM/GFU archives.

38. *Actas de la Junta Anual*, 1966–1981, January 1974, NWYM/GFU archives.

39. BMC Minutes, August 7, 1973, NWYM/GFU archives.

concern among the mission council, sensing that the INELA was not ready for exposure to Friends of a more liberal theological persuasion.[40] Council chairman Ron Stansell tempered this concern, noting that "Bolivian Friends *could* be a blessing and have a ministry elsewhere in the world," through these kinds of encounters.[41]

The INELA did not participate on the planning committee, but they eagerly accepted the invitation to attend the conference. In January 1977, the representatives chose Francisco Tintaya as a member of the *mesa directiva* and Enrique Tito, then director of the Patmos Bible Institute, to travel to Kansas.[42]

Tintaya and Tito traveled to the United States, visited Friends churches and attended the FWCC gathering, reporting on the INELA. They followed this up with a visit to Oregon where they visited more churches and participated in NWYM's annual sessions, thus becoming the INELA's first official visitors to the NWYM. They reported on their trip in the January 1978 annual representatives meeting in La Paz, giving an overview of church visits and noting that Quaker worship services in many places are not noisy, are in fact largely silent. They also noted that many Quaker churches in the United States are not evangelical. It's interesting that from their visit to Northwest Yearly Meeting, the main observation came from their exposure to the budget of the board of missions. They reported that while the board gave $40,000 toward the needs of the national churches in Bolivia and Peru, a considerably larger amount went for support of the missionaries.[43]

Development of the Youth and Women's Societies

Another important aspect of the INELA's organizational growth during the 1970s was the further development of the national youth (UJELAB) and women's (UFINELA) societies. Established in the 1960s, as we saw in the last chapter, both these groups had their own *mesa directiva* on the national level. Both the youth and women's *mesa* members traveled widely in order to facilitate the development of district and local branches. Annual and quarterly conferences added to the schedule of activities.

A frequent topic of debate was the relation of these two societies to the overall leadership of the national church. Both groups presented their annual reports to the representatives and brought forth activity proposals for approval. The tension between the needs for broader participation and the need for control defined some of this debate.

The urge for the leadership to "control" was especially felt in regards to the UJELAB. The traditional respect for age and experience in Aymara culture came head to head with the forces of modernization and the higher education of young people

---

40. BMC Minutes, June 4, 1974, NWYM/GFU archives.

41. Ron Stansell, letter to NWYM, June 5, 1974, NWYM/GFU archives.

42. *Actas de la Junta Anual*, 1966–1981, January 1977, INELA archives.

43. *Actas de la Junta Anual*, 1966–1981, January 1978 INELA archives.

across the nation. Church leaders felt concern about the threat of youth rebelling against authority, and several times applied disciplinary measures to UJELAB leaders.

In the 1979 annual representatives meeting, UJELAB president David Tintaya presented the organization's annual report. It included the information that their 1978 annual youth conference was a time of deep discouragement, mainly due to "the scant help we have received from adult leaders; all they do is criticize us." He concluded with a recommendation that the 1979 annual UJELAB conference be cancelled, due to these misunderstandings.[44] The representatives denied this request and asked that the ad hoc *mesa directiva* in charge of the gathering meet with the youth leaders that very week to come to a solution.[45] That meeting was successful, with the youth leaders feeling affirmed rather than criticized.

The annual 1979 youth conference took place as planned with a record attendance of around four hundred young people from all the districts. The positive activity report for 1979 shows that, in addition to youth conferences in all eight districts, UJELAB organized an evangelistic campaign in INELA's new work in Tutimaya, near the city of Cochabamba, where twenty young people "carried out the total evangelization of the village, going house to house, handing out literature and teaching the word of God." In their overall evangelistic work for the year, they reported distributing 49,660 gospel tracts.[46] UJELAB was determined to contribute to the advance of the INELA. (One interesting note concerning the dynamics of the negotiations between the *mesa directiva* and UJELAB at the end of the decade was the fact that while David Tintaya was the UJELAB president, his father, Francisco Tintaya, was the INELA president.)

The women's society, UFINELA, also demonstrated a passion for activities to advance the work of the INELA. Their annual reports to the representatives meetings show numerous trips to encourage women's organizations on the district and local levels.[47] The annual women's conference became a high light of the year. Outstanding were their initiatives in special fund-raising projects that allowed them to turn over to the INELA gospel films and even a movie projector, for use in conferences and evangelistic campaigns.[48] The UFINELA *directiva* turned the projector over to the INELA at the end of the 1977 UFINELA annual conference with the admonition that the projector "be administered by a person who knows how to run it because the ladies of the seven districts gave an immense sacrifice in order to purchase it." Their letter concludes by saying that if the *mesa* takes good care of the projector for the Lord,

---

44. UJELAB annual report, January 1979, INELA archives.

45. *Actas de la Junta Anual*, 1966–1981, January 1979, INELA archives.

46. UJELAB annual report, January 1980, INELA archives.

47. For example, note the annual UFINELA report for 1977, January 1978, INELA archives.

48. See BMC Minutes, August 7, 1973, NWYM/GFU archives, and *Actas de la Junta Anual*, 1966–1981, January 1977, INELA archives.

"then we will have even greater desire to work and receive another blessing from God, because God is great to bless us."[49]

UFINELA gives a movie projector (H. Thomas)

In contrast to the youth society, the UFINELA showed itself more submissive to the authority of the INELA. This is best demonstrated in the society's most ambitious project of the decade, the purchase of a plot of land in Magallanes, in the lowland Caranavi-Alto Beni District. The entrepreneurial purpose of this purchase was the cultivation of coffee, with the profits to be donated to the INELA for its evangelistic program. The INELA representatives in their annual 1974 meeting approved the coffee-planting plan.[50] Yet problems with the property title, personal interests of the different people involved, and the difficulties of the actual work forced the *mesa directiva* to call a special meeting with the UFINELA leaders and the presidents of all six districts later in 1974. As a result the UFINELA was ordered to turn the project over to a newly formed cooperative, *El Buen Samaritano*, and focus on more spiritual activities.[51]

49. UFINELA annual report, September 4, 1977, INELA archives.

50. *Actas de la Junta Anual*, 1966–1981, January 1974, INELA archives.

51. *Acta* of a called meeting, August 25, 1974, INELA archives.

THE OUTREACH DEVELOPMENT OF THE CHURCH

The president of the *mesa directiva* and the secretaries of evangelism traveled every weekend and often during the week in an attempt to encourage every district and, if possible, every church. While not all conferences were evangelistic in nature, almost every gathering contained a service where non-believing neighbors were invited to hear the gospel and become Christian.

The activity reports of *mesa directiva* members leave one breathless. For example, in the annual representatives meeting of January 1974, the two secretaries of evangelism gave separate detailed reports for their activities in 1973. Arturo Tito prefaced his report by saying, "During the church year I made all the visits I possibly could with the help of God." He noted the purposes of his visits as "strengthening the faith of the believers, helping people find reconciliation before God, and realizing campaigns with the goal of helping the church grow with new believers." He reported visits to forty different places in the six districts and new areas.[52]

In the same annual meeting, the other secretary of evangelism, Cipriano Copa, reported a total of ten quarterly meeting visits (with 113 converts), and fifteen evangelistic campaigns held in different churches (with 162 converts), as well as teaching in five short courses for leadership training.[53] In addition to these two reports, the INELA president, Pascual Quispe, and the director of the new missionary society, Severino Bartalama, also presented detailed travel activity reports. The leadership of the INELA was hardworking and placed a high priority on maintaining contact with all the far-flung congregations that made up the national church.

Santa Cruz

A highlight of the decade was the expansion of the INELA into the lowland department (state) of Santa Cruz, to the east of the department of La Paz. Many Aymara people from the *altiplano* and the Yungas valleys were migrating to the department of Santa Cruz, an area seen as ripe for development and economic growth. Among these migrants, members of the INELA sought a better way of life and wanted the Friends Church to be a part of it. The migrants included Eugenio Ramos, a leader in the INELA, and the new work developed around his leadership with the first congregation being organized in 1972.[54] Francisco Quispe and Javier Quispe also gave leadership.

---

52. Arturo Tito, annual report of secretary of evangelism, January 1974, INELA archives.
53. Cipriano Copa, annual report of secretary of evangelism, January 1974, INELA archives.
54. Quisbert and Ramos, "El espíritu de hacer misiones," 96–98.

J. Quispe, E. Ramos, and F. Quispe, leaders of the Santa Cruz work (NWYM)

The *mesa directiva* became interested in promoting this new work.[55] In 1974 Quentin Nordyke accompanied a commission of nationals on a visit to Santa Cruz. Nordyke reported that a group of about one hundred persons gathered for meetings over the weekend and that the group had already bought and paid for a lot on which to build their church. Leaders expressed a desire to have a North American missionary assigned to the new area. Mission council expressed hesitancy, feeling that "a strong and healthy church can be planted without the help of a missionary."[56]

The national church intended to incorporate the new work into the INELA and continued to express its desire that the mission place a family in Santa Cruz.[57] The mission, in consultation with the board of missions, finally came to the same conclusion and the board appointed Mark and Wilma Roberts.

In July 1976, the Roberts moved to Santa Cruz. In addition to encouraging the existing churches, Mark Roberts set up a center of the extension Bible school and made several evangelistic trips. In his report to the mission council in January 1977, Roberts emphasized that the future of the work would likely be among the more responsive Aymara peoples colonizing the areas outside the city of Santa Cruz.[58] Considering

55. BMC Minutes, September 19, 1973, NWYM/GFU archives.

56. BMC Minutes, June 4, 1974, NWYM/GFU archives.

57. BMC Minutes, December 8, 1975, NWYM/GFU archives.

58. BMC Minutes, January 29, 1977, NWYM/GFU archives.

the long-term possibilities of this work, the mission decided to buy property for a missionary residence.

Two of the challenges of the new work were its geographical distance from the rest of the INELA and the cultural differences between the two areas. Mission council minutes from May of 1977 recommend "that the fact be recognized . . . that while [the] Santa Cruz work is technically a part of the Bolivian INELA, distance and culture make it really a 'separate' work and that its own unique development be pursued."[59]

The Roberts left for furlough in mid-1977, and in early 1978 Roscoe and Tina Knight returned to Bolivia to take up residency in Santa Cruz. As in their previous experience as pioneer missionaries in the Yungas, one of their first tasks was to fix up a place to live, and in Santa Cruz that meant overseeing the construction of the new missionary residence. But, as in the Yungas, Knight did not let that postpone the work he felt called to do. In October 1978, he wrote home about the first church plant in a jungle colony in San Julian:

> We now have a new church! Away out in the jungle. Forty homesteaders, some with their families, arrived the first part of September at the government colonization project of San Julian. Of these 40, about 10 were Protestant, with a majority being from our Friends churches of the Altiplano. We had been expecting them for weeks but they never arrived. So we were really pleased when I checked one day at the Colonization office, to learn that they had arrived just 3 or 4 days previously. So Tina and I made the trip, 5 hours each way, to see if we could find them. We stopped at different places for directions and finally located them away out in the virgin jungle. There is just a small clearing, made by government tractors, and the rest of the hard labor of clearing all that heavy jungle growth and huge trees is up to the colonists. They each own over 120 acres so they will be years clearing it all.
>
> They were really glad to see us as many were discouraged and disillusioned. They had expected a paradise; instead they found heat, lonesomeness, hard work and worse of all, the biting insects; not to mention poor water and 20 families having to live in one small building. We encouraged them and I have since made 3 more trips with different brethren from Santa Cruz to help them organize a church and start regular services.[60]

This gives a flavor of the challenges the new colonists faced and the pioneer type work required to build a church among them. A year later Knight wrote home about this same group of colonists, saying that all the Friends had become discouraged and gone back home to the *altiplano*, and that the small church plant had collapsed. He now wondered if a Friends work was even possible in the colonies but noted that the work in the city was slowly progressing.

59. BMC Minutes, May 14, 1977, NWYM/GFU archives.
60. Roscoe Knight, letter to NWYM, October 4, 1978, NWYM/GFU archives.

In his report to mission council at the end of 1979, Knight reiterated the slowness of work in the city, but again encouraged outreach in the San Julian colonies, despite the difficulties of travel there during the rainy season. He reported that most people were of Quechua background, and that he was working with four groups that were meeting regularly, one of which had already been organized as a Friends congregation. He encouraged the council to continuing maintaining a missionary family in the area.[61]

The Santa Cruz congregation (being a monthly meeting unrelated to any INELA district) reported directly to the annual gathering of representatives in La Paz. In their report for the 1979 year, Eugenio Ramos informed that they were currently supporting two new congregations in the San Julian colonies.[62]

National Missionary Society

Another highlight of the decade was the initiative of the INELA in forming their first missionary society. While the secretaries of evangelism of the *mesa directiva* did their evangelistic ministry mainly through already established churches, many were sensing the need to go to unevangelized areas.

INELA president Pascual Quispe proposed the creation of a new national mission work in the 1973 representatives meeting. He named the provinces of Aroma, Camacho, and North Yungas, and proposed that two national missionaries go and live in these areas in order to evangelize and plant churches. He proposed that the *mesa directiva* plan and administer the program, and that special offerings be raised throughout the yearly meeting to support it. The representatives approved the plan and set up a preliminary society to study how to bring it to reality.[63]

The missionary society officially came into being on April 22, 1973, in the annual Easter conference in the tabernacle. The first officers included president Severino Bartalama and vice president Arturo Tito; Tito also served as secretary of evangelism on the *mesa directiva* and was the link between the two groups.[64]

The first appointed missionary, Mario Surco, a native of the Ambaná area (a mountainous region north of La Paz), had become a Christian through Friends in Yungas where he had moved to colonize. He discovered a gift of evangelism and in the 1960s the Yungas District sent him as their missionary to Caranavi.[65] Eventually he returned to his native area on the highlands to begin a church, and in 1973 the society appointed Surco as their missionary to Ambaná. By the end of the year, the society reported three small congregations in the area and a total of forty-nine believers.[66]

---

61. BMC Minutes, October 25, 1979, NWYM/GFU archives.

62. *Actas de la Junta Anual*, 1966–1981, January 1980, NWYM/GFU archives.

63. *Actas de la Junta Anual*, 1966–1981, January 1973, INELA archives.

64. Domingo Mamani was treasurer and Jesús Tórrez secretary.

65. Mario Surco, interview with Félix Huarina, 2013, Caranavi.

66. Annual report of the missionary society, January 1974, INELA archives. Also Humberto

A second national missionary, Eusebio Quispe, was sent to the village of Berenguela in the Pacajes area southwest of La Paz, in the mountainous land bordering Peru and Chile. Two brothers, José and Pascual Sánchez, had earlier begun a small church, and Quispe arrived to minister to the new believers. After five months of service, he was killed in a truck accident, leaving a wife and three children. The society then sent national missionary Bacilio Angulo. Francisco Kunurana, a believer who lived in Catacora, also in the Pacajes area, began a church in that community and was also considered a national missionary.[67] During the 1974 annual representatives meeting, a total of twenty-two new churches were reported having been planted in 1973, seven of them through the new missionary society.[68]

Severino Bartalama continued leading the missionary society during 1974. The high point was clearly the development of the two strongest churches, Villa Exaltación in Berenguela with 180 believers (including children) and Catacora with 120 believers. Both churches had built their own chapels, and Villa Exaltación had already planted two dependent congregations. National missionary Luis Tola served in Villa Exaltación and Bernardo Flores in Catacora. An extension Bible school center began functioning in Catacora. On the basis of this success, the missionary society proposed that the area be officially recognized by the INELA.[69] This proposal was accepted by the representatives, and in January 1975 the Pacajes District, with two monthly meetings and three dependent churches, became the seventh national church district.[70] (Note: by the 1970s the church was using the word "district" rather than "quarterly meeting" to describe the organizational divisions. "Quarterly meeting" was still used for the actual four-times-a-year gatherings of these districts.)

The work in Ambaná, to the north, experienced a setback when the appointed national missionary, Mario Mamani, became discouraged and abandoned the work midyear, but another national missionary candidate, Humberto Gutiérrez, stepped forward and began working in the area with four potential new churches.[71]

For the next few years, the missionary society carried out its work with both advances and setbacks. The pattern that developed was that of short-term missionary service by a variety of people, partly because of the difficulties of the assignment. Humberto Gutiérrez's story exemplifies the experiences of these national missionaries.[72]

Gutiérrez became involved with Friends in La Paz in 1968, while still an idealistic university student with communist tendencies. He became a Christian through

Gutiérrez, interview with Harold Thomas and Nancy Thomas, January 26, 2016, La Paz.

67. Annual report of the missionary society, January 1974, INELA archives.

68. BMC Minutes, February 27, 1974, NWYM/GFU archives.

69. Annual report of the missionary society, January 1975, INELA archives.

70. *Actas de la Junta Anual,* 1966–1981, January 1975, INELA archives.

71. Annual report of the missionary society, January 1975, INELA archives.

72. Humberto Gutiérrez, interview with Harold Thomas and Nancy Thomas, January 26, 2016, La Paz.

his contact with Friends, although people didn't seem to trust him because of his background. In 1974 while working in a shoe store, he was falsely accused of stealing money and jailed (and subsequently released). The crisis caused him to promise God that he would respond to the first request to minister, no matter where that might be.

That same year, 1974, when the national missionary in the Ambaná area resigned, Bartalama asked Gutiérrez to go as a missionary. He had no idea where Ambaná was, but he said yes. The missionary society gave him no training and had no ministry plan. In January 1975, Bartalama drove him out to Ambaná and left him in the village of Comaptía where a small group of five believers was regularly meeting. Gutiérrez lived wherever he found a place, usually in the home of a believer, and he ate on the level of the people, which was not much. The agreement was that he would stay there a year. He left his wife of one year and baby daughter in La Paz.

He taught Bible and Christian life, and led worship services with the group of believers. He determined to talk to everyone in the village. It was hard at first. He greeted everyone he met, but at first people would not return his greeting. They were suspicious of strangers and at one point even discussed killing him.

At the end of the first two weeks, he was weak and exhausted, partly from lack of a good diet. It had been a poor year for crops, and there were no meat or eggs. The diet consisted of a weak potato soup, salt, and animal fat. He returned to La Paz for his health, to rest and gather his strength to go back. This became his pattern for the eight months he spent in Ambaná: two weeks in the field, one week in La Paz. Petrona, his wife, stayed in La Paz and put together a small business of chickens and eggs, and this helped sustain Gutiérrez. The missionary society gave him a small stipend at the end of each month that basically covered his travel expenses.

He began to walk to other villages regularly, where his practice was to go to the schools and community organizations, introduce himself to the community leaders and teachers, tell them who he was and what he wanted to do. He was then usually invited to speak to people, often in the community center or school. Raised in the city, he was familiar with the Aymara language from his parents and grandparents, but he had never spoken Aymara. In the Ambaná area no one spoke Spanish, so this was a learning stretch for Gutiérrez. He learned to speak Aymara.

National missionary Humberto Gutiérrez (H. Thomas)

He remembers especially the community of Copusquía, where Friends had no contacts. He befriended the community leader, Alejandro Quispe, and Quispe himself gathered all the people of the community in the schoolhouse, and Gutiérrez preached the gospel to them. That first service two people converted. He spent the night in the community center for guests, and was given a can of DDT to help keep the fleas under control. He used it. That was the first contact Copusquía had with the gospel. Today there is a strong Friends Church there.

Gutiérrez had to leave his work after only eight months because the missionary society ran out of money. As there were not yet trained leaders in the different communities he had worked in, it felt like he was leaving nothing behind. But the national church continued to visit the small groups of believers, even as the missionary society itself floundered, and little by little some of these groups developed into churches.

In 1977 Gutiérrez accepted a call to pastor the Villa San Antonio Church in La Paz. In 1979, he led his local church in reaching out to the very area where he had served his eight months as a missionary: Ambaná. He was thus able to carry on what he and the other national missionaries like Mario Surco had begun.

In spite of the gains the missionary society made, which were many, administrative and financial struggles would eventually bring it down. In the 1978 annual business meeting, the representatives decided to again restructure the national missionary work, temporarily placing it under the *mesa directiva* secretary of evangelism, thereby effectively disbanding the society.[73] The society had been a noble experiment; it bore good fruit, and the church learned from it. In the 1980 representatives meeting, Lago Norte, a result of the missionary society's labors, was accepted as the eighth district of the INELA, with two monthly meetings and four dependent congregations.[74] The actual work begun by the society went forward, but new means would need to be discovered.

A New Ministry Focus in Social Outreach

The INELA had been involved in social work from its inception in 1924 with its schools. These continued through the decade of the 1970s, under the direction of the *mesa directiva's* secretary of education and his committee. The secretary of education reported that in 1970, twenty-one rural schools hosted 720 students; an urban school continued to function in La Paz.[75] This number fluctuated throughout the decade, dipping down to sixteen rural schools with some 583 students in 1979.[76] In 1974 administrative and disciplinary problems forced the *mesa* to close the La Paz school.[77]

In other areas, a social consciousness was slowly growing in the INELA, especially among young adults. In the 1976 representatives meeting, the youth organization, UJELAB, proposed that the church add to its *mesa directiva* a secretary of health.[78] In its 1977 session, the representatives formalized the role, naming Humberto Gutiérrez as the new secretary of health;[79] he served in that position through the end of the decade, forming the social action committee of other young Friends challenged to make a contribution toward bettering the physical and material well-being of people in the church and in the country as a whole.

One of the purposes of the new role was to administer the pastors' medical fund, one of the benefits that the mission gave to the church in the form of a regular financial donation. This was in recognition of the low salaries pastors and church leaders received, a condition that put them at risk when accidents or illness struck. Since the 1950s, the mission had administered the fund, and they willingly turned that task over to the national church, letting the secretary of health receive the petitions for help and disburse the funds as needed. But the intentions of the INELA went beyond the administration of this fund to the possible creation of new programs to promote the health of its constituency.

Meanwhile the mission was also growing in its consciousness that a holistic gospel necessarily needed to include the social aspect. In the 1976 Christmas retreat of

73. *Actas de la Junta Anual, 1966–1981*, January 1978, INELA archives.

74. *Actas de la Junta Anual, 1966–1981*, January 1980, INELA archives.

75. *Actas de la Junta Anual, 1966–1981*, January 1971, INELA archives.

76. *Actas de la Junta Anual, 1966–1981*, January 1980, INELA archives.

77. *Actas de la Junta Anual, 1966–1981*, January 1975, INELA archives.

78. *Actas de la Junta Anual, 1966–1981*, January 1976, INELA archives.

79. *Actas de la Junta Anual, 1966–1981*, January 1977, INELA archives.

both the Bolivian and Peruvian mission councils in Cochabamba, Bolivia, the joint mission council concluded by reaffirming its priority on spiritual ministry, but also noted that this needed to include addressing the physical/economic/social needs of people. The final report recommended that the initiative in this area should come from the INELA, but that missionaries could encourage it.[80]

In January 1977, NWYM Quaker Stuart Willcuts (son of Jack Willcuts), who was serving with Christian NGO World Vision, visited La Paz, and Hal Thomas put him in contact with Gutiérrez and the INELA's social action committee. Following that encounter, Thomas wrote to the board of missions that "what is especially exciting is that there is high interest and capable leadership in the INELA for meeting some of the pressing social needs of the Aymara community if there are funds available. I will be working with a group of INELA leaders during the next two months drawing up proposals for specific projects. . . . There is grass roots concern and planning and leadership to begin some far-reaching social programs in the INELA."[81]

During 1977, the social action committee proposed forming a medical clinic on the Max Paredes property. Gutiérrez worked with his committee and in constant consultation with Hal Thomas and Stuart Willcuts until the proposal was ready to be presented to World Vision. That same year World Vision accepted to cooperate with the INELA in the project, offering seed money of $15,000, and asking the INELA to itself raise and contribute a portion of the start-up costs, equivalent to $1,000.

In a letter to the board of missions at the end of 1977, mission council president Ron Stansell wrote,

> We note some concern from you, Jerry,[82] regarding this $15,000 grant to the INELA. We have made no minutes on it since the negotiation and connections have not been through [Mission] Council, but rather directly between World Vision personnel and the MD of the INELA, which we feel is healthy and fine. Hal has met with them a time or two and the Sec. of Health of the MD has counseled with Hal. . . . The goal: bring higher quality health facilities within closer geographic and economic reach of believers coming and going through Max Paredes.[83]

The *mesa directiva* made available several rooms in the old mission home on Max Paredes Street to be set up and used as consulting rooms, a lab, and a small pharmacy. (The clinic thus would share the building with the Patmos residency Bible School and different INELA offices.) During 1978, Gutiérrez and the social action committee made the necessary purchases, prepared the rooms, and contracted medical personnel. In April 1979, the clinic opened for business, with one doctor and two nurses. The

---

80. NWYM Joint Mission Council, December 22–26, 1976, NWYM/GFU archives.

81. Harold Thomas, letter to NWYM, February 7, 1977, NWYM/GFU archives.

82. At the time, Gerald Dillon was president of the board of missions.

83. Ron Stansell, letter to NWYM, November 28, 1977, NWYM/GFU archives.

committee hoped that in time the low fees charged for services, plus offerings from the INELA, would make the clinic solvent and self-sufficient. Fund-raising efforts among the churches continued and in his 1980 report to the INELA representatives, Gutiérrez reported having raised most of their required amount of start-up costs.[84]

While the clinic was the main focus and contribution of the new social action committee in the 1970s, the annual reports of the secretary of health showed a range of other projects carried out, including medical and dental checkups as a part of the annual pastors' conference and health and nutrition classes in other church conferences.[85] Vision was high and participation in these projects energetic.

INELA AND THE MISSION IN A CHANGING RELATIONSHIP

Throughout the decade the mission and the national church struggled to redefine a changing relationship.

The Cochabamba Retreat and Changing Mission Perspectives

As noted above, a joint Bolivia/Peru mission retreat was held in November 1976, in the city of Cochabamba, Bolivia. Different missionaries presented position papers. These show certain changes in mission philosophy and strategy, in addition to the concern for a more holistic approach.

Jack Willcuts, clerk of the Department of Missions, was visiting the field, and he presented a paper on the aims and goals of the mission, noting that a previous sense of needing to withdraw from the world was being replaced by a sense that the church needed to penetrate and influence its context, to be salt and light. He asked, "How can the strengths of the past in our own mission become stepping stones to not only increased evangelistic outreach but a maturing church of the future? A church that enlarges its concern to all sociological factors including education, agriculture, politics, economics, health and standards of living?" Willcuts reaffirmed the mission's policy of indigenization, "continuing a non-directive role, a non-authoritative voice."[86]

Willcuts also reaffirmed the mission's strategy of cultural affirmation, as part of the indigenous process:

> Fortunately, the Spirit led our mission years ago to discern that the Indian fiesta was not evil in itself, only the immorality which accompanied the music, the eating together, the fellowship, the fun of dressing in one's best clothes and visiting with neighbors. This all became in the Quaker context, the church conference and eventually the Junta Trimestral. So, let the dignity of the Aymara cultural scene, the patterns of community and national life be cleansed

---

84. Annual report of secretary of health, January 1980, INELA archives. They had raised b$17,000 of the required b$20,000.

85. Annual report of secretary of health, January 1980, NWYM/GFU archives.

86. Jack Willcuts, unpublished manuscript, November 1976, NWYM/GFU archives.

not abolished, let national music be written and shared, not downgraded or Americanized. This may be one of the great strengths and break-throughs of Friends work. And this has resulted in an effective conversion of family, and entire communities rather than just individuals. . . . It isn't a matter of syncretism or adjustments to the Gospel, but rather to allow people expression in their own manner, to communicate their own mental and linguistic structures, etc. It is a matter of giving people and their cultural heritage their proper worth.[87]

Quentin Nordyke's presentation of the changing role of the mission, affirmed the indigenous principle, but also acknowledged that sending churches (like NWYM) also have a sense of mission that may, at times, conflict with a national perspective causing tension between the groups. He used the example of the mission's emphasis on the extension Bible school and the seminary, while the INELA favored the residency Bible school program.[88]

Hal Thomas continued with this emphasis in his challenge to be missionary advocates, being both respectful of culture but also true to a prophetic calling that occasionally challenges local perceptions:

> The missionary as Advocate will approach his target culture as a guest. He is not to condemn a culture or to be a judge over it. That is the role of the Holy Spirit as the missionary is faithful to communicate clearly. The missionary comes to move within the forms of culture, not to transplant his own way of life. He does not have the right to force change. His constant attitude will be that of the learner. His constant questions, "Why?, How do you do it?" . . . Does the missionary have the right of advocacy in areas where he sees the church is weak or immature? What about the situation where the people he is working with do not seem to share his concern? . . . The missionary is also a prophet in that he is responsible to speak forth the councils of God.[89]

The sense of the retreat was that God was leading the mission to continue to encourage the indigenous development of the national church, but at the same time to be free to take the initiative and advocate for change when appropriate.

Crisis Points

During the decade of the 1970s, several crisis points illustrate the changing roles between the church and the mission. These include struggles over property, conflict over a revision of the Aymara hymnal, the threats of sects, and authority/discipline issues in general.

---

87. Jack Willcuts, unpublished manuscript, November 1976, NWYM/GFU archives.
88. Quentin Nordyke, unpublished manuscript, November 1976, NWYM/GFU archives.
89. Harold Thomas, letter to NWYM, November 16, 1976, NWYM/GFU archives.

Struggles over Property

We have seen how during the 1960s and into the early years of the 1970s, the INELA led the effort to build a new tabernacle on the Alto. While the mission made major contributions (such as funding the roof, doors, windows, and platform), the national church took the initiative, supplied the labor, and brought the project to completion. This allowed over four thousand believers to gather in the annual Easter conference, a boast to the morale of the whole church.

While the mission council discussed the possible need to strengthen the support for the huge tabernacle roof, time and other activities prevented that from happening. Then in April of 1976, a major hailstorm collapsed the roof. This caused great alarm, but both the INELA and the mission tried to downplay the seriousness of the event, not giving it much importance in official minutes or annual reports. Leaders began planning immediately how to raise the funds to rebuild the roof, as the rest of the building had remained standing.

This became the opening scene of a drama that would extend into the next decade. This time the mission remained firmly in the background as the national church navigated some murky waters. Part of the moneymaking plan involved selling off small parcels of the land surrounding the tabernacle, and this became incredibly complex. At one point, an INELA leader was jailed for corruption as he had sold and then resold the same plots for personal profit. Not until 1979 did the national church concede that a rebuilding of the tabernacle was not going to happen. The representatives voted to reserve ten lots for the local church and sell off the rest of the property to pastors of the INELA.[90]

Another major conflict involved church property in an area of La Paz called Calacoto. Originally this had been rural property, but as the city grew this particular area rose in value. Being at a lower altitude, it became prime real estate for the middle and upper classes. The mission had contributed toward the original purchase and later transferred the title to the INELA. But, as in so many cases, the official papers were not entirely legal and the ensuing battles over this particular property went on for years and involved corruption, injustice, and even jail sentences for INELA leaders.[91] The mission contributed to the legal expenses in the early 1970s, but left the handling of the case to the INELA. Not wanting to let go, the church carried the battle on into the next decade.[92]

90. *Actas de la Junta Anual*, 1966–1981, January 1979, INELA archives.

91. For example, in 1970 INELA president Antonio Mamani was jailed as a representative of the church. Eugene Comfort, letter to NWYM, December 14, 1970, NWYM/GFU archives.

92. For backgroup details on the Calacoto property conflict, see Harold Thomas, letter to NWYM, November 16, 1976, NWYM/GFU archives.

The Aymara Hymnal Dispute

We have seen that since the early years of the work, believers worshiped in their own Aymara language. Juan Ayllón began the work on what would become the official INELA hymnal as he translated favorite hymns from Spanish into Aymara. (Some of these had been first written in German, then translated into English, and from the English into Spanish.) This translation work continued through others as a body of hymns became available to the church. Early versions of the hymnal were diglot, including both Spanish and Aymara versions of the hymns on facing pages.

In the 1940s and 1950s, with the encouragement of CALA (the Commission on Aymara Literature and Literacy, a Wycliffe supported organization), the movement to produce original Aymara hymns, using Aymara music, added a richness to the hymnal. Various Friends artists participated in this effort. Both the mission and the national church supported the work of CALA by serving on its board of directors. CALA's own hymnal of entirely indigenous Aymara music became a great favorite in rural churches.[93] Urban churches often preferred the Spanish option.

For many years the mission's contribution was the republishing of the INELA hymnal. Gains made from a subsidized sale of the hymnals went back into a fund for the next edition. The INELA hymnal served as an aid to worship and as a unifying tool for the whole church. The popular hymnal was also made available to other national churches and enjoyed good sales. The reprints were a continuing item of business for the mission council.

Early in the 1970s the mission decided to do more than reprint the hymnal. They decided it was time for a revision of the older Aymara translations. This was partly at the suggestion of Carmelo Aspi, himself a gifted musician and writer. So the mission decided to cooperate with Aspi, paying him a stipend for his work.

The mission released the revised hymnal in 1974, and controversy immediately ensued. The conflict was not just between the mission and the INELA, but also between the conservative and more forward-looking members of the national church herself.

In their January 1975 meeting, the *mesa directiva* listened to the concerns of Julio Kuno, an INELA member who was leading a faction of protesters. He presented his case for the divine inspiration of the old hymnal. Kuno began by attacking the CALA hymnal of indigenous music, stating that "this hymnal does not have God's inspiration because the music and the words are very cold. The music is 75% worldly and one can dance to it. The words are superficial, saying nothing of sin or holiness." He went on to state that the new revised INELA hymnal "doesn't contain right doctrine ['knowledge']. It lacks blessing because of its forced and liberal translations and because it's

---

93. For the history of CALA's contribution to an Aymara hymnody, see CALA, *Breve historia*.

been mixed with CALA hymns."[94] (In 1979, Kuno would be disowned by the INELA for heresy.)[95]

The *mesa* responded positively, noting in the minutes that "the exposition of brother Kuno was accepted as a good observation, wholesome and edifying. We were reminded that we need to carry out the 1974 decision of the representatives to reprint the new edition but also to recuperate the older version."[96] Ironically, Carmelo Aspi was serving as the newly appointed president of the national church, and as a result of this discussion, he presented his resignation in the same meeting. It was not accepted. In their March meeting, the *mesa* decided to completely support the older version.[97] In the meantime, different unauthorized leaders were stirring up the controversy among the churches, preaching against both the CALA hymnal and the newly revised INELA hymnal.[98]

The mission decided to hold steady with its plans to support the new version, having received testimony as to its linguistic superiority. The council rejected a request by the *mesa* to reprint the older version, and reported that the new hymnal was selling well among the churches, despite the controversy.[99]

In 1975 the mission acknowledged that the problem was not going away and decided to be flexible with the next revision, due that very year because of strong sales of the 1974 reprint. Council decided to change a few of the old favorites back to the original translation, but to keep most of the revisions in light of all the newer believers in Peru and Bolivia who were now familiar with these.[100] Actual changes made to the seventh edition (1975) were minimal.

In 1978, Tina Knight wrote home describing how one of the UFINELA leaders had disrupted the annual women's conference, giving some background into her mind-set:

> Gregoria is sure that God gave her a vision one morning at 4 a.m. and told her to go thru' out the churches to warn them against using the new edition of the hymn book, the new edition of the Aymara N.T., and the new choruses and songs sung to Aymara tunes. . . . She goes around to the churches saying this or that is of Satan. . . . She spoke of a vision and of angels. . . . She said that she remembered Doña Julia [Pearson] placing her hymnal in her Bible and saying that these two books were sacred and that we weren't to use anything else.[101]

94. *Actas de la mesa directiva, 1974–1977*, January 6, 1975, INELA archives.

95. BMC Minutes, February 27, 1979, NWYM/GFU archives.

96. *Actas de la mesa directiva, 1974–1977*, January 6, 1975, INELA archives.

97. *Actas de la mesa directiva, 1974–1977*, March 31, 1975, INELA archives.

98. *Actas de la mesa directiva, 1974–1977*, June 30, 1975, INELA archives.

99. *Actas de la mesa directiva, 1974–1977*, June 30, 1975, INELA archives.

100. BMC Minutes, April 8, 1975, NWYM/GFU archives.

101. Tina Knight, letter to NWYM, September 1978, NWYM/GFU archives.

The controversy continued through the decade, with the *mesa directiva* reporting in 1978 ten thousand pirated copies of the old version (produced by several denominations) available to tempt believers to buy them illegally.[102] Hal Thomas wrote home to the Board of Missions, explaining the seriousness of the situation, noting that "the idea of two official hymnals, or freedom to select a hymnal, is completely strange to them [the church leaders]. The hymnal is to them one of the identifying marks of the INELA. . . . Pray with us that such a small issue won't split the churches, especially in the La Paz Quarterly Meeting."[103]

This controversy demonstrated tensions within a basically conservative church that was growing and incorporating new elements and new perspectives.

OTHER CRISIS POINTS

Many other smaller crisis points occupied the leaders of the church, including false teaching and various moral disciplinary issues. Temptations to sexual transgression and mishandling of funds kept cropping up. The *mesa directiva* dealt with such matters, sometimes in consultation with the mission, but more often on their own. In one of his mission council cover letters in 1975, Ron Stansell noted that "the Mesa Directiva is involved in a couple of difficult disciplinary measures and we're doing our best to support them in prayer and encouragement, but keeping our noses out."[104]

Negotiations over Transportation

For the mission, one of the stickiest problems of the decade concerned their service of transportation to the national church. During the 1960s, the mission continued its policy of pulling back from active ministry in the churches, wanting to encourage national leadership. At the same time the wide-flung network of churches to be visited and discipled, plus the economic hardships of the times, caused the mission to increasingly take up the role of chauffeur, especially on the weekends as the missionaries drove national leaders and teams to quarterly meetings, district conferences, evangelistic campaigns, and other ministry opportunities.

A regular item of mission council minutes during the decade of the 1970s was a long list of trips each male missionary had taken that month. The list was impressive (as well as oppressive). For example, in July 1974, between them, Mark Roberts and Hal Thomas made six quarterly meeting trips and four extension Bible school trips, transported leaders to a pastors' short course, and drove on four other occasions.[105] Many of these were weekend trips, some going from Thursday through Sunday evening. From time to time, a missionary would be invited to teach a class or preach, but

---

102. Harold Thomas, letter to NWYM, July 4, 1978, NWYM/GFU archives.
103. Harold Thomas, letter to NWYM, July 4, 1978, NWYM/GFU archives.
104. Ron Stansell, letter to NWYM, September 11, 1975, NWYM/GFU archives.
105. BMC Minutes, August 1, 1974, NWYM/GFU archives.

their main task was transportation. The transportation fund soon became the largest item in the mission's annual ministry budget.

Hal Thomas and believers on a ministry trip (H. Thomas)

This began to be a frequent topic of discussion in mission council meetings and *mesa directiva* meetings, with both groups considering possibilities for a new arrangement. Different experiments were tried, including a transportation fund given to the *mesa directiva* for them to handle, without missionary chauffeurs involved. The mission designated that this was to go for evangelistic or educational trips, not administration or church maintenance. This arrangement proved less than satisfactory. Ron Stansell discussed this in a letter to the board in 1975:

> Regarding the national transportation fund, we'll continue to muddle through best we know and don't really have any clarity of leading what we think should be done. Basically it's the old tension between indigenous policy and worthy and profitable use of money—subsidies, if you please—that does appear to further church growth. We want to help evangelize, but we don't want the church to grow up thinking they cannot evangelize without our money! . . . If we saw exactly eye to eye on how to use the funds, there would be no problem, but we do not want them responsible to report to us, yet we do not feel it wise policy to be subsidizing the INELA for administration and maintenance items. Clear as mud? In the meantime, we're loving each other and finding relations going fine.[106]

106. Ron Stansell, letter to NWYM, September 11, 1975, NWYM/GFU archives.

Even with the fund to enable the national leaders to travel without missionary presence (sometime in a mission vehicle), the missionary travel load continued heavy throughout the decade. Not all missionaries saw this as negative, however, and all appreciated the chances to develop relationships while on the road. In 1977 new missionary Gil George offered this six-month evaluation of the missionary/national church relationship in regards to travel:

> My role to this point has been almost exclusively travel. Quarterly meetings, evangelistic trips, youth conferences, women's conferences, all the pastor's *cursillos*, and assorted other trips for discipline, church visits, etc. I am personally convinced that the trips are not only necessary but are among the most important ministries we offer. And by that I mean even aside from the opportunities to preach or teach. . . .
>
> We found in answering Quentin's priority questions at retreat that we had very little idea of what the MD was thinking as far as their own priorities and goals were concerned, yet one thing was clear to us all: the MD thought that our top priority ought to be trips. It is strange to me that that which the MD sees as being very important for us to do is our lowest priority. No one wants to be just a taxi driver. Myself least of all, but there is far more involved than driving and sitting through a conference. There is tremendous opportunity for ministry on a much more personal level than in a classroom or behind a pulpit. . . . The pickup is a counselling room on wheels; a pulpit and classroom combined. It is the best opportunity I see for really influencing the church through its leaders.[107]

This particular situation and the discussions it engendered among missionaries and with the national leaders would continue into the decade of the 1980s, with some notable developments.

INELA/Mission Cooperative Outreach

While the mission council accepted George's perspective as valid, recognizing the value in the quiet accompaniment that took place through the service of transporting national leaders, the search for a more proactive form of ministry according to priorities continued. In the annual mission field report for the 1977/78 year, council chairman Ron Stansell wrote, "Both the Mesa Directiva and mission need to carefully avoid locking themselves into too much maintenance church work at the expense of new evangelistic groundbreaking. The Quarterly Meeting and local leadership do a certain amount of evangelism and establishing of new works, but the mission council is concerned that the mission and the Mesa Directiva of the INELA keep setting the example in evangelistic concern."[108]

---

107. Gil George, letter to NWYM, February 15, 1977, NWYM/GFU archives.
108. Ron Stansell, letter to NWYM, August 1978, NWYM/GFU archives.

In 1979 the mission council presented a proposal to the national church representatives that had one missionary family cooperating with national leaders in a focus on outreach in a particular geographic area, while another missionary would continue with the current schedule of trips to quarterly meetings and conferences. The church accepted the plan, and Hal Thomas was named to work in the Ancoraimes/Camata area north of Lake Titicaca, while James Roberts served as chauffeur to the *mesa directiva*. The Villa San Antonio church in La Paz, under the pastoral leadership of Humberto Gutiérrez, had adopted the Camata area for their own mission outreach, partly based on the fact that Gutiérrez had served as national missionary there previously. The church had already begun traveling and ministering in the area. Council minutes note that "Hal, Nancy, Humberto Gutierrez and a few others traveled to the Camata area last weekend to visit churches and explore the church planting possibilities. After a leadership training course in late February, Thomases and a team of nationals will concentrate in this area for three months."[109] Thomases would partner with the local Villa San Antonio congregation, under the leadership of Gutiérrez.

In mid-1979, Ron Stansell wrote to the board that the work in Camata was proving fruitful, but that more time was needed:

> To this point this church-planting "experiment" has been quite successful. Four congregations are meeting regularly in the area, and while only one of those is new in the last year, the other three have been considerably strengthened and a number of other contact points where there are believers have been nurtured. The objective as spelled out by the Mesa Directiva is to build this together as a new Quarterly Meeting. Thomases feel we are about half way along toward that goal, and should encourage the MD to continue with this area for the present.[110]

The mission council and the *mesa directiva* agreed to extend the time Thomases would cooperate in this venture. In November 1979 the INELA formed the Lago Norte District, with six congregations.[111] It was recognized in the 1980 representatives meeting.

This cooperation in outreach between the mission and the INELA would continue into the decade of the 1980s, with the INELA taking the leadership role.

OTHER ACTIVITIES OF THE MISSION

In two other areas the mission invested time and resources, apart from any cooperation with the INELA. These ministries would potentially affect the national church, but the mission felt free to take the initiative and work apart from its relationship

---

109. BMC Minutes, February 27, 1979, NWYM/GFU archives.
110. Ron Stansell, letter to NWYM, June 2, 1979, NWYM/GFU archives.
111. BMC Minutes, November 26, 1979, NWYM/GFU archives.

with the church. These were in the areas of Bible translation and national evangelistic campaigns.

Since the days of Carroll Tamplin and Juan Ayllón, the mission had a tradition of involvement with translations of the Bible into the Aymara language. In the 1970s, the United Bible Society invited Ron Stansell, and later, Hal Thomas, to become part of the team to translate the Old Testament into Aymara. Ron and Hal would alternate their times of service to this project, acting as biblical exegetes or cultural consultants, with different Aymara Christians doing the base translation. INELA leader Francisco Mamani had by this time become an employee of the Bolivian Bible Society, and he led the team in this project that would require the missionary's active presence one to two mornings a week for some seven years. It was a significant, but quiet, contribution. The new translation, a complete Bible in Aymara, would be presented to the community in the mid-1980s.

Hal Thomas lead in another initiative, that of encouraging participation in the interdenominational evangelistic campaign under visiting evangelist Luis Palau. The INELA, along with other Protestant denominations in La Paz was invited to participate in the planning phase during 1977. Francisco Tintaya represented the INELA. Due to cultural differences, the *mestizo* leaders of the planning committee inadvertently insulted Tintaya, as well as other Aymara leaders, and the INELA officially decided not to cooperate. Thomas gave some cultural orientation to the committee, but the damage had been done.

Yet the forward-looking youth of three INELA churches in the city wanted to participate with Thomas in the campaign. In a letter home, Thomas promoted the value of this level of interdenominational cooperation: "At this point in time there is more cooperation and good feeling among the churches of La Paz and interdenominationally than I have ever seen, and the middle-class population is ripe for harvesting and church-planting."[112]

The results of the citywide week of meetings were impressive with 10,756 total conversions reported, mostly among people under twenty. The Friends Church on Max Paredes Street was assigned the names of 439 people with whom to follow up, with the Villa San Antonio church receiving between two hundred and three hundred names.[113] Pre-campaign strategy had included follow-up techniques meant to lead to an increase of membership in local churches all over the city. Yet in the following months, actual church growth in the INELA as a result of the campaign was not significant. This underscored, among other things, the difficulty of working across social class and cultural barriers among the Bolivian population. Eventually the mission council would conclude that mass evangelistic campaigns were not a strategy they should follow. But the campaign did make it clear how open the youth of the city were becoming, and this included young adults from an Aymara background.

112. Harold Thomas, letter to NWYM, October 11, 1978, NWYM/GFU archives.
113. Harold Thomas, letter to NWYM, October 25, 1978, NWYM/GFU archives.

CHURCH AND MISSION AT THE END OF THE DECADE

As mentioned at the beginning of this chapter, the decade of the 1970s proved to be one of growth, with the church expanding from around one hundred churches in six districts to approximately 165 churches in eight districts by the beginning of 1980. New ministries in leadership formation, along with a growing missionary vision highlighted the work of the Spirit, in spite of the very real struggles toward maturity and the difficult changing relationship with the mission.

Yet in his annual field report for 1979, council president Hal Thomas noted that for the last several years of the decade, growth of the church had actually plateaued.[114] He suggested the following reasons: communication problems with a geographically spread out church, transportation bottlenecks, administrative problems, leadership training problems, and uncertainty about Quaker doctrinal positions (especially the sacraments and worship on Sunday, under the influence of other denominations). Thomas also noted the challenges of a rapidly urbanizing and increasing youthful population.[115] The moral failure of various leaders also contributed to the plateauing of the church. All of these would require serious strategic refocusing. And prayer.

REFLECTIONS ON THE DECADE

As stated in the introduction, the work of the church in the decade of the 1970s was to establish its own identity. An important aspect of this was the need for the church to primarily reflect its Aymara culture, and not the culture of the mission or even of the Friends. An example of how this happened (or didn't happen) comes out in the controversy over the 1974 revision of the INELA hymnal. Artistic expressions, such as music, are close to the heart of a culture. The mission apparently assumed that opposition to the revised Aymara translations of the hymns came from the conservative nature of rural Aymara Christians, adverse to any change. This conservative clinging to tradition undoubtedly played a part. But it seems that a deeper reason, come to light in more recent investigation, was that Juan Ayllón's translations, from the 1920s and 1930s, were dynamic equivalent translations from the Spanish; these captured the meaning of the originals but expressed it in ways that sounded pleasing to the Aymara ear. People refer to the language in these older translated hymns as "sweet." Some claim that Carmelo Aspi, in his translations, followed a more literal method, and that the result sounded stilted and unpoetic in Aymara.[116]

For this reason, perhaps more than any other, the controversy went on for years. With the reprinting of the hymnal now entirely in the hands of the INELA, new revisions have included a mix of the older and newer translations of Spanish hymns. The

---

114. Harold Thomas, annual field report, 1979, NWYM/GFU archives.

115. Harold Thomas, letter to NWYM, January 31, 1980, NWYM/GFU archives.

116. Humberto Gutiérrez, David Mamani, and Félix Huarina, focus group, November 22, 2017, La Paz.

sixth edition, published in 2014, includes a restoration of all Juan Ayllón's old Aymara translations (twenty-six of them), and also includes six of Carmelo Aspi's translations, along with those of many others as the hymnal has expanded.

One of the most interesting missiological conundrums of the decade was the struggle of the mission to balance its commitment to indigenization, walking behind as the national church assumed leadership, with its commitment to follow the leading of the Spirit, even when this meant taking the initiative, sometimes in opposition to the wishes of the INELA. Sponsoring the Aspi revision of the hymnal may provide an example of when the mission should have backed down in sensitivity to national sentiment. But mission initiative in the extension Bible school (TEE), the San Pablo Seminary, and more active participation in outreach exemplify obedient response to what the missionaries sensed as the leading of the Spirit. That some of these programs did not ever become "owned" by the national church, in spite of their strengths, shows the complexity of the indigenous goal.

Perhaps the most "Quakerly" thing that happened to the church in the 1970s was the recognition of the INELA as an official yearly meeting, according to the custom of Friends around the world. That the leadership of the INELA had no idea of its significance is not surprising as their contacts up to that point had been limited. Perhaps the mission should have done more to educate the church and helped them celebrate the recognition.

We can discern the movement of the Spirit of God during the 1970s in the very struggles of the INELA to grow into its own identity. God was calling to himself a people among the Aymara population of Bolivia, and the process of becoming the church in this particular place was not easy. We see the church stretching toward maturity in the formation of its own national missionary society and in its growing consciousness of the social aspects of the gospel. We sense the movement of the Spirit in persons of deep commitment and a willingness to sacrifice, persons such as Mario Surco, Humberto Gutiérrez, Pacual Quispe, Francisco Tintaya, David Tintaya, and Carmelo Aspi. Little by little the INELA was coming into its own as the people of God and a part of the family of Friends.

We sense the Spirit moving in the struggles of the Friends mission as people responded to God's call to the work of facilitating the development of a mature and independent INELA. That both the mission and the national church persisted through the struggles and misunderstandings is further testimony to the fact that something more than the construction of a religious organization was going on. God was building a people, a church, on the high planes and lowland valleys of Bolivia.

8

Broadening Contacts and Perspectives

INELA in the Decade of the 1980s

As the INELA entered the decade of the 1980s, the clash between military and civilian politicians continued to rock the nation. The INELA faced its own challenges as disappointment at the failure of its first organized national missionary society was balanced by a growing social consciousness. Events in the 1980s would offer challenges to both the social and evangelistic ministries of Bolivian Quakers.

HISTORICAL OVERVIEW

If the 1960s and 1970s were marked by military regimes, the decade of the 1980s is recognized as the beginning of Bolivia's experiments with democracy under a multiparty political system. For a couple of years the political chaos of the late 1970s continued, but in September 1982, the congress chose as the new president, Hernán Siles Zuazo, one of the old MNR politicians, thus bringing to an end eighteen years of authoritarian military rule.

For the rest of the decade presidents served their full terms, with new elections held on a regular basis. The multiplication of political parties added to the complexities of democracy, and each election seemed to have a balance of candidates from the right, the center, and the left. These included an indigenous party, the *Movimiento Revolucionario Tupac Katari*, whose development hinted at the direction the country would go in future decades.

The economy Siles Zuazo inherited in 1982 was in ruins. Added to the declining price of tin, agricultural production suffered under the effects of the El Niño currents, causing drought on the *altiplano*, followed by flooding in different areas of the country.

Siles Zuazo's answer was to print more money, a practice begun as early as 1980 by former politicians. "Between 1980 and 1984, the total stock of money in circulation increased by over 1000 percent. Prices were quickly affected, and by May 1984, Bolivia was experiencing hyperinflation with rates of price increases of over 50 percent per month."[1] By 1985, the inflation rate was a stunning 8,170 yearly percent,[2] the highest in the world since pre-World War II Germany.

The 1985 elections brought in Victor Paz Estenssoro, now seventy-seven years old, for a fourth term as president. According to Klein, "To the surprise of both enemies and friends, this seeming relic of a past era proved to be the most dynamic and able civilian politician to rule in the last decades of the twentieth century."[3] His most important act was the radical New Economic Plan, an attempt to confront runaway inflation, huge national debt, and the overall economic stress of the population. The act devalued the currency, freed exchange rates from government control, along with price and wage controls, and placed severe limitations on government spending, including reduction of government employee wages. While such drastic measures were probably necessary, these resulted in growing unemployment and "increased social misery."[4] The collapse of the tin market in 1985 and the rising parallel coca economy added to the multiple tensions. The so-called "Drug War" began to define the uneasy relationship between Bolivia and the United States.

The economic struggles of the decade impacted the constituency of the INELA more than the political upheavals. It was the lower social classes, including the indigenous populations, that were most affected. As Aymara Friends believers on the *altiplano* and in the semitropical valleys struggled for survival, leaders in the organization were increasingly conscious of the social dimensions of the gospel and attempted to address these in their programs and ministries. They worked with the mission in these areas, as well as with different Quaker organizations around the world known for their humanitarian efforts. It was a decade of broadening contacts. At the same time, both the INELA and the mission struggled to maintain the evangelical emphasis on expanding the church in new areas, including the growing urban populations.

INELA AND THE MISSION IN THE DECADE OF THE 1980S

Representatives in the January 1980 annual meeting recognized Lago Norte as the eighth district of the national church, a result of the joint evangelistic/discipleship effort of the church and the mission. Leaders reported between 161 and 170[5] congregations throughout the field. The various educational programs of the church were moving forward, with 583 grade school students in sixteen centers, and a combined

---

1. Klein, *Concise History*, loc. 4329.

2. Klein, *Concise History*, loc. 4334.

3. Klein, *Concise History*, locs. 4372–77.

4. Klein, *Concise History*, loc. 4415.

5. The president reported 161 congregations, while the mission in their field report gave the number as 170 (annual field report, 1980, NWYM/GFU archives).

number of over one hundred theology students studying in Patmos Bible School (residence and extension centers) and the San Pablo Seminary.[6]

The failure of the national missionary society was somewhat offset by the opening of the medical clinic in 1979, under the supervision of the secretary of social action (formerly known as the secretary of health).

Key leaders throughout the decade of the 1980s included those elected to the role of president of the INELA: Francisco Tintaya (1976–1981), Pascual Quispe (1982–1984), Humberto Gutiérrez (1985), Venancio Quispe (1986), and Francisco Mamani (1987–1989). The service of several missionaries would span the decade: Ron and Carolyn Stansell (1980–1985), Hal and Nancy Thomas (1980–1989), and James and Gail Roberts (1980–1988). Others would make significant shorter-term contributions: Randy and Mary Morse (1981–1982), Dwaine and Becky Williams (1985–1988), Steve and Janelle Baron (1985–1987), Roscoe and Tina Knight (1988, 1989), Wayne and Bev Chapman (1988–1989), and Ed and Marie Cammack (1989).

ADMINISTRATIVE DEVELOPMENT

During the decade of the 1980s, the *mesa directiva* made a gradual attempt to decentralize, encouraging the districts and local churches to handle their own ministries and solve their own problems.[7] *Mesa directiva* minutes for the decade deal much less than previously with local church issues.

Another step forward in decentralization came in the emphasis on the commissions under each secretary on the *mesa directiva*. By 1985, the working committees at the national level included an administrative committee, a finance committee, an *Estatutos* revision committee, and committees under the secretaries of education, evangelism, social action, and literature.[8] The districts also had their secretaries of education, evangelism, and so on.

While the naming of committees was an attempt to widen the base of leadership participation, their actual functioning was often problematic, with confusion over authority and competition between ministries. This needs to be understood in light of the political and economic chaos in the country at large, which included corruption in high places. People were more distrustful of political leaders than ever, and it is not to be surprised that this atmosphere of suspicion would exist within the church.

A look at the representatives meeting of January 1982 illustrates this. At this time, Francisco Tintaya came to the end of his six-year presidency under a cloud, caused partially by the mismanagement of a former INELA leader who had been

6. The secretary of education reported thirty students in Patmos residency, fifty-three in the extension centers, and twenty-four INELA students in San Pablo for the 1979 school year (annual report of secretary of education, January 1980, INELA archives).

7. James Roberts, letter to NWYM, July 1984, NWYM/GFU archives; *Actas de la Junta Anual*, 1981–1993, January 1985, INELA archives.

8. *Actas de la Junta Anual*, 1981–1993, January 1985, INELA archives.

given the task of selling lots on the old tabernacle property.[9] The funds were then to be disbursed among the districts. Districts leaders were asking where the money was; all of this was compounded by the high levels of inflation.[10] As president of the INELA during the time when the money somehow disappeared, Tintaya was forced to take on much of the blame. The discussion during the meetings was loud and controversial, and criticism hounded Tintaya for several years, leading to a breakdown in his health.[11]

Other controversies dominated the 1982 representatives meeting. Financial insecurity seemed to make everyone nervous. It was announced that the medical clinic would be closed, with the doctors accusing the clinic director of poor administration and financial mismanagement. Controversy circled the management of the fund designated for reprinting the hymnal. The literature committee, newly formed the year before, complained that the *mesa directiva* had not turned over the funds they needed to operate, and the whole committee resigned. The committee for the revision of the *Estatutos* also resigned, for similar reasons, as did the president of the national youth organization (UJELAB).

In contrast and during this same time, the *mesa directiva* showed administrative maturity in their handling of the transportation issues that had so plagued them in the previous decade. Early in 1982, the mission turned over one of their vehicles, a 1979 Toyota jeep, to the *mesa directiva* for use in their travel, along with an amount of $75 a month for the first half of the year. Later that year, upon seeing the progress the church was making in managing the use and upkeep of the vehicle, the mission replaced the '79 vehicle with a new 1982 Toyota pickup, and an agreement to help train drivers and cover insurance costs for the next year. The offering for the purchase came from the Friends Youth of NWYM.[12]

The presidencies of Francisco Tintaya (1976–1981) and Pascual Quispe (1982–1984) gave a certain stability to the INELA, even while they lacked in vision for outreach. This lack of vision partly stemmed from the sheer demand for survival which most Bolivians felt during these years. The years 1985 and 1986 rocked the boat with two short-lived presidencies. Humberto Gutiérrez (1985) represented the younger generation. He was a dynamic leader and had made contributions as a national missionary in the 1970s and as the INELA's first secretary of health, also during that decade. But he was a first-generation Quaker, raised and educated in the city, and

---

9. Arturo Tito, the leader in question, was later apprehended and jailed. In 1987 he confessed and asked pardon of the *mesa directiva*, handing over all the legal documents in his possession (NWYM Mission Council Minutes, May 6, 1987, NWYM/GFU archives). The money was never recovered, partly due to the wildly fluctuating inflation the first half of the decade.

10. *Actas de la Junta Anual*, 1981–1993, January 1982, INELA archives.

11. In the following year's representatives meeting, Tintaya publicly apologized for the mismanagement (although not personally responsible) and promised to pay back the money that was lost (*Actas de la Junta Anual*, 1981–1993, January 1983, INELA archives). This he did over the next few years (interview with David Tintaya by Harold Thomas and Nancy Thomas, February 2016, Santa Cruz).

12. BMC Minutes, September 25–27, November 26, 1982, NWYM/GFU archives.

mistrust from the rest of the largely conservative, rurally formed leadership of the church created tensions that forced him to resign after a year. Gutiérrez was followed by Venancio Quispe (1986), a more traditional Aymara Quaker with a family background in the church, thus making him more acceptable to the majority of INELA Friends. However, the pressures of the office plus personal/family tragedies forced him to resign after only one year.

In their 1987 annual session, the representatives elected Francisco Mamani as INELA president, thus ushering in a three-year term of both stability and vision (1987–1989). Mamani represented the best of the two previous presidencies. He was a young, second-generation leader, and at the same time, he came from a rural family that had been part of the INELA almost from the beginning. His father, Antonio Mamani, had previously served as INELA president (1959–1960, 1966–1967, 1969–1970). Francisco Mamani had served as director of the Patmos Bible School (residency program) and as a local pastor. At the time of his election to the presidency, he was also working full time with the Bible Society, directing the project to translate the Old Testament into the Aymara language.

Mamani introduced and promoted a visionary three-year plan for evangelism, discipleship, and church planting for the whole field, in full cooperation with the mission. He switched the focus from social action projects back to evangelism, while at the same time encouraging the different social projects to continue.[13] This switch was possible due to the new economic and political stability in the country at large; survival was no longer the only priority.

Administratively, the INELA continued to form new districts as the church grew. As mentioned above, the Lago Norte District was named in January of 1980. In 1981, Santa Cruz became the ninth district. Santa Cruz presented a different scenario because the area was so far removed from the rest of the INELA and actually represented a different cultural grouping (although many of its members came from Aymara believers who had migrated to the lowlands). So Santa Cruz was named a "departmental district" (*departamento* being the Spanish equivalent of "state") to distinguish it from the other districts of the INELA which were located in the department of La Paz. During the rest of the decade, Santa Cruz developed its own *mesa directiva*, Bible institute, and annual representatives meeting, while maintaining a loose relationship with leadership in La Paz. This differentiation would eventually lead to conflict within the wider INELA organization.

Other new districts formed during the decade include the division of the Yungas District into the North Yungas and South Yungas Districts (1984), and the creation of the El Alto District (thus making a division between the lower city of La Paz and the upper city of El Alto), and the Altiplano Sud District, both in 1988. Thus, during the 1980s, the number of INELA districts grew from seven to twelve.

---

13. *Acta* of a called meeting, January 17, 1987, INELA archives.

BROADENING CONTACTS

The 1980s saw the INELA broaden its contacts with other churches and organizations, both within its borders and with other countries.

Contacts within the Country

Within Bolivia, the National Association of Bolivian Evangelicals (ANDEB) was founded in 1966, with the Friends Mission and the INELA both being founding members. But the INELA soon dropped out of ANDEB, partly because of the cost of membership and partly because its interests focused more on its own internal issues. But in 1980 the INELA requested a renewal of their membership and was accepted. This contact proved to be a part of the INELA's broadening perspectives. Membership in ANDEB proved helpful to the INELA in its response to the drought. For example, in 1983 ANDEB and the INELA worked together in twenty-one communities where Friends had a presence, in distributing seed potatoes and relief food supplies.[14]

Another interdenominational organization that the mission had been involved in was the Commission for Aymara Literature and Literacy (CALA). During the 1980s the INELA increased its contribution. Jesús Tórrez served as treasurer of the organization for a time,[15] and Salustiano Aspi became involved in both administration and in transcription of Sunday school materials. Eusebio Aspi served as an illustrator and Humberto Gutiérrez as a writer. Other INELA leaders, as well as missionaries,[16] became board members. More and more local churches were encouraged to use the materials for children, as well as the popular collection of original Aymara hymns.

The United Bible Society's translation project also provided a point of contact and interaction with the larger Christian church. As seen in the previous chapter, in the 1970s the Society had invited Ron Stansell and Hal Thomas to become part of the team as exegetes and biblical resource people in a new project to translate the Old Testament into Aymara. By the beginning of the 1980s Francisco Mamani had been promoted as director of the project. This was a major responsibility and he handled it well. In 1987, the Bolivian Bible Society publicly presented the gathered representatives of all denominations the first copy of the entire Bible in the Aymara language. Mamani was honored for his significant role in the project; at that time he was also serving as INELA president.

The mission and the national church joined in another major cooperative effort with other denominations in the founding of the *Universidad Evangélica Boliviana* (UEB, Bolivian Evangelical University) in the city of Santa Cruz. Both groups became

---

14. *Actas de la Junta Anual, 1981–1993*, January 1984, INELA archives.

15. *Actas de la Mesa Directiva, 1987–1990*, July 9, 1987, INELA archives.

16. Hal Thomas was CALA board president several terms in the 1980s and Nancy Thomas served as a consultant and trainer of writers.

part of the UEB's first board of trustees in 1980.[17] When the university officially opened in 1982, Javier Quispe, a Quaker from Santa Cruz, and Ron Stansell served on the faculty. In 1983 Stansell not only served on the board of trustees and taught theology classes, he also chaired the theology department. The UEB would go on to develop and serve the INELA as a resource for pastoral training, as well as a means for its young people to become professionals in many fields. The INELA, along with the mission, continued to be a part of the board of trustees.

The INELA also increased its contact with other Friends denominations in Bolivia, especially Central Friends and the Holiness Friends. This took place mainly through programs initiated by the supporting missions: participation in the extension Bible school teacher training workshops, the production of extension textbooks, and San Pablo Seminary.

International Contacts

Partly due to the physical and economic disasters of the decade, it was natural that the INELA would seek help from international sources, many of these Quaker organizations.

During 1982 five INELA leaders participated in workshops sponsored by World Relief on project development. At this stage the information about how to construct a project proposal proved especially helpful. In the INELA archives we found dozens of copies of form letters that Pascual Quispe sent out during his three-year presidency (1982–1984), presenting the needs of Bolivian Friends and requesting donations or the sponsorship of projects. These went out to organizations, Quaker and otherwise, Christian and otherwise, around the world. Some responded.[18]

One of the most significant outside Quaker contacts was with the Friends World Committee for Consultation (FWCC). As we saw in the last chapter, this contact began in the 1970s, and it would deepen during the 1980s. In early 1980 Francisco Mamani attended a meeting for Latin American Friends associated with FWCC. There in San José, Costa Rica, the Organizing Committee for Latin American Friends (COAL) was founded.[19]

In 1984 representatives in the January annual gathering approved requesting official membership in COAL. Their letter of request reported that "our greatest longing and desire is that all Friends always be united in the Lord so that we can help one another."[20] The *mesa* accompanied this letter with another that contained a list of

---

17. BMC Minutes, October 13, 1980, NWYM/GFU archives.

18. For example, the INELA archives contain copies of letters from Quispe to the Quaker UN lobby, Friends General Conference, the Quaker Council for European Affairs, Lutheran World Relief, Food for the Hungry, Heifer Project, World Neighbors, and numerous yearly meetings around the world.

19. BMC Minutes, February 25, 1980, NWYM/GFU archives.

20. INELA *mesa directiva*, letter to COAL, January 1, 1984, INELA archives.

eight projects, also approved by the representatives, that they hoped COAL would finance.[21]

COAL accepted the application for membership, and throughout the rest of the decade this organization would make significant financial contributions to the INE-LA. These contributions helped sponsor university training to assist young Quakers to become professionals (especially in the medical professions), relieve the effects of the drought and flooding, sponsor the medical clinic, handle administrative costs, and encourage inter-visitation among Quakers.[22] As a result of the help with inter-visitation, many Bolivian Friends traveled to COAL meetings, FWCC Triennial Conferences, and other gatherings.

The reception of this generosity did not come without its problems. Occasionally infighting concerning who got to travel took place, along with the pressure for those traveling to bring home money or new project agreements. And, even as the mission was slowly withdrawing its financial support in order to promote the development of an indigenous self-supporting church, the possibility of the INELA's forming new dependencies was ever present.

Overall, the INELA's contacts with the FWCC throughout the decade seemed to have a positive impact. In 1982 Humberto Gutiérrez and Patricio Medrano participated in the FWCC Triennial Conference in Kenya. They returned reporting "surprise" at liberal Friends, but stated that "they did not compromise their beliefs."[23] In 1984 the FWCC funded travel for several Bolivian young people to attend a world gathering of young Friends in North Carolina. As these young leaders reported back to the *mesa directiva*, Dionisio Aspi noted that he had been able to share the gospel with other Friends. Following the North Carolina conference, the same young people visited in the annual sessions of NWYM.

In January 1987 COAL held its annual business meeting in La Paz, just after the INELA's annual representatives meeting, at which FWCC representative Alex Morrisey spoke. Representatives from Mexico and Honduras, as well as Morrisey, along with the members of the INELA's *mesa directiva* met for several days to hear reports and plan for the coming year. In a report home, Hal Thomas made the following observations: "I was impressed with the high sense of participation our leaders exhibited in the COAL meetings. They consider the organization to be theirs. Although funding (this last year over $16,000) comes from FWCC, the COAL leaders decide the budget and administer the funds. Alex participated well in the meeting, but was careful that decisions were those of the representatives."[24] Thomas noted the positive projects COAL was promoting, with a focus on publications and inter-visitation. He also noted that INELA leaders were acting with maturity and responsibility and making their

21. INELA *mesa directiva*, letter to COAL, January 20, 1984, INELA archives.
22. Exact amounts of FWCC offerings would vary but averaged around $6,000 a year.
23. BMC Minutes, September 25, 1982, NWYM/GFU archives.
24. Harold Thomas, letter to NWYM, January 23, 1987, NWYM/GFU archives.

own contributions. He closed this section of his report by observing that "less our leaders are seeing COAL as a source for funding projects, and more as a way of relating to the wider family of Friends."[25]

Other Quaker organizations contributed financially to the INELA during the decade, including an offering from the evangelical Taiwan Friends Church in 1984. These distant Friends sent $2,000 to help with drought relief.[26] In 1989 a Quaker organization in New York state offered to fund science equipment for the Friends high school in the *altiplano* area of Villa Alicia.[27] These are but two examples.

In November 1987 the Evangelical Friends Alliance (EFA) sponsored an intercontinental conference on evangelism in Guatemala City. The INELA participated with fifteen delegates. The weeklong conference, conducted in both Spanish and English, increased the sense of family among evangelical Quakers throughout the Americas.[28]

In May 1989 the EFA invited Friends leaders from around the world to an organizational meeting in Houston, Texas. Francisco Mamani, INELA Bolivia president, and Constantino García, INELA Peru president, were among the delegates. The gathered representatives organized the new Evangelical Friends Church International (EFCI), a group that would prove to be a positive uniting force among Christian Quakers around the world in the coming years.

In addition to outside Quaker contacts, the INELA interacted with other Christian organizations during the 1980s. These included World Vision, World Relief, World Concern, Compassion International, and the Billy Graham Evangelistic Association. The INELA sent representatives to the Billy Graham–sponsored conference on evangelism in Amsterdam in 1986. Another group of leaders and pastors attended a continent-wide church growth conference in Buenos Aires in 1987.

Clearly the INELA's horizons were broadening as they realized their place as part of the larger Quaker and Christian movements.

OUTREACH AND DISCIPLESHIP

As noted above, up until 1987, the INELA focused more on internal administrative issues, relief from natural disasters, and development projects than on evangelism and outreach. Survival was understandably the priority.

Evangelistic Efforts of Congregations and Individuals

The fact of a lack of emphasis on the official denominational level does not mean that evangelism and efforts to plant new churches were not happening. The INELA continued to send the secretary of evangelism out to the districts on evangelistic campaigns,

25. Harold Thomas, letter to NWYM, January 23, 1987, NWYM/GFU archives.
26. BMC Minutes, October 5, 1984, NWYM/GFU archives.
27. Roscoe Knight, letter to NWYM, December 21, 1989, NWYM/GFU archives.
28. *Actas de la Mesa Directiva*, 1987–1990, December 7, 1987, INELA archives.

and new churches were reported at every representatives meeting (along with losses). In addition to these efforts, various congregations and individuals carried on evangelistic activities throughout the decade.

For example, Francisco Mamani, the pastor of the New Jerusalem Church in La Paz at the beginning of the decade,[29] had a clear gift of evangelism and a charismatic ability to inspire and mobilize people in his congregation. The church organized an evangelism society and, as members of this congregation had done in years past, began traveling out to unreached areas. They especially focused on the El Alto area of La Paz and a rural area to the south of the city. Both the secretary of evangelism of the *mesa directiva* and the mission offered to partner with this congregation in their outreach, seeing this as the leading of the Spirit.[30]

In addition to congregations reaching out in evangelism and church planting, some individuals also arose to follow this calling. One example was Gregorio Vargas. Vargas came from an *altiplano* community in the Cordillera District of INELA. He completed his ministerial training in the Patmos Bible Institute (residency program). In 1981 Vargas went to the village of Umanipampa-Tocotoconi in the Larecaja Province as the assigned public school teacher. This was an area on the *altiplano* north of La Paz, close to the INELA's Cordillera District. It was an area with no INELA churches or contacts.

Vargas had no official assignment within the INELA, but he had been trained as a pastor and had a strong call to evangelize. He called himself "a voluntary missionary." He writes of entering the village on a Thursday night and then going to his public reception the next day. He refused the alcoholic drinks the families offered him, according to custom, considering this as part of his Christian testimony. The following day he writes of leading one of the men of the town to an experience of Christian conversion, the beginning of the church in that village.[31]

Vargas attended to his school duties during the week, and on weekends he evangelized and discipled the new believers. He began visiting people in nearby villages also, with the same evangelistic zeal. He writes of people accepting Jesus as their Savior in family groups, of beginning to teach the new Christians every night in their homes, and slowly forming a church.

---

29. One of the two oldest congregations in the INELA, sometimes referred to as the La Paz Friends Church or the Max Paredes church, from the name of the street. Eventually the name was changed to the New Jerusalem Friends Church.

30. BMC Minutes, January 23–24, February 25, 1980, NWYM/GFU archives.

31. Gregorio Vargas, "Historia de la Iglesia," unpublished manuscript, n.d., INELA archives.

Gregorio Vargas (front row, far right) and the new church in Umanipampa-Tocotoconi
(G. Vargas)

In November 1981, the Friends Church in Umanipampa-Tocotoconi was formally organized, with the participation of INELA officials. Between 1981 and 1987, Vargas planted six Friends churches in the Larecaja Province, sometimes with the help of leaders from the Cordillera District, but mostly with only the cooperation of his wife and son. He continued supporting himself as a public school teacher.[32]

Gregorio Vargas serves as an example of men and women among Friends who followed the call of God outside of any officially named capacity in the church, since the beginnings of the INELA in the 1920s and 1930s. Many will remain unnamed in the history books, but their influence nurtured the church and contributed to its growth.

Combined Mission / National Church Evangelistic Efforts

As noted above, while the INELA as a denomination did not emphasize evangelism between 1980 and 1987, the mission continued with this as a priority, and they labored to include the church in a partnership which was often more one-sided. The work included continued efforts in the Santa Cruz Departmental District, in urban La Paz/El Alto, and in outreach to the Peruvian INELA.

SANTA CRUZ

The mission had made a priority of the Santa Cruz work, both in the city and in the outlying colonies. The families who served in this area in the 1980s, successively, were

32. Gregorio Vargas, "Iglesias fundadas," unpublished manuscript, n.d., INELA archives.

James and Gail Roberts, Ron and Carolyn Stansell, and Dwaine and Becky Williams, with missionary presence there until June 1988. Their assignments included encouraging the maturity of the main church in the city, working with local believers to begin other congregations in the city, training leaders through the Bible school program, participating in the Bolivian Evangelical University, and partnering with national evangelists and pastors to plant and nurture Friends churches in the jungle colonies.

The San Julian colonies seemed an open field to the mission, and evangelistic outreach, begun in the 1970s, continued into the decade of the 1980s. The annual mission field reports of 1981 and 1982 mention groups of new believers in three San Julian colonies.[33] In 1983 the mission decided that the best way to move forward in the colonies would be through the services of a national missionary/pastor, and in December of that year Pío Villca, a Patmos Bible Institute graduate and pastor from La Paz, moved with his family into one of the San Julian colonies. For the next two years he was active in pastoring the new groups and in evangelism and discipleship programs. The mission paid his salary.

Villca served as national missionary in San Julian for two years but left because of personal difficulties. He was replaced by Hilarion Aranda, a believer from the Caranavi Friends Church who had been living in San Julian. In the first six months of Aranda's ministry, three new groups of regularly meeting believers were established. Theological extension education centers had been set up in the colonies for leadership training,[34] as well as day schools for children in the colonies.

Friends day school in San Julian (NWYM)

33. Nancy Thomas, annual field report, 1980–1981; annual field report, 1981–1982, NWYM/GFU archives.

34. Dwaine Williams, annual field report for Santa Cruz, 1985–1986, NWYM/GFU archives.

But the work proved difficult, partly because of the constant turnover of people in each community, as some adjusted to life in the tropics, and others didn't. This made training a stable local leadership extremely difficult. Aranda resigned after only one year, and in April of 1987, Pascual Quispe, former *mesa directiva* president from the Caranavi District, stepped up as the next national missionary to San Julian.[35] He would remain there for the rest of his life. When Dwaine and Becky Williams retired in June 1988, the mission decided not to send any more mission personnel to Santa Cruz. The work would go forward in the city and the San Julian colonies under the administration of the national church, although mission funds continued for a time to underwrite the national missionary's salary.[36]

URBAN LA PAZ/EL ALTO

The mission's attempted cooperation with the INELA in urban church planting throughout the 1980s provides an enlightening case study in mission/national church relationships. In January 1980, the mission council approved cooperating with the New Jerusalem Church in La Paz in their evangelizing efforts in El Alto (upper La Paz).[37] The council also expressed concern for outreach to Spanish-speaking youth in the city, a controversial ministry that Francisco Mamani had begun with services in Spanish for these people. Some national leaders shared this concern and others were opposed.[38]

In 1984, the Department of Missions commissioned Hal and Nancy Thomas to dedicate their fourth term on the field to church planting in La Paz, with emphasis on the emerging middle class. The Thomases spent the year of 1984/85 sharing the vision of the project with INELA leaders, visiting existing churches, trying to raise consciousness of the situation of the rising Aymara middle class and the possibilities for work among them.

Because of illness, the Thomases returned to the Northwest in 1985. During that time, several members of the *mesa directiva* visited the NWYM's annual yearly meeting sessions. While there, they criticized the Thomases to the Department of Missions for deviating from their indigenous policy and working outside the authority of the *mesa directiva*. The initiative of the mission to begin a middle-class Spanish ministry threatened some of the more conservation leadership of the INELA. The department responded by instructing the Thomases to cooperate more with the program of the *mesa directiva*. This was probably a necessary corrective to the urban work, although one result was that it ended the attempt to reach the Spanish-speaking middle class.[39]

35. Dwaine Williams, annual field report for Santa Cruz, 1986–1987, NWYM/GFU archives.

36. BMC Minutes, November 2, 1986, NWYM/GFU archives. In 1999, the mission once again sent a family, Ed and Marie Cammack, to Santa Cruz.

37. BMC Minutes, January 23–24, 1980, NWYM/GFU archives.

38. BMC Minutes, September 10, 1980, NWYM/GFU archives.

39. Thomas and Thomas, Urban Church Ministry Report, June 1989, NWYM/GFU archives.

Under the direction of the Department of Missions and in submission to the INELA's *mesa directiva*, the Thomases returned to La Paz in 1986 and worked with the *mesa* to organize the Urban Commission for Church Growth. This group was composed of the *mesa directiva's* secretary of evangelism, officers of the La Paz District, all city pastors, and the Thomases, representing the mission. The group met weekly for over a year "to share concerns, pray for one another, and plan strategy for reaching the city. From this group came the series of discipleship books . . . thus meeting one of our goals. Perhaps one of the greatest values of this Commission was the personal encouragement and ministry the pastors received. The meetings were well attended."[40]

But the existence of the commission provoked more controversy among INELA leadership; some members of the La Paz District leadership felt threatened, and various leaders in the rural areas criticized the mission for discriminating against rural churches. So even though the meetings themselves were going well, the La Paz District officers disbanded the urban commission, leaving the mission without any vehicle by which to cooperate with the *mesa directiva* in planting city churches.

So the Thomases, with mission council consent, "decided that the only way we could proceed would be to quietly offer our services to any churches or individuals who had caught the vision."[41] The mission involvement with the new congregations varied in each situation, in some cases with more direct participation, and in other cases with encouragement to local leaders who were moving forward. The mission sponsored workshops on aspects of church growth, leadership, and intercessory prayer. The mission program of a matching fund to help with urban property purchase played an important role in the effort. As much as possible, the mission encouraged churches to use local resources such as the Bible school programs, the San Pablo Seminary, and available Friends literature.

The mission's cooperation in the urban church-planting project ended in 1989. The final report to the Department of Missions states that "throughout the five-year period [1985–1989], we have cooperated with different established churches in starting fourteen new groups. Eleven of these have become recognized dependent congregations."[42]

The Resurgence of Evangelistic Outreach as an INELA Priority

With the election of Francisco Mamani as INELA president in 1987, the national church shifted its sense of priority back to evangelism and church planting. This took place partly because of the political and historic changes in the country and the growing economic stability. But a large part of the change was undoubtedly due to the passion and character of the INELA's new leader, Francisco Mamani.

---

40. Thomas and Thomas, Urban Church Ministry Report, June 1989, NWYM/GFU archives.

41. Thomas and Thomas, Urban Church Ministry Report, June 1989, NWYM/GFU archives.

42. Thomas and Thomas, Urban Church Ministry Report, June 1989, NWYM/GFU archives.

We noted above that Mamani was a force behind the aggressive outreach of the New Jerusalem Friends Church in La Paz at the beginning of the decade. He brought the same perspectives and gifts to his leadership task as INELA president. The three years were carefully laid out with training goals to equip the churches for outreach. The hope was that by the end of the third year (1989), each congregation would have planted one new congregation. The mission cooperated by coordinating the production of the three discipleship booklets and by focusing its efforts in church planting in La Paz / El Alto and in the San Julián area of Santa Cruz.[43] For the next three years, this plan set the agenda for the INELA. A new atmosphere of vision and hope pervaded the church. While not meeting the optimistic goal of each church having planted a new church, the number of congregations grew by twenty-two during the three years of the program, from a reported 177 churches at the beginning of 1987[44] to some 199 at the end of 1989. The church had renewed its vision for outreach.

Evangelistic Outreach beyond Cultural and National Borders

In addition to evangelism within Bolivia, the INELA extended its missionary vision to other countries during the decade of the 1980s.

PERU

In May of 1980 the Bolivian and Peruvian expatriate missionaries met in a joint mission council meeting and minuted a suggestion that a Bolivian missionary be sent to Arequipa, Peru in a teaching or evangelistic capacity. The hope was that the Bolivian INELA would come to own this outreach and provide the financial support for the missionary.[45]

The Bolivian *mesa directiva* accepted the challenge and named Antonio Mamani (father of Francisco Mamani) as their missionary to Arequipa, taking an all-church offering for his support in early 1981.[46] But the arrangements for the program were not entirely satisfactory to the INELA, and later that same year, they sent their own fact-finding team, Humberto Gutiérrez and Sabino Chipana, to Arequipa to investigate possible missionary activity. They came back with a proposal for the NWYM mission to support an INELA missionary program, including salary and benefits similar to those received by North American missionaries. Antonio Mamani, meanwhile,

---

43. *Acta* of a called meeting, January 17, 1987, INELA archives.

44. Again, the statistics are problematical, with the mission council showing reported differences between 157 and 177 for 1987 (BMC Minutes, July 1987, NWYM/GFU archives). The *mesa directiva* report of churches for 1989 was 190, but these did not include the Santa Cruz District ("Datos Estadísticos," 1989, INELA archives). Mission Council included Santa Cruz for a count of 199 churches (BMC Minutes, July 1989, NWYM/GFU archives).

45. Joint Mission Council Minutes, May 17, 1980, NWYM/GFU archives.

46. BMC Minutes, March 3, 1981, NWYM/GFU archives.

resigned and came home.[47] The mission did not accept the new proposal, but the NWYM missionaries did sit down with the *mesa directiva* to listen to their input, and later minuted the following decision: "Arequipa still is important, and the mission is dedicated to evangelizing there. However, the question now has become, what does Bolivia see as its needs for outreach? Do they really feel a call to work in coastal Peruvian churches? How can the mission help the Bolivian Church in its outreach program? The Council agrees to listen carefully to their thinking on the issue. The Council desires to function along the lines of the MD's leading on outreach."[48]

In the following several years the idea of sending Bolivian missionaries to Peru was set aside, especially as the economic crisis and the drought claimed the attention of both national church and mission. But Bolivian leaders continued visiting Peruvian Friends, partly encouraged by the FWCC's funding of inter-visitation, and partly through the concerns of INELA leaders to be of help. By 1987, the missionaries and church leaders from both countries again began to explore the possibilities and make plans.[49] A minute from a joint mission council meeting in August notes that the Peruvian Friends are requesting a missionary from the Bolivian Friends but that the Bolivians are less than enthusiastic.[50]

The talks went forward, and in January 1988, Leonardo Tola presented to the Bolivian *mesa directiva* his calling to go to Peru as a missionary.[51] Tola, a Friends leader from an *altiplano* community near Jesús de Machaka, had graduated from both the Patmos Bible Institute (residency program) and San Pablo Seminary, as well as completing his high school education. For ten years he had been serving as a pastor and schoolteacher in the Yungas community of Arapata.[52] And now he was sensing a call to mission work.

The yearly meeting representatives commissioned Leonardo Tola and his wife, Delia Virginia, that same January 1988, and the couple arrived at their destination in Areuqipa in February. Tola was named pastor of one of the Arequipa churches that was struggling and given the role to encourage and teach in other congregations in Arequipa and the coastal towns of Tacna and Ilo.[53]

As part of the arrangement, the Tolas were to be supervised by the Peruvian *mesa directiva*, under a form of contract that the Peruvian church had set up, agreeing to give a certain monthly stipend to the family, as well as providing an apartment and ministry expenses. In September, Tola wrote home to the Bolivian *mesa directiva*, lamenting the rising cost of living in Peru (another case of runaway inflation) and

47. BMC Minutes, July 28, 1981, NWYM/GFU archives.

48. BMC Minutes, October 30, 1981, NWYM/GFU archives.

49. *Actas de la Mesa Directiva*, December 7, 1987, INELA archives.

50. Joint Mission Council Minutes, August 12, 1987, NWYM/GFU archives.

51. *Actas de la Mesa Directiva*, January 2, 1988, INELA archives.

52. Edwin Cammack, "Leonardo," *Keeping Current* (May 1988), NWYM/GFU archives.

53. Edwin Cammack, "Leonardo," *Keeping Current* (May 1988), NWYM/GFU archives.

complaining that the Peruvian church was subtracting ministry expenses from their small stipend, and that his family was suffering.[54]

The Bolivian *mesa* then contacted Ramón Mamani, the president of the Peruvian INELA, to try and resolve the situation. The Bolivian leaders also sent a letter to Tola to encourage him, not only in his economic trials, but with questions and suggestions about his missionary service to the Peruvian church.[55]

Benito Apaza, a second Bolivian missionary, joined the national missionary team in April 1988 and began serving with his wife and four daughters on the Peruvian *altiplano*.[56]

ARGENTINA

The INELA experience in outreach to Argentina in 1987 was initiated and promoted entirely by the national church.

In February 1987, the *mesa directiva* named five men to go to a church growth conference in Buenos Aires.[57] The conference was sponsored by the Korean Paul Yonggi Cho; Cho's growth method was being explored by the INELA's Commission for Urban Church Planting, and the men named were participants on the commission. The mission and the INELA, as well as the local churches of those being sent, together funded the trip.[58]

The conference encouraged the attenders, but what happened afterward was more significant. The Bolivians pastors had made contact with various Bolivian Friends who had immigrated to Buenos Aires, and on March 15 they celebrated with them and with others who had joined them in a worship service. Following that they organized the first Friends church in Argentina, with appointed leaders and instructions for regular meetings.[59]

After returning home to La Paz, three of those sent—Humberto Gutiérrez, Sabino Chipana, and Elías Mamani—developed a detailed proposal for a new mission work and presented it to the *mesa directiva* of the INELA in May 1987. The proposal presented objectives that included establishing a Friends church that would lead to other such churches in Argentina, and detailed methods that focused on the sending of a Bolivian missionary family under the administration of the INELA, with the participation and funding of Friends congregations in La Paz, the whole La Paz District,

54. Leonardo Tola, report, September 14, 1988, INELA archives.

55. INELA *mesa directiva*, letter to Ramón Mamani, November 12, 1988, INELA archives. Partly due to the problems the Tolas faced in Peru, including the lack of adequate support, after their return to Bolivia the couple split up and eventually divorced.

56. Ken and Tonya Comfort, "What Exactly Is a Missionary?," *Keeping Current* (November 1989), NWYM/GFU archives.

57. *Actas de la Mesa Directiva*, February 7, 1987, INELA archives.

58. BMC Minutes, March 3, 1987, NWYM/GFU archives.

59. "Project for a Missionary Work in Buenos Aires," May 1987, INELA archives.

the INELA, and the Northwest Yearly Meeting in the United States. The proposal also included a realistic budget based on cost of living in Buenos Aires.[60]

Both the mission and the INELA enthusiastically discussed the proposal throughout the rest of 1987, but there was no concrete response, and no new outreach effort was organized. Several reasons for this include the focus of the INELA on the three-year plan for evangelism and church growth within the country, the failure to name a specific committee or secretary within the INELA for carrying forward the discussion, and internal conflicts that included growing criticism of Humberto Gutiérrez, one of the project's key proponents, for not holding strictly to Friends doctrines.[61] These factors distracted from the proposal and interest gradually died out.

However, the contrast in the two missionary outreach proposals submitted by INELA leaders in the 1980s shows considerable growth in both insight and vision for mission work. It's fascinating that the same two leaders were involved in both proposals. Humberto Gutiérrez and Sabino Chipana had traveled to Arequipa in 1981, as we have seen above, and returned with a missions proposal that hinged on foreign funding. But the proposal they submitted for the work in Buenos Aires in 1987 shows Bolivian ownership and growth in insight as to the complexities of mission outreach as well as the possibilities for partnering in addressing those complexities.

The Friends congregation planted in Buenos Aires in 1987 continues to this day.

LEADERSHIP TRAINING

The leadership training programs established in the 1970s continued throughout the 1980s: the Patmos Bible Institute residency school under the direction of the INELA; the Patmos Extension Bible Institute under the joint direction of the INELA and the mission; and San Pablo Seminary under a board of cooperating missions.

All three programs had their ups and downs during the decade. The INELA appointed a director for the Patmos Bible Institute, which was still referred to as a "residency" program even though students no longer lived on campus and classes were held at night. Student enrollment was strong the first half of the decade, varying between twenty-four and thirty-eight students each year; only about half these students were from the INELA.[62]

---

60. "Project for a Missionary Work in Buenos Aires," May 1987, INELA archives.

61. *Actas de la Mesa Directiva*, February 6, 1988, INELA archives.

62. Statistics are problematical as different entities reported different numbers each year: The secretary of education made his annual report, as did the director of Patmos; these usually varied. The mission's annual field report often gave another number for the same year. Some of the variation comes from whether or not the figure factored in students who enrolled and then dropped out. These discrepancies in numbers of students also apply to those in the Bible school extension program, those in San Pablo Seminary, and those in the rural general education program. Nobody, except the missionaries, worried much about it.

In 1985, the residency program of Patmos took a downward turn, reporting only twelve students,[63] and for the rest of the decade this level of low attendance contrasted with the numbers of students in the extension Bible school and the San Pablo Seminary.

INELA students continued to take advantage of the opportunity to study theology at a higher level in the San Pablo Seminary. Overall attendance at the seminary grew from forty-nine students (twenty-four of whom were INELA) in 1980 to 120 in 1985.[64] A report made in 1983 showed that in the eleven years of the seminary's existence, over eighteen denominations had participated and of those, 41 percent of the students were from the INELA.[65]

The extension education branch of Patmos was felt by some INELA leaders to be a threat to the success of their preferred "residency" institute. The program grew during the decade, reaching a high point in 1984 with over 360 Friends students in twenty-seven centers.[66] From that date, enrollment dropped, and in 1989, fourteen extension Bible school centers were functioning.[67]

Extension center in Pacajes District, 1983 (NWYM)

63. *Actas de la Junta Anual*, 1981–1993, January 1986, INELA archives.

64. NWYM Minutes, 1980, 21; BMC annual field report, 1984–1985, NWYM/GFU archives.

65. Harold Thomas, report to INELA, January 1983, NWYM/GFU archives.

66. *Actas de la Junta Anual*, 1981–1993, January 1985, INELA archives; James Roberts, annual field report, 1985, NWYM/GFU archives.

67. Wayne Chapman, annual report on theological education, 1989, NWYM/GFU archives.

James Roberts took on the role of cooperation with the INELA in theological education from 1986 to 1988. Until the end of the decade, the mission assisted with extension centers in new districts, always hand in hand with national teachers.

Yet the tensions continued. In the annual field report of 1988, Hal Thomas observed, "After eighteen years with the TEE program, and many pastors trained through this method of education, we are aware that it is still the mission that provides the impulse for this part of the Bible school. We are the writers, we are the main teachers in teacher retreats, we are the promoters. In view of our mission purposes to work alongside the INELA, we are questioning whether this educational program can become indigenous."[68]

In 1988, Wayne and Bev Chapman moved over from Peru to spend a year on the mission staff in La Paz. At the request of the *mesa directiva* and with mission council approval, Wayne Chapman was named as director of Patmos Bible Institute, both the residency and extension programs. At the end of the year he also observed that the INELA "has very little interest in the [extension] program" and "very little participation in the [San Pablo] seminary program."[69]

GROWTH IN THE SOCIAL ASPECTS OF THE GOSPEL

The context of the 1980s encouraged the church to development in the area of its responsibility to the surrounding social, political, economic, and ecological reality. As we have already seen, the reality of the 1980s included significant political change from military dictatorship to democracy, runaway inflation, and natural disasters that went from drought to flooding. While the constituency of the INELA struggled for survival, the church could not help but look around and realize that the whole country had needs, needs that the church had a responsibility to address. This was especially felt by the youth and young adults in the church, people who were becoming increasingly restless for a more holistic ministry.

Schools

One way the national church had always reached out was in its system of primary schools, serving not only the children of believers, but the surrounding communities. The INELA school system continued throughout the decade. The program reached a high point in 1985 with nineteen schools and 859 students.[70]

A notable effort of the decade included the organization of Friends middle and high schools in the *altiplano* area of Villa Alicia and on El Alto, next to the local Friends church on the property that formerly belonged to the tabernacle.[71]

---

68. Harold Thomas, annual field report, 1987–1988, NWYM/GFU archives.

69. Wayne Chapman, annual report on theological education, 1989, NWYM/GFU archives.

70. *Actas de la Junta Anual*, 1981–1993, January 1986, INELA archives.

71. Raul Mamani, annual report of secretary of education, January 1987, INELA archives.

The Clinic

As noted above, the small medical clinic on the Max Paredes property in La Paz was forced to close in 1982 due to the economic crisis and poor administration. Although the country still struggled economically, the clinic reopened in July 1984, with Humberto Gutiérrez acting as director and employing two part-time doctors.[72] During 1985, the clinic added a laboratory and dental services.[73] Through the rest of the decade, donations from FWCC helped the clinic sustain its ministry. The end of the 1980s saw a stronger program with the part-time help of two doctors, several lab technicians, a dentist, a physical therapist, and an X-ray technician.[74] Dr. Lucio Moya, the director from 1987 through the end of the decade, efficiently administered the program, promoted ministries of health education in rural areas, and encouraged young Quaker men and women to become medical professionals.

Responses to Disasters

The most dramatic stories of the 1980s come from the INELA's and the mission's responses to the traumatic events of the decade, both political and economic.

RELIEF EFFORTS

As mentioned in an earlier section, both the mission and the INELA cooperated with other organizations in relief efforts addressing alternating droughts and flooding, with the resulting losses of crops, animals, and housing. International organizations, such as USAID, found working through religious groups a more reliable way of getting relief directly to the victims of disasters, and these groups included Friends. ANDEB, the national association of evangelicals, also coordinated with Friends and other groups in the distribution.

THE GREENHOUSE PROJECT

One of the most notable responses to the ecological crisis was the greenhouse project. The mission initiated the project in 1980 when Hal Thomas was named a member of an advisory committee for World Concern missionary Jon Wilson. Wilson, a young agronomist, specialized in greenhouse technology, and Thomas learned from him. After Wilson left Bolivia, the mission council decided to experiment further, building six greenhouses in different areas of the *altiplano* between 1982 and 1984, with the financial help of World Concern.[75]

---

72. *Actas de la Junta Anual*, 1981–1993, January 1985, INELA archives.

73. *Actas de la Junta Anual*, 1981–1993, January 1986, INELA archives.

74. Annual report of the secretary of social ministry, January 1990, INELA archives.

75. NWYM, Department of Missions, Task force paper on social development, January 1984, NWYM/GFU archives.

Several INELA leaders had been observing Wilson's work and were interested in pursuing the possibilities. They began by incorporating the project into the extension Bible school work in Pacajes, one of the areas most affected by the drought.[76] Thomas, various INELA leaders, and the students in the Pacajes extension center built two experimental greenhouses (and, as additional projects with the students, they dug a community well and vaccinated the llama and alpaca herds). Later, as the fruit of community development workshops with World Concern, INELA leaders wrote up their own greenhouse project proposal.[77]

In January 1984, the Department of Missions appointed a task force to consider the place of social development projects in light of the mission's priorities of evangelism and discipleship.[78] The task force affirmed, "We see the need of balance in our mission program, taking into account that the Aymara peoples are one of the poorest in Latin America. While we reaffirm that the main thrust of the mission should be its ministry in church planting and leadership training, we also see that ministering to the social and physical needs of people is also part of what it means to be the Church."[79] The task force recommended, among other things, that the mission board appoint a specialist in greenhouse technology to be part of the field staff for a term.

The Department of Missions acted quickly, and in December of that same year, 1984, Steve and Janelle Baron arrived in La Paz to begin their term of service. Steve, an agronomist, and Janelle, a nutritionist, came prepared professionally to undertake a new cross-cultural adventure.

In reporting home after his first few months on the job, Baron mentions the INELA leaders and how the team was working together:

> I've been impressed and encouraged by the interest and enthusiasm that the Aymaras have for this project. Félix Huarina, the coordinator for the project, has done a lot of thinking, planning, and physical work to get the project off the ground. Besides that, he has taken me on as his own "special project." Mateo Mamani is one of two men that will be trained to eventually take charge of the construction, maintenance, and operation of the greenhouses after we're gone. He has one greenhouse, already, out by Lake Titicaca and we are building the "experimental greenhouse" on his property in the upper part of La Paz. Policarpio Rodríguez will eventually control the purse strings for the project, but right now he is quietly helping us build, with enthusiasm, the adobe walls of our first greenhouse. Pasqual Quispe is the craftsman of the group. Having been the former president (superintendent) of the Yearly Meeting, he is able

76. BMC Minutes, July 17, 1982, NWYM/GFU archives.

77. BMC Minutes, January 22, 1983, NWYM/GFU archives.

78. Members of the task force were Hal and Nancy Thomas, home on furlough, Geraldine Willcuts, David Myton, and Gerald Dillon.

79. NWYM, Department of Missions, Task force paper on social development, January 1984, NWYM/GFU archives.

to contribute in many ways. He's had experience in agriculture and is a woodworker. All of these men, and others, have accepted me so well.[80]

The greenhouse project, 1980s (H. Thomas)

This style of teamwork with Bolivian Friends leaders would characterize the Barons' two years in Bolivia, as together they experimented with materials and design plans, and worked with the communities and churches who supplied the land, some of the materials, and the labor. The project included courses in greenhouse construction and gardening, as well as intensive family gardening techniques in the lower Yungas valleys, where greenhouses were not necessary, but agricultural improvements were. They also developed a manual so the project could carry on into the future. When the Barons left in early 1987, the national church planned to continue the project. The mission council turned over its greenhouse funds to the *mesa directiva* for the national church to administer, and this signaled the formal end of the mission's participation.[81]

The families that directly participated in the project were able to grow some vegetables and fruit during the time of draught. But because the only plastic available for the roofs did not last more than a year under the rays of the *altiplano* sun, the greenhouses built during that time did not last. Yet the technology presented was solid, including instructions on the rotation of plants for the improvement of the soil.

80. Steve Baron, "I Write Our First Official Contribution," *Keeping Current* (May 1985), NWYM/GFU archives.

81. BMC Minutes, March 3, 1987, NWYM/GFU archives.

A few years later, with the availability of a more durable plastic, many people not even related to the project were able to take advantage of this technology. It may be that the greatest long-term contribution of the project was the manual the Barons developed.

During the years of the project, although it was considered a cooperative effort by the church and the mission, the 1984 annual report of the secretary of social action reflected the perception that the church was assisting in a mission project.[82] After the Barons returned to Oregon, the energy seemed to leave the project. The attention of the INELA turned to other endeavors, cooperative ventures with other Quakers organizations involved in community development and willing to provide financial help.

SETALA

In the first half of 1983, various leaders who had participated in the community development workshops sponsored by World Relief and ANDEB formed a new INELA organization to help administer projects. They named it the *Sociedad Amigos Evangélicos para Tecnología Apropiada* (SETALA, Friends Evangelical Society for Appropriate Technology), with Julio Quispe, a young Quaker agronomist and engineer, as its first director.[83] The organization defined itself as "under the INELA with the purpose of discovering, adapting and adopting technologies and using these as means to design and propose projects in community development, faithful to the commandment to love our neighbor."[84]

One of SETALA's tasks was to raise funds from organizations around the world for their different projects. One of the first of these projects was the care and raising of guinea pigs as a food source, approved for funding by the Friends Mission in Guatemala and New England Yearly Meeting (1983). Through the rest of the 1980s, other projects were in the care of various animals, the setting up of small businesses such as bakeries, and projects in the areas of health and nutrition. Training workshops in veterinary medicine, through the sponsorship of World Concern, were especially appreciated. In the years from 1985 to 1989, FWCC alone divided its offerings to the INELA between the medical center ($4,010), SETALA projects ($3,522), university scholarships for professional formation ($2,988), and administrative costs ($880).[85]

Although under the umbrella of the INELA, it was not clear how SETALA would relate to the *mesa directiva*'s secretary of social ministries and his committee. It began apart from any *mesa* decision. As it turned out, coordination between the secretary of social action, as representative of the *mesa directiva*, and the director of SETALA worked well for most of its approximately ten-year history. However, the continual

---

82. Annual report of the secretary of social ministries, January 1984, INELA archives.

83. Letter from SETALA to INELA churches, July 20, 1983, INELA archives.

84. Letter from SETALA to BMC, March 20, 1984, INELA archives.

85. Report of FWCC contributions to INELA, July 4, 1990, INELA archives.

turnover of *mesa directiva* members and consequent lack of continuity became a problem, as we shall see in the next decade.[86]

Growing Awareness of a Holistic Gospel

The consciousness of the holistic demands of the Christian gospel was growing on individual and congregational levels, as well as on the denominational level. It was expressed in many small unofficial acts. One notable example of this took place in 1985, in the context of a citywide strike of miners from surrounding areas.

The plight of Bolivian miners had always been hard, but in the 1980s, with the collapse of the international tin market, the situation turned more serious. In March 1985, the central workers' union (COB) called a general protest strike of all workers in the country, with a special call to miners to leave their mines and converge on La Paz. Nancy Thomas wrote this firsthand description: "From all directions they came, from the tin mines to the north and south, from the gold and wolfram mines to the east. Wearing their hard hats like a flag, 16,000 miners marched the streets of La Paz for two weeks, chanting slogans, blocking traffic, setting off dynamite caps. Explosions reverberated throughout the city, doing little more than breaking windows and frightening people, but voicing a deeply felt protest."[87]

Félix Huarina, one of the members of SETALA, reacted with compassion rather than fear to the presence of the miners, realizing that their strike allowance allowed them barely enough for one meal a day. He suggested to other Friends leaders in La Paz that they provide a meal for some of the strikers. Reaction to this suggestion was, understandably, mixed.

> A former president of the church said perhaps they could manage to give one meal to 50 miners. But Humberto Gutiérrez, current president of the Bolivian Friends Church, countered, "Let's add a zero to that number and feed breakfast and lunch to 500 miners. And let's do it tomorrow!" . . . I asked Félix later if they had sufficient money at that time to feed 500 miners. He replied, "No, we didn't have any money, but we knew it would come in, so we went ahead with plans."
>
> By Tuesday night, resources on hand included one kerosene burner, several large pots belonging to the local church, a donation of cocoa bars from a Quaker cooperative chocolate factory, and the assurance that God was with them. Before going home, Félix wrote up a radio announcement inviting workers from four specific mines to come to the church for breakfast and lunch the following day. He also asked that individual Quakers donate whatever they could to make the project successful. Félix's parents are bakers, and that night Félix and his wife stayed up baking bread for the breakfast.

86. Félix Huarina, interview with Harold Thomas and Nancy Thomas, November 2, 2017, La Paz; Bernabé Yujra, interview with Harold Thomas and Nancy Thomas, November 23, 2017, La Paz.

87. N. Thomas, "Hard Hats in a Friends Church," 11–12.

Wednesday morning 700 miners entered a Friends church, most for the first time, and received two pieces of bread and a large mug of hot chocolate. As the morning progressed, many Friends believers responded to the need, the first being a widow from the upper part of the city who had walked several miles with a sack of bread on her back. Others came bringing food, plates, pots, money and time. By 10:00 a.m., a crew of workers was busy peeling potatoes and carrots for the soup that was slowly cooking on the eight borrowed kerosene burners. At noon the brethren served two bowls of a thick vegetable-rice soup to each of the same 700 grateful men. Several confirmed, "This is the best meal we've had all week." . . . after everyone had eaten his fill, Félix was able to announce, "We have so much food left over, we'd like to invite you to come eat with us again tonight." The miners broke out in spontaneous applause.[88]

That evening after supper, the miners stayed on in the sanctuary for a movie on the crucifixion and a short message by pastor Francisco Mamani, followed by a time of testimonies. Several spokesmen for the miners expressed their gratitude, one remarking, "I never thought something like this would happen in a church." One result of the day was that other denominations followed suit, and the next few days saw soup lines in other parts of the city.

This example could be multiplied in other unpublished expressions of compassion from Friends congregations and individuals around the yearly meeting.

From 1987 to the end of the decade, these efforts to address the social and economic realities took place in the context of a major INELA effort to reach out evangelistically and plant new congregations. The two types of ministries, evangelism/discipleship and social development, seemed to be moving forward simultaneously. In general, we can say that at the end of the 1980s, the church was more aware of its context and its responsibility to minister holistically.

THEOLOGICAL AND STYLISTIC CONTROVERSIES

Growing contact with other Christian groups, in country and internationally, increased the possibilities of what some began to interpret as doctrinal "contamination." Controversies arose over issues of Friends doctrine and over other matters that had more to do with worship style than theological positions.

The most significant of these controversies had to do with the Friends positions on the sacraments, specifically baptism and communion. To a certain extent, these had been difficult positions from the beginnings of the Friends movement in Bolivia. The early missionaries taught the Friends' spiritual interpretation of the sacraments, but the context of both Catholicism and Aymara animism caused problems in comprehension. Symbolic expression plays an important role in an animistic worldview, and the absence of these particular Christian symbols would, from time to time, trouble

88. N. Thomas, "Hard Hats in a Friends Church," 11–12.

the INELA. Some have observed that the Bolivian Friends were very good in their evangelistic ministries, persuading many people and families to become Christians. But down through the years many of these converts left Friends for other groups, often drawn by the need to receive public baptism. It's been said that the INELA has a wide front door but an even wider back door.

Many of the early believers accepted the missionaries as patriarchs of the faith, not to be lightly questioned, and these believers became the staunchest defenders of Friends' positions in later years. But new believers, not yet grounded in the faith, and young people becoming educated, would observe the rest of the Christian movement in Bolivia and read the Bible, questioning, and, sometimes, leaving Friends for another church. The controversy over the Friends position on the sacraments surfaced several times in the 1980s. The mission's efforts through teaching and literature production did not lay the confusion to rest.

In the annual representatives meeting in 1981, another committee was appointed to further revise the *Estatutos* of the INELA. Committee members were instructed to include a clearer section on Friends doctrines of baptism and communion.[89]

Humberto Gutiérrez, at that time pastor of the Villa San Antonio Church in La Paz, had been for many years on his own quest, committed to Friends but also wanting to obey the Scriptures. He was questioning whether or not Quakers might be mistaken on the sacraments. Willing to take risks, he experimented in his congregation, and elsewhere, with use of the physical elements of water, bread, and wine. He did not try to hide this, and controversy arose, especially considering his positions of leadership.

In late 1987, Gutiérrez wrote to the La Paz District as well as to the *mesa directiva* of the INELA, explaining his concerns over the issue of water baptism and asking permission to practice this sacrament in the Villa San Antonio Church in La Paz. The La Paz District then wrote to the *mesa directiva* a letter that gently sums up the controversy:

> This is a very sensitive issue for the La Paz District and we lack a clear understanding of the doctrinal distinction between water baptism and the Baptism of the Holy Spirit, which is the actual spiritual practice of our believers.
>
> Because of this we recommend that the INELA M.D. carefully consider, in the light of the Bible, this aspect, without personal or congregational prejudice, taking into account the doctrine of Friends down through its existence and in all parts of the world.
>
> In second place, we want to point out that in the small new churches in our district, this is a serious problem because of other denominations that practice water baptism. This is the reason we can't keep many of our new believers.

89. *Actas de la Junta Anual*, 1981–1993, January 1981, INELA archives.

But we also note that there are many believers and leaders well founded in our doctrines, including the Baptism of the Holy Spirit. For these believers, water baptism is unnecessary, and these very different perspectives are causing confusion in some of the INELA churches.

With these considerations, and others that you can analyze, we are asking that the INELA M.D. impartially, if at all possible, present this matter before the Group of Representatives.[90]

Ironically, Gutiérrez himself was elected president ad hoc of representatives gathering in January 1988, and the topic of water baptism was not discussed. But the *mesa directiva* decided in their regular February meeting to respond to the Villa San Antonio church's letter, reminding them of the Friends position and pointing out the pertinent section in the *Estatutos*.[91] The *mesa* then wrote a very gentle letter to the church, encouraging them to comply and suggesting future conversations.[92]

This, of course, did not end the matter. In January 1990, Jesús Tórrez, a member of the *mesa directiva* as well as of the Villa San Antonio church, accused the church of not respecting the *Estatutos* of the INELA by practicing water baptism and communion with the elements and, thus, "rejecting the doctrine of Friends." He wrote to the *mesa*, encouraging them to formally adopt (or, as it were, re-adopt) the Friends position on the sacraments in the upcoming representatives meeting. This, he said, would help prevent "the Friends church from falling into deep chaos and confusion over such practices. . . . [It was,]" he insisted, "a matter of grave importance for the institutional life of the Friends Church."[93]

This story will continue in the next chapter.

In addition to the issue of the sacraments, contact with other Christian groups fomented other types of controversy in the INELA, most of these having to do with worship forms rather than theological content. One of the controversies involved Campus Crusade for Christ, an organization that had deeply influenced some young leaders in La Paz and in the Caranavi District. A young man from Caranavi, Elías Copa, had formed a group of disciples whose enthusiasm and lively style of worship threatened older believers, and several times Copa was put under discipline. He eventually did move into heresy and was still a cause of concern to the INELA at the end of the 1980s.

The INELA also struggled with the influence of the growing Pentecostal/charismatic movement. The movement strongly attracted young Aymara Quakers with the exuberance of the worship and claims of miraculous healings. This, too, threatened the older generations of the INELA, including much of its leadership. Tensions between

90. Annual report of La Paz District, January 2, 1988, INELA archives.
91. *Actas de la Mesa Directiva*, 1987–1990, February 6, 1988, INELA archives.
92. INELA *mesa directiva*, letter to Villa San Antonio church, March 11, 1988, INELA archives.
93. Jesús Tórrez, letter to INELA, January 4, 1990, INELA archives.

the generations and those arising from social class differences would continue into the 1990s.

THE STORY OF FRANCISCO MAMANI

Several younger leaders served the INELA in the 1980s, among them, Francisco Mamani. We saw him at the beginning of the decade as the pastor of the New Jerusalem Friends Church in La Paz, leading in an aggressive church planting project that later resulted in a new district. Mid-decade, as an employee of the Bible Society, he participated in the presentation of the complete Bible in the Aymara language. At the end of the decade, as president of the INELA, he led the whole yearly meeting in evangelizing and planting churches. He clearly was one of the key leaders of the decade.

Francisco was born in 1945 in the small community of Calata on the shores of Lake Titicaca.[94] His parents, Antonio and Eustaquia Mamani, were not Christians at the time of his birth, and not part of the Friends church in the village, although certainly aware of its presence. Pancho (as Francisco was known) was admittedly a bit of a rascal. He loved soccer, but his mother opposed his playing, possibly out of fear of his being injured. So Pancho played the game on the sly. At times when he came home late, his parents locked him out of the house.

But they loved their son, not behaving too differently from other non-Christian parents in the village. While still a young boy, Pancho became very sick, and his parents took him to a neighboring village for treatment under a reputed animistic healer. When that didn't work they decided to take him to the Amacari Friends Church, drawn by the church's reputation for prayer. The believers prayed for Pancho and he recovered. As a result, Antonio and Eustaquia became Christians and members of the small Friends church in Calata.

Francisco attended a local grade school. There were no high schools in their area of the lake, so when he came of age, his parents took him to the Baptist school in the town of Huatajata, also on the lake, but many miles distant. They left Pancho there, enrolled in the school, but they did not have the resources to leave him with sufficient bedding or food. He attended school, but this time of his life involved much suffering. His parents had arranged for his room and board as much as they could. But he often went hungry, or made soup from onions, or even fish that had washed up on the shores. He managed to finish high school in a Nazarene institution in El Alto.

Francisco's desire to train for Christian service took him to Santa Cruz where he enrolled in the Berea Bible Institute, sponsored by the World Gospel Mission. There he came under the positive influence of Marshall and Catherine Cavit, who discipled him and encouraged him toward pastoral ministry. He became engaged to a local girl, but when she two-timed him, the Cavits persuaded him to consider another student, Juana Ott, a girl who had grown up in the *altiplano* town of Viacha, part of the

94. Information for this story comes from a lifetime of friendship and many conversations, plus a confirming interview with Juana Ott de Mamani, his wife, in La Paz on February 19, 2016.

Bolivian Holiness Church. Although they didn't know each other well, Pancho and Juana decided to marry.

Pancho and Juana marry, with the Cavits as their sponsors (NWYM)

They married in the New Jerusalem Friends Church in La Paz, and theirs was the first "fancy wedding," according to Juana, having been persuaded by their sponsors, the Cavits, to have a ceremony complete with white dress, bridesmaids, groomsmen, ring bearer, and flower girl (novelties at the time, commonplace today). Some members of the church criticized them, saying they were "copying the world." Nevertheless, the INELA recorded Pancho as a pastor and sent the newlyweds to the Yungas to pastor the Arapata Friends Church.

During their two years in Arapata, Pancho taught in the Friends grade school during the week and attended to his pastoral duties on the weekends, leading the worship services and visiting in homes. Juana taught children in the church and accompanied Pancho on his home visits. According to Juana, they won the hearts of the people and enjoyed their pastoral experience.

The *mesa directiva* of the INELA then asked Pancho to come to La Paz and direct the Patmos Bible Institute (residency program), which he did from 1969 to 1971. He soon added to this role the pastorate of the New Jerusalem Church. And in 1972 the Bolivian Bible Society invited him to become one of their promoters and colporteurs, a job he held for the rest of his life, graduating from promoter to director of the project that translated the Old Testament into the Aymara language.

In this chapter we have seen how Francisco Mamani again took on the pastorate of the New Jerusalem Church in 1980 and served as INELA president from 1987 to 1989. We have seen how his vision, enthusiasm and charismatic leadership style stimulated the church to move outside itself and minister in the surrounding context.

Pancho's leadership inspired many, and people still tell stories about him. One has to do with his love of soccer, a game he continued to play throughout his adult life. One Sunday, Pancho, as pastor of the New Jerusalem Church, called in sick, asking that someone else preach in his stead. That was no problem, as the church had many gifted and trained people who could preach or teach at a moment's notice. The congregation prayed for their sick pastor.

This was a special Sunday, the day the leading Bolivian soccer team was facing its key opponent in a World Cup elimination game, to be played in the La Paz stadium. La Paz won the game, and the next day the leading newspaper featured the event. Two photos covered the front page, one of the game in action and the other, a close-up of the crowd going wild. In the center of that close-up, Pancho stood tall, arms lifted, yelling his heart out.

Most of the congregation thought the exposure hilarious, while some, of course, criticized him. He never did live it down.

Francisco Mamani (NWYM)

Francisco earned his reputation as a preacher of excellence. Grounded in the Scriptures, no one could tell a Bible story like Pancho, in Spanish or Aymara. His influence on young people was also notable, and he took the time, not only to play soccer and preach in youth camps, but to spend one-on-one time in discipleship.[95]

Francisco's life was not all ministerial success. Toward the end of his term as INELA president, certain conflicts came to a head and he faced harsh criticism, as had many leaders before him. Early in the 1990s Pancho and Juana decided to leave the INELA and move to Cochabamba. They were without a church connection for a time, but at some point the Evangelical World Church (related to the World Gospel Mission) invited him to pastor one of their churches in Cochabamba. From that date, Francisco worked himself up in the denomination to become one of their key leaders.

Although the Mamanis were never officially reconciled with the INELA, they kept up many of their relationships with Friends believers and missionaries. Their home in Cochabamba became a place of hospitality for many, including the authors of this volume.

Francisco Mamani died suddenly and unexpectedly of a heart attack in his home in 2004. Many people in the INELA today still consider him as one of their own, an important part of the history of Friends in Bolivia.

CHURCH AND MISSION AT THE END OF THE DECADE

In this chapter we have seen how the missionaries struggled with the impulse to address needs by initiating ministries, balancing this with their commitment to encourage the development of an indigenous national church that would be empowered to initiate and carry out its own ministries. We have also seen the struggles for authority within the different branches of the INELA, with steps forward and backward.

In 1988, Hal and Nancy Thomas presented a paper on mission-national church relationships to the mission council and the Department of Missions. It gives insight into the state of mission/national church relationships at the end of the 1980s.[96]

The paper quoted the philosophy statement in the document "Bolivian Field Policy Statements": "It is recognized that the Friends Mission-INELA relationship is to be constantly changing as the National Church grows and matures. The division of responsibilities must be regularly reviewed and redefined to meet new opportunities of church growth. The spirit of trust, love and cooperation will be the only constant. . . . In all his endeavors, the missionary will make an effort to withdraw from certain aspects of the work, training Bolivians to eventually assume full responsibility."[97]

---

95. Our own son, David, counts himself as one of Pancho's young disciples.

96. Thomas and Thomas, "Thoughts on Missionary-National Relationships," 1988, NWYM/GFU archives.

97. Thomas and Thomas, "Thoughts on Missionary-National Relationships," 1988, NWYM/GFU archives.

The Thomases described the relationship of the mission and the national church at the end of the 1980s as that of equal associates: "The National Church plans and executes its own programs, sometimes asking cooperation from the Mission, sometimes not. The Mission likewise carries out its own programs, sometimes with and sometimes without the cooperation of the National Church. The relationship is cordial."[98]

And yet there existed ambivalence. The paper admitted to some attitudes of paternalism on the part of the mission and recognized that "some national leaders (of the older generation) long to go back to the 'good old days,' literally refer to us as their 'spiritual fathers' (even men who've been Christians longer than we've been alive!), and tell us about the old missionaries who took better care of them and did more things for them than we do."[99]

The paper concluded by recommending a recommitment of the mission to following the INELA's priorities and limiting missionary personnel to only one family in La Paz. It stated that this change "does not necessarily mean that the Mission ceases to share its financial resources. We still have to face the reality that we, as North Americans, are rich, and Bolivia is one of the poorest countries in the world. . . . The change in relationship involves a change in the way we share our resources (as well, perhaps, as the amounts)."[100]

Throughout 1988 and the first half of 1989, the mission and the *mesa directiva* labored together to define a new working relationship. The timing was significant; in June of 1989 both the Thomas and Chapman families were retiring from the field, and the Department of Missions was sending in only the Ed and Marie Cammack family at that time as Bolivian field staff. While experienced as missionaries in Peru, this would be their first term in Bolivia. Roscoe and Tina Knight would also come as roving missionaries between both Bolivia and Peru. It was important for carryover and stability that the new agreements be in place by June 1989.

The new plan stated that it was not a contract, but rather a description of ways the mission and the national church had agreed to cooperate going into the 1990s. The gradual decrease in the mission's financial contribution to the pastors' medical fund shows an intentional lessening in mission presence over a ten-year period. The plan included turning over to the INELA the entire stock of literature on hand, including hymnals; this whole program would now be entirely in the INELA's hands. The plan made limited provision for mission cooperation with INELA in evangelism projects and in teaching support in the Patmos residential Bible school. It continued to detail mission involvement in the extension Bible school, the San Pablo Seminary,

98. Thomas and Thomas, "Thoughts on Missionary-National Relationships," 1988, NWYM/GFU archives.

99. Thomas and Thomas, "Thoughts on Missionary-National Relationships," 1988, NWYM/GFU archives.

100. Thomas and Thomas, "Thoughts on Missionary-National Relationships," 1988, NWYM/GFU archives.

and the Bolivian Evangelical University in Santa Cruz. Mission help for urban church property purchase was limited to funds on hand, but mission support for a national missionary in Santa Cruz would continue.[101]

Another significant change came with the decision that the INELA would have more input in missionary placement and supervision. Knowing that the Ed Cammack family would be coming to Bolivia, the *mesa directiva* requested that they be placed, not in La Paz, but in Caranavi. Both the mission council and the Department of Missions accepted this recommendation. Before the Cammacks' arrival in June 1989, the *mesa directiva* and the Caranavi District leaders met to plan the priorities and activities that would guide the Cammacks' ministry during their three-year term.[102]

The beginning of the decade of the 1990s saw the INELA with almost 200 congregations in its twelve districts, including Santa Cruz. The presence of the mission was intentionally decreasing, as the relationship between the two bodies would continue to change.

REFLECTIONS ON THE DECADE

The natural and economic disasters of the 1980s affected the development of the INELA. The loss of crops, animals, and even homes forced both the national church and the mission into unified action, including cooperation with other groups such as ANDEB, USAID, World Concern, and the FWCC. This action was expressed in both short-term relief efforts and new projects and organizations (the greenhouse project, the clinic, and SETALA, for example). A longer-term result was the continuing development of an unwritten theology of holistic mission, a perspective which was both more Quaker and more Christian.

A recurring problem that affected the decade of the 1980s (as well as previous decades and those to follow) was that of marital infidelity. The Aymara cultural ideal of the man and woman joined to form the whole person (the *jaqi*) clashes with the common reality of infidelity, perhaps part of the breakdown of traditional culture. This carries over into the church in all denominations, and is especially harmful as it affects leadership. The INELA has not been free from this, in spite of its inherited emphasis on personal holiness.

In the 1970s and 1980s, the problem of moral failure affected ministry at the highest levels of INELA leadership, touched pastors, and was problematic in the national missionary movement. In some instances, repentance and restoration allowed ministry to reignite. In other cases, families were lost to the church. This situation remains one that the INELA needs to recognize and find biblical life-giving ways to address. The issue has, undoubtedly, affected the development of the church.

101. BMC, "*Plan de Cooperación entre la Misión 'Los Amigos' y la INELA*," 1989, NWYM/GFU archives.

102. BMC Minutes, March 2, 1989, NWYM/GFU archives.

Missiologically, the decade provides a fascinating case study of the tension between a strict adherence to the indigenous policies of the mission (being careful to follow the *mesa directiva* and play a background supportive role) and the need to follow the perceived leading of the Holy Spirit, even when this leading involved taking the initiative and exerting a strong leadership role. A discussion of why the INELA never adopted as theirs the Bible extension school program or the San Pablo Seminary enters this territory. Leaders today admit that both programs were good, designed to adequately meet the need of the times to form pastors. They suggest that INELA opposition came primarily because the programs were mission initiated, as opposed to the Patmos residence program designed by the INELA.

The mission had made a deliberate decision to initiate both programs in the 1970s, taking into consideration the urgent need for pastoral formation in a national church that was quickly out-growing its current leadership resources, and also taking into consideration the INELA's apparent inability to see the problem or to address it. It was a matter of obedience to the perceived leading of the Spirit, and this sense of both urgency and leading continued through the decades of the 1980s and 1990s.

It must also be noted that opposition to the extension program came from some of the leaders at the top level of the organization (*mesa directiva*), but that ground-level support was strong. The hundreds of students, the teachers being trained, and the national administrators were encouraged and engaged. Before the program faded away sometime before 2005, it had succeeded in forming a whole generation of pastors for the INELA.

While admitting the failure to successfully transfer the extension program to the INELA, perhaps it accomplished what it was meant to accomplish. At any rate, this story demonstrates the difficulty the mission experienced in following an indigenous goal and giving primacy to the Spirit's leading.

Other case studies of the decade that illustrate the mission's attempts to achieve this delicate balance include the greenhouse project and the cooperation in urban outreach.

In terms of the INELA's development as a specifically Quaker denomination, the highlight of the decade would have to be the church's growing relationship with outside Quaker organizations, part of its expanding perspective. The mission's concern that exposure to theologically liberal Quakers might harm the church was largely unrealized. INELA Friends leaders proved themselves capable of holding their Christian Quaker convictions while respecting and learning from other traditions.

Some in the national church today claim that during the 1980s, INELA Friends were interested in relating to FWCC, COAL, QBL, and other Quaker groups mainly for the financial benefits and the project support these relationships seemed to promise. This is probably too cynical a view. Not only were the broadening perspectives such relationships provided enriching to the INELA, the Bolivian Friends contributed their own perspectives of faith, their exuberance in worship, their practices of prayer and fasting, and their focus on Jesus as the center of the church. The enrichment went both ways.

We see the Spirit at work in the decade of the 1980s as the INELA slowly continued walking the path to maturity. We see Jesus alive and teaching his people in all the extension centers scattered across the *altiplano* and down into the Caranavi and Yungas valleys as leaders-in-formation gathered to discuss the Bible, apply its teaching to the daily challenges of their people, and learn to be ministers of the gospel.

We see the Spirit among leaders, church members, and missionaries working together to deliver quinoa and seed potatoes to villages suffering from the drought. We see the Spirit working alongside the classes on crop rotation in greenhouses, veterinary medicine, and the raising of guinea pigs. We see the Spirit in the clinic on Max Paredes Street attending to the needs of the poor without discrimination. We see the Spirit stirring soup and feeding striking miners. And we sense the work of God as God's people more and more realized that ministering the gospel included attending to the physical, material needs of human beings. This, too, is mission.

And, of course, we see the Spirit in the lives of so many exemplary people, men and women not perfect but in the process of being transformed and built up as leaders of the church. We see God at work in people like Gregorio Vargas, Francisco Mamani, Humberto Gutiérrez, Félix Huarina, and Leonardo and Delia Virginia Tola. God was building God's church, using people like these.

9

Redefining the Structure

INELA from 1990 to 2002

During the decade of the 1990s, while Bolivia as a nation struggled forward in its development as a complex, multiethnic democracy, so the INELA slowly advanced in its growth as an independent, self-governing national church. Alongside the church, the Friends Mission worked through its own battles over how to let go and when to actually leave.

HISTORICAL OVERVIEW

The evolution of a multiethnic democracy was the major theme of Bolivian history and politics for twenty years, from the first democratically elected president in 1982 to the 2002 elections when indigenous leaders, both men and women, filled a third of the legislature.

Although progress was not smooth or without violence,[1] and the political swings from left to right seemed extreme, all governmental changes during this period came about through democratic elections, not revolutions or coups.[2]

The names of Felipe Quispe and Evo Morales began to become part of the national scene, especially in the approach to the 2002 elections. Both Aymara leaders, Quispe represented the *altiplano* communities, whereas Morales gained his political experience as leader of the coca-growers union in the Chapare valleys between the cities of Cochabamba and Santa Cruz. In 2002, Morales came in second to Sánchez de Lozada who was elected president under the MNR. Morales's party, the MAS

---

1. In fact, twice during this period of time, in 1995 and in 2000, the current president declared a state of siege, giving the government extraordinary powers to respond to protest and violence. Grindle, "Shadowing the Past?," 322.

2. For a good overview of the period of 1982–2002 in Bolivian history, see Klein, *Concise History*, ch. 9.

(*Movimiento al Socialismo*), would continue to gain influence in the years ahead, as would indigenous participation in the life of the nation.

Another important event of the decade was the constitutional revision of 1994. The new first article of that constitution defined Bolivia not only as a "free, independent and sovereign country," but also as "multiethnic and pluricultural," "the first time this was formally recognized."[3]

The year 1994 was also significant for the passing of the Education Reform Law. This widespread reform attempted to make education accessible to boys and girls in the whole population, not just in certain privileged sectors. It aimed to improve the quality and relevance of education. And it emphasized the bilingual nature of the population, making it possible for children to learn in Aymara, Quechua, or Guaraní, as well as Spanish. While the ideals of the reform were not uniformly accomplished, this did mark an upward trend in both the accessibility and quality of education throughout the country.[4] In fact, by 1999, 87 percent of the nation's primary-age children were enrolled in school, and 38 percent of secondary school–age children. (This compares to 1950 when only 25 percent of children were in primary school.)[5]

Related to the rising level of general education, two other social changes had been gradually taking place. The first of these was the overall literacy rate for adults over the age of fifteen. In 1950 only 31 percent of the adult population was literate; that had risen to 67 percent by 1976; but in 2000 fully 86 percent of the Bolivian population knew how to read and write.[6] The significance of this to indigenous peoples cannot be overstated.

The other related social change has to do with language identification. Because of a more universal education, Spanish was acknowledged to be the dominant language of the country in the 1992 census. Even though 62 percent of the population identified as indigenous, these people were rapidly becoming bilingual, making them literate in the official language, a decisive advantage to their active participation in the life of the nation. Interestingly enough, this growth in bilingualism did not seem to diminish the use of traditional languages such as Aymara.[7]

The growth in life expectancy from the age of 40.4 in 1950 to 60.5 in 1995[8] gives an indication of the rise in overall standard of living throughout the nation. This was accompanied by an urban population shift; whereas in 1950 only 20 percent of the population lived in cities of over twenty thousand, by 2001 over half of the population was urban. But at the same time, as Klein points out, at the turn of the century,

---

3. Klein, *Concise History*, loc. 4580.

4. Contreras, "Comparative Perspective," 283.

5. Klein, "Social Change in Bolivia," 245.

6. Klein, "Social Change in Bolivia," 248.

7. Klein, "Social Change in Bolivia," 249–50.

8. Morales, "National Revolution," 221. Based on the Human Development Index, developed by the UN in 1998.

"the incidence of extreme poverty among national households was 24 per cent in the urban areas and 59 per cent in the rural ones. On the *altiplano*, 70 per cent of the rural population was listed as living in extreme poverty."[9]

In this political and social context, the INELA struggled to meet the growing demands of its membership and to define and govern itself as a "free and independent" body. And, just as on the national level, constitutional revision also marked the decade in the life of the church, as leaders wrestled with issues of structural identity and maturity. The end of this period in mid-2002 would see the Friends Mission officially leaving Bolivia, cutting formal ties to the INELA in an attempt to encourage independence and maturity.

INELA AND THE MISSION BETWEEN 1990 AND 2002

Since the 1950s when the Bolivian government recognized the INELA as a legal organization and approved its constitution, the *Estatutos*, the church has struggled with revising and perfecting those *Estatutos*. This struggle came to a head in the decade of the 1990s and in many ways dominated the life of the church.

This reflected in part the changes in Bolivia's own national constitution and new legal regulations that sought to govern all religious organizations. It also reflected the changing geographical reality of the Friends Church. In previous decades the INELA had spread from its concentration in the department (state) of La Paz to the lowland department of Santa Cruz. The 1990s would see the church expanding to the departments of Cochabamba, Chuquisaca, and Oruro. The difficulties of administering this expanding organization served as further motivation for revising the *Estatutos*. Understandably, the process proved controversial and extremely difficult. Power struggles and confusion of authority played their part in this chapter of the church's history.

INELA leaders who administered in the role of INELA president during the period of 1990 to 2002 were as follows: Patricio Medrano (1990–1991), Remigio Condori (1991–1994), Sabino Chipana (1995–1997), Sabino Chalco (1998–1999), Cirilo Aruquipa (2000–2001), Exiquiel Chipana (2001), and Silver Ramos (2002–2004). For several very confusing years, the INELA actually had two competing presidents when Remigio Condori (1998–1999) and Tomás Rodríguez (2000–2001) filled the role of president over all the districts in the La Paz region, with the national and the regional presidents uncertain as to which was actually the leader of the church. Constitutional revision was clearly in order.

Aside from administrative struggles, strong INELA leaders arose in the areas of education, mission, social ministry, and work among women and youth.

The Friends Mission continued to work alongside the INELA during this time, although its priorities differed. The working out of the indigenous principles the mission had adopted from the beginning of its time in Bolivia in the 1930s would

---

9. Klein, "Social Change in Bolivia," 251.

dominate in the 1990s, with an evolution in thought, going from a focus on recruiting more missionaries to one of a pullout of all foreign personnel. This pullout actually happened in 2002, when the Friends Mission closed its office in La Paz and brought its missionaries home to the Northwest.

NWYM missionaries serving full-time with the Friends Mission in Bolivia during this time were Ed and Marie Cammack (1989–2001), and Jerry and Keri Clarkson (1995–2002). Roscoe and Tina Knight made several short-term visits, and Hal and Nancy Thomas rejoined the mission in 1999, stationed in Santa Cruz.

Comparing the minutes of the Friends Mission with those of the INELA *mesa directiva* for these years, one almost gets the sense of reading two separate stories. Issues of focus, priorities, and perceptions differed, although significant points of intersection also mark the narrative.

ADMINISTRATIVE STRUGGLE AND DEVELOPMENT

Organizational and administrative growth marked the decade of the 1990s, but progress seemed at times like a battle through chaos. In 1991 the *mesa directiva* committees included departments of administration (that met weekly for the nitty-gritty running of the church), of evangelism, of social ministries, of pastoral care, of finances, and of education (including both secular and theological programs).[10] The entire *mesa directiva* continued to meet monthly, and for additional meetings as situations arose. And "situations" did, indeed, arise.

Under all this organization on the national level, the separate districts (formerly called "quarterly meetings") had their own *mesa directivas*, quarterly and annual gatherings, programs and finances. Local churches, both monthly meetings and dependent congregations, fit at the bottom of the chart, but, according to Friends practice, these embodied the life of the church, and each congregation sent representatives to the annual representatives' meeting. The voice of each meeting mattered.

On paper it all looked neat and manageable, but the reality was otherwise.

In spite of the growing horizontal sharing of leadership on the district and local levels, the administrative load at the top was becoming increasingly heavy. In his annual report to the representatives meeting in January 1995, INELA president Remigio Condori observed that for most of 1994 his work was tied up in the legal and administrative problems of the INELA,[11] giving him as president little time to focus on the spiritual needs of the church or outreach to the surrounding context.

The heaviest administrative burden of the decade had to do with the INELA's legal constitution, the *Estatutos*. Revision of the *Estatutos* proved to be a complicated process that involved committees that labored for months over both content and form, an approval process that circulated the document among all the INELA

---

10. *Actas de la Mesa Directiva*, 1990–1993, February 29, 1991, INELA archives.

11. *Actas de la Junta Anual*, 1994–2001, January 1995, INELA archives.

districts, multiple reworkings based on community input, until the final approval at representatives meeting. This approval enabled the *mesa directiva* to submit the revision to the government, and the document would then be returned to the INELA for more adjustments and further approvals. Both Quaker practice and Aymara cultural values demanded this slow and highly participative process.

Most of the adjustments had to do with defining the balance of power between the representatives meeting, the *mesa directiva*, the districts, and the local churches. The church was slowly defining its legal identity, not an easy task. Each set of representatives meeting minutes from the decade contains discussion, much of it heated and controversial, on the latest *Estatutos* revision.

The expansion of the INELA from the department of La Paz into other distant departments made this process particularly complex. The differences between La Paz and Santa Cruz included more than distance. The cultural and socioeconomic realities made it difficult to administer both areas under the same plans and programs. In 1990 Roscoe Knight wrote home to the mission board that "the La Paz INELA is not involved with the Santa Cruz work nor do they feel responsibility toward it. . . . Not that they are against it, but it is too far removed from their center of interest."[12]

The Santa Cruz *mesa directiva's* demands for autonomy in government, voiced throughout the decade, sometimes went as far as to suggest they become a separate yearly meeting.[13] The different *Estatutos* revision committees finally resolved this issue by creating a new level of government, that of regions. Under the national *mesa directiva*, the church would divide into two regions, based on the two geographically separate departments: La Paz in the Andean highlands and Santa Cruz in the tropical lowlands. Again, on paper it all looked well balanced. But in reality, the La Paz Region included all eleven established districts and up to two hundred congregations, while the Santa Cruz Region represented some six small churches. It was laughably lopsided. Yet the two regions, under this organizational plan, were legally equal.

The *Estatutos* revision that spelled out this solution gained approval of the INELA representatives in a special called meeting in October 1996,[14] and by January of 1998 the Bolivian government had also signed off on it. In the representatives meeting of 1998, the new *Estatutos*, along with the official government resolution, were read aloud in the sessions. Ironically enough, the Santa Cruz delegation expressed its disapproval of this new official version.[15]

But the greatest organizational awkwardness of this new *Estatutos* was not the relationship between La Paz and Santa Cruz, but the chaos introduced into the administration of the eleven districts and multitude of churches in the region of La Paz.

---

12. Roscoe Knight, letter to NWYM, December 17, 1990, NWYM/GFU archives.

13. Edwin Cammack, letter to NWYM, November 11, 1991, NWYM/GFU archives.

14. *Actas de la Junta Anual*, 1994–2010, January 1997, INELA archives.

15. *Actas de la Junta Anual*, 1994–2010, January 1998, INELA archives.

In the same representatives meeting, election of officers now took a new turn. Sabino Chalco was elected as the new national president, along with two secretaries, representing each of the two regions; this would be the new three-person national *mesa directiva*.[16] Then elections were held for the La Paz Region, with Remigio Condori being named as "executive secretary" (often referred to as "president" in the ensuing confusion of titles), and committee secretaries were chosen for the other positions previously held by the national *mesa directiva* (one each over the areas of finances, missions, human development,[17] and pastoral ministries).[18] (The Santa Cruz Region was left to have its elections on its own, as most of its representatives had not shown up.) What this did was to set up a division between a national executive body with its president and a regional executive body with its president. Actual authority and roles were not clearly spelled out, and for the next few years confusion reigned.

The difficulty of making the new structure work was becoming clear to everyone, but figuring out what to do about it proved challenging. Special emergency meetings were called in 1999 with the two regional executive bodies trying come up with a new proposal. Both regional groups agreed that a "two-headed" church was unworkable, that the INELA needed to return to having one national executive body. Yet another *Estatutos* revision committee was appointed.[19]

In the 2000 representatives meeting, Cirilo Aruquipa was elected INELA national president, with Tomás Rodríguez as executive secretary of the La Paz Region.[20] Interestingly enough, both of these men had earlier in the decade been involved in other church controversies needing intervention by the *mesa directiva*. Rodríguez had recently been restored to fellowship after three years under disciplinary measures. With these two men in conflicting places of leaderships, possibilities for a peaceful resolution to the dilemma were not looking good.

In May of 2000 Aruquipa called a special representatives meeting to present a "spiritual plan" for the INELA and to establish his authority as national church president. Although the fifty-seven people gathered did not represent a quorum, Aruquipa went ahead with the meeting and reminded people that the present legal *Estatutos* gave his three-person *mesa directiva* "maximum authority" over the INELA.[21]

In November of 2000, the La Paz regional executive secretary, Rodríguez, called for the first regional representatives meeting. During those sessions, the gathered representatives agreed that they held "maximum authority" for the areas under their

---

16. *Actas de la Junta Anual*, 1994–2010, January 1998, INELA archives.

17. "Human development" was the new term for the "social ministries" committee.

18. *Actas de la Junta Anual*, 1994–2010, January 1998, INELA archives.

19. *Actas de la Junta Anual*, 1994–2010, September 4, November 8, November 13, 1999, INELA archives.

20. *Actas de la Junta Anual*, 1994–2010, January 2000, INELA archives.

21. *Actas de la Junta Anual*, 1994–2010, May 10, 2000, INELA archives.

jurisdiction, which included most of the churches in the INELA. They also formed another commission with people from all districts for revision of the *Estatutos*.[22]

Aruquipa and Rodríguez had a lengthy public argument during the 2001 January INELA representatives meeting, confirming that they could not work together. Each stated that he would be willing to resign if the other also resigned. The gathered representatives could not come to consensus about anyone resigning, so they called for a vote on whether or not to follow the current legal *Estatutos*. The yeas won, so the representatives told the two leaders they would just have to learn how to get along. They called them forward for a public reconciliation, to which they both complied, at least going through the motions.[23]

In February of 2001, Aruquipa, apparently fed up with the ongoing battle, called a special meeting of the members of his *mesa directiva*, all three of them. Apparently only two showed up, Aruquipa and Jhonny Santalla. They wrote out an official "Minute of Suspension," and fired not only the regional executive secretary, but also his entire council of elected secretaries.[24] The regional officers ignored the action and continued in office.

On April 1, an assembly under an ad hoc team of leaders heard accusations and arguments from both sides, read letters about the situation from the different districts of the INELA, and then unanimously fired the whole lot, both national and regional presidents, with their officers and councils. They set up a transitional *mesa directiva*, named the officers, and gave them freedom to run the church up until the next representatives meeting in January 2002. Exiquel Chipana took on the temporary presidency of the INELA. The final action taken that day was to name a commission of reconciliation for all the former members of the two executive bodies.[25]

The INELA managed to survive the crisis, and in January 2002, the gathered representatives decided that the church would go back to the former structure of one executive body, the *mesa directiva*, over all the districts of the church. They would coordinate with Santa Cruz, trying to find a way that this group of churches could function separately from La Paz, yet still be a part of the INELA. While this did not follow the legal *Estatutos*, the revision commission would do the hard work assigned to them, hoping that the changes would soon be legalized. Silver Ramos was elected for a three-year term as president.[26] The brethren laid down their arms.

DEVELOPMENT OF THE SOCIAL MINISTRIES ARM OF THE INELA

While the INELA continued to declare the outreach ministries of evangelism, church planting, discipleship, and pastoral training as its priorities, in terms of actual time and

22. *Actas de la Junta Anual, Región La Paz*, November 23, 2000, INELA archives.

23. *Actas de la Junta Anual, 1994–2010*, January 2001, INELA archives.

24. Minute of Suspension, February 14, 2001, INELA archives.

25. *Actas de la Junta Anual, 1994–2010*, April 27, 2001, INELA archives.

26. *Actas de la Junta Anual, 1994–2010*, January 2002, INELA archives.

finances the church placed an equal if not a greater emphasis on its social ministries of education, health, and agriculture. This was partly due to the influx of outside funding as international Quakers (and others) generously responded to project proposals sent north from INELA leaders. It also came from a maturing social consciousness on the part of many who were beginning to understand the gospel in more holistic terms.

Educational Ministries

The INELA continued its program of rural primary schools, gradually expanding into the cities with middle and high school levels. At the beginning of the decade, secretary of education, Elías Mamani, reported on sixteen schools, with 681 students attending the five largest. The rural school in Villa Alicia, begun in the 1980s, was now offering primary, middle, and high school levels,[27] and the new urban school in El Alto (upper La Paz) was making plans to broaden its levels as well. The school in La Paz, on the Max Paredes property, reopened in 1991.

Numerical growth reached a high point between 1997 and 1999 with over 1,200 students, most of them concentrated in La Paz, El Alto, and Villa Alicia, each of which included middle and high school levels.[28] But by the end of the decade, most of the rural schools had closed, some due to poor administration, others due to the fact that the growing number of government schools lessened the need for faith-based schools. Five Friends schools remained in 2002, the urban La Paz and El Alto schools especially marked with growing student bodies.

Again, administration was the struggle of the decade. The question of administrative authority tipped and balanced between the sponsoring church (all schools were attached to local congregations), the director of the school, the faculty, and the *mesa directiva* of the INELA through the secretary of education. No one seemed to know who was in charge. In spite of the tensions, the schools functioned, and children received what was considered by many to be a superior education.

One of the most prominent examples of working through chaos to order took place in El Alto, the sprawling extension of La Paz that was by the 1990s a separate municipality. The Friends school there was begun by members of the church that met on what had formerly been the site of the tabernacle in the 1960s and 1970s. The property itself was problematical, with the national church, the local church, and different individuals claiming ownership of parts and parcels. Legally, the national church held church and school properties in its name, so in the 1980s the local congregation and the INELA had agreed on opening a Friends school on this strategic location.

From the beginning, uncertainty surrounded the matter of who held responsibility for securing the legal papers for the school to function, for administering the school, and for financial accountability. This uncertainty reached a peak in 1990 when

27. Report of the secretary of education, April 5, 1990, INELA archives.

28. *Actas de la Junta Anual,* 1994–2010, January 1997, January 1998, January 1999, INELA archives.

Cirilo Aruquipa, pastor of the sponsoring Hebrón Friends Church, took charge of the school and fired a teacher who happened to be the wife of an INELA leader. The *mesa directiva*, as well as faculty and others involved in the school, got up in arms, and the ensuing battle stretched out for months. The *mesa* dismissed Aruquipa from the pastorate of the Hebrón Church as well as the leadership of the school. It reinstated the teacher who had been fired. Some of the meetings between church members and the *mesa* were so volatile, local police were needed to monitor the discussions and keep the peace.[29]

Of course, as the INELA expanded, it became more difficult for the *mesa directiva* to be directly involved in all the inner workings of the organization, including the running of the schools. One solution for the educational program was the formation of an administrative council for each school.[30] In addition, the INELA began developing an internal document of rules and processes to standardize administration in all the Friends schools. This went through various versions, but the results contributed to a more stable administration of the schools.[31]

Several international Quaker organizations played an important role. Notable among these were the FWCC and its arm, International Quaker Aid (IQA), and a group from England, the Quaker Bolivia Link (QBL). These groups, sometimes working through the *mesa directiva*, sometimes working directly with a particular school, sponsored scientific lab equipment in the Villa Alicia school,[32] library books and infrastructure for several different schools,[33] property for a school in Israel[34] (near Caranavi), and even computers for the Villa Alicia school in 2000,[35] something that would have been inconceivable to the parents of these young people ten years previously. A report to the La Paz regional gathering at the end of 2000 informed that nearly $19,000 had been spent on new buildings for the school on the Max Paredes property in La Paz.[36]

Compassion International also continued working with Friends schools (as well as individual congregations without schools) throughout the decade.

The Bolivian Evangelical University (UEB) in Santa Cruz, founded in the 1980s with the participation of both the INELA and the Friends Mission, thrived in the 1990s, offering numerous different majors in addition to theology. David Tintaya represented the INELA on the board of trustees and by 1992 had actually been made

---

29. *Actas de la Mesa Directiva*, 1987–1990, April 18, 1990, INELA archives.

30. *Actas de la Junta Anual*, 1981–1993, January 1993, INELA archives.

31. *Actas de la Junta Anual*, 1994–2010, January 1994, January 1996, INELA archives.

32. INELA *mesa directiva*, letter to Alex Morisey, May 22, 1990, INELA archives.

33. *Actas de la Junta Anual*, 1994–2010, January 1997, January 1998, INELA archives.

34. *Actas de la Junta Anual*, 1994–2010, January 1998, INELA archives.

35. *Actas de la Junta Anual*, 1994–2010, January 2001, INELA archives.

36. *Actas de la Junta Anual de La Paz*, November 23, 2000, INELA archives.

president of the university's board of trustees,[37] a position he carried for six years. This represented a significant contribution of the INELA to the nation.

Medical Ministries

As in the case with educational ministries, the INELA's continued involvement in medical ministries was characterized by administrative challenges and financial contributions from outside organizations throughout the 1990s. The decade opened with the case of the stalled ambulances. In the late 1980s, the INELA had presented to the FWCC the project of an ambulance for the clinic in La Paz. The FWCC accepted the project, purchased the ambulance, and notified the secretary of social ministries that the vehicle was waiting in Miami to be collected.[38] But the department of social ministries couldn't do the legal work or raise enough money to ship the ambulance to La Paz, so they decided to sell it in Miami and try to collect the money, hoping to buy another ambulance.[39]

In 1994 the INELA was able to purchase a Toyota Land Cruiser for $31,300, with $16,968 coming from FWCC funds (through International Quaker Aid) and $14,532 coming from rental money from the clinic on the Max Paredes property. The department of social ministries was supposed to share the vehicle with the *mesa directiva*, but the secretary of social ministries expressed his concern that this wasn't the understanding of the FWCC in giving their money toward the project to be used in medical work.[40] And although the original purpose of the vehicle was to equip it as an ambulance, this never happened. It gradually became a *mesa directiva* vehicle, thus violating the terms of agreement with the FWCC.

The medical clinic on the Max Paredes property in La Paz continued functioning throughout the decade, but the administration and ministry focus radically changed. At the beginning of the decade, a document listing projects sponsored by International Quaker Aid included $10,000 for the INELA's medical program, focused on the clinic.[41] In 1994, the INELA received outside offerings of $15,110 for the clinic.[42] Yet during the early part of the decade, the *mesa* changed from directly administering the clinic to renting out space to different specialists who would then set up their private practice, still with the overall goal of giving economic medical attention to the public.[43]

---

37. *Actas de la Mesa Directiva*, 1990–1993, November 12, 1992, INELA archives.

38. *Actas de la Junta Anual*, 1981–1993, January 1990, INELA archives.

39. *Actas de la Junta Anual*, 1981–1993, January 1992, INELA archives.

40. Bernabé Yujra, report of the secretary of social ministries, January 1995, INELA archives.

41. FWCC, IQA, 1990. The amount given to the INELA, $10,000, was matched by the same amount given for the Soweta Meeting House in South Africa, and to the Friends Center in Costa Rica. The rest of their project money, $47,000, was spread in small amounts around the globe, INELA archives.

42. *Actas de la Junta Anual*, 1994–2010, January 1995, INELA archives.

43. *Actas de la Junta Anual*, 1994–2010, January 1994, January 1995, INELA archives.

These specialists included a general practitioner, a lab technician, an X-ray technician, a dentist, and a nurse. The *mesa* benefitted from the rentals, but had little say about how the clinic was run. Rental collection became problematic, and the vision of the clinic as ministry seemed to morph into a way to gain income for the programs of the INELA. Outside project money paid for equipment.

Dr. Lucio Moya had offered his services to the clinic in the 1980s, and at the beginning of the 1990s an FWCC project sponsored his further training at a university in Mexico City. His vision was to study, then come back and again help in the clinic. Something interfered with those plans, and we find that in 1994, Moya returned to La Paz and discovered that in the changeover of the *mesa directiva*, he no longer had a place in the clinic. The INELA leaders he had previously worked with were now out of office and the current leaders did not feel obligated to keep the church's agreements with him. Moya made a formal denouncement against the INELA to the Ministry of Labor,[44] but he did not follow through on it, and the matter was eventually dropped. This effectively ended Moya's cooperation with the INELA, and undoubtedly discouraged the FWCC from further projects with the church.

As early as 1997 another medical project was developing. This project, a proposal for a medical clinic in the lake community of Amacari, originated with the Friends in Amacari, under the leadership of Daniel Ticona. Ticona presented the original proposal directly to Quaker Bolivia Link (QBL) whose personnel were developing relationships with Friends in La Paz. QBL responded with enthusiasm and committed to raising funds in England and Ireland. In 1998 the INELA secretary of social ministries reported to the representatives meeting on the plan to finance and build the medical center, and a more developed project proposal was designed.[45] By 2000, property had been purchased in Amacari, and by 2001 a building had been constructed. QBL had followed through, raising most of the money through the Ireland Yearly Meeting of Friends.[46] In 2002, the clinic was inaugurated under the name *Centro Médico Boliviano Irlandés*, with a representative of the Irish government attending the ceremony.[47] The INELA would continue to promote it in the following decade.

SETALA

Another aspect of the social ministries of the INELA during the 1990s concerns SETALA, the organization set up in 1983 by young idealistic Friends as part of the department of social ministries. SETALA had its own director, apart from the elected secretary of social ministries on the *mesa directiva*. During the first half of the 1990s,

44. *Actas de la Junta Anual*, 1994–2010, January 1994, January 1995, INELA archives.

45. *Actas de la Junta Anual*, 1994–2010, January1998, INELA archives.

46. *Actas de la Junta Anual de La Paz*, November 23, 2000, INELA archives; Bernabé Yujra, interview with Harold Thomas and Nancy Thomas, November 23, 2017, La Paz.

47. Bernabé Yujra, interview with Harold Thomas and Nancy Thomas, November 23, 2017, La Paz.

SETALA continued active in soliciting project funds, some coming from World Concern,[48] some from FWCC, and some from local government agencies.[49] Projects included training of veterinary workers, seminars on health and first aid, nutrition classes, vaccination campaigns, development of small businesses, and various agricultural projects.[50]

But the reports began to show a gradual diminishing of funding and projects. World Concern dropped its support for the program in 1994.[51] The 1995 field report from the mission notes that "the Social Action Program of the INELA [a reference to SETALA] is at a standstill due to poor leadership which was a major cause for losing funding from international sources."[52] The report of the mission board to NWYM in July of 1996 informed that SETALA was no longer functioning,[53] although it did continue to limp ahead for a few years.[54] By the end of the decade, what was once a vibrant, active and idealist group of young Quaker activists had shrunk to a diminishing and disillusioned organization working on a few small projects as outside funding would come in. The INELA's department of social ministries continued to function, but in a greatly reduced manner with the drying up of outside funds.

In spite of the administrative problems that plagued SETALA, the various projects contributed to the welfare and training of many people. According to Bernabé Yujra, who worked with SETALA as INELA secretary for social ministries between 1992 and 1994, "SETALA opened the eyes of many people to the possibility of this kind of holistic project as well as to the possibility of raising funds from outside groups to sponsor the projects."[55]

Growth toward Holistic Mission

Throughout the decade of the 1990s, one notices a separation and even competition between the social ministries of the INELA and its evangelistic/spiritual ministries. Many of the INELA's ministries seemed to depend on outside funding, and the different nature of the resources may help explain the separation. In the 1990s the Friends Mission returned to their emphasis on evangelism, church planting, discipleship, and

---

48. In 1991 alone World Concern gave over $10,000 to SETALA projects, (SETALA report, January 1992, INELA archives).

49. SETALA director Julio Quispe reported in 1992 a project with the Rural Development Fund (Fondo de Desarrollo Compesino) for $20,000 for pig-raising in the community of Coromata, (SETALA report, January 1992, INELA archives).

50. *Actas de la Junta Anual*, 1981–1993, January 1992, January 1993; *Actas de la Junta Anual*, 1994–2010, January 1994, INELA archives.

51. *Actas de la Junta Anual*, 1994–2010, January 1994, INELA archives.

52. Edwin Cammack, annual field report, 1995, NWYM/GFU archives.

53. NWYM Minutes, 1996, 44, NWYM/GFU archives.

54. *Actas de la Junta Anual*, 1994–2010, January 1998, INELA archives.

55. Bernabé Yujra, interview with Harold Thomas and Nancy Thomas, November 23, 2017, La Paz.

leadership training, although the 1980s had been marked by a more holistic approach. All the financial aid from the mission to the INELA was in these areas (with the exception of the medical fund for pastors), and mission personnel focused their activities according to their priorities. On the other hand, as long as outside funds were coming from international Quaker organizations, as well as from other NGOs, these focused on the social/economic side of ministry. Thus funding and administration for the different types of ministries were forced to be separate, contributing to an either/or perspective of evangelistic outreach and social ministry.

A closer look shows that this was not the whole story. Occasional voices were raised in favor of a holistic approach to ministry. Some of the most notable of these spoke out in March 1994, in a workshop called by the INELA secretary of social ministries, Bernabé Yujra. Members of the *mesa directiva*, UJELAB, and UFINELA, as well as volunteers with experience in the areas of missionary work, education, agriculture, and public health came together to devise a ministry plan for the future in reaching out to the poor.[56]

In his opening remarks, Yujra presented the purpose of the workshop as an integration of the ministries of health, agriculture, education, and mission outreach in order "to give witness to our being Friends with our Lord and Savior, Jesus Christ." Experienced people in all the different areas (including young adult men and women) made presentations, followed by discussion and recommendations for an integrated ministry plan. In speaking about education, Yujra and Eduardo Mamani reminded people that the Friends schools were originally created with the purpose of giving children a formation rich in Quaker Christian principles, and these children often made the best evangelists for the gospel back in their homes and communities. They also noted the need to cooperate with the national educational reform movement, upgrading technology and equipping young people to make contributions in areas of social reform.

Paulino Ruiz, presenting in the area of agriculture, told the participants that "it's important to recognize that the social ministry of the INELA is a ministry of our Lord and Savior, at the service of humanity."[57] Concerning the financing of projects, he encouraged the participants to let resources come from within the church and the communities served as part of their missionary outreach. He expressed the view that some of the early social ministries of the INELA, such as the clinic and the work of SETALA, were misguided and actually created dependencies. But the later work of SETALA, he claimed, in empowering veterinary workers in their communities was exemplary; it demonstrated how to support "transformational holistic development that is sustainable and values the neighbor as a child of God, worthy of life."[58]

---

56. All references to this event come from the report on the planning workshop for INELA's social ministry, March 12, 1994, INELA archives.

57. Planning workshop for INELA's social ministry, March 12, 1994, INELA archives.

58. Planning workshop for INELA's social ministry, March 12, 1994, INELA archives.

The workshop concluded with recommendations for projects that focused on transformation, were locally sustainable, and that integrated the spiritual and social/ material sides of ministry. The report states that "the leaders of the INELA need to affirm the conviction that the social ministries of Friends are part of the ministry of our Lord and Savior Jesus Christ."[59]

While the ideals of this workshop were not necessarily carried out in either the social or the spiritual ministries of the INELA in the rest of the decade, we note the stirrings toward a more holistic (and more genuinely Quaker) perspective.

DEVELOPMENT OF THE SPIRITUAL OUTREACH ARM OF THE INELA

Each INELA administration throughout the decade of the 1990s declared the spiritual ministries of the church as priorities. These ministries included training of pastors and leaders, the maintenance of programs such as the quarterly meetings and conferences, doctrinal teaching, and missional outreach into new areas.[60] In mid-decade the title "secretary of evangelism" changed into "secretary of missions," emphasizing the focus on entering new areas and even new cultural groups. This became one of the bright points of the 1990s.

In all of these ministries, the Friends Mission encouraged and worked with the INELA, although the dance steps became more complicated, and at times it seemed as though the two groups were moving to different tunes.

Leadership Training

The need to train pastors and leaders for the church continued. While the mission maintained its focus on theological education by extension and the San Pablo Seminary, the national church emphasized its preference for a more traditional residential Bible school program.

In January of 1992, the *mesa directiva's* secretary of education announced that the Patmos Bible School residency program had been suspended because of lack of students. In contrast, during 1991 the extension Bible school had been functioning in twenty-two different centers. The gathered representatives agreed to rethink both the extension and residency programs, reorganizing and adding technical and first aid courses.[61]

This reorganization would continue throughout the decade as the INELA attempted to replace the Patmos Bible Institute. These efforts reflected the needs both for a higher level of education for church leadership and for legal degrees to match

---

59. Planning workshop for INELA's social ministry, March 12, 1994, INELA archives.

60. "Triennial Plan, 1990–1992," January 1990; departament of evangelism activity plan, January 1990, INELA archives.

61. *Actas de la Junta Anual*, 1981–1993, January 1992, INELA archives.

the demands of educational reform in the country. Planners also wanted to include vocational and secular courses for a more holistic formation.

The first paragraph to a 1992 proposal sheds lights on the perspective of some of the INELA leaders concerning the mission's role in pastoral training:

> The Patmos Bible Institute was officially born in 1966, that is, 26 years ago. In its first years it played an admirable role, but because it did not take into consideration the realities of its context, little by little it diminished. Finally, the missionaries stepped in and, instead of helping us in the formation of leaders, they founded the Extension Institute and a Seminary. They superficially began forming leaders for the work, neglecting the human and relational aspects. Although some of us tried to restructure the Institute, we failed because of the lack of financial support that would pay a director or at least provide the same scholarships that were given to students in the Extension or San Pablo programs.[62]

Blaming the mission for the struggles of the residency program highlights the disconnect and misunderstanding between the church and the mission.

Between 1990 and 2002, leaders came up with six different proposals for an institute for pastoral formation, with six different names and plans. Some of these functioned for a few years, but the difficulties spelled defeat for all but the final program.[63]

In 2000 an innovative program emerged, known as the *Centro de Educación Teológica Integral* (*CETI*, Center for Holistic Theological Education), and by the end of 2000, some sixty students were studying in centers in La Paz, Caranavi, and the Yungas.[64] This program continued through 2001, but already leaders were upgrading the program so that it could gain government approval and offer a legal two-year degree in religious studies. The name changed to the *Instituto Superior de Educación Teológica los Amigos* (*ISETA*, Friends Institute for Theological Higher Education), and by 2002 had replaced CETI. This program would survive.

An overall description of INELA pastoral formation for the decade could be "creative instability."

---

62. Proposal for the *Instituto Bíblico "Patmos" (Politécnico)*, 1992, INELA archives.

63. The proposals were as follows: the Patmos Polytechnic Bible Institute (IBPP) in 1992; the Friends Center for Theological Studies (CETA) in 1993, an attempt to unite all Quaker denominations in one school; the Friends Higher Education Technical-Theological Center (CESTTA) in 1995; the Friends Higher Education Theological Center (CESTA), with these last two functioning for three years, 1995–1998; the Center for Holistic Theological Education (CETI), which functioned from 2000 to 2001; and finally, the Friends Institute for Theological Higher Education (ISETA), which replaced CETI in 2002.

64. *Actas de la Junta Anual de La Paz*, November 23, 2000, INELA archives.

Mission Involvement in Leadership Training

In general, throughout the decade of the 1990s, the Friends Mission worked with the national church, and sometimes apart from the national church, in the formation of leaders and pastors. Ed and Marie Cammack arrived in June 1989, and, in response to the *mesa directiva's* request, were stationed in Caranavi for three years. In their first annual report back home to the mission board, Cammack refers to "many spiritually weak churches and a critical lack of trained pastors and lay leaders." He mentions churches discouraged by the influence of false doctrines and that 90 percent of the youth had been "lost to other churches or to the world." In full cooperation with Caranavi District leaders and pastors, in that first year the Cammacks restarted the Bible school extension program with over fifty students, began an extension center of San Pablo Seminary with seven students, and energetically visited all the twenty-four functioning congregations in order "to minister sound doctrine to them, give encouragement and get acquainted with them."[65]

Ed Cammack leads extension center in Caranavi District (E. Cammack)

This set the pace for the next two years of the Cammacks' cooperation with the national church in the Caranavi District. Ed Cammack always traveled and ministered in team with national leaders, and his own pastoral spirit and gifts did much to encourage churches in the district during that time. While maintaining a spirit of cooperation with the national church, Cammack also affirmed the educational priorities of the

65. Edwin Cammack and Marie Cammack, reports, July 1990, NWYM/GFU archives.

mission, promoting the theological education by extension and San Pablo Seminary programs.

For the next three years of their service in Bolivia (1994–1997), the Cammacks lived in La Paz and continued serving the national church as counselor to the *mesa directiva*, promoter of pastoral training through the extension Bible school and San Pablo Seminary, and encourager of the growing national missionary movement. The Cammacks spent their last three years (1998–2001) in Santa Cruz where, among other activities, they were influential in beginning the Friends Theological Center (*Centro Teológico de los Amigos*, CTA), connected to the theology department of the Bolivian Evangelical University. The CTA existed to organize and encourage students from the different Friends denominations preparing for pastoral leadership in the university. Diego Chuyma, a young INELA leader from the *altiplano*, was named director, having returned from theological studies at Barclay College in Kansas and Azusa Pacific University in California.

For five and a half years, the Cammacks were the only full-time missionary family in Bolivia, but in December 1995, Jerry and Kerri Clarkson joined the staff and set up their home in La Paz. The Clarksons served two terms in La Paz (1996–1998, 1999–2002), focusing on pastoral training, giving encouragement also to the national missionary program. Most of their activity centered around the extension Bible school and San Pablo Seminary, not only teaching, but working with INELA leaders in attempts to transfer ownership and responsibility of these programs to the national church. The mission also encouraged Jerry Clarkson to work with the INELA initiatives in pastoral training,[66] and he actively participated with the INELA planning for CETI and ISETA.

The Patmos Extension Bible Institute flourished in the decade of the 1990s, in large part due to mission involvement, but always with a view toward encouraging national ownership. But by 2002 only thirty-eight students participated in the extension program, renamed as EBAD (*Educación Bíblica a Distancia*).[67] This compared to some 360 students reported earlier.[68] By this time the INELA was considered to be in charge of the extension program, with funds from the mission destined to be cut in the future. The inter-denominational mission agency in charge of textbook production had also nationalized, with INELA participation on the board.

While the interdenominational San Pablo Seminary continued to grow and develop, fewer INELA students were considering this an option for theological education. In 2000 only seven INELA students were studying in San Pablo.[69]

---

66. Joint Mission Council Minutes, June 24–25, 1999, NWYM/GFU archives.

67. Gregorio Vargas, report of secretary of theological education, January 2003, INELA archives.

68. *Actas de la Junta Anual*, 1994–2010, January 1999; report of secretary of education, November 22, 2000, INELA archives.

69. Report of secretary of education, November 22, 2000, INELA archives.

The mission's promotion of theological education by extension and San Pablo Seminary did not ultimately result in INELA ownership. Nor did mission support for the Friends Theological Center in Santa Cruz result in a permanent program. As long as mission personnel and funding were in place, these programs functioned and made significant contributions to the formation of men and women as leaders for the INELA. While not permanent, the national church seemed to take aspects of these mission-initiated programs, refine, and adapt them in its attempts to come up with its own programs for leadership training.

National Missionary Outreach

In the INELA's official three-year plan (1990–1992), the one underlined sentence defined the task as to "Oversee the growth of the Lord's Church through the plan for evangelism."[70] The specific plan called for more district coordination, with the national secretary of the department of evangelism (missions), Luis Laura, meeting four times a year with all the district secretaries of evangelism to pray, plan campaigns and encourage each other. Preference would be given to "new and distant areas."[71]

Santa Cruz

At the end of the 1980s, Pascual Quispe, former INELA president, had moved with his family to the town of San Julián and had begun serving as national missionary in the colonies. At the beginning of the 1990s, Santa Cruz District president, Eugenio Ramos, reported congregations in the town of San Julián and in five colonies, some of them quite small, but meeting regularly.[72] Quispe served as a missionary pastor to all these groups, being supervised by the Santa Cruz District and supported financially in large part by the mission, at least in the beginning of the decade.

In 1991 Bernardo Flores, a graduate of the Patmos Bible Institute, joined Quispe as a national missionary to San Julián.[73] Ramos's annual report to the INELA for 1991 showed his understanding of national ownership of the mission work in San Julián, stating that the NWYM missionaries turned the work over to the Santa Cruz INELA in July of that year.[74]

The history of the work in San Julián from that point on is sketchy. Quispe and Flores served together in San Julian from 1991 through 1993. Esteban Ajnota served as a national missionary to the whole Santa Cruz region from 1994 to 1996. Gradually mention of San Julián as a place of mission outreach was dropped from the reports and the minutes. It appears that the colonists' dream of secure farms in the tropics proved

70. "Triennial Plan," January 1990, INELA archives.

71. Department of evangelism activity plan, January 1990, INELA archives.

72. *Mesa directiva* of the Santa Cruz region, letter to the INELA and the BMC, June 1990, INELA archives.

73. Roscoe Knight, letter to NWYM, March 9, 1991, NWYM/GFU archives.

74. Eugenio Ramos, letter to INELA, December 5, 1991, INELA archives.

difficult to achieve, so that a gradual migration away from the colonies took many of the believers, and most of the small church plants disappeared. Pascual Quispe continued living in San Julián as a volunteer pastor and Friends leader.

NATIONAL MISSIONARY MOVEMENT

Secretary of missions Luis Laura ended his report to the representatives in 1991 with a plea for more full-time evangelistic workers, for evangelistic equipment, for adequate funds, and for a better system of communication and coordination among the districts in the La Paz department.[75] The *mesa directiva* took Laura's challenge seriously and in July 1991 sent an elaborate and well-thought-out project proposal directly to NWYM, bypassing the mission council. It suggested that for the cost of sending one foreign missionary to Bolivia, the NWYM could instead use that money to help support five full-time national workers. These would be missionary-pastors assigned to the districts that needed the most help: Lago Norte, Pacajes, North Yungas, Frontera, and a new area to be developed. They were asking the NWYM to invest $86,267.50 over a five-year period; they proposed raising $35,750 locally.[76]

The NWYM mission board responded graciously that while they did not have the amount of funds requested, they were interested in the project and were willing to invest $3,000 a year for five years if the INELA would choose one of the districts for a pilot project and invest in the project themselves.[77] The INELA chose to focus on the North and South Yungas Districts for 1992 and issued a call for national missionary candidates. Antonio Mamani Balboa, a young Friends pastor (to be distinguished from the older Antonio Mamani who had served as INELA president in the 1960s) was accepted, placed under the supervision of the secretary of missions, and sent off to the Yungas. He was to alternate months between the North and South Yungas Districts, working with district officials in organizing specific activities. To cover Mamani's salary and basic ministry expenses, the INELA would pay 30 percent, the districts would provide places to live and products for food, covering another 30 percent, while the mission would pay 40 percent.[78]

The report of Mamani's activities for that first year leaves one panting. It included eighteen evangelistic campaigns in churches, thirty-six revival meetings, three new communities evangelized, 158 days dedicated to visiting the families of leaders, 156 days traveling to and participating in quarterly meetings and conferences, preaching in forty-five churches, the organization of three extension centers with thirty-two students, ten short courses given to leaders, three music classes given to twenty-one students, five families brought back to the faith, and twelve newly converted families. Mamani worked with the district leaders, meeting with them eighteen times for

75. *Mesa directiva* report, January 1991, INELA archives.

76. *Mesa directiva*, letter to NWYM, July 3, 1991, NWYM/GFU archives.

77. Board of Missions Minutes, November 8–9, 1991, NWYM/GFU archives.

78. *Mesa directiva*, letter to NWYM, May 30, 1992, INELA archives.

planning. The report began and concluded with the observation that Mamani's work was well received by the districts.[79] One would hope so.

Thus began a new phase in INELA's national missionary movement. The national church, through its department of missions, supervised the work. The Friends Mission cooperated in short courses for missionary training and in serving as consultants to the secretary of missions. Financially the mission carried up to 50 percent of the support of the program, while the national church raised the rest through special offerings and the sacrificial giving of many individuals.

By January 1993, the INELA department of missions had developed a detailed application form for missionary candidates, a list of requirements, and a general job description, all in a very professional manner. The twelve requirements included a sense of missionary call, Bible school graduation, at least five years of pastoral experience, marriage, commitment to the INELA, ministerial aptitudes (including preaching, teaching, leadership, organization, and ability to get along with people), an absolute commitment to the "original biblical doctrine of Friends," willingness to be subject to the authorities and regulations of the INELA, and, in general, to be an understanding, positive, hardworking person.[80]

The general job description gives insight into the national church's priorities in this new effort. First on the list was the spiritual strengthening of the churches, in second place the training of leaders and, thirdly, evangelistic efforts in new areas. The description includes monthly and annual reports, as well as activity plans.[81] Each missionary would meet with district leaders to come up with activity plans.

That second year, 1993, the INELA department of missions accepted new candidates who would join Antonio Mamani to make up the national missionary force. Sixto Gutiérrez was assigned to the Lago Norte District, to be replaced the following year by Victor Quispe. Dionisio Lucasi went to the Pacajes District where, interestingly enough, the Alliance Mission of Norway helped support the project.

Antonio Mamani's intense dedication to work, as noted above in his activity report, characterized the attitude of the more than eleven men (often with their wives) who served as national missionaries in the years between 1992 and 2002. Others who served throughout the department of La Paz included Zenón Gallegas (North and South Yungas), Sixto Mamani (South Yungas), and Simón Ticona (Pacajes). In 1996 Dionisio Lucasi transferred from the Pacajes District to begin a new missionary work below Caranavi in the Alto Beni area, a place called Palos Blancos, a work which would soon capture the interest of the national church.[82]

79. Antonio Mamani Balboa, report, February 15, 1993, INELA archives.

80. "*Requisitos para ser misionero*," January 17, 1993, INELA archives.

81. "*Descripción de funciones*," January 17, 1993, INELA archives.

82. NWYM Minutes, 1997, 44.

Antonio and Julia Mamani, missionaries to Cochabamba (E. Cammack)

In 1994, Antonio Mamani left his missionary work in the Yungas to serve for three years as INELA's secretary of missions. At the end of that time in 1997, he was sent to the city of Cochabamba, where he and his wife, Julia, served as missionaries for the next several years. This marked the extension of the national missionary program into a new department. In 1998 Demitrio Poma was sent to the city of Sucre in the department of Chuquisaca where a small congregation had been established two years previously; Emilio Villca served in Sucre in 1999 and Crispin Cruz in 2000. Also in 2000 Valerio Corani went as a missionary to the city of Oruro, in the department of the same name.[83] Thus the national missionary program had extended the work of the INELA to five different states by the end of the 1990s. In addition to the encouragement of the churches and the training of believers, new churches were planted and the INELA recognized two new districts, the La Asunta District and the Alto Beni District, both in 2000. This brought the total of INELA districts to fourteen.

Part of this national missionary extension was cross-cultural as the church plants in Cochabamba and Sucre were among both Aymara and Quechua speakers. Dionisio Lucasi's work in Alto Beni extended into the Mosetén and Chimane tribal groups.[84]

---

83. These appointments are named in the reports of the NWYM Board of Missions to NWYM in the minutes of 1997–2000.

84. NWYM Minutes, 2001, Report of the Board of Missions, 42.

Victor Quispe, National Missionary

The long-term missionary commitments of Antonio Mamani, Dionisio Lucasi, and Victor Quispe stand out during this period. These men not only served as national missionaries, they each worked for three years in the role of INELA secretary of missions. Victor Quispe's story exemplifies their experiences.

Quispe was born into a Quaker family on the *altiplano* in 1958. The family moved to the tropical Caranavi area when Victor was still a child. He grew up as part of the Villa San José Friends Church and attended a Friends elementary school. After a few years in a secular high school, he enrolled in the extension Bible school and upon his graduation in 1985 was recognized as an INELA pastor. He then pastored two churches in the Caranavi District. He married Modesta Huanca and the couple eventually had five children.[85]

Looking back on his youth, Quispe writes about a formative time in the Villa San José Church where he grew up. It was Christmas Day, 1978; it was also the day the local soccer team had a championship game. Quispe was twenty years old and an avid soccer player. As he impatiently sat through the Christmas Day church service, the Spirit of God began to convict him. The pastor's message "bared my soul," he writes. "All my impurities, bad habits and vices" marched before him and he realized that he had come to love sports more than God. Facing the choice of leaving the service early to play in the game or going to the altar to begin a life of dedication to God, he chose to go forward. The church leaders gathered around him, prayed, and "I received the baptism of the Holy Spirit. . . . In that moment I felt reconverted, my life now consecrated to God's service."[86] Quispe looks back on that experience as a turning point in his life, the beginning of preparation for a life of ministry

In 1991 and 1992, Victor and Modesta Quispe both suffered serious illnesses, and Victor was forced to leave the pastorate. They went to El Alto to live. The whole family began crying out to God for healing. Victor promised to return to ministry. He heard God reply, "I will heal you so that you can give witness to those who don't yet know me." The couple repented, and Victor promised to accept the first ministry position offered to him. Healing came slowly, but it did come.

In addition to pastoring churches in the Caranavi District, Quispe had become active as a district officer, helping to oversee many churches before the time of his illness. Even so, Quispe did not have experience of the INELA on the national level, not being accustomed to travel to La Paz for the yearly representatives meetings. In 1993 he decided to present himself to the *mesa directiva* in La Paz. He met INELA president Remigio Condori and told about how God had helped him through the trials of his life.

---

85. Curriculum de Vitae and pastoral census form, April 1993, INELA archives.

86. The rest of the material for Victor Quispe's story comes from his testimony, written after 2007 and entitled "Mi testimonio de mi vida real" (My real life testimony), n.d., INELA archives.

Condori immediately responded with a challenge: "We need a missionary pastor for a distant district. Would you be willing?"

"Yes, I'm ready," came the instant reply.

Next came the formalities of application forms and interviews, according to the newly developed list of requirements. After consulting with Modesta and deciding that she and the kids would remain at home in El Alto, he gave his consent. Things moved quickly after that. Quispe was assigned to the Lago Norte District on the *altiplano* and left within weeks.

"And so," he writes, "I left on my journey without knowing where I was going or what exactly my mission would be." He was told he should get off the bus in the town of Copusquía and that the local Friends leaders would help him get organized and begin his work.

Thus began Quispe's contribution to the INELA's national missionary movement. He would end up dedicating more than twenty years to this endeavor.

Victor Quispe, missionary on the altiplano, with wife, Modesta (E. Cammack)

Immediately upon arrival in Cospuquía, Quispe was faced with what would be a part of the context of all the national mission work: the conflict between the gospel and the animistic practices of the local culture. When asked to perform a marriage ceremony that combined Christian and animistic practices, Quispe refused to comply and demanded that the church leaders decide whether to give in to cultural demands or hold to their Christian principles. The church's decision to follow Christ would turn out to be a major step of Christian commitment for many in the district.

Another event in the neighboring community of Chipo gives insight into the national missionary experience. Quispe wrote about that event:

> One day as I was visiting the homes of the brethren according to my custom, an older lady named Carmen approached me. She said, "How good you've come to visit. I've been waiting. My neighbor's pigs are sick with a contagious disease, and it will probably spread next to my pigs. Please pray that my pigs don't die."
>
> I replied, "Yes, I'll pray. But first why don't you give one of your pigs in offering to the church? God will protect all the others."
>
> She immediately brought me a pig, saying, "This is now God's pig." Together we prayed that God would cover and protect her pigs from the disease. Then I left for another village.
>
> Within four days, the Chipo community leader came and said to me, "Brother pastor, they've told me you prayed for the pigs of this lady and that not one of her pigs has died. Learning this, all the people in our village have sent me to bring you back to pray for all the pigs in town."
>
> I told him, "I'm not a diviner or magical healer. I work according to God's will, the same God who is over your pigs. If you desire to know this God, I can come back to a meeting of all the villagers, and we can pray and you can repent of all your sins, and God will hear us and heal, not only your pigs, but your land as well."
>
> The community leader replied, "We will agree to a meeting of all the community if you come." We set the date.
>
> Indeed, the whole community came together, with their children. That day was such a blessing as we watched everyone become reconciled among themselves, asking God for pardon on bended knees for a whole hour without getting tired. As a result, the whole community converted to God. Since then they've taken all the "saints" out of their old Catholic chapel and turned it into an evangelical church. And that's the way it is up to today. There are no more pagan festivals in the community, although not everyone goes to church.[87]

Concerning the role of missionary, Quispe's observations are provocative. He wrote about a visit to one of the communities where a new work was beginning:

> At first it was difficult to break the image of missionaries as tall, blond men who come from the North and bring a lot of money in order to help the poor. That was what being a missionary meant to people at that time. When I showed up at a Quarterly Meeting, the program had on it a preaching service by the national missionary. People were waiting for this person to show up,

---

87. Victor Quispe, "Mi testimonio de mi vida real," n.d., 4, translated from Spanish by Nancy Thomas, INELA archives.

but I was already there. So I made myself known, and those present responded with, "What?! You're the missionary?" Then they went on, "Here's our list of requests. We want you to help us with windows, doors, stucco, and cement so we can do the finishing work on this church building."

I responded, "Surely you have enough yourselves to finish this work."

"We have nothing, we're poor," they replied.

But looking around, I noted the 300 to 400 llamas and alpacas they owned, knowing that I myself did not own even one llama. Yet they considered themselves poor. I thought to myself that I needed to teach them to give. So with the Holy Spirit's help, I said, "Brothers and sisters, let's give an offering according to our possibilities. It's true that you have built this meetinghouse with much effort, and now all that's left are the finishing touches, and you need help with this. I'm going to give a window. Now appoint someone to make a list of what everyone else is willing to give."

Everyone offered to supply something, some a window, others a door, or stucco, or cement. Others promised to come and work. In this way the need of the church was covered, and a way of thinking that they needed to depend on outside help also began to change in all the churches.[88]

Quispe served as a national missionary to Lago Norte District from 1993 to 1997. As a result of his work and of those who followed him, nine new congregations were planted, and eventually the area was divided into two districts, partly because of the large distances between congregations.[89] Quispe took on the role of INELA secretary of missions from 1998 to 2000.

Bolivian Missionaries to Peru

In the 1980s, Bolivian missionaries had gone to Peru to cooperate with the leaders of the Peruvian INELA. Benito Apaza served from 1988 to 1992, when he was succeeded by Emilio Villca (1993–1996). Both Apaza and Villca served on the Peruvian *altiplano*. In 1997, Esteban and Gaby Ajnota, a young couple who had been giving leadership in the Santa Cruz region, accepted the call to go to Peru as INELA missionaries, destined for the city of Arequipa. Both Esteban and Gaby had been educated in the Bolivian Evangelical University's theology program and were recognized as Friends pastors. In addition to pastoring they had been named as national missionaries in the Santa Cruz District from 1994 to 1996. Esteban writes that

after many experiences as missionaries in Santa Cruz, we were invited to be foreign missionaries, in this case sent to the Republic of Peru, in the coastal zone, the city of Arequipa for the years 1997 to 1999. There we experienced radical changes, passing from one culture to another, from one country to another. The challenge of working with the churches was huge, as their needs

88. Quispe, "Mi testimonio de mi vida real," n.d., 5, INELA archives.
89. Quispe, "Mi testimonio de mi vida real," n.d., 5, INELA archives.

were pronounced. All three of us had to work. Our four-year-old son became part of our ministry, a co-laborer in the Kingdom of God. We began to train brothers and sisters in the Friends churches of Arequipa, emphasizing the growth and development of the church and missions.[90]

As with the Bolivian missionaries before them, the Ajnotas served under the supervision of the Peruvian INELA's *mesa directiva*, with their support coming from the INELAs of both countries. They gave training and leadership to different programs of the church, especially in the city of Arequipa. The Ajnotas were to be the last of the Bolivian Friends missionaries to the Peruvian Friends Church, as the Peruvian brethren were now themselves forming national missionaries in their own context.

THE STRUGGLE TO BE QUAKER

The controversy over water baptism continued into the 1990s. With all the changes coming into the *Estatutos*, several times the demand was made that this document hold steady in its affirmation of Friends doctrine, particularly on the sacraments; other sections could change, but that one, no.[91] Yet different leaders and even congregations continued to question the Friends position, causing confusion and controversy in the rest of the churches; many felt that if Friends were wrong on this position, they ought to change and bring their practice more in line with the Bible. The majority of the churches felt the Friends position was the true biblical position. This one doctrinal point seemed to take precedence over all others.

The representatives meeting of January 1993 gave a day to a plenary doctrinal session, considering the cases of the Villa San Antonio and Eben Ezer city churches, both of which now practiced water baptism. Representatives from each district expressed their concerns. Some of the opinions expressed and minuted were as follows: "We shouldn't disobey the established authority of the institution." "There can be freedom of worship without creating problems in the national church." "We've taught Friends doctrine for many years; changing now would be an error, as if saying we've been false, thus creating doubts." "This situation is painful; we need to come to a decision." "It's painful that we're arguing over the baptism practiced by John and the baptism in the Holy Spirit; it causes problems and divisions; the brethren need to recognize their errors." "Those who are not in agreement with our doctrine should just leave."[92]

Consensus was reached on continuing with Friends doctrine. The representatives then suspended the Villa San Antonio and Eben Ezer churches, along with pastors Ildefonso Limachi, Tomás Rodriguéz, and Humberto Gutiérrez.[93] (Later in the decade, the Villa San Antonio Church and all three pastors successfully petitioned to

---

90. Ajnota, "Volviendo para servir," 67, translated by Nancy Thomas.

91. *Actas de la Junta Anual*, 1981–1993, September 26, 1992, INELA archives.

92. *Actas de la Junta Anual*, 1981–1993, January 1993, INELA archives.

93. *Actas de la Junta Anual*, 1981–1993, January 1993, INELA archives.

be readmitted to the INELA. The Eben Ezer Church joined the Assemblies of God.) In spite of the consensus agreement, this issue would continue to rise up, in different churches and with different leaders.

Another relatively small incident demonstrates some of the confusion about Quakerism in general. The secretary of education in 1994 was Hipólito Llanque, an educated and innovative thinker who had been doing a good job overseeing the Friends schools amid all their administrative controversies. He had been instrumental in restarting the school in La Paz on the Max Paredes property and in writing the guidelines and policies that would bring order into the whole educational system.

As part of his leadership role Llanque had been able to travel abroad and had become acquainted with non-programmed Friends. He was attracted to their form of worship and use of silence. He organized a small group of unprogrammed Friends in El Alto. They called themselves the Bolivian Quaker Community (*Comunidad Cuaquera Boliviana*). (The word "Quaker" or *cuaquero* had not before been part of INELA's vocabulary; they had always used the term "Friends," *Amigos*.)

In 1994 this group sent a letter to the representatives meeting, asking the INELA to recognize them as a separate yearly meeting. The fact of their existence came as a "sad surprise" to some, and no one was ready to give such a small group yearly meeting status.[94] In an extra called meeting of the representatives in February 1994, Llanque was confronted and made to choose: "Are you with the silent Quakers or with us?" Apparently the existence of such a group, no matter how small, seemed to threaten INELA leaders. Llanque then said he would peacefully leave the INELA, asking pardon of all present. Later that year he resigned his post as secretary of education, and the INELA lost, for a time, one of its promising young leaders. (The silent meeting slowly disappeared. Llanque later successfully asked to be reinstated in the INELA.)

INELA leaders continued relating with unprogrammed Quakers around the world, especially those in England and those connected to the FWCC. They also maintained their relationship with the NWYM and with Evangelical Friends International.

THE END OF A CHAPTER IN MISSION / NATIONAL CHURCH RELATIONS

Previous chapters have documented the Friends Mission's philosophy of indigenization, putting the mission ahead of its time, especially in the first thirty years, 1930–1960. The goal had always been to eventually lead the national church to a place of independence and sustainability. At times it seemed that progress was measured in inches, not miles.

During the 1980s the mission staff had begun to look toward the time when the mission would actually leave the field. But in the 1990s, with a complete change of personnel as well as its reduction, the mission seemed to be backing up, reconsidering

---

94. *Actas de la Junta Anual*, 1994–2010, January 1994, INELA archives.

the timing of dissolving the mission. In fact, from 1990 to 1995, both the mission staff and the mission board spoke of the need to increase the number of missionaries coming to the field.[95]

Because of the low number of missionaries on the field, the Bolivian and Peruvian mission councils began regularly meeting together, and the joint mission council replaced the individual field councils. In their retreat in Cochabamba in December of 1990, the joint council minuted a request for the mission board to work toward four families in Bolivia and four in Perú.[96]

The Bolivian mission and the national church continued negotiating their working agreements, as in years past, with a focus on financial benefits. The mission was still subsidizing church property purchases (limiting this to funds on hand), medical care for pastors, theological education (focusing on the extension Bible school, San Pablo Seminary, and the new Friends Theological Center in Santa Cruz, all mission initiatives), and the national missionary program, attempting to encourage national church contributions to these programs as well. The INELA's perspective of the mission's role continued to have the flavor of entitlement.

The hint of a change came during the mission board's midyear meeting in January 1996. Under the leadership of co-clerk Ron Stansell, board members spent time not only considering how to know when the work in Bolivia and Peru would end, but whether or not the board should be looking for new fields of mission work. Change was in the air. The board appointed a task force to explore these two issues.[97]

Gradually the mission staff came alongside the board, and in a proposal presented at midyear board meetings in January 1997, Ed Cammack and Ron Stansell listed possible goals and job descriptions for a limited staff in Bolivia, with several scenarios for what they began describing as a "phase-out."

The conversations continued over the next few years, as the board explored mission possibilities in Ramallah, North Africa, China, and Russia. A necessary part of this expansion was the phase-out plan concerning Bolivia and Peru. The joint mission council sent another draft of what they were now calling a "phase-over plan" to the board in July 1998, proposing that the missions focus on pastoral training in the immediate future, while gradually bringing to a close financial assistance to the national church in all areas. It stated, "We perceive that the work here is progressing to the point that the churches would mature better without constant contact with and support from the mission."[98]

The INELA had no idea that this conversation was taking place. The joint mission council asked the mission board in February of 1999 for its official approval of

95. Edwin Cammack, letter to NWYM, August 14, 1990, NWYM/GFU archives.

96. Joint Mission Council Minutes, December 28, 1990; see also July 16, 1991, NWYM/GFU archives.

97. Board of Missions Minutes, January 26, 1996, NWYM/GFU archives.

98. Joint Mission Council, "Next Stage," July 6, 1998, NWYM/GFU archives.

the phase-over plan so that they could begin dialoging with the Bolivian and Peruvian INELAs, preparing them for the change.[99] Concern was expressed for the national church in both countries, that the shock of this change, with the removal of personnel and funds, not be too damaging.[100]

In July 2000, the Bolivian mission staff informed the *mesa directiva* of the phase-over plan and began to prepare the national church for the change. Meanwhile, Stansell and Cammack continued working on the final draft of the plan, which the administrative council of the mission board approved in November. This spelled out the remaining financial benefits in the categories of theological education and the national missionary movement. The mission was giving the national church just over $10,000 a year in each of these funds in 2000. For the next several years, the offerings would decrease by a third each year, and be terminated by the beginning of 2004. The INELA would be working and planning for ways to financially sustain their programs.[101]

This phase-over plan listed three reasons for the pullout and its timing, claiming that the final change from mission leadership to Bolivian leadership would impart a greater sense of empowerment and authority to the INELA. While not affirming that the national church was perfect, the plan saw the church as ready. The reasons listed were as follows:

> Because of the maturation of the Bolivian INELA. We desire to affirm our confidence in the Christian leadership and Spirit-led discernment of Mesa Directiva leadership, of pastors, of teachers and of the rank and file of INELA membership. We perceive of less and less need for expatriate presence and expatriate resources to assist them (personnel, vehicles, and financial subsidies).
>
> Because Bolivia Yearly Meeting of Friends can and will be increasingly healthy as it generates new internal funding and personnel resources to sustain missions and theological programs. We believe that our deferring to Bolivian leadership and funding in these two critical fields will actually strengthen rather than weaken the work of the Lord.
>
> Because NWYM senses a call to new fields where the gospel has not yet been preached. By phasing over, our limited resources can be redeployed elsewhere. As we do so, however, we invite Bolivian INELA to also consider possible partnership or networking or participation with us in the opening of new fields.[102]

Ed and Marie Cammack retired from the field in June 2001, followed by Jerry and Keri Clarkson in June 2002, the last of a long list of full-time missionaries sent

---

99. Joint Mission Council Minutes, February 13, 20, 1999, NWYM/GFU archives.

100. Board of Mission Minutes, December 18, 1998; July 22–28, 2000, NWYM/GFU archives.

101. Edwin Cammack, letter to NWYM, July 25, 2000; Joint Mission Council Minutes, October 10, 2000, NWYM/GFU archives.

102. Ron Stansell and Edwin Cammack, "Bolivian Friends Mission Phase-Over," October 27–28, 2000, NWYM/GFU archives.

from the Northwest. Hal and Nancy Thomas remained in Santa Cruz, directing the missiology program in the UEB, and giving part-time as counselors and encouragers to the INELA.

The missionaries had expressed concern that the INELA not be shocked or damaged from the loss of personnel and funding. On a first glance, it appears their prayers were answered. At least in the official documents, the INELA appears to have under-reacted to this change. Part of this may be due to the fact that the phase-over was taking place at the same time the church was struggling with the organizational chaos of the *Estatutos* revisions, the various controversies over properties and doctrine, the problems with coming up with an acceptable plan for theological education, and the difficulties in administering both the educational and social action projects. Their focus was naturally on activities for which they were directly responsible. The mission phase-over was deliberately slow and gradual, giving leaders time to get used to the idea.[103]

In his end of the year field report for the Bolivian Friends Mission in 2001, Hal Thomas summed up the state of the INELA and the significance of the phase-over:

> We have partnered with Bolivian Friends in INELA for 71 years. . . . We are now entering a fourth generation of INELA leadership. Our consistent vision has been that the church grow in its own Andean context. We did not propose to reproduce Friends in the Northwest. We aimed to see local and national leaders forming worshipping communities, making their own decisions, visioning and supporting their own programs, discipling their own people, reaching out to new communities in mission, theologizing from Scripture and their unique experience and formation, establishing their own identity. In the 1950s the Mission first stated these goals in terms of indigenization. In today's context of mission we would restate those goals in terms of contextualization—that it reflect the good news and mission of God in this world incarnated in thoughtful Bolivian Aymara experience and perspectives. Because of our own formation as Friends missionaries, Bolivian Friends are part of the evangelical Quaker tradition, and have joined Northwest Yearly Meeting in this calling within the wider Christian movement. They also face their own unique challenges as a distinct church in a distinct culture, and increasingly bring fresh perspective and vision to us all.[104]

Thomas ended his 2002 report by affirming, "We also look forward to those who will partner in new ways and ventures in the coming years. We have encouraged ourselves many times by remembering that the church is not ours, but belongs to and depends on its faithful Creator and Head, Jesus Christ."[105]

---

103. In addition, *mesa directiva* minutes from June 2000 to January 2001 are missing. These may have contained some reaction to the mission's plans.

104. NWYM Minutes, 2001, Harold Thomas report, 44, NWYM/GFU archives.

105. NWYM Minutes, 2002, Harold Thomas report, 44, NWYM/GFU archives.

INELA AT THE END OF AN ERA

In June 1999, a singular event took place in the town on Amacari, on the shores of Lake Titicaca, the site of the first gathering of Aymara believers in what would one day become the Bolivian Friends Church. Now over four thousand believers came together to celebrate the INELA's seventy-fifth anniversary. Seventy-five years previously, in 1924, Juan Ayllón had returned to Bolivia as the first Quaker missionary dedicated to establishing the Friends Church (INELA) on Bolivian soil.

Celebrating 75 years, Amacari, 1999 (E. Cammack)

People came from all the corners of the yearly meeting: from the different districts on the *altiplano*; from districts in the tropical valleys of the Yungas and Caranavi; from the cities of La Paz, Santa Cruz, Sucre, and Cochabamba. Friends from Peru, Central America, and the United States joined, along with representatives from other Bolivian denominations. Aymara Friends gathered to sing, worship, celebrate, and remember over seventy-five years of God's faithfulness to them.

Ed and Marie Cammack described the celebration:

> There was no building large enough to seat them all. The only area which was adequate to accommodate everyone was a large athletic field. A temporary platform was built. Light wires were temporarily installed for night services. Big loud speakers were used to make it possible for everyone to hear. Sunday the local electric company official decided too much electricity was being consumed by the celebrants, so he pulled the switch. Services continued

on schedule, using a small battery-powered speaker. . . . These people enjoy music! Bands came from various churches and united as one large band. . . . People were challenged to live out God's word in their lives, in their homes, churches, communities and the world around them as they go into the next century. They were also challenged to do the mission of the church in making new disciples.[106]

During the period from 1990 to 2002, the INELA increased from twelve to fourteen districts, including Santa Cruz. Statistics of churches and believers varied too widely to be considered reliable. At the beginning of 1990, the INELA reported on two hundred churches. Hal Thomas in the 2002 field report wrote, "Accurate statistical reporting in the INELA continues to be problematic. We have no firm study for 2002, or for previous years in this last decade, to be able to give numbers of members, faithful attending believers, or community. Annual reports identify more than 200 congregations at the present time."[107] This shows a plateaued church, with no numerical growth.

This was certainly an era for the INELA to look back and remember, and to look forward with faith. The period from 1990 to 2002 had its fill of controversies, but the INELA moved forward in important ways, including its ability to administer increasingly complex programs. With the Friends Mission stepping out of the scene, this ability would be put to further testing in the years ahead.

REFLECTIONS ON THE PERIOD

It's interesting to compare events in national history with the development of the INELA in these years. Bolivia's constitutional revision of 1994 was parallel with the INELA's struggle to legally adapt its *Estatutos* to the widening reality of its churches, resulting in the 1998 revision, although this would not end the church's efforts to find an appropriate structure. Likewise, the increasing participation of Bolivia's indigenous peoples in the country's political life was concurrent with the nationalization of the INELA as the Friends Mission left after over seventy-two years of service.

Within the INELA, this period saw a shift from the proliferation of social ministry projects with outside funding to the drying up of that funding and the failure of several larger endeavors (e.g., the shift of the clinic from ministry to source of income and the disappearance of SETALA). This was largely due to lack of administrative experience, including in the area of financial accountability, with some of the problem being the custom of yearly assigning responsibilities with little regard for continuity or the abilities of those given the job. This parallels the traditional community system of assigning *cargos*. This all may have been more a matter of a gradual maturity rather

---

106. Edwn and Marie Cammack, *Keeping Current* (August 1999), NWYM/GFU archives.
107. NWYM Minutes, 2002, 41, NWYM/GFU archives.

than failure, as many in the leadership of the INELA were realizing that specific training in areas of organizational and financial management was necessary.

Missiologically, the most significant event of the period was the dissolution of the mission in 2002.[108] As leaders of the INELA look back at this event, they are divided in their sense of its timing, with many saying that the mission should have stayed longer (and continued sharing its funds), a few sensing the mission should have left sooner, and most people indifferent. The mission's perception of a lack of response on the part of the church at the time has proved correct. By the time the mission left, its personnel in La Paz had been reduced to one family that was focused on education and did not travel widely. While the leaders were aware the mission was leaving, the majority of the people in the church had no idea, and it did not seem that anything had changed. The reduction of mission funding had been gradual and programs had already been turned over. While it did take a few years for the INELA to find ways to fund mission outreach and theological education, it eventually happened. The lack of a big send-off or the fact of the church's under-reaction may mean that the mission successfully met its goal of not causing trauma. "While there was no lament, at least neither was there rejoicing," as one Bolivian Friend put it.

Looking back on the goal of an indigenous church and all that led up to the mission's exit, Friends theologian and historian Humberto Gutiérrez writes the following:

> There were times of tension between the mission and the national church, as the mission pushed us toward independence, while national believers wanted to still depend on foreign resources. These times of tension, even crisis, were part of the church's maturing process. Now the Bolivian Yearly Meeting has its own rhythm of institutional life and continues to develop under the initiative of its own leaders, second and third generation believers. In the future we hope to work more closely with NWYM as partners with shared mission goals in other contexts. The church will continue because it belongs to the Lord.[109]

In considering the development of the INELA as a Friends denomination, what obviously stands out in this period is the continued controversy over the issue of baptism. This is not surprising in a culture that values religious symbolism in both its animistic and Catholic/Christian expressions. But while this particular issue negatively affected the unity of the church, the majority of the people maintained an emphasis on the basic Quaker/Christian essentials: a Christocentric theology, an active belief in the living presence of Jesus as people gather in his name, and a commitment to let the living Spirit lead on both personal and corporate levels. Add to this the growing understanding of the good news of the gospel to include ministry to the whole person

---

108. While the Friends Mission ceased its activity and left the country in 2002 and was dissolved as far as NWYM was concerned, its formal dissolution in Bolivia didn't take place until after 2019, due to legal complexities.

109. Humberto Gutiérrez, letter from La Paz to NWYM, August 2017, NWYM/GFU archives.

and community—a basic Quaker tenet—and we see a people who could rightly identify as both evangelical Christian and Quaker.

Where was the Spirit moving among the INELA in this tumultuous period of its development?

Some leaders responded to this question with a touch of humor in saying that with all the controversy and trauma of the period, "we see the hand of the Spirit in the fact that the church did not destroy itself. We're still here today."

In looking at the drying up of outside money and the loss of social ministry projects during the period, seen as calamities at the time, some see the grace of God as the losses forced the church to refocus on its priorities of discipleship and evangelism. (This is not to say that the failure of the projects and organizations was God's will, but rather that God used loss to bring a needed change.)

And, of course, we see the Spirit of God active in the lives of many persons and congregations where loyalty, faithfulness, and great commitment flourished in the midst of the problems. This is especially evidenced in the national missionary movement in the lives of people like Antonio Mamani Balboa, Victor Quispe, Dionisio Lucasi, and Esteban and Gaby Ajnota.

Finally, we see the presence of the Spirit in the courage and dedication of the Friends Mission in seeking God's will about leaving Bolivia, and then acting on their understanding. The mission and the board went through a difficult time of discernment, with setbacks and doubts, with genuine concern about the effect of a pullout on the national church, but with a commitment to walk this hard path. This was accompanied by the necessary acknowledgment that the church in Bolivia belonged to God and that God would take care of his people.

10

The Post-Mission Years

INELA from 2002 to 2017 (and Beyond)

The historical movement of the nation and the advances of the INELA ran parallel during the years between 2002 and 2017. The key that united them was indigenization. As Bolivia experienced its first indigenous national president, the INELA began functioning without the physical presence of the NWYM mission. This chapter looks at the post-mission years from 2002 through 2017, and beyond.

HISTORICAL OVERVIEW

From the beginning of the new millennium, the political party of indigenous leader Evo Morales, MAS (*Movimiento a Socialismo*), was growing in power and popularity, while the traditional elite parties were diminishing. This reflects what historian Herbert Klein terms the *mestizaje* of Bolivian society.[1] Klein defines the new *mestizo* class as "Indians who entered the labor force, adopted urban norms, bilingualism, and moved into small towns and cities throughout the nation."[2] The city of El Alto (formerly upper La Paz) was the growing center of *mestizaje* and political power.

In the December 2005 presidential elections, Morales won 56 percent of the votes, the first candidate to win over a 50 percent majority since the years of the military dictators. It also marked the first time the president of Bolivia (or any Latin American nation) was a person who self-identified as indigenous. The tide had turned. Morales would go on to easily win reelection twice, in 2009 and 2014, thus making him the longest-running president in the nation's history.

Morales's first term as president was characterized by wide-scale nationalization of companies, beginning with the oil and gas industries, telecommunications, and the electric company, and included the takeover of numerous foreign industries. It was also characterized by its distancing from the influence of the United States, partly

1. Klein, *Concise History*, loc. 4954.
2. Klein, *Concise History*, loc. 4713.

because the focus of this super power was now the Middle East, and partly due to Bolivia's rejection of US attempts to curtail the production of coca. (Morales had previously led the coca growers' syndicate.)

Another mark of Morales's presidency was, not surprisingly, his promotion of indigenous culture, including its values, ceremonies, and customs. Part of his inauguration celebration took place in the ruins of the Tiahuanacu civilization on the *altiplano*, complete with animistic rituals and prayers to the *Pachamana* (Mother Earth), most of it in the Aymara language. Morales carried these customs over into the presidential palace on numerous occasions. He refused to don the formal black suit and tie and dressed in custom-made colorful indigenous fabrics.

A highlight of Evo Morales's first term was the creation of a new constitution, approved by a national referendum in 2009. Klein notes that in its affirmation of the indigenous populations, the Constitution of 2009 "called for the recognition of their dignity and worth as full citizens, especially for those who traced their origins to pre-conquest times. Respect, dignity, and the recognition of individual and traditional community rights and beliefs were declared a fundamental aspect of state policy."[3] Bolivia as a nation began to be officially referred to as the *Estado Plurinacional de Bolivia*.

During these years, general health and living standards continued to rise, although still low in comparison to other Latin American countries. Even more impressive was the rise in literacy and educational levels, placing Bolivia on a par with other South American nations and above the Central American republics and Haiti. By 2012, 87.1 percent of the nation's boys between six and nineteen years old attended school, along with 87.4 percent of the girls.[4] The 2012 census figures placed literacy rates at 94.9 percent of the total adult population.[5]

Another important statistic that affects the life of the church is the change from a rural to an urban population. By 2012 67.5 percent of the population lived in the cities with only 32.5 percent in the rural areas.[6]

Related to the rural/urban migration patterns is an increase in migration out of the country. By 2010 Klein estimates that half a million Bolivians (out of a population of roughly ten million) were living abroad.[7] The 2012 census reconfirmed these figures, showing the majority of Bolivians overseas living in Argentina, Spain, Brazil, Chile, and the United States.[8] These moves were by and large economically moti-

3. Klein, *Concise History*, locs. 5050–55.

4. INE, *Características*, 190.

5. INE, *Características*, 37.

6. INE, *Características*, 15.

7. Klein, *Concise History*, loc. 4916.

8. INE, *Características*, 70–71.

vated, and people living in other cities or countries regularly sent money back home to their families.[9]

Perhaps the most significant revelations from the 2012 census concern the self-identification of the Aymara population. In a country that was beginning to recognize its multiethnic composition, 1.6 million Bolivians identified themselves as coming from Quechua and Aymara roots, accounting for 34.2 percent of the population. Those who identified Aymara roots composed 16 percent of the entire population,[10] but 47.6 percent of the population of the department of La Paz.[11] At the same time the number of people registering a preference for the Aymara language had shrunk to 10.7 percent of the population. This shows the Aymara people becoming a significantly diminishing distinguishable percentage of Bolivia population, indicating a greater assimilation of the Aymara culture into the general Bolivian culture, especially in the city.[12]

In this context of change, the INELA, an indigenous Aymara Friends Church, experienced its first years without the physical presence of the mission. It was a time of stretching toward stability.

INELA FROM 2002 TO 2017

As the INELA entered the next phase of its institutional life, it was struggling and growing administratively, but clearly plateaued in its expansion. In 1990 the church had reported some two hundred congregations spread out over twelve districts. In 2002, while the number of districts had risen to thirteen, the number of congregations was roughly the same. Through the years between 2002 and 2017, the reported number of congregations fluctuated from 210 in 2002[13] to a high of 228 for 2004,[14] leveling out at 209 churches in 2014,[15] and dipping down to somewhere between 184 and 200 at the end of 2017.[16] Losses of some twenty churches were reported in 2013,

9. In 2007 Klein reports that money sent home from family members abroad amounted to 7.4 percent of the nation's GDP (*Concise History*, loc. 4916).

10. INE, *Características*, 29, graph 17.

11. INE, *Características*, 36, illustration 17.

12. INE, *Características*, 12.

13. *Actas de la Junta Anual*, 1994–2010, January 2001, INELA archives. Twelve districts reported 175 churches. El Alto District and Santa Cruz failed to report, and their statistics would have brought the total up to roughly 210 churches.

14. *Actas de la Junta Anual*, 1994–2010, January 2005, INELA archives.

15. *Actas de la Junta Anual*, 2011–2017, January 2014, INELA archives. The La Paz *Directiva* reported 199 churches. Santa Cruz failed to report statistics, which would have brought the total up to around 209.

16. Yearly meeting reports, January 2018, INELA archives. The statistical reports to the 2018 yearly meeting sessions varied, with the president reporting 184 churches and the districts reporting 191 churches. The history team named and counted churches in each district, coming up with around 200 total.

2014, and 2015, probably a repeated reference to the same churches, spread out over the different districts.[17] We sees gains and losses evening out.

In 2000, La Asunta was the last area recognized as a new district. In 2004, Camacho would become the fifteenth district, with no new districts being formed during the next fourteen years.

Leaders who served as INELA president during this time were Silver Ramos (2002–2004), Mario Chávez (2005–2007), Félix Nina (2008–2010), Daniel Limachi (2011–2013), Timoteo Choque (2014–2016), and Hector Castro (2017–). La Paz departmental (state) presidents included Dionisio Lucasi (2012–2014), and Eusebio Aspi (2015–2016).

The struggle for stability would prove greater than the vision for expansion in the years between 2002 and 2017.

ADMINISTRATIVE SETBACKS AND ADVANCES

Administrative issues the INELA faced during this time included the revision of its *Estatutos*, financial sustainability, continuance of ministry programs, project management, and the administration of its school system.

The Continuing Saga of the Estatutos

As has been noted previously, since the first government approval of the INELA's constitution, the *Estatutos*, in 1956, the church had been in a continuous process of revision, trying to get it to match an appropriate Aymara way to administer the church and, at the same time, to keep it legal. We learned in the last chapter that the 1997 *Estatutos* (actually approved in 1998) had proven awkward and controversial for various reasons, and in 2002 the annual representatives meeting decided to go back to the former organization where the church had only one executive body, the national *mesa directiva*, and this in spite of the fact that it was not the legal version. This put the church in a vulnerable position with the Bolivian government.

The revision of the *Estatutos* continued and proved even more difficult with the changes in government, the new national constitution (2009), and attempts the government of Evo Morales was making to regulate religious communities.

In the 2005 January representatives meeting, the assembly unanimously approved the latest revision of the *Estatutos*, with the expectation that the *directiva*[18] would do the legwork to get it approved and legalized by the government. In the same meeting, the assembly decided to elect a completely new *directiva*, not satisfied with

---

17. *Actas de la Junta Anual*, 2011–2017, January 2013, January 2014, January 2015, INELA archives.

18. By this time the INELA had begun to drop the term *mesa directiva*, using simply *directiva* to refer to the executive body of the national church.

the former body's conduct and decisions;[19] this insured that previous ministries and plans would be cancelled and much of the work begun from scratch.

In the representatives meetings of the following three years, the *directiva* would report that the *Estatutos* were not yet approved. In the 2008 meeting, the assembly reiterated that while the 1997 version was legal, internally they would continue operating by the revised (but not yet government approved) version with one national *directiva*. During the same meeting, controversies surfaced, and the assembly again demanded a complete turnover of the *directiva*. None of the newly elected officials had previously served on the national level of the church; they chiefly represented the rural populations of the church.[20] Once again, many past programs and plans were effectively quashed and ministries started from scratch.

In 2011, the representatives felt uneasy enough about the illegality of the form of government they were actually following that they voted to once again practice the 1997 version and elected a three-person national *directiva*, with Daniel Limachi as president.[21] Again, the new officers represented a complete turnover of personnel. This was followed in 2012 with the actual election of both a national *directiva* (with Limachi continuing as national president) and a departmental (state) *directiva*[22] to administer the some two hundred churches in the department of La Paz. Dionisio Lucasi was elected president of the La Paz *directiva*, along with the secretaries of finances, missions, education, and pastoral ministries.[23] (The election of the Santa Cruz *directiva*, to oversee its five or six churches, was left to the Santa Cruz churches to take care of themselves.)

Once again, the INELA found itself with what many were calling a two-headed organization. The awkwardness and confusion over authority continued for the next five years, but without the traumatic conflict that afflicted the church between 1997 and 2002. The two heads (national and La Paz *directivas*) seemed to move forward in an uneasy dance. In the meantime, work on the revision of the *Estatutos* went on, spurred by the need to adapt the revision to changes in the country.

The election of Timoteo Choque as national *directiva* president in the 2014 representatives meeting was fortuitous. Choque, a second-generation Quaker, had been educated in La Paz and was working professionally as a lawyer in a government office. He represented a growing generation of young educated Aymara professionals whose presence in the church was perceived as both opportunity and threat. As INELA president, Choque was charged with continuing the work of the revision, and this

19. *Actas de la Junta Anual*, 1994–2010, January 2005, INELA archives.

20. *Actas de la Junta Anual*, 1994–2010, January 2008, INELA archives.

21. *Actas de la Junta Anual*, 2011–2107, January 2011, INELA archives.

22. For the two lower-level *directivas*, the representatives changed the name from *regional* to *departmental* directiva, to reflect the emphasis of the national constitution.

23. *Actas de la Junta Anual*, 2011–2107, January 2012, INELA archives.

he did from a base of legal understanding, working with the named commission and getting input from all the districts.

In 2016 the representatives unanimously approved the latest revision of the *Estatutos*, and Choque spent much of that year going from one government office to another. With all the governmental changes, the government was not able to give the final stamp of approval (the official fees not yet having been decided), but Choque was assured that this would be just a matter of time. So the 2017 INELA representatives rejoiced and accepted the revision as their new (almost approved) *Estatutos*. This enabled them, after twenty years of confusion, to once again put into practice the governance of one national executive body (the *directiva*), overseeing the work of the fifteen church districts, including Santa Cruz. Although going back to the way it was in the beginning (1956), this was considered by all a major step forward.

Financial Stability and Ministry Programs

With the diminishing of outside funding, the INELA more than ever looked to the tithes of pastors, congregations, and districts to funds its administration. The clinic housed on the Max Paredes property in La Paz had ceased to be a ministry administered by the INELA, and become, rather, an economic resource for the church. The rental of rooms to medical personnel (doctor, dentist, lab technician) became one of the main sources of income for the church, along with tithes from the income of the school on the same property.[24] Up through the beginning of 2004, NWYM continued supporting theological education and the national mission program, in diminishing amounts.

During the years from 2002 to 2012, administrative costs swallowed the bulk of the INELA's budget, with smaller amounts going out for ministry programs.[25] While this in part reflects the fact that some of the ministries had their own, separate, budgets (the school, for example), the church's challenge was to contain administration and focus more on its ministry outreach programs. This imbalance was gradually changing and seems to have taken a turn in 2013, with increasing percentages of the budget beginning to be spent on ministry programs.[26]

---

24. In 2004, for example, the tithe from UEELA, the school, came to b$41,852, income from rentals amounted to b$20,191, and income from tithes of leaders and churches was b$15,730. In 2010, from a total of b$199,777.60 income, b$76,389 came from rental income, with the second largest source of income coming from tithes at b$55,233.80 (2004 financial report, January 2005; 2010 financial report, January 2011, INELA archives).

25. For example, in 2010, b$74,069.20 was spent on administration (the largest amount being *directiva* stipends), another b$21,119.90 spent on legal costs, office expenses and transportation, while b$44,480.60 was spent on ministry programs in missions, schools and social service projects. The two other expenditure items in the report were labeled "Various General Expenses" (b$23,314.60) and "Other Expenses" (b$43,090) (2010 financial report., January 2011, INELA archives).

26. The financial report for 2013 (January 2014) shows increases in giving from tithes, rentals and missionary offerings. For the first time, ministry program expenditures (missions, education, pastoral) are reported to be greater than administrative expenses. The same carries through in the

Closely related to financial sustainability was the continuation of ministry programs that had been partially supported by the Friends Mission and other outside sources. Some of these the INELA was able to carry forward, with appropriate adaptations. With the hymnal replacement fund, for example, the INELA successfully administered the sale of hymnals and oversaw the reprints as needed, a program that continues through the present time.

The literature program went beyond what the mission had previously done in providing tracts and booklets for distribution. The INELA decided to create its own series of adult Sunday school lessons, developing certain theological themes for the year that would be considered in all the churches. The themes for 2005, for example, were the Christian family, leadership, and Friends baptism. In 2012, the theme was Friends history and practices, addressing issues that were currently controversial or points of attack from other denominations (e.g., baptism, women's ministry, and speaking in tongues). With oversight by the *directiva*, writers were all INELA volunteers. Copies were sold at a reasonable rate and local churches encouraged to use them. Funds collected went toward future printings.

The program for medical assistance to pastors and teachers has been more difficult to sustain as it has no reciprocal source of income but has had to be budgeted from the INELA's general funds. During the post-mission years, the *directiva* has continued to consider individual petitions for help and to make decisions on a case-by-case basis. In addition, the INELA has consistently attempted to provide help to retired pastors. They have managed, off and on, to do this, at least in minimal amounts. The national church continues to wrestle with these issues. Meanwhile, in so many cases, family members and local churches have found ways to help meet the medical and retirement needs of the men and women who have served among them.

Another area in which the mission had made significant contributions in matching funds was in property purchase and church building construction. After several years of diminishing offerings, the mission cut funding for property purchase near the end of the 1990s. Again, the INELA has found this level of help to congregations difficult to sustain. They continue to consider appeals and make decisions on a case-by-case basis, according to available cash on hand.

But what the national church has not been able to sustain, increasingly local congregations are finding local resources to both buy land and put up their own buildings, a healthier model.

We could cite many examples, but one of the most notable is the rebuilding of the New Jerusalem Friends Church on the Max Paredes property in La Paz. Many people in the INELA consider this congregation to be the "mother church." It was the first organized Friends Church, dating back to 1924 and the ministry of Juan Ayllón. The original construction of the church building in 1938 saw heavy financial contributions from OYM, alongside the contributions of many local believers in labor and

---

report for 2014 (financial report, January 2015, INELA archives).

materials. (See chapter 3.) This church hosts the annual representatives meetings and serves as a center for much of the activities of the INELA.

In February 2008, the monthly business meeting of the New Jerusalem Friends Church unanimously decided that it was time and adopted the theme "Let Us Arise and Build" (Neh 2:18). The meeting appointed ten commissions to work on different aspects and began planning. On May 11, the congregation held a thanksgiving worship service, and the next day began demolition of the building that had served INELA believers for over seventy years. It was reported to be a day of "tears and nostalgia," as well as of breaking down the walls. The demolition took two months, with members of the local church doing the labor, much of it during the evenings.[27]

Rebuilding the New Jerusalem Friends Church (H. Thomas)

During the next eleven months, many people joined with the local believers, offering labor, materials, food and finances. The dream of local believers was that "the New Temple, 'New Jerusalem,' will be house of prayer, a place of salvation and new life, a place of reconciliation, a place of rejoicing and celebration, and also a place from which many will leave this world to enter the presence of God for all eternity."[28]

The financing of this huge project was an important part of the story. We read in the church's news bulletin, "We went through some difficult times when we had not even one centavo left in the treasury to let us continue the work. . . . So we got on our knees and cried out to the owner of all wealth. The answer came immediately, and

27. New Jerusalem Friends Church, "Informative Bulletin #3, INELA archives.
28. New Jerusalem Friends Church, "Informative Bulletin #3, INELA archives.

many brethren joyfully gave their offerings. It's unbelievable, but true. And because of this, we never stopped working, not even one day."[29]

Other financial offerings came from a local hospital, some Catholic believers, other Friends churches, and former NWYM missionaries. The women of the local church contributed through work projects, sometimes cooking all night in order to sell meals during the day. Other people organized sales of used clothing, and many people contributed physical labor.[30]

On May 17, 2009, the church celebrated the final roofing with a parade and a worship service that lasted from 8:30 a.m. to 7:00 p.m., with times out to eat together.[31] The building included a parking basement and five stories, with the second story meeting room and balcony able to seat over eight hundred persons. While the finishing work went on for several more years, the building had effectively been erected in a little over a year, largely through local resources.

This example was repeated in other congregations, some on the same scale as the New Jerusalem Friends Church (e.g., the Tabernacle Church on El Alto and the Laja Friends Church on the *altiplano*). It demonstrates an area in which the national church has clearly grown from dependence to independence. It's especially significant that it happened, and is happening, on the local level.

National and International Connections

Part of the INELA's organizational development has been the cultivation of relationships with other organizations, both within the country and internationally. During this post-mission period the INELA has continued contact with the National Association of Evangelicals of Bolivia (ANDEB), especially important in coming to understand how the new laws of the country affect churches; but the INELA continues to resist becoming members of ANDEB.

Connections between the INELAs of Bolivia and Peru are strengthened through the annual "bi-national" conference as Friends from these neighboring countries gather to worship, learn, and discuss matters of mutual interest.

Although the FWCC no longer financially supports large projects in Bolivia, the INELA is an active member of its American division, COAL, and this has proven an important link to the larger Quaker family. COAL funds transportation for INELA leaders to attend annual and triennial meetings throughout the world. FWCC has continued, on a limited basis, to contribute to smaller projects, such as joining with NWYM to sponsor writer-training workshops. The INELA has maintained loose connections with two other Quaker organizations: Quaker Bolivia Link (QBL) out of England and the Bolivian Quaker Education Fund (BQEF) from the United States.

---

29. New Jerusalem Friends Church, "Informative Bulletin #3, INELA archives.
30. New Jerusalem Friends Church, "Informative Bulletin #4, INELA archives.
31. New Jerusalem Friends Church, "Informative Bulletin #4, INELA archives.

The INELA also continues to relate to the family of evangelical Friends around the world, mainly through its membership in Evangelical Friends Church International (EFCI) and, of course, in its ongoing relationship with the Northwest Yearly Meeting of Friends (NWYM). In 2010 the Board of Global Outreach of NWYM organized a permanent committee to encourage the ongoing relationship of the two yearly meetings (as well as the Peruvian INELA). The board sponsored the 2015 visit of INELA president, Timoteo Choque, and his wife, Elisabeth, to yearly meeting sessions in Newberg. Choque gave a state-of-the-church address for the INELA and expressed the INELA's gratitude for the years of investment and ministry. Cooperation between the two yearly meetings in mission outreach continues to develop.

Another important link between the INELA and NWYM, and a point of administrative development, has been the joint history project that resulted in this book. The team of investigators and writers from both yearly meetings worked together for over five years (2013–2018) to better comprehend how the INELA has come to this point in its story. The project necessitated inter-visitation and many online conversations.

LEADERSHIP TRAINING PROGRAMS

The designated funds from the mission continued through the end of 2003, and as long as these were in place the extension Bible school program limped ahead, but after a brief surge of thirty-eight students and seven graduates in 2003,[32] it gradually ceased to exist. The locally organized ISETA training program had a component of distance education as well as a central site in La Paz, and this program seemed to replace the older extension Bible school. Mission funds in support of the San Pablo Seminary also ceased at the beginning of 2004, and while this interdenominational program continued, the INELA no longer chose to use it for the preparation of its pastors.

In spite of setbacks, ISETA continued. In the 2015 representatives meeting, ten ISETA students had finished their year of practice and were brought forward for recognition as pastors. In 2016, the center in La Paz offered night classes for twenty-six students, while the residential center in Israel (Caranavi District) hosted nineteen. Centers in Laja, Cullucachi, and Tunari together saw an additional thirty-two students finish the year.[33] In 2017, the number of students in five centers grew to ninety-nine.[34] While half the students in the La Paz center come from other denominations, students in the outlying centers are young adults who hope to serve in the INELA.[35]

In Santa Cruz, the Friends Center of the UEB continued to function for a few years, representing the different Friends denominations in Bolivia and Peru, but its distance from La Paz made it difficult for the INELA to consider it as a serious component in its theological education program. In addition, many students from the La

32. Report of INELA secretary of theological education, January 2004, INELA archives.

33. Hector Castro, annual president's report, January 6, 2017, INELA archives.

34. Nelson Sullca, interview with Harold Thomas and Nancy Thomas, November 27, 2017, La Paz.

35. Nelson Sullca, interview with Harold Thomas and Nancy Thomas, November 27, 2017, La Paz.

Paz region or from Peru who went to the UEB for their theological education decided to stay in the more pleasant Santa Cruz region upon graduation, instead of returning to pastor churches in the high lands as their sponsors had hoped.

In addition to the efforts to facilitate a formal theological training program, the INELA continued sponsoring pastors' conferences and short courses, and these were a source of encouragement to leaders. Both the youth organization, UJELAB, and the women's organization, UFINELA, sponsored leadership seminars that gave training. One member of the national (or regional) *directiva* was charged with the oversight of ministry to the pastors, but the problem of the training of the next generation of leaders for the INELA continued to challenge the church. In the statistics for the 2016 year, it was noted that of the 202 functioning congregations, 170 had pastors, leaving thirty-two churches without pastoral ministry.[36]

SOCIAL OUTREACH

We have seen how the strength of the INELA's social ministries began to wane in the 1990s, partly through administrative struggles that resulted in the drying up of outside funding. This tendency continued on through the post-mission years. Yet, on district and local levels, the church continued to reach out to help meet the social and economic needs of its context.

Educational Programs

The focus on education continued, with five schools functioning in 2002. Administrative and financial problems with the large Rey Salomón school in El Alto (including failure to pay back taxes and teachers' benefits) prompted the INELA to shut it down in 2004. The school in Villa Alicia also folded in 2004, leaving the large school on the Max Paredes property in La Paz to be administered by the INELA and two small rural schools that were put under the care of local churches (Israel and Suriquiña).[37]

In spite of the loss of the majority of the INELA's schools, the school on the Max Paredes property in La Paz flourished in the post-mission years. The annual report for the 2003 school year showed 396 children (almost as many girls as boys) in the primary, intermediate, and high school levels.[38] It became known as UEELA (*Unidad Educativa Evangélica Los Amigos*). The INELA's secretary of education, Raúl Mamani, communicated in his 2005 report the goal to make the school one of the finest in that section of La Paz and noted that "what the parents and the surrounding neighborhoods value is the high quality of our educational services."[39] His committee was cooperating with the broader educational reform in the country, following the basic

---

36. Pablo Sossa, annual report of secretary of pastoral ministries, January 4, 2017, INELA archives.
37. Report of the secretary of education, January 2005, INELA archives.
38. Report of the secretary of education, January 2004, INELA archives.
39. Report of the secretary of education, January 2005, INELA archives.

national plan, and adding courses and extracurricular activities, setting up science labs and supplying computers. Part of the INELA's stated purpose was to impact with Christian education that would affect character, behavior, and even the family life of the students.[40]

Friends school in La Paz, UEELA (H. Thomas)

By the end of 2014, pre-kinder and kindergarten levels had been added and attendance was up to 556 students;[41] that number grew to 584 for the 2016 year.[42] In addition, a counseling department was offering services to troubled students and their families. The stated aim continued to be a Christ-centered education.[43]

Yet, with all the good things happening in the UEELA, administrative and financial troubles plagued the school. With a growing student body, the school was soon handling more money than the INELA,[44] with some of that money going into the gen-

40. Report of the secretary of education, January 2005, INELA archives.

41. Report of the secretary of education, January 2015, INELA archives.

42. Hector Castro, annual president's report, January 6, 2017, INELA archives.

43. Report of the secretary of education, January 2014, INELA archives.

44. In 2009, for example, the school's income came to b$648,486.81, with b$533,118.69 going out in expenses (*Actas de la Junta Anual*, 1994–2010, January 2010). The general income of the national church was b$151,037.57 and its expenses b$142,322.10 (report of the secretary of finances, January 2010, INELA archives).

eral funds of the church. In his 2010 annual report, the secretary of finances reported on the unclear financial reports of the school, noting that "the hen that lays the golden egg is in trouble."[45] Some of the income was being deposited in the name of different leaders for "safe keeping," and in other cases the surplus funds on hand tempted leaders to borrow money to use in other programs, and then finding it difficult to pay back. Tax records for several years were unclear, and receipts from purchases hadn't been kept. Several times during this period leaders had to be publicly reprimanded and dismissed from their positions because of financial mishandling.

In 2011 the school advertised for the position of accountant and interviewed several candidates, finally choosing a young Friend from the South Yungas District who had completed her university work in accounting. Sonia Quispe was at the time attending the New Jerusalem Friends Church and was active in the youth group. She accepted the position and immediately proposed a strict plan for managing the school's complicated accounts. Although problems from the past still threaten the school, since 2011 with the application of professional standards of management, the school has shown itself to be sustainable and is functioning well.[46]

Another educational program the INELA continued to cooperate with was Compassion, International. In previous decades, several rural schools had run after-school Compassion programs, offering extra help to students with their schoolwork. During the post-mission period these programs continued, even after the rural schools closed. Friends churches in the communities could still offer the Compassion program in cooperation with the local public schools, with kids coming to the church after school to get needed help. Through most of this period, ten different Compassion centers worked through Friends churches, providing help to kids in their communities, not just to children of believers.

The Bolivian Quaker Education Fund (BQEF), although not a program of the INELA, has benefited the church's young people, and, indeed, INELA young adults have provided most of the local leadership of the program. BQEF's scholarship program began in 2003 through the initiative of Newton Garver, from New York Yearly Meeting, who was concerned to help young people from all the Quaker groups in Bolivia get a university education. While the state universities were free, the incidental costs (books, transportation, room and board) made it impossible for many Friends young people to get the higher education that would allow them to become professionals and advance in life. So Garver gathered concerned Quakers from various unprogrammed yearly meetings in the United States and formed the non-profit BQEF. The group gives scholarships to Quaker students for incidental university costs, beginning in 2003 to work with fifteen students and a budget of $15,000. By 2008, the group was supporting forty students with a budget of $60,000.[47] Bernabé Yujra, an

45. INELA *Actas de la Junta Anual,* 1994–2010, January 2010.

46. Sonia Quispe, interview with Nancy Thomas, November 9, 2017, La Paz.

47. *Actas de la Junta Anual,* 1994–2010, January 2008, INELA archives.

INELA employee of BQEF, reports that between 2005 and 2019, the organization has helped some 98 INELA young people finish their university education and become professionals.[48] The program fills a need and continues to this day.

The Bolivian Evangelical University (UEB) in Santa Cruz provides another higher education option for Friends young people. The INELA continued its presence on the UEB Board of Trustees in the person of David Tintaya, an INELA Friend who served different terms as president, secretary, or treasurer on the board. Friends students participated in many of the UEB programs, in addition to the training in theology.

Medical Programs

While the clinic on the Max Paredes property had begun to function as a source of rental income, no longer directly as a medical service of the INELA, the challenge to offer this type of service continued. The focus shifted to the development of a health center in the community of Amacari, scene of the beginnings of the Friends work in Bolivia. As noted in the previous chapter, the English non-profit organization, Quaker Bolivia Link (QBL), had invested heavily in this project prior to 2002, the first building had been constructed, and the health center had begun to function. Most of the finances had come from Ireland Yearly Meeting of Friends, through QBL. In honor of the Irish Friends, the clinic was named the "Bolivian Irish Medical Center."[49]

Yet the project was plagued with administrative confusion, and the struggle for leadership shifted back and forth from the INELA *directiva*, to the Peninsula District, to the town of Tiquina, to QBL, and even to the neighboring Catholic University (UAC) that cooperated with the hospital for several years.

The complete changeover of the INELA *directiva* in 2008 once again made it difficult to carry on with established programs and plans, and this naturally affected involvement in the Amacari medical project. While the center continued functioning in 2008 and 2009, with some support from QBL, by January of 2010 its administration had been passed over to the municipality of Tiquina (the county center). This marked the end of the INELA's involvement, after a twelve-year effort.[50]

The Amacari hospital was still functioning at a minimal level in 2018, under the administration of the municipality of Tiquina.

The Buen Amigo

Several smaller social projects functioned in the post-mission years, some of these with QBL support. But one of the most significant efforts originated from the grass

48. Bernabé Yujra, report to INELA, March 12, 2019, INELA archives.

49. In 2006 QBL leader Juan Aparicio reported that start-up costs had been shared by QBL (US$41,294), the local town, probably Amacari ($10,127), the surrounding community, probably Tiquina ($5,190), and INELA ($2,836); report to QBL, October 18, 2006, INELA archives.

50. *Actas de la Junta Anual*, 1994–2010, January 2010, INELA archives.

roots concern of young INELA Quakers wanting to respond to the social and economic needs of people in rural churches.

In 2010, Sonia Quispe was serving as president of the La Paz District youth organization, UJELAB. Sonia and her executive body were experiencing a sort of holy restlessness, wanting to do something active in response to the needs they sensed among the INELA constituency. So they decided to undertake a simple project in the community of Copusquía in the Lago Norte District where a Friends Church had been established. The Christmas season was approaching, so the group began collecting toys and clothes from the various Friends churches in La Paz.[51]

After the planning phase, they were ready to serve. A small group of young people gathered at the New Jerusalem Friends Church in the middle of the night to load up and begin their adventure. The trip proved quite an adventure in itself. The bus broke down mid-journey and they managed to get all the people and materials into a van. They traveled for two days and nights, having to park the van in a village after the first night and go forward on foot the next day and, later, with the help of some burros. Rain and the need to cross rising rivers added to the excitement.

The actual experience in Copusquía proved "hugely satisfying," in Sonia's words. The brethren put them up in their homes. The young people on the team were impacted by the needs they encountered in the community and surrounding area and felt both sorrow at these needs and joy at the chance to give something. They also felt a sense of respect for the people in the community.

The team presented evangelistic services in the evenings and during the day interacted with around 150 excited kids. They served them hot chocolate, and one member dressed up as Santa Claus as they distributed the clothes and toys.

At this point, the young people had no plans of forming an organization. This was an isolated project of the La Paz District UJELAB. Even so, they gave themselves the name *Buen Amigo* (Good Friend).

In 2012, Quispe and those who had participated in the project met with other motivated young people and adults in both the La Paz and El Alto Districts. They shared their strong desire to be of service and began organizing and making plans for further projects. They continued calling themselves *Buen Amigo*. All of this was outside the formal structure of the INELA. During 2012 the group responded to needs in the Camacho and Pacajes Districts. They distributed toys and clothes in Friends churches during the Christmas season, and provided the services of a doctor and a dentist as well.[52]

In 2014, major flooding in the Bolivian lowlands resulted in an emergency situation, affecting Friends in the Asunta and Alto Beni Districts. *Buen Amigo* mobilized

---

51. Much of the information for this section comes from an interview with Sonia Quispe, Rubén Maydana, Francisco Mamani, and Reynaldo Mamani, conducted by Humberto Gutiérrez, 2017, La Paz.

52. *Actas de la Junta Anual,* 2011–2017, January 2013, INELA archives.

INELA leaders to join them and provided leadership to a relief effort, gathering and distributing food, water, clothing, and temporary shelter for those affected. Members of the women's organization, UFINELA, and the missions commission of the INELA also participated, and many young adult volunteers gave of their resources, time and energy.[53] People worked together to meet the need, all under the coordination of *Buen Amigo*.

The group presented a formal proposal in the 2015 representatives meeting, asking to come under the umbrella of the INELA. The proposal showed a clear vision for holistic mission, with an emphasis on social help to communities in need, but with an accompanying evangelistic outreach. It based itself theologically on the twin mandates to preach the word of God and to love one's neighbor. The proposal also contained detailed activity and financial reports, showing the project to be totally self-supporting, with no outside financial resources, nor intent to solicit any. The assembly enthusiastically approved the project.[54]

Rubén Maydana, a leader in UJELAB, joined *Buen Amigo* in 2012 and has been involved in its leadership since that date. He reported that the fundamental idea behind the group is social service as part of the historic testimony of Friends. Becoming part of the INELA as a youth, he was impacted by missionaries who came with the gospel, but also with a profession they could use to help others. He talks about how impactful the actual experiences of service have been to those involved, such that they can't now consider not serving the needs of others and are always wondering how to do more, or how to serve in better ways.[55]

WOMEN AND THE YOUTH

The organizations representing the women (UFINELA) and the youth (UJELAB) of the INELA also continued to develop during the post-mission years. In fact, this is where much of the health and vitality of the church was expressed.

The Spirit of UFINELA

As had been the case in previous decades, the women of the yearly meeting were known for their hard work and sacrificial spirit, especially for the cause of mission outreach.

The annual UFINELA reports to the representatives meeting were normally a list of activities and special offerings, signifying a tremendous amount of work and outpourings of generosity. In her 2005 report, UFINELA president Marcela Mamani gave the typical impressive list (including visits to all fourteen districts and mission trips to

---

53. *Actas de la Junta Anual*, 2011–2017, January 2015, INELA archives.

54. *Actas de la Junta Anual*, 2011-2017, INELA archives.

55. Sonia Quispe, Rubén Maydana, Francisco Mamani, and Reynaldo Mamani, interview with Humberto Gutiérrez, 2017, La Paz.

the cities of Sucre, Oruro, Cochabamba, and Potosí) and summed it up by saying, "Everything went forward normally," in typical Aymara understatement.[56] After a similar report in 2009, the yearly meeting minutes record that "the report was approved with much applause,"[57] not a typical reaction, but an appropriate recognition of value.

The reports always included fund-raising and special offerings taken for national mission projects. During these years, the women helped rent a meeting place in Potosí, pay for the property for the new church in Oruro, purchase bricks for the construction of the New Jerusalem Church in La Paz, clear the land and put up a fence for a project in the Alto Beni District, as well as support national missionaries with their regular offerings.[58] Almost all the work and the fund-raising of the UFINELA were directed outward, in support of missions.

Again, in the 2015 meeting of the representatives, the assembly not only approved the UFINELA's annual report, the entire gathering applauded. (The authors of this text were present and joined in the applause.) The only observation made to the report was to say that the rest of the church should be doing more to support and encourage the women in their work.[59]

UFINELA officers send greetings, 2013 (H. Thomas)

56. *Actas de la Junta Anual,* 1994–2010, January 2005, INELA archives.

57. *Actas de la Junta Anual,* 1994–2010, January 2009, INELA archives.

58. See reports in the *Actas de la Junta Anual* for 2008 to 2015.

59. *Actas de la Junta Anual,* 2011–2017, January 2015, INELA archives.

THE STORY OF MARCELA MAMANI

Marcela Mamani served as UFINELA president from 2004 to 2005. Her simple story represents that of many of the women who have worked in the church. When elected to the position in 2003, she was an unmarried and relatively young woman in her early forties. This was definitely a leadership position she had to grow into.[60]

Marcela grew up in a mountain village east of La Paz where some thirty believers gathered in a Friends church. She attended the local grade school, but the teacher taught in Spanish and Marcela, with the rest of the children, spoke only Aymara. When economic circumstances forced her to migrate to La Paz as a teenager, she says she could not read or write in any language, and she felt insecure speaking Spanish.

The city frightened Marcela, but she knew she could find a spiritual home among Friends. Wanting to serve God, she talked with the president of the New Jerusalem Friends Church on Max Paredes Street, who said she could provide flowers for the worship services. So Marcela began a small business, selling candies and fruit drinks on the street, and dedicated it to survival and flowers for the church.

Through church attendance and contact with believers, she began perfecting her Spanish, eventually teaching herself to read, using the Spanish Bible and hymnal. She was invited to join the local branch of UFINELA, and at her first meeting she was named treasurer. She protested that she could not read, write, or do math, but the other ladies told her God would help her learn. She began copying words and numbers into a notebook, teaching herself to write. She served as treasurer for several years and was then named secretary. She gradually became literate in both Spanish and Aymara. She continued in the following years serving in the local women's society and visiting other Friends churches as opportunities arose.

During the annual women's conference in November 2003, held as usual in the New Jerusalem Friends Church, Marcela stayed outside selling fruit drinks, planning to donate the money to an UFINELA missions project. She had been praying that God would help the ladies choose the right officers for the coming year.

On the Saturday of elections, one of the ladies came outside to ask her to join them. She agreed, intending to help in prayer. But when she was asked to sit up front with the officers, it dawned on her that her name was on the list as a candidate for UFINELA national president. She felt moments of panic, sensing her lack of formal education. But because of the way she had prayed, she felt she should submit to the process. She silently asked God to let the other candidate win.

But Marcela Mamani was chosen president of the national UFINELA for the 2004/2005 term. She came to enjoy the role, especially the opportunities to visit all the districts and encourage women all over the yearly meeting. A natural leader and businesswoman, she learned to lead administrative meetings, organize conferences, promote projects, and encourage other women to join her in the work.

60. Marcela Mamani, interview with Nancy Thomas, July 7, 2004, Santa Cruz.

After her term as president ended in January of 2006, Marcela again took up her job of selling candies on the streets of La Paz, until summoned to a new assignment. The New Jerusalem Friends Church called her to pastor its mission outreach congregation in the city of Cochabamba. Marcela gladly accepted the challenge and served in this pastoral role for two years, until coming down with cancer. She had to be flown home to La Paz and once there the leaders of UFINELA and the women in the New Jerusalem congregation took charge of caring for her until her death in 2012. While Marcela Mamani would not be considered a major leader in the INELA, she was a much loved and appreciated servant of the church and its Lord, typical of many others.[61]

The Spirit of the Youth

Along with the women's organization, the national Friends youth organization, UJELAB, continued to develop. This organization now represented a new generation of young Friends who were more educated than their predecessors and, in many ways, more restless and wanting to interact with their context in positive ways. Many were becoming professionals.

In response to the needs of the church and the context, young Friends became involved in two large projects during the post-mission years: the development of a retreat center in the Palos Blancos area of the lowland Alto Beni District and the organization of the volunteer group for social ministries, the *Buen Amigo*.

THE PALOS BLANCOS PROJECT

Palos Blancos is a jungle town in the Alto Beni District. The INELA's mission outreach to the Alto Beni area began in 1996 when national missionary Dionisio Lucasi moved there and began evangelizing and discipling groups of new believers in five villages, Palos Blancos being one of these and serving as the center of the new work. Both the UFINELA and the UJELAB desired to be involved in the INELA's mission work and participated in the effort in Palos Blancos from the beginning. NWYM missionary Jerry Clarkson also encouraged this work,[62] and mission funds helped support it, contributing US$4,000 for property purchase (half the actual cost) in 1997.[63] The INELA had great hopes for the development of this property.

In the years following its purchase, the potential of the Palos Blancos property continued to capture the attention of the INELA, but its development was to prove problematic. Comprised of 11,646 acres, problems with property titles took time to resolve. Several proposals such as beginning a school or planting orange trees seemed to get nowhere. Yet delegations from the national *directiva*, UFINELA, and UJELAB

---

61. Teodora de Aspi, interview with Nancy Thomas, November 12, 2017, La Paz.

62. *Actas de la Mesa Directiva*, 1996–1999, December 7, 1996, INELA archives.

63. *Actas de la Mesa Directiva*, 1996–1999, January 4, 1997, INELA archives.

continued to visit to encourage the local believers and envision the development of a ministry.

In the 2009 representatives meeting, the assembly honored the work of the women and the youth in promoting the work in Palos Blancos and decided that from that point on, the UJELAB and the UFINELA would together be in charge of the project.[64] Under the leadership of president Rubén Maydana, UJELAB presented a five-year project proposal (2009–2013) to develop a Friends Retreat Center that would host camps, spiritual retreats, and workshops, primarily in support of leadership development for the INELA.[65]

Members of the *directivas* of UFINELA and UJELAB seemed to work well together, and the next few years saw them traveling frequently to Palos Blancos, being active in clearing and fencing the land, drawing up and getting approval for the building plans, and beginning construction on the first building. None of this went smoothly, of course, partly due to administrative confusion over leadership of the project.

While the women and youth may have worked well together, others were also involved. An INELA Palos Blancos commission,[66] Alto Beni District, and the local Palos Blancos church each felt entitled to leadership in the development of the project. Once again, administrative confusion seemed to reign, with too many "heads" vying for control.[67]

The projected 2013 date for completion of the Palos Blancos project came and went, with the annual reports of UFINELA and UJELAB informing of limited activity, but obviously no longer giving leadership to the project. In the representatives meeting of January 2017, the INELA turned the property back to the Alto Beni District, to develop or not as they would.[68] The property titles are still not clear, but the local Friends church continues to meet there.

THE STORY OF RUBÉN MAYDANA

In looking at the contributions of youth in the post-mission years and at the development of leadership in the future generations of Friends, the name of Rubén Maydana has come up several times, both in regards to the Palos Blancos project and to the organization of the *Buen Amigo*.

Rubén Maydana was born in La Paz in 1978.[69] His parents were not involved in any evangelical church, but they were good people with strong values. His father worked as an electrical engineer; his mother stayed at home to attend the family.

---

64. *Actas de la Junta Anual*, 1994–2010, January 2009, INELA archives.
65. *"Proyecto Palos Blancos,"* 2009, INELA archives.
66. *Actas de la Junta Anual*, 1994–2010, January 2010, INELA archives.
67. *Actas de la Junta Anual*, 1994–2010, January 2010, INELA archives.
68. *Actas de la Junta Anual*, 2011–2017, January 2017, INELA archives.
69. Information for this story comes from an interview with Rubén Maydana, conducted by Nancy

Rubén attended primary and high school in La Paz, and upon graduating from high school, he attended an industrial training school, finishing with a license as an electrical technician. He worked in industry for several years, including a stint in the Bolivian Naval Forces.

As a young man, he discovered the charismatic Pentecostal megachurch called Ecclesia. He was drawn to the vibrant youth program, and at fourteen years old he decided to become a Christian. The young people studied the Bible, learned how to teach and preach, and went out to put their training into practice. Rubén, a timid youth at the time, gradually developed leadership skills and learned to speak in public. The pastor modeled leadership and genuinely cared for the youth under his care. But when this pastor fell into moral sin and had to leave the church, Ruben, disillusioned, also left.

The next several years were rough, yet the Spirit of God continued to speak to him, drawing him back into Christian fellowship, in spite of his resolution to stay away from churches. Some young people from his neighborhood invited him to the Golgota Friends Church, and he saw something so positive in their lives that he responded. For about two years he did nothing but "warm the bench," as he puts it. He was unsure of himself and did not feel that God could pardon him for his past failures. That changed little by little, and his friends persuaded him to become active in leadership in the youth group. He began studying the Friends way of being the church and found himself entering in.

After a time of leadership at the local level, he was elected to a position on the *directiva* of the La Paz District youth organization, UJELAB.

In 2009 Rubén was elected president of the national UJELAB, a position he served in for four years. As such he was involved in leading the Palos Blancos project, a task that proved challenging. He experienced the tensions in the national church between the youth and the adults, as well as between urban Friends, such as himself, and rural Friends, representing much of the leadership of the INELA. The failure of the Palos Blancos project was a source of deep disappointment. But he learned much from that experience and gained the respect of his elders as well as his peers. During those years of leadership in UJELAB, Rubén had left off full-time employment, and gained his living by contract work on specific projects in his profession, thus freeing him to devote most of his time to the church.

In 2012, now free of the UJELAB role, Rubén joined the leadership team of the *Buen Amigo* organization, and this has proved a source of life and hope. Since 2014 he has been employed full-time at the Friends high school (UEELA) on Max Paredes Street. He teaches computer science and Christian education and finds satisfaction in this role.

Thomas, November 7, 2017, La Paz.

Rubén Maydana with computer students (H. Thomas)

In 2016 he married Abigail, a young woman from another Friends church in La Paz. He continued to hold his membership in the Golgota Friends Church and served a term as church president. In 2016 he was named president of the La Paz District of the INELA. Rubén has also been active in FWCC and COAL activities and has had the privilege to travel and get to know the wider family of Friends.

Looking back, Rubén remembers reading a manuscript by Carmelo Aspi on the history of the INELA and being impacted by the missionaries who integrated evangelistic work with humanitarian service, noting the schools for children, literacy work, the farm, medical help, and other acts of service. This has become for him a vision of what the church should be, and his dream is that INELA members come to have a deeper biblical understanding of Christian service, followed by obedience in acts of service.

INELA IN RESPONSE TO COMMUNITY OBLIGATIONS AND CULTURAL PRESSURES

The Aymara culture is highly communal in nature, as we have seen, along with its paradoxical emphasis on individualism. The rural Aymara family lives in a specific community, and that community offers the family certain advantages and makes of it certain demands. The community obligations have been a part of Aymara life centuries before the beginnings of the Friends Church in this culture. These obligations to fulfill certain *cargos* or leadership tasks in the running of the community affect every man (and, by extension, every woman who shares the *cargo* with her husband).

And yet these obligations and pressures are, in a sense, the "elephant in the room" of the church. They are rarely addressed in sermons or classes. Part of the heritage of the holiness movement the missionaries brought with them included a strong theology of separation from the world. This brought a prohibition on political activity that somehow filtered down to the level of local community service. And yet the pressures the community exerted, part and parcel of the culture, were strong. The individual believer was left, as it were, to decide on his own how to respond, knowing there were consequences for compliance and consequences for refusing to fulfill local obligations. These obligations always involved the pressure to participate in the animistic offerings and the ritual drunkenness, which is a large part of the reason Christians held back. This has been part of the unspoken history of the Friends Church (along with every other Protestant group in the country) since the beginning.

Historically, individual believers have responded in different ways. Some have refused participation in community service, and of these, some have suffered persecution including loss of their lands. Others have gotten by because of community indifference. Many have announced that they are retiring from church for their year of community service; they then give in to the unacceptable aspects of this service; some return to the church after the year is up, publicly confess, receive forgiveness and are reinstated. Many never return to the church.

And then there are those believers who manage to serve their communities and maintain their Christian testimony. This is a more difficult way.

During the years this chapter addresses, 2002–2017, the negative pressures involved in community service have intensified, due to the presidency of Evo Morales. Especially in the early years of his presidency (2006–2010), Morales pushed indigenous values in all levels of national life. A law was passed requiring all members of a community to respect and practice the *usos y costumbres* ("practices and customs") of that community, a reference to whatever cultural customs the majority of community members followed. In most Aymara communities that meant honoring the ancient animistic practices. Concurrently, the national constitution guaranteed freedom of religion and the right to refuse to engage in religious practices according to one's conscience. But this right was not widely known among the people in the communities who felt only the pressure to conform.

In all of this the Friends Church remained largely silent.

In recent years, since 2010, the pressure has grown lighter as people have come to know their constitutional rights. Yet an adequate response to the challenge of community service remains to be articulated by Bolivian Friends.

In spite of this, there are Bolivian Quaker leaders who have found a way to express their Christian testimony through service to their communities. The stories of

Eusebio Lecoña and Remigio Condori serve as examples as the rest of the church wrestles with this challenge.

The Story of Eusebio Lecoña[70]

Eusebio Lecoña is a member of the Ch'ojasivi Friends Church, part of the *altiplano* Frontera District of the INELA. As a young man, soon after his conversion in 1975, he moved to La Paz to attend the Patmos Bible Institute. Upon graduation he completed his military service, married, and moved back to his community of Ch'ojasivi, serving a few years as pastor of the church.

When Eusebio decided to go ahead and fulfill his obligatory responsibility of service to the community, he asked the congregation to support him and pray for him, telling them of his determination not to compromise his Christian testimony. During that first year, he discovered that he could apply to his new role all that he had learned in Patmos in terms of administration (the importance of doing things carefully and in order, following the established rules and regulations, careful financial accounting, and so on). This contrasted to how the tasks had been carried out previously, and other community leaders noticed this and affirmed him. His work made a difference, and Eusebio discovered a new vocation in community service. He continued year after year, fulfilling different roles, gradually climbing the ladder of responsibilities, coming to serve on the provincial as well as the local community level. As of this interview, he had dedicated more than thirty years to community service.

Eusebio Lecoña in official costume (E. Lecoña)

70. Eusebio Lecoña, interview with Harold Thomas and Nancy Thomas, December 26, 2017, La Paz.

Since community work demands so much time, Eusebio found it necessary to resign leadership roles in the church (including pastor), but the church approved of his calling and has continued supportive, in contrast to Friends churches in other communities. Eusebio has been able to keep up faithful attendance at church. He began the practice of coming to the church every Sunday morning at 5:00 to pray until the services begin. Sometimes others join him; often he prays alone.

From the beginning of his service, Eusebio let it be known that he was an evangelical Christian and as such was not rich and could not invert a lot of money into sponsoring fiestas, and that he would not drink or buy beer for meetings or fiestas. Once, when obligated to sponsor a fiesta (it was his turn) he refused but offered as an alternative to sponsor a meal for the whole community after the fiesta (a more expensive alternative than just buying the beer). The result was much appreciated by the community. Because of his refusal to compromise and his firm commitment to hard work and honesty, the community and surrounding region respect him and automatically ask him to pray at the beginning of meetings and events.

Some of the concrete contributions Eusebio has made for his community of Ch'ojasivi are the construction of a clinic, a police station, and a military training center. He has worked with a committee for reforestation, setting up a tree nursery. He has also served four years as a high school music teacher.

Eusebio tells the story of when he was serving on the mayor's council in the provincial town of Pucarani in 2008. Evo Morales, president of Bolivia, had called for a gathering of provincial mayors and council members in the department of La Paz. The mayor of Pucarani was a friend of Morales and sat across from him at the banquet. At the start of the meal, Morales loudly asked if there was anyone present who was a Christian and could pray for the meal. (Eusebio says it was hard to tell whether the president was serious or doing this as a kind of joke.) The mayor pointed to Eusebio, who then felt a moment of panic, but complied by offering a sincere grace while all stood and bowed their heads.

Afterward, Morales engaged Eusebio in conversation, asking him how long he had been a Christian, telling him that his grandmother used to take him to a Baptist church when he was a boy. Morales especially remembered the song "I Have Decided to Follow Jesus," which he enjoyed singing as a child. When the waiter served the drinks, Morales asked that they serve a soft drink to Eusebio.

Eusebio testifies that since the beginning of his years of community service, he has not once compromised his Christian testimony. His testimony is not just negative—a refusal to drink, participate in pagan fiestas, or give offerings to the spirits—but a commitment to serve with honesty and integrity, bringing the best of his education and abilities to better life in his community.

Eusebio has a deep concern that the church—on the level of the INELA administration, down to the local churches—has not taught the brethren about their community obligations or how to carry them out, nor is it preparing young people for what they will face in the future.

The Story of Remigio Condori[71]

Remigio Condori is from the *altiplano* community of Kera, part of the Altiplano Sud District. He is well known in the INELA, having pastored several Friends churches and serving as president of the INELA from 1992 to 1994 and as executive secretary of the La Paz Region of the church from 1998 to 1999. He also served a two-year term as a national missionary among the Mosetén tribal peoples in Alto Beni.

Concurrent with his service to the INELA, Remigio has kept up his community service in Kera, and now that he is a "retired" pastor, he puts even more time into the community.

Kera currently has about seventy-five families and around 250 persons. There are three evangelical churches in this small community: the INELA Friends, the Bolivian Church of God, and the Seventh-day Adventists. The three churches cooperate with each other and with the community, a rather unusual situation. Town meetings take place in the churches, with the three taking turns. Remigio has been key in bringing about this level of cooperation.

Remigio first became involved in community service as a youth, mainly because he was one of the few who knew how to read and write, and because he had taught himself Spanish. So he grew up in community service, as well as in the church and found no disparity between the two.

He says he's involved in his community because as a Christian he's concerned for the community and wants to help address its problems. He sees the importance of love for both the community and for the church, and he understands the role of his Christian testimony partly as the responsibility to fight corruption wherever he sees it. His consistent reputation for honesty, integrity, and generosity has gained him the respect of the community. People routinely ask him to pray before their official meetings.

Remigio says that the Kera Friends Church has always supported him and prayed for him. That may in part be due to his teaching.

In contrast to Eugenio Lecoña, Remigio has resisted climbing the levels of service and becoming involved on the regional and provincial levels. He has chosen to limit his service to the local community of Kera, partly because he observes the corruption and political infighting at the higher levels.

Remigio sees the changes that Evo Morales has brought as positive, that now more people are aware of indigenous people and their rights. More government help has come to rural communities such as Kera as a result, although he observes that this has also brought more temptation to corruption. As for the law that demands respect for local *usos y costumbres*, Remigio says it's not been a problem in Kera because of

71. Remigio Condori, interview with Harold Thomas and Nancy Thomas, January 7, 2018, La Paz.

his years of service. People don't insist on the old Aymara animistic practices and the custom of heavy drinking as part of the fiestas, knowing this is not acceptable to the Christians. "We're working well together," he says.

He mentions that one of the good things President Morales has done is to restore cultural pride in their traditional costumes. For a man that means his colorful poncho, his *gorro* (knitted cap), and his authority whip. Remigio always uses these in ceremonies; they signify responsibility and respect.

Remigio tells the story of something that happened around 2012. According to Aymara customs, twice a year the community gathers in the fields to perform the animistic sacrifices to the mother earth, asking for protection from the elements and for a good crop. These happen at the time of seed-sowing and again at harvest. Blood offerings are sacrificed (sheep or llama) and the blood is sprinkled on the ground. For two years in a row the Christians refused to cooperate, and after the offerings were made, hail destroyed the crops, putting the community at risk.

On the third year, under Remigio's leadership, the three evangelical churches proposed to the town that instead of the traditional offerings, they spend three days in prayer and fasting for the fields. The community agreed, and each church sponsored one of the days of fasting, with the whole community in attendance. At the end of each day, the fast was broken with a feast, and the community leaders themselves provided the food.

That year hail did not come and the harvest was abundant. Now this is the new custom of the community, with the three-day prayer and fasting services in the three evangelical churches happening twice a year. While this does not mean the whole community has become evangelical, it does signal a new level of cooperation between church and community, and an openness to the working of God.

MISSION OUTREACH OF THE INELA

In 2002 Dionisio Lucasi was named the new INELA secretary of missions, a position he held for the next three years. Previously he had been serving as national missionary in the Alto Beni tropical area, which was recognized as a district of the INELA in 2000. He brought a personal sense of passion for missions to the job, as well as his years of experience.

During the years of Lucasi's service, and with the support of offerings from the NWYM, the church was able to maintain support of national missionaries most of the time in the outposts of Cochabamba,[72] Sucre,[73] Oruro,[74] the Lago Norte and Camacho

---

72. Antonio Mamani Balboa in 2002.

73. Victor Quispe in 2002, Crispin Cruz in 2003.

74. Valerio Corani, 2002–2004; Celso Cutile in 2004.

Districts,[75] and in a new work in the city of Potosí.[76] The INELA supported four national missionaries in 2002 and three in 2003 and 2004.[77]

In 2003, Lucasi promoted a new church plant in the city of Potosí, in the department by that name, following up on a vision to have Friends churches in each of the departments of Bolivia. Lucasi and others began house-to-house evangelism in Potosí for three months, inviting Hugo Flores, an Assemblies of God pastor, to work with them. Flores was from the Alto Beni area where Lucasi had formerly worked and he spoke Quechua, the language of Potosí. Flores began gathering the new believers together for Sunday worship in September of that year.[78] During 2004, the INELA gave Flores a small stipend to pastor the work in Potosí, as they did with their other national missionaries.[79]

Early in his term of service, Lucasi began encouraging the district and local churches to be active in their own mission outreach, not depending on the national church to carry the full weight of the church's outreach program.[80] This would become more and more important as the INELA began to feel the loss of funds from the outside. Several churches and individuals responded in practical ways, such as supplying pulpits and benches for the new congregations in Oruro and Potosí.[81] Some of his training workshops for mission workers were aimed at the secretaries of mission on the district level.[82] And, as mentioned earlier, the women's and youth organizations of the INELA continued to actively support the mission effort.

In 2005, another seasoned national missionary, Victor Quispe, was named INELA secretary of missions. Quispe brought the same level of passion and experience to the job as had Lucasi, but in the following three years, the lack of outside financial resources impacted the work.

During the years that Quispe served, 2005–2007, the representatives meeting minutes make no mention of national missionaries. Hugo Flores continued to pastor the new work in Potosí, and Quispe made regular trips to Sucre, Oruro, Potosí, and other places, often accompanied by members of the UFINELA *directiva*. He was also able to visit the congregation planted in Buenos Aires, Argentina back in 1987 (see chapter 8), and get in contact with a gathering of Friends in Sao Paulo, Brazil, sending them hymnals and literature.[83]

---

75. Esteban Anamuro in Lago Norte in 2003 and in Camacho in 2004.

76. Hugo Flores, 2004.

77. See the INELA annual reports of the secretary of missions, January 2003, January 2004, January 2005, INELA archives.

78. Report of the secretary of missions, January 2004, INELA archives.

79. Report of the secretary of missions, January 2005, INELA archives.

80. *Actas de la Junta Anual*, 1994–2010, January 2003, INELA archives.

81. *Actas de la Junta Anual*, 1994–2010, January 2005, INELA archives.

82. *Actas de la Junta Anual*, 1994–2010, January 2004, INELA archives.

83. *Actas de la Junta Anual*, 1994–2010, January 2007, INELA archives.

Yet the national missionary program was clearly running low on enthusiasm, as well as funds. Quispe reported to the 2008 representatives that he had tried to offer missionary training courses in 2007, but that no one seemed interested.[84]

The election in 2008 of all new *directiva* officers, none of whom had had experience in leadership on the national level, set all the programs of the INELA back. This included the national missions ministry. The work in Potosí dwindled and died, while the new church in Oruro went forward, pretty much on its own, with some encouragement from the El Alto District.

Even so, in 2011 the missions commission began to dream and pray and plan how to reignite the spark. They planned to again place national missionaries in three areas—the Camacho District, the Beni lowlands, and the city of Oruro. They began to raise money locally and plan how to bring in funds from the outside. Early in February 2011, the national *directiva* sent a letter to the NWYM Board of Global Outreach, requesting its participation in a mission project by giving $5,000 a year to support three national missionaries.[85]

Meanwhile, the board had been considering how to encourage the INELA, without reintroducing a dependency on outside funds. For several years, former missionaries Hal and Nancy Thomas had been making short visits to Bolivia to facilitate the writers' seminars, begin the history project, and encourage the church. After discussing the INELA's proposal and recognizing the need, the board gave the Thomases permission to meet with INELA leaders and together design a program that would encourage in a healthy way the mission outreach of the church, including limited outside financial support.

The two yearly meetings worked out the plan in 2011, and in March 2012 representatives of the national and La Paz regional *directivas*, together with Hal Thomas on behalf of the NWYM Board of Global Outreach, signed a five-year agreement. Under this plan, the INELA would make a yearly mission plan that included national missionaries, then raise the money locally to carry out the work. Each year, the NWYM mission board would contribute an offering equal to 30 percent of what the INELA had raised, up to a limit of $5,000 a year. The plan included regular activity and financial reports from the INELA, and visits of encouragement and teaching from NWYM personnel.[86]

84. *Actas de la Junta Anual, 1994–2010*, January 2008, INELA archives.
85. *Mesa directiva*, letter to NWYM, February 14, 2011, INELA archives.
86. "*Convenio Proyecto Misionero*," March 6, 2012, INELA archives.

**NWYM representative Hal Thomas and INELA president Daniel Limachi
sign missions agreement, 2012 (H. Thomas)**

Although the bulk of the fund-raising and all of the mission work would be carried out by the INELA, the encouragement of the partnership of the NWYM, plus the additional financial support, was enough to once again fan the flames of enthusiasm for the missionary endeavor of the church. In 2012, the first year of the partnership, the INELA managed to raise US$6,632 in offerings, with the NWYM board contributing just under $2,000. Between 2012 and 2016, the INELA locally raised a total of $30,509, and the NWYM board gave an additional $9,152. The men of NWYM took this offering on as their contribution.[87]

Under the umbrella of the secretary of missions and his commission, national missionaries were again sent out to the Camacho District, to the city of Oruro, and to different areas in the lowland department of Beni.[88] The missionary training seminars began again and evangelistic campaigns were carried on in the districts that requested them.

87. Harold Thomas, "Cummulative Report: INELA Bolivia and NWYM the Mission Project, 2012–2016," March 27, 2017, NWYM/GFU archives.

88. Report on Joint Bolivia INELA-NWYM Missions Project, December 20, 2017; report of the mission work 2013, January 2014; report of the mission work 2014, January 2015, INELA archives. These national missionaries included Benito Guerrero, Eugenio Poma, Fernando Camara, Estaban Anamuro, Valentín Mamani, Benita Mamani, Gabriel Villaba, and Rogelio Parijahua.

From the beginning of the agreement, finances went through the La Paz regional *directiva* into a special fund ably administered by the regional secretary of finances, with regular reports to the INELA as well as to the NWYM board. Throughout the whole period of the project, financial accountability was sound and transparent, with spending focused on the ministry rather than overhead costs.

The annual missions report for 2012 gives a sense of the focus and approaches of the program. This report was jointly prepared by Daniel Limachi, national president of the INELA; Dionisio Lucasi, president of the La Paz departmental *directiva*; and Emilio Villca, secretary of finances for both the yearly meeting and the department:

> In the [state] of Beni we are with the Chimane tribal people, native to the area, and who live near the town of Yucumo. . . . Most of these people live at a low economic level, do not have stable housing, and still maintain their traditional lifestyle. They cultivate few agricultural products. But the community where we are working as a church has become aware [of other alternatives] and, as a result of having received the teachings of the Word of God, are trying to move out of this life of poverty.
>
> Another point of mission [in the state of Beni] is in the town of Piedras Blancas, which is 17 hours from La Paz [and passes through Caranavi and the region of Alto Beni where we have many churches]. . . . The inhabitants are Chimane and Tacana tribal people, plus the Quechua and Aymara immigrants [who have come to farm and trade] from the states of Oruro, Potosí, and La Paz. Here we have a multi-cultural church and different languages where we are able to communicate through the Spanish language. . . . It is the gospel that unites us in love.
>
> Benita Mamani is our single missionary here.
>
> In the state of La Paz we are working in the mountainous province of Camacho. . . . We have two churches there in the high mountains and valleys north of La Paz in an area of very traditional Aymara culture where the current policies of the national government encourage the traditional religion with its rituals. Our work here is very difficult.
>
> Our missionary here is the Benito Guerrero family.
>
> In the state of Oruro we are working in the city of Oruro to consolidate our believers through a process of discipleship and formation of leaders who are developing good understanding of the Bible and Friends principles.
>
> Our missionary here is the Fernando Camara family.[89]

The report includes a section detailing the activities of the secretary of missions and his commission and a recognition of the responsibility of missionary outreach having passed from the Bolivian Friends Mission of NWYM to the INELA:

---

89. "Report on Joint Bolivia INELA-NWYM Missions Project," July 20, December 20, 2012, INELA archives.

We have coordinated and supported the activities of our missionaries through visits, letters, the Internet, and telephone contact. In all of this we recognize the contribution and example of the Bolivian Friends Mission that, through your missionaries, was present with us for 80 years. And now we are patiently supporting and encouraging our own missionaries in these three states, expecting that the new converts and leaders in these mission points will also mature and take their place [along-side us] in the INELA. We recognize that we must be persistent and patient in this task.[90]

The INELA continued its mission emphasis on the three areas of Beni, Camacho, and Oruro up through 2016, supporting national missionaries in each area.

Another aspect of the mission outreach of the INELA in these years was the growing awareness of the presence of Friends churches in Brazil and Argentina. In the 2014 and 2015 representatives' meetings, members from the church in Buenos Aires attended, José Sosa in 2014 and the church's pastor, Tiburcio Cruz, in 2015. Sosa reminded the assembly of the history of the church, having been established in 1987 with the visit of three INELA leaders from La Paz, one of whom was his brother, Elías Mamani. In the intervening years several INELA leaders had visited, and the group continued to meet.[91] Cruz reported that the church had recently purchased property for a building, having formerly met in homes, and that attendance now averaged fifty people. The representatives enthusiastically received these visitors with their reports and recommended that Argentina be officially a part of INELA's mission outreach.[92]

In January 2017, the missions commission of INELA presented a five-year proposal that contained a detailed administrative manual and expressed a desire for continued financial cooperation with NWYM.[93] Part of the proposal reads, "We understand that evangelization and the extension of the Kingdom of God through missionary work has no borders. In recognition of this great truth, the *mesa directiva* of INELA Bolivia will create mission works in other countries, in coordination with the Global Outreach Board of Northwest Yearly Meeting, to evangelize and plant Friends churches in Argentina, Brazil and other countries."[94]

The philosophy underlying the plan is clearly holistic and Christo-centric, as reflected in its mission statement: "To expand the Kingdom of God through evangelization and discipleship in places where Christ has not yet been preached with the goal of making converts who will live transformed and free lives, who will themselves promote human and community development, resulting in men, women and families

---

90. "Report on Joint Bolivia INELA-NWYM Missions Project," July 20, December 20, 2012, INELA archives.

91. *Actas de la Junta Anual, 2011–2017,* January 2014, INELA archives.

92. *Actas de la Junta Anual, 2011–2017,* January 2015, INELA archives.

93. *Proyecto de Obra Misionera en Bolivia y el Exterior, 2017–2021,* January 2017, INELA archives.

94. *Proyecto de Obra Misionera en Bolivia y el Exterior, 2017–2021,* January 2017, 2, INELA archives.

that are agents of change, contributing to a state of well-being, dignity, and peace-with-justice as signs of the Kingdom of God."[95]

In 2017 the men of NWYM approved entering into another five years of cooperation, agreeing to annually contribute 30 percent of what the INELA itself would raise for its mission outreach.

INELA AT THE END OF THE PERIOD

Throughout this period between 2002 and 2017, the INELA attempted to develop and administer several major projects, but with uneven results. There has been a pattern of ambitious and well-developed project proposals, enthusiastic endorsement by the national church, but followed by a failure to carry them out. Chief examples include the closing of most of the INELA's schools, including some that had received substantial outside financing (e.g., Batallas, Villa Alicia, and Rey Salomón). Other examples are SETALA, the medical centers in La Paz and Amacari, and the Palos Blancos project.

But the successes were there, too, chief among them the growing school on the Max Paredes property in La Paz, the UEELA. Although plagued by administrative problems, the school has grown in reputation as well as in number of students and provides a quality education for urban children. The *Buen Amigo* project and the project to write the history of the INELA are other large endeavors that appear to be succeeding. Large building projects have been carried to completion on the local level, a significant accomplishment.

The joint national missionary project could also be seen as an example of a large project that is succeeding. This, along with the history project, are examples of limited outside contributions helping, while not causing dependency.

But questions remain. As stated at the beginning of this chapter, overall numerical growth of the INELA remained plateaued throughout this period at around 200+/- reported congregations. In bringing his statistical report to the representatives in January 2017, Jesús Huallpa reiterated the problem of inaccurate statistics: "I wasn't able to gather statistics for all INELA members because not everyone [referring to local churches] responded to the form I sent out, and the numbers that were sent in were not real."[96] While the national missionary emphasis has strengthened the church and planted new congregations in the targeted areas, the unexplained losses of over twenty congregations in other areas leveled out the gains.

Undoubtedly, by the end of 2017 the INELA could be described as an autonomous, independent yearly meeting. In addition to dealing with the situation of plateaued growth, the challenge will now increasingly turn to becoming an interdependent yearly meeting, maintaining healthy relationships with NWYM, EFCI, other

---

95. *Proyecto de Obra Misionera en Bolivia y el Exterior, 2017–2021*, January 2017, 4, INELA archives.

96. Jesús Huallpa Cutipa, report, January 4, 2017, INELA archives.

Quaker groups, and the wider church, relationships with a more mutual character, allowing Bolivian Friends to make their own unique contributions.

REFLECTIONS ON THE PERIOD

It is obvious that the presidency of Evo Morales throughout this period has exercised a powerful influence on the development of the INELA, as well as on the country as a whole. The growth of the sense of dignity, worth, and autonomy of all indigenous peoples took place simultaneously with the fact of the INELA's independence from the presence of the mission, and this has contributed toward the INELA's maturity as a yearly meeting.

Perspectives of different church members about the Morales government reflect a certain ambiguity. While the government has strengthened the Aymara people's sense of identity, it has not solved their economic and social problems, and the president's popularity is slipping even as he attempts to extend his presidency beyond the limits allowed by the national constitution.

There is more tension between rural and urban Aymaras, as the president has repeatedly affirmed the status of traditional rural people, resulting in less attention to urban Aymaras. The INELA is roughly divided half and half between rural and urban believers. As mentioned in previous chapters, this division has long been a source of tension in the church and this particular conflict has been acerbated in the last fifteen years.

Another tension has to do with the government's insistence on a return to indigenous practices in the rural communities, putting believers under pressure to conform to traditional customs as part of their community service. On the other hand, this has encouraged many to speak up for their constitutional right of freedom of religion, leading some to strengthen their Christian testimony even as they serve their communities. A challenge that the INELA still needs to live up to is to provide its constituency with guidance in how to do this well.

In considering the missiological significance of the period extending from 1990 to 2017, the fact of the INELA's plateaued growth is a cause of concern among the leaders. As noted above the planting of new churches through the national missionary movements and other evangelistic efforts has been offset by the closing of just as many congregations. The church needs to reflect long and hard on this situation.

The causes are complex. In our times of joint reflection, different leaders offered several possible explanations. The fact of migration to the cities affects rural churches. As young people make permanent moves to La Paz and El Alto, many rural churches are left with older people, and when these die, the church closes. Young migrating Friends sometimes connect with urban Friends churches, sometimes they find a more exiting Pentecostal option, and others simply drop out of church altogether.

A fairly recent phenomenon is the reaffirmation of rural roots, and many urban Aymaras are making an effort to maintain ties to their communities of origin, returning home to register and vote in elections, for example. Some Friends living in El Alto travel out to their communities to attend church. Even with this situation, urban migration is one of the reasons for the loss of rural congregations.

Some people insist that confusion about Quaker baptism drives people away, causing loss of membership. And it is true that other denominations have criticized the INELA for their lack of water baptism, accusing the church of heresy. New believers often struggle with this issue, and several churches have been lost over it.

Other young Friends are troubled by the continued conflict within the church, as well as what they perceive as the dysfunction of the perpetually changing leadership and the consequent lack of stability. Inadequate training of national evangelists and missionaries is offered as another reason for decline. Dedicated service but without unified and consistent strategies makes for uneven results. Others suggest that the leadership and pastoral training programs need to come into step with the times, recognizing that young adults today are better educated and need levels of theological studies in tune with their educational development and professional status.

And it may be that Quaker leadership and administrative practices are not conducive to large numbers of congregations. The values of a horizontal level of leadership with high participation of the whole church encouraged, while matching similar values in the Aymara culture, are simply not efficient if the church grows beyond a certain point. Actually, this can be seen in Quaker yearly meetings around the world that tend to be small. It may be that around two hundred congregations is the maximum of what the present administrative model can maintain.

These are all issues the church is beginning to wrestle with, seeing the needs and desiring to expand into the surrounding populations.

In terms of maintaining its Quaker testimony, the INELA continues to strongly affirm the Christocentric position that dates back to George Fox in seventeenth-century England. They affirm the Bible as God's written word and the Spirit as the living Word able to speak to God's people today. These are basic Quaker positions. They struggle to maintain the horizontal egalitarian approach to leadership, partly because the surrounding Christian culture is strongly influenced by a hierarchical leadership model (complete with "apostles" whose word may not be disputed) and an insistence that only men may minister publicly. They also struggle to balance evangelistic outreach ministry with service to the poor.

There is a growing desire on the part of many young adults in the church to understand and affirm their evangelical Quaker roots. This grows along with contact with Quakers worldwide, both programmed and unprogrammed.

Reflecting on a deeper level, it seems clear that the Spirit of God has been at work among God's people in the years since the mission left in 2002. With all the struggles and even the conflicts, the church persists and matures. The INELA has become an independent yearly meeting in its own right.

We especially see God's Spirit in the church at worship, as Friends gather to sing (loudly, long, and with great sincerity), pray out loud, and listen to leaders share from the Word. We see the Spirit's movement in the lives of people dedicated to service, such as the women and the way they pray and sacrificially offer their funds and goods for the missionary movement. We see the Spirit in the holy restlessness of young people in the Palos Blancos project and in beginning the *Buen Amigo* organization. We see the Spirit in the new administrative maturity of the school on the Max Paredes property and in developing the new *Estatutos* after so many years.

We see Jesus alive and well in people like Marcela Mamani, Rubén Maydana, and Sonia Quispe, and in brave rural Quakers such as Eusebio Lecoña and Remigio Condori who are keeping their Christian testimony strong while serving the needs of their local communities.

There's a way yet to travel, but the INELA is still walking that mountain trail.

11

Faithfulness through the Generations

The Tintaya Family Story

The relationship of the Tintaya family to the Bolivian Friends Church extends from the early gathering of believers in Amacari (estimated 1915–1924) on the shores of Lake Titicaca and the Laja Friends Church on the *altiplano* (early 1930s). Their lives move through generations and geography to reflect the development of the INELA, projecting on to its future. The story of this one family, exemplary of so many others, serves as a specific narrative review of the hundred-year history of the INELA.

As of the writing of this chapter (2018), David and Arminda Tintaya live in the lowland city of Santa Cruz. David pastors the Friends Christian Congregation (CCA) in the city and also serves on the Board of Trustees of the Bolivian Evangelical University (UEB). Arminda works as registrar in the same university. Their two older daughters, Anabel and Anahí, have both graduated from the UEB, and Joana is still in high school.

The David and Arminda Tintaya family (D. Tintaya)

David and Arminda are leaders in the church as well as in their professions and, along with their daughters, exemplify how the profile of Bolivian Quakers has changed. Yet their roots go back to their rural Aymara communities and their ancestors made vital contributions to the development of the INELA in each period.

THE GRANDPARENTS

In the early 1900s, the fishing village of Amacari nestled on the east side of Lake Titicaca as a free community. Adobe houses gathered around the central plaza, along with a Catholic church. Other small homes lay scattered throughout the village and out into the countryside. Individual plots of crops provided for each family, and small fishing boats lined the docks each evening.

Through some kind of spiritual spontaneous combustion, Amacari became the scene of the first group of Christian believers in what was later to become the *Iglesia Nacional Evangélica de Los Amigos*, or INELA. (See chapter 1.) As we have seen, the believers met for several years with no denominational affiliation, under the leadership of men like Cruz Chipana and Manuel Alvarado, new believers themselves. In 1924, Bolivian Quaker missionary Juan Ayllón began visiting the group, and at some point the believers decided to become part of the Friends denomination that Ayllón was forming. In 1931, newly arrived OYM missionary Carroll Tamplin appointed Cipriano Mamani as the first Friends pastor of the Amacari Friends Church, and soon a small grade school was also organized.

David Tintaya's paternal grandparents, Mariano Tintaya and Nicolasa Mamani, were part of this small protestant church. Mariano Tintaya was probably a fisherman, along with most of the other men in the village. Among their other children, Francisco, David's father, was born in Amacari. The year was 1929.[1]

Arminda's maternal grandparents, Mariano Jahuira and Leandra Huanca, were among the founders of another early Friends church, located in the small *altiplano* town of Laja, just northwest of La Paz.[2] Mariano grew up in the *altiplano* community of Sullcataca Alta, where he went to primary school. He moved to La Paz as a young man.

Mariano became a Christian when a missionary took him to the Friends church in La Paz where he responded to an altar call. That missionary may have been Juan Ayllón who later discipled the new believer. While still young in his faith, Mariano Jahuira helped found the congregation in Laja. He was named the first leader of the new church (an *encargado*, or "the one in charge" of leading services), not because of any pastoral training, but because he was the only one among the three founding couples who could read and write. This would have been in the early 1930s.[3] In its beginning days, the Laja congregation was a dependent of the church in La Paz. Mariano married his wife, Leandra, in the new Laja Friends Church, and Juan Ayllón served as an official witness, signing their marriage certificate.

---

1. Information about David's grandparents and father comes a recorded interview David conducted with Francisco Tintaya, 2014, El Alto.

2. Information about Mariano and Leandra Jahuira comes from an interview with their granddaughter, María Rosa Tazola, conducted by Nancy Thomas on January 19, 2014, Laja.

3. Carroll Tamplin, letter to OYM, January 22, 1932, NWYM/GFU archives.

Leandra Huanca had been raised by a Christian mother (this would be Arminda's great-grandmother) in the small village of Jank'ok'ala on the *altiplano*, a place where persecution of Protestant Christians was the norm. When Leandra's father died, her mother took the three kids and escaped to La Paz. There her mother and one sister died. Leandra somehow managed to keep her faith in God, finally finding stability in marriage to Mariano Jahuira.[4]

Mariano's granddaughter María Rosa Tazola, who lived with her grandparents in Laja as a child, remembers that her grandfather had the gift of evangelism and was tireless in his efforts. He visited all the houses in the community and beyond, invited people to church, and was apparently fearless and fervent. "He talked with everybody," she reports.

When he spoke out in the community, people listened quietly because he had the voice of authority. He preached powerfully and with gestures. María Rosa even remembers being told about his advice to newly converted young people, counseling them to live lives of purity and holiness. He told the young men, "Watch out that your pants don't fall down," and to the young women, "Watch out that your skirt doesn't come off."

God blessed Mariano Jahuira with abundance, reports María Rosa. He supported his family as a farmer and also served as the town's midwife. His character as a hard worker extended to the church as well. The family tells stories of his bringing rocks from the mountains on his burro to help build the first temple for the La Paz Friends Church on Max Paredes Street in 1938. He would ride his bicycle across the *altiplano* running errands for people, ever attentive to the needs in the local congregation.

Mariano and Leandra served in their church for over three decades until sometime in the 1970s when the sect known as the "Prophecy Friends" caused division in the Laja church. This was the group led by Eugenio Nogales of the New Jerusalem Friends Church in La Paz. (See chapter 6.) The Jahuiras left to join the sect, taking with them other members as well as benches and even pictures off the walls. As we have seen, this sect caused confusion among several churches, but gradually grew smaller and smaller. Mariano and Leandra stayed with it, but just before they died, sick and in bed, they asked members of the Laja Friends Church to come to their bedside where they asked forgiveness, saying they might have been mistaken in changing their allegiance.

THE PARENTS

David's Parents, Francisco Tintaya and Francisca Quispe de Tintaya

Francisco Tintaya, David's father, was born in 1929 in Amacari.[5] As noted above, his parents were part of the newly organized Amacari Friends Church, still considered

---

4. Quispe Jahuira, "Mi historia," 88.

5. Information about Francisco Tintaya's life comes from an interview David Tintaya taped with

a missionary outpost at that time. Francisco and his three brothers grew up in the church and he remembers Cipriano Mamani, pastor of the congregation, and Juan Ayllón, the denominational leader. He recalls the coming of the first Anglo missionary, Carroll Tamplin, especially the little launch that Tamplin used to travel around the lake. He was acquainted with Howard Pearson and Helen Cammack. He recalls that the group of churches was called by the brethren "The Oregon Friends Church."

But all was not easy growing up in Amacari. Francisco did not receive any formal education. When still a boy, he lost his father, and his mother's remarriage made life difficult for him. His stepfather beat him, not an uncommon situation, so the adolescent Francisco ran off alone to the big city, not an uncommon response.

The city of La Paz overwhelmed him at first, with its crowds and noise. Francisco slept out in the open for his first weeks in the city, but he soon found a way to survive by selling ice cream on the streets. But within that first year, a stranger, a worker in a candy factory, kidnapped him, took him into his home, and forced him to work in the factory. This went on for two years, and all this time Francisco had no contact with his family back in Amacari.

After two years, Francisco's "keeper" rewarded him by dressing him in nice clothes and letting him go to the movies. Francisco took advantage of the opportunity, and after the movie ended he caught a city bus up to the Friends Church on Max Paredes Street, effectively escaping his captivity. At some point shortly after his escape, he ran into his stepfather at the church. This man angrily asked him where he'd been, telling him his mother was worried. After hearing the story, the stepfather confronted the man who had sequestered Francisco, but no legal action was ever taken.

Francisco gradually became skilled as an electrician, working with machinery. This gave him employment in the city and, coupled with his growing commitment to the local church in La Paz, introduced a stability into his life. He also met his wife-to-be in the La Paz Friends Church.

David's mother, Francisca Quispe, was born in the village of Ch'ojasivi on the shores of Lake Titicaca. (There is a Friends church in the village today.) While still a young girl, Francisca's father, Isidro Quispe, was murdered, and local leaders, wanting to take his land, forced Francisca's mother, Marcela Aruquipa, to take the kids and abandon the village.[6] Marcela and several of her children soon died of fever and diarrhea, common causes of death among the poor. One brother and sister, along with Francisca, survived to adulthood. So, like Francisco, she tried to adjust to the big city of La Paz and finally found work as a domestic maid. She also made her way to the La Paz Friends Church where, not only did she become a Christian, she found a family among the believers. Francisco and Francisca were married in La Paz.

---

his father in 2014, and interviews between the authors and David Tintaya (February 12, 15, 16, 2016), Santa Cruz.

6. Oscar Tintaya, letter to Nancy Thomas, June 5, 2017; interview with Harold Thomas and Nancy Thomas, December 19, 2017, La Paz.

Little by little the couple became involved in the life of the local congregation. Francisco repaired and maintained the equipment in the church, keeping the loud speakers and microphones functioning. They began traveling to the different quarterly meetings and other INELA gatherings, thus becoming acquainted with the whole denomination. During the same period, the two began practicing with the newly forming choir of the La Paz Friends Church, the beginning of what was to become a rather famous choir among the churches of the Bolivian highlands. They started traveling out with the choir to sing in different churches.

Francisco found a job as caretaker on the mission's property in El Alto, La Paz, and he and Francisca lived there until they were able to buy the land from the mission and build their own home. Three boys were born to the couple on El Alto: Jaime, David, and Oscar.

Francisco, Francisca, Jaime, and David (NWYM)

Neither Francisco nor Francisca had much formal education. They did not learn to read or write as kids because they had to concentrate on survival. But as young people and adults they undertook their own education. They taught themselves to read using the Bible, although Francisca never became very adept. David says of his father, "He was very disciplined. He dedicated every Saturday afternoon to reading and writing. It was a sacred time."[7] They bought books, especially from the Wycliffe related organization, CALA, and, as David recalls, "They were always reading."[8] The grown kids later discovered among their possessions two books that had especially influenced their parents: Spanish language translations of *The Small Woman*, the story of Gladys Aylward, missionary to China, and a book on prayer by Hudson Taylor.

David remembers being in his father's Sunday school class in the La Paz church: "I saw him as an impassioned teacher. I don't remember his methodology, but I remember his passion and that he motivated us kids."[9]

Slowly, through his service in the local congregation and through his visits to other churches, Francisco began to sense the call of God to ministry. Sometime in the 1950s, the INELA named Francisco an official "worker" (*obrero*, a title that comes before *pastor*), and called him to serve in several churches, successively: Wajchillo, Jawircatu, and Yanari (all three in the valley south of La Paz), and Llojeta (now a barrio in the city of La Paz). Again, one thing David especially remembers about his father in the role of pastor was his passion for the work. And he remembers that the title, whether "pastor" or "worker," didn't matter that much to him.

The change from serving in La Paz to pastoring rural congregations was drastic. The family continued living in El Alto, and Francisco traveled out early Sunday mornings, returning late at night. In the dry season he took a bus, but in the rainy season he could only travel as far as the first river, and he had to cross on foot, the water sometimes coming up to his chest. The river ran swift and the crossing could be treacherous. Sometimes Francisca accompanied him, and on special occasions, the boys came along. David remembers stepping into the river, lifting their stuff high in the air, praying their way across. But for his father, "there was no impediment or inconvenience too great to prevent him from getting to his congregation."[10]

When Francisco began pastoring in Jawircatu, only ten believers gathered on a Sunday morning. He introduced himself to the general secretary (political authority) of the community, explaining why he was there; this man eventually became a believer and joined with the others, a group that grew to thirty people by the end of his three-year pastorate. During that time, the congregation planted another Friends church in the community of Yanari (that eventually became two congregations, Yanari Alto and Yanari Bajo).

7. David Tintaya, interview with Harold Thomas and Nancy Thomas, February 12, 2016, Santa Cruz.

8. David Tintaya, interview with Harold Thomas and Nancy Thomas, February 12, 2016, Santa Cruz.

9. David Tintaya, interview with Harold Thomas and Nancy Thomas, February 12, 2016, Santa Cruz.

10. David Tintaya, interview with Harold Thomas and Nancy Thomas, February 12, 2016, Santa Cruz.

After pastoring the church in Jawircatu, the INELA called Francisco to serve the new congregation in Yanari. That meant travel to Jawircatu, then on foot up the mountain several hours further. Sometimes he traveled at night on trails and through passes that had a reputation for evil spirits, but David claims that his father rejected their power over him as a Christian and went forward without fear. Nothing bad ever happened to him on those trails.

Francisco served his next pastorate in the community of Llojeta, which is now a *barrio* of the city of La Paz, on the side of the canyon stretching up to the *altiplano*. David remembers many weekends when his father didn't have enough money for transportation and had to walk down from El Alto, where the family still lived, across the city, and up the canyon edge to Llojeta, a journey of some fifteen miles. He especially remembers one time, on the church's anniversary, when the celebration went late and his father didn't get home until the early hours of the morning. He had lugged a big basket all that way, but he was happy, the basket full of the food offerings of his grateful congregation. Sometime during the years he pastored at Llojeta, a friend gave him a knife because of the high crime rate in the streets of La Paz at night. Francisco battled within himself, but finally decided not to carry the weapon. "I'm going to trust in God instead," he told his family.

Francisco Tintaya at his home on El Alto (H. Thomas)

These years when Francisco pastored the four rural churches, during the 1950s and 1960s, corresponded to the 1952 birth of the INELA and its reorganization toward further independence in 1964. Significant years in the development of the national church, as a pastor Francisco would surely have participated in the excitement as well as the challenges that led to administrative growth.

After this service of pastoring in rural areas, Francisco Tintaya was called to pastor the La Paz Friends Church in the late 1960s. Then beginning about 1970 he served three years as treasurer on the INELA *mesa directiva*, followed by three years on the *mesa's* pastoral oversight committee. These roles enabled him to travel throughout the districts of the yearly meeting and become better acquainted with the whole work of the INELA.

In the representatives meeting of January 1976, Francisco Tintaya was elected president of the INELA. Three years later, in January 1979, he was reelected, allowing him to serve six years (1976–1981) as president of the national church, an unusual length of time for this role.

As INELA president, Francisco, along with Enrique Tito, was the first INELA Friend to officially visit Oregon and the annual sessions of NWYM, an addendum to the FWCC trip to Wichita in 1977.

During his six years as INELA president, Francisco Tintaya tirelessly visited throughout the yearly meeting and oversaw, along with other *mesa directiva* members, the ministries of the church. It was a time of rapid church growth, with the decade of the 1970s showing an increase of roughly 100 to 165 churches. (See chapter 7.) A national missionary society rose up during that decade, and the church developed a consciousness of its social responsibility as part of the gospel. The INELA added the role of secretary of health to the *mesa directiva*, and the clinic on Max Paredes Street began functioning. They were exciting and challenging years.

It was a crucial time to be serving as president, and it included the usual conflicts. David Tintaya remembers that his father's commitment to serve was firm, as were his attempts to protect his family from the tensions that naturally came with this position. He was not willing to sacrifice his family to his own leadership role. He instructed his sons that they were not to suffer on his account and, especially, that they were not to get angry at people who might criticize him.

Criticism did come. In January 1982, Francisco left office under a cloud, due mainly to financial controversy surrounding sale of land on the tabernacle property in El Alto. Although most of the problem was due to the mismanagement of a colleague, the representatives forced Francisco as outgoing president to carry the blame. Discussion during the representatives meeting was loud and controversial, and he bore what he perceived as deep shame for several years, eventually suffering a breakdown in his health. He was forced to pay back some of the money lost, a task which took several years.

This is a difficult memory for the family to deal with, even today. David Tintaya notes that this type of bitter experience has happened to other INELA leaders, and that it is not unusual for people who leave leadership roles to isolate themselves in their shame and never again take part in the life of the church. Indeed, David remembers that for a brief time after leaving office, Francisco no longer wanted anything to do with the church in La Paz or the yearly meeting as a whole.

Even so, some still saw Francisco's gifts and appreciated his leadership abilities. That very year (1982) the La Paz Friends Church, now known as the New Jerusalem Church, asked Francisco to begin visiting one of their dependent congregations, in Achocalla, up the hill behind Llojeta where he used to pastor. His deep commitment to God caused him to agree. When he visited the church for the first time, he found only three believers. He promised them he would come for a year to be with them on Sundays. He kept his word, traveling once a week, partway by car, then up the hill on foot. By the end of the year, twenty believers were worshipping together. Looking back, he says simply, "It's very good to be in the work of the Lord."[11]

At the conclusion of his year of visitation, the New Jerusalem Church asked Francisco to be their pastor, a call he accepted and a role he served for several years. He was invited back as pastor of this church again early in the 1990s, a position he served together in team with Sabino Chipana. These good experiences served as a restoration to ministry.

Later in the 1990s Francisco took on the pastorate of the Villa Alicia Friends Church in the Cordillera District of the *altiplano* and served there for about ten years. David reports of this pastorate that his father was greatly valued in the whole district and honored for his years of service. While there he showed his heart for a holistic gospel and helped in the school and in different social projects. One time he joined the leaders of the community as they climbed the highest hill to give their offerings as prayers for rain. Rather than join in the animistic practices, Francisco prayed, long and loud, for God to send the rains and an abundant crop. The community appreciated his participation and people later referred to him as the one who helped give them food that year.

He liked to introduce people to new experiences, so once he asked Francisca to help him fix pancakes for all the people in the church (something she had learned when working as a maid for missionaries). People still remember the pancake feast at Villa Alicia.

After his time in Villa Alicia, Francisco pastored a small church on El Alto for several years. Since his official retirement, he has felt a special call to other older people and emphasized ministry to this age group as he participated as a member of the Tabernacle Friends Church. He also felt called to a prayer ministry and for several years led the early Sunday morning prayer meeting in his church. He only stopped when his hearing and visual challenges become too much of a problem. At the time of this writing (2018), he devotes himself to prayer and reading the Bible. He says that in 2017 he read the whole Bible through three times. He continues to attend the Tabernacle Church as he is able. He considers intercessory prayer as his main ministry, and

11. Francisco Tintaya, interview with Harold Thomas and Nancy Thomas, March 2, 2018, El Alto.

he includes former missionaries in his prayers, saying, "They have left behind a good work for the Lord. A strong church. Your work has not been in vain."[12]

Francisca Quispe de Tintaya, David's mother, served as a faithful wife and mother during the years of Francisco's pastoral and administrative ministries.[13] But she served in her own leadership role as well, especially in the development of UFINELA, the Bolivian Friends women's organization. Formally organized in the mid-1960s, Francisca was in on the ground level. David remembers its beginnings as coming from the times the pastors' wives would gather together to cook for the various conferences and meetings their husbands were involved in. As a child he played on the floor and listened to their conversations as the ladies peeled potatoes and stirred the soup. He remembers Gregoria de Tito, Gregoria de Ticona, María de Mamani, Juana Ott, and Salomé Huarina.

The women talked about wanting to form their own organization, complete with a feminine *mesa directiva*, like the men had, and like the youth were beginning to form. Their motive was to support the national church. But David also remembers that the men became defensive and suspicious that what the women really wanted was power; they feared competition. He even remembers his parents arguing about it at home, and he suspects that the same thing was happening in the families of other leaders.

Francisca Tintaya, center, joyful servant (NWYM)

Regardless of opposition, real or imagined, the women kept up the pressure, and the UFINELA was officially organized in 1965. Francisca was active from the beginning and especially loved traveling out to the rural conferences and quarterly meetings. She was elected secretary of evangelism in 1971[14] and later served as president.

The women were entrepreneurial, and many of them, including Francisca, were skilled with handwork. They sold crafts and food to raise money for different projects, such as a projector, Christian movies, and a large evangelistic tent which they donated to the national

12. Francisco Tintaya, interview with Harold Thomas and Nancy Thomas, March 2, 2018, El Alto.

13. Information about Francisca de Tintaya comes from an interview conducted by Harold Thomas and Nancy Thomas with David Tintaya (February 12, 2016, Santa Cruz).

14. Ron Stansell, letter to NWYM, August 31, 1971, NWYM/GFU archives.

church. Francisca loved to distribute tracts as she traveled and taught in the difference conferences, and at one point, the Bolivian Bible Society presented her with a special recognition for this labor. She was especially concerned with the need for the women of the churches to understand about good nutrition and hygiene and developed a series of well-received classes on these subjects. Francisca de Tintaya, along with the other leaders of UFINELA, became known and respected for sacrificial service and promotion of the mission outreach of the national church.

David was an adolescent during the years his mother was especially active in UFINELA. Still unsure about her education, Francisca welcomed David's help with preparing her monthly and annual reports. David remembers that she was open not only to his help with writing and math, but listened to his suggestions for the ministry. It marked a change in their relationship and was an important part of David's formation as a young leader. (He also helped his father with his reports.) When not active on the national level, Francisca continued to support the branches of UFINELA at the district and local levels until her death.

Arminda's Parents, Francisco Quispe and Dora Jahuira de Quispe[15]

Arminda's father, Francisco Quispe, was the oldest of five children born to Tiburcio Quispe and Asencia Plata in the village of Llojeta, close to La Paz. They were part of the La Paz Friends Church. Francisco trained as a carpenter and worked in La Paz as a young man. He met his wife, Dora Jahuira from Laja, at the La Paz church and they were married there.

Dora grew up the daughter of Mariano and Leandra Jahuira, part of the team that founded the Laja Friends Church. In the 1940s when Dora was a child, people didn't see education as being important for a girl. As the oldest daughter, Dora was especially needed for chores in the home. Dora's daughter, Rufina Quispe, remembers her mother telling her how she longed to go to school. She would beg her father, promising to get all the housework done, in addition to her school assignments. He finally gave in, but he held her to her word. She had to use all her recess and lunchtime at school to do her homework, but it wasn't enough. She had to drop out of school after the second grade.[16] Her mother told her, "Now you can count and sign your name. That's all you need."[17]

At one point during the period when she with still living with her parents in Laja, Dora remembers her mother taking her to the mission farm at Copajira. Leandra served as a cook for some of the special classes. Dora played with other kids on the

---

15. Some of the information about Francisco Quispe and Dora Jahuira comes from interviews conducted by Harold Thomas and Nancy Thomas with Arminda Quispe de Tintaya (February 12, 2016; January 29, 2018, Santa Cruz) and with Rufina Quispe Jahuira (October 10, 2004, Santa Cruz).

16. Quispe Jahuira, "Mi historia," 88.

17. Rufina Quispe Jahuira, interview with Nancy Thomas, October 10, 2004, Santa Cruz.

farm, including the missionary kids, but the tall white missionaries themselves scared her. She was especially frightened of the vivacious Tina Knight.

Dora's father, while a respected Friend and leader in the local church, was also a strict man who would occasionally beat his wife or children for disobedience. So, at the age of thirteen, Dora decided to leave home to make her own way in the city. With her parents' consent, she traveled to La Paz and began work as a domestic maid. Her parents made sure that her employers would give her Sundays off to attend church, and in this way Dora began to attend the La Paz Friends Church where she met Francisco Quispe.

One day Dora ran into Francisco in the Alvaroa Plaza in La Paz, and they began talking. It so happened that one of the believers from the Laja church saw them together. Dora became frightened of how her father might react, so much so that she decided the only thing she could do would be to marry Francisco immediately, although they hardly knew each other. It was not a good way to begin a marriage. Dora was sixteen years old.

The couple lived in La Paz for a few years and had two children, a son who died in infancy and Arminda. For Arminda's birth, Francisco and Dora traveled to Laja so her father, Mariano Jahuira, the town midwife, could attend at the birth of his granddaughter. In their early years of marriage, Dora suffered at the hands of her mother-in-law (not an uncommon situation), so when Francisco felt an impulse to study at the Bethesda Bible Institute in the city of Santa Cruz, the couple decided to make the huge change and moved from La Paz down to the low-lands.

Francisco Quispe in the 1970s (NWYM)

While in Santa Cruz the couple had their second daughter, Rufina. The tropical climate proved too hot and humid for these highlanders and they returned to La Paz for two years. While in La Paz, Rufina got sick and almost died, and the doctors told them to get the baby back down to the lower altitude of Santa Cruz to save her life. That and the continuing domestic violence among their relatives caused the young family to return, and in time they bought property, built a home, and settled down in Santa Cruz.

Although their marriage was far from perfect, Francisco and Dora did manage to break the cycle of family violence, in large part through the influence of the church. Both their daughters say they treated them well and encouraged them to get a good education, something that had been denied to Dora. Francisco's skill as a carpenter assured him of work, and Dora set up a stall in the local market. The girls went to the local schools.

From the beginning of their time in Santa Cruz in 1969, Francisco and Dora joined with the Javier Quispe and Eugenio Ramos families to begin a Friends church. The believers met in homes for several years, then managed to purchase property for a church building. The church was officially founded in 1972 and over the years several other Friends congregations were planted in the city. Both the INELA and the Friends Mission supported the Santa Cruz outreach efforts.

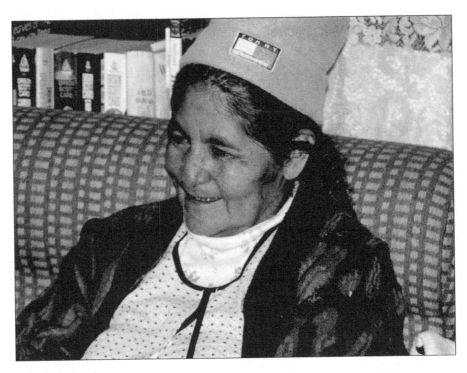

Dora Jahuira de Quispe, 2005 (H. Thomas)

Francisco died in 1993 and Dora in 2009. Before her death, Dora was able to see her dream of education fulfilled in her daughters. They both graduated from the Bolivian Evangelical University, Arminda in communications and Rufina in psychology. Her granddaughters would follow suit within a few years.

DAVID TINTAYA AND ARMINDA QUISPE DE TINTAYA

In 1986 the Tintaya and Quispe families joined forces as David Tintaya, son of Francisco and Francisca Tintaya, married Arminda Quispe, daughter of Francisco and Dora Quispe. The place was El Alto, in the department of La Paz.

David's Story

The three sons of Francisco Tintaya and Francisca Quispe—Jaime, David, and Oscar—responded differently to the pressures of being children of a pastor and denominational leader. The oldest, Jaime, rebelled against the church.[18] While still an adolescent he left home to live independently and pursue his own lifestyle. Even so he kept up a relationship with his parents, visiting them at least once a week. One week when he failed to show up, Francisco and Francisca got suspicious and began looking for him. They searched two weeks until they discovered his body in the morgue. Police told them he had been robbed, murdered, and dumped by the side of a road out in the country. Jamie was eighteen at the time of his death.

Oscar, the youngest son, also wrestled with his father's hardships as an INELA leader, but his talents presented him with other options.[19] Today Oscar Tintaya enjoys a reputation as an accomplished artist. His paintings, in oil, acrylic, or watercolor, range from realistic nature depictions to abstract studies of Aymara culture and the landscapes of the *altiplano*. He has had exhibitions in the cities of La Paz, Cochabamba, Oruro, and Santa Cruz, and in 2000 he was among of a group of four Bolivian artists invited to exhibit their works in Austria. His works also appear in private collections in Bolivia, Argentina, Germany, France, Austria, and the United States (including the headquarters of the NWYM of Friends in Newberg, Oregon). His natural depictions of the flora and fauna of Bolivia appear in three published collections, one on the salt flats of southwestern Bolivia, and two guidebooks to the birds of the country.[20] He is sometimes referred to as "the Audubon of Bolivia."

Today Oscar lives with his aged father, Francisco, in the family home in El Alto. He sometimes accompanies his father to services in the Tabernacle Friends Church, but he has distanced himself from any ministry or active leadership role in the INELA. Oscar remains single.

While David Tintaya also grew up in the reality of being the son of parents actively involved in the ministry of the church, his memories are colored with gratitude. He writes,

> As a child I had to accompany my parents to all the church services. I went with them on home visits, to monthly meetings of the local church, to Quarterly Meetings, to Yearly Meetings, to pastors' conferences, to women's conferences, to leaders' meetings and to all the other church sponsored events. As a small child I didn't understand much of what was happening, but as time went on I began to grasp the nature of each event. But my place was to listen and

18. Information about Jaime Tintaya comes from an interview with David Tintaya, conducted by Harold Thomas and Nancy Thomas, February 16, 2016, Santa Cruz.

19. Information about Oscar comes from Oscar Tintaya, letter to Nancy Thomas, June 5, 2017; interview with Nancy Thomas, December 19, 2017, La Paz.

20. Illustrations in Jammes, *Salar de Tunupa*; illustrations in Hesse, *Algunas Aves del Chaco*; illustrations in Hertzog, *Aves de Bolivia*.

observe; I had no opportunity to give my opinion about the affairs they were dealing with.[21]

David also speaks of his memories of his father as an impassioned Sunday school teacher, and as a pastor who gladly faced all sorts of inconveniences to serve in the rural congregations he pastored. Of the influence of those early years, he writes,

> The experiences I had with my parents have been very useful to me, and I consider that my family was the first school in my formation as a leader. They weren't thinking about this, but rather they had me by their side because of a sense of responsibility as parents, providing care and protection. They had no one to leave me with at home.
>
> . . . I believe that this was the principle base for my development as a leader in the church, as well as in the other positions I have held.
>
> . . . Those moments in early childhood, next to my mother and father, have proved invaluable. Thinking back on them helps me, comforts me, and encourages me to keep on developing myself responsibly, so that I can in turn serve my church, my community and my own family.[22]

In his adolescent years, as his parents became more involved in wider leadership roles in the INELA, David was able not only to learn from their example, but to be of service to them in helping with activity and financial reports. His parents began encouraging him to express his opinions and to start to take on his own leadership roles.[23]

Also during those adolescent years, David's friends in the church influenced him. David literally spent his childhood in the church and he ran around with the sons of other leaders, friends of his father, the sons of Carmelo Aspi, Domingo Mamani, Pascual Quispe, and others. These boys actually formed a rather exclusive gang.

Elías Copa, son of Cipriano Copa, an INELA leader from the Caranavi District, became a special friend. Elías was lighter skinned, a medical student in the university, and actively involved in the local branch of Campus Crusade for Christ, an international Christian organization from the United States that emphasized aggressive evangelism. Elías had the ability to relate to people in the middle classes as well as the indigenous people from which he came. He represented a new emerging younger generation of Quakers, better educated and in touch with the wider world around him. He exercised a great deal of influence over his peers in the INELA as he became involved in the youth group of the New Jerusalem Friends Church in La Paz.

Among Friends in those days, no one spoke of "receiving Christ as your personal Savior." Children were not "evangelized"; they were simply brought up in the

---

21. Tintaya, "Mi escuela," 99.

22. Tintaya, "Mi escuela," 100–101.

23. Information about David Tintaya comes from interviews with Harold Thomas and Nancy Thomas (February 12, February 15–16, 2016, Santa Cruz).

faith. David first heard this phrase from Elías as he shared in the youth group. For a time Elías served as the local youth group president, and he put pressure on the kids to "receive Christ," according to the teachings of Campus Crusade. David resisted because that was not a teaching he had ever heard in the church. But sometime in the late 1970s, in a large Luis Palau crusade in La Paz, he gave in and went forward at the invitation to publicly receive Christ.

Soon Elías began winning other young people from the middle classes of the city, and some of these kids began coming to youth group at the church. This posed a threat, not only to the adults in the congregation, but also to some of the other youth, especially the sons of the INELA leaders, David's old gang. Elías fought with the church council, not willing to respect his elders in silence. The leaders told him, "Here we don't 'receive Christ'; we 'practice holiness.'" The new style of Christian music certainly contributed to the tensions between both social classes and age groups.

Elías took a special interest in David, giving him personal Bible studies and discipleship lessons. Once during a youth meeting Elías announced that David would be leading the service that night, without warning David. David struggled through the meeting, but after that the fear left and he found himself able to lead events, often called on to be a "master-of-ceremonies." He now says, "All the things I was learning at that time, I learned by force."

Elías tried to teach the youth in the church to evangelize, Campus Crusade style. David now reflects that not all his strategies were legitimate. For example, a group would enter a plaza and Elías would have the kids spread out and mingle among the crowds. He would find a prominent place and begin to loudly preach on the "Four Spiritual Laws." The scattered youth would pretend they didn't know him, but would make positive comments, like, "What's this?! Let's go see!" and draw people by their enthusiasm to approach and listen.

The controversy in the New Jerusalem Church grew, until most of the middle-class kids, realizing they were not welcome, left. Elías himself was eventually forced to leave.

David stayed with the church, and around 1977 he became involved in the national youth organization, UJELAB. He served first as secretary and then as president from 1978 to 1979. This allowed him to travel widely throughout the different INELA districts, encouraging the youth and expanding his own knowledge of the church.

This period in David's life is especially interesting because it coincided with his father's presidency of the INELA during a time when tensions were being felt between older leaders and young people with more education. The established leaders tried to control the youth. What had happened in the local New Jerusalem Church was duplicated to some extent on the national level.

As we noted in chapter 7, David Tintaya's annual UJELAB report in the 1979 representatives meeting informed the gathering that the 1978 annual youth conference was deeply discouraging, chiefly because of "the scant help we have received from [the church's] adult leaders; all they do is criticize us."[24] The representatives met with the UJELAB officers during those meetings, listened to them and finally managed to affirm the group.

Under David's leadership 1979 was a better year. The annual youth conference saw a record four hundred young Friends in attendance, representing all the INELA districts. The youth leaders carried out smaller conferences in the different districts, with a special mission trip to boost the INELA's new work in the village of Tutimaya, outside the city of Cochabamba. David continued to develop his organizational and leadership abilities. He says that through these early leadership experiences, "I developed a sense of confidence along with my capacity to lead. I learned to develop and carry out projects related to evangelism and the formation of young leaders."[25]

David spend 1980 doing his obligatory year of military training.

The year 1982 was a turning point, due to the controversy attending the end of his father's term of service as INELA president. Although Francisco had not caused the financial problems, as outgoing president he bore the brunt of the criticism, even being forced personally to pay back to the INELA some of the money that had been lost (which, eventually, he did). The family moved back up to their home on El Alto and for a time no one had any desire to even attend church. As noted above, Francisco was soon again involved as a pastor.

David admits that he went into a period of frank rebellion, not against his parents, but against the church. He questioned all he had been taught. Relations between the adults and the youth in the New Jerusalem Church continued tense. At one point the church council put a padlock on the door of the youth meeting room. They asked David to take over the presidency of the youth group, "not knowing who I really was," says David. When that didn't work out, David stepped down from his leadership role with the youth.

He reunited with his old group, the by-now very rebellious sons of INELA leaders. They called themselves "The Black Tribe," and began experimenting with "sports, drinking, and sleeping in the streets." Once they set up a street discotheque in front of the church during worship time. They turned the volume up as loud as it would go. The gang frequently spent the night in the street kiosk of one of their parents. "It was great fun," remembers David.

One adult leader who was alert to what was happening was New Jerusalem pastor Francisco Mamani, known to the kids as Pancho. Pancho loved sports, soccer in particular, but he refrained from the post-game drinking parties that were the norm and that these young men were experimenting with. Pancho began regularly following up on the youth, sometimes showing up at the kiosk in the early mornings. "He never scolded us," says David. "He was our friend."

24. UJELAB report, January 1979, INELA archives.

25. Tintaya, "Mi escuela," 100.

Little by little, David returned to the faith and the church. The others followed later. This experience and the way Pancho cared for them has impacted David's leadership as a pastor. Years later, sometime around 2000, David, by now an established and respected leader, returned to the New Jerusalem Church and publicly confessed his involvement in the problems of the 1980s. He asked for and received pardon. Since that time, his ministry of preaching and teaching has grown throughout the INELA.

David met Arminda in 1978. At the time he was a developing leader in UJELAB and was scheduled to travel to the youth conference in Santa Cruz. Actually, David did not want to go to this conference; it was a difficult time in his life and, furthermore, he had no extra money for the trip. But his friend Benjamin Huarina felt so convicted that David needed to travel, he not only talked him into it but paid his way. Unfortunately (or not) while in Santa Cruz, David got sick. So the Francisco Quispe family invited the group to move from the hostel where they were sleeping to their home to better care for David. Arminda, Francisco's oldest daughter, remembers the other members of the group laughing and playing around in the patio, while poor David suffered indoors, trying to recuperate. Out of pity, she went inside to keep him company. The two started talking and a friendship began.

Their friendship developed long distance over the next eight years, until it just seemed that the next step was marriage. They married in El Alto in 1986, with the reception in the Tintaya family home. (The writers of this history attended the event.) The couple immediately moved down to Santa Cruz, partly because Arminda was in her second year of studies in the Bolivian Evangelical University. They made their home with Arminda's parents, in the very house where they first met (and where they live today). They eventually became parents to three daughters: Anabel, Anahí, and Joana.

Santa Cruz proved to be the land of opportunity for this generation of the Tintaya family. David soon found a job with APRECIA, an educational institution for the blind. His gifts of administration and leadership became evident, and the organization gradually increased his responsibilities until finally naming him executive director, where David oversaw all the educational programs and employees of the organization.

At the beginning of his fourteen years at APRECIA, his superiors had told him not to be "overtly Christian" in carrying out his duties. But by the time he had become executive director, the board of directors told him to try to employ as many other Christians as he could, especially from the Friends Church. When he felt his time there was up, he left the organization with honors and continues to serve on its board of directors.

David had found a calling, working with people with disabilities or special problems. After APRECIA, he helped found and served as board director of an institution for unmarried pregnant girls, "Center of Life."

In addition, David has poured much of his time and energy voluntarily into the Bolivian Evangelical University as a member of the board of trustees. Both the INELA and the Friends Mission had been founding members of this university in the early 1980s. Because he lives in Santa Cruz and because of his abilities, the INELA has consistently named him as their official representative to the UEB board. As his gifts became known, he was given more responsibility and actually served six continuous years as board president. He has also served many terms as secretary or treasurer, in addition to representing the INELA.

But at the heart of his life and work, David Tintaya is a Friends pastor. But before we tell that story, let's focus on Arminda.

Arminda's Story

Francisco Quispe and Dora Jahuira de Quispe had three children. As we have seen previously, the first-born, a son, died in infancy. Arminda, the middle child, was born in La Paz, and the youngest, Rufina, in Santa Cruz. Arminda and Rufina both grew up in Santa Cruz, were raised in the atmosphere of the growing Friends church of that city, and enjoyed educational privileges that had been denied to their parents and grandparents.

Rufina majored in psychology, graduating from the Bolivian Evangelical University. About herself today, she writes,

> Actually, I exercise my profession as an educational psychologist working with pre-school and school aged kids with special needs. I thank God for choosing me as his instrument. God helps me balance my time between my further studies, my profession, and my church. But God comes first. My mother used to tell me that even though I obtained a good job, gained lots of money, and became a professional, never should I distance myself from God.
>
> In these ways, God formed me. I'm thankful for the two congregations that God used in my life. But I recognize that my family was my first school. I'm grateful to my great-grandmother who had to flee persecution in order to faithfully follow God. I'm also grateful to my grandmother and my mother, women who didn't have the opportunity to study, but who were women of faith and prayer, God's instruments in my life. Finally, I want to say that all my life accomplishments are now the means God has placed in my hands that I might better participate in his work, just as did my grandmothers and my mother, women of courage.[26]

Arminda Quispe[27] was four years old when her parents moved from La Paz down to Santa Cruz. She remembers well that first day. The family had found shelter in a room in the back of an evangelical church in town. Her parents had brought some chuños[28] and fat with them, and they fried the chuños; the meal left them still hungry.

26. Quispe Jahuira, "Mi historia," 90–91.

27. Information about Arminda Quispe comes from interviews conducted by Harold Thomas and Nancy Thomas, February 2, 2016, and February 12, 2016, Santa, Cruz.

28. Freeze-dried potatoes from the altiplano.

The family was too shy to venture outside and go to church. When the church service ended, the people gathered in the patio for a meal. Francisco made Arminda go out and mingle with the crowd in the hopes that someone would offer her food. No one did. She felt hungry and very sad.

The little family had several strikes against them from the first. Not only was it a challenge for people from the highlands to adjust to the tropical climate of Santa Cruz, this more predominantly middle-class population still clung to their prejudices against indigenous peoples. So after the birth of their second daughter, Rufina, the family returned to La Paz.

Rufina's illness in the high altitude forced the Quispes to once again move down to Santa Cruz, and this time the move was permanent. Francisco, a skilled carpenter, found work making furniture, and in time, his work prospered, allowing him and Dora to purchase land, build a house, and establish the family.

But Francisco's heart was especially focused on planting a new Friends church in Santa Cruz, working together with the Eugenio Ramos and Javier Quispe families. Arminda's memories of those times are mixed. While the three families worked and prayed together, sometimes they would argue about where and how to plant the church. She remembers one of the local believers who offered the Friends hospitality and became involved in their new work. Pedro Ticona's charismatic personality attracted people into his home where the believers met for a while. Arminda says that "he gave them hospitality and then forced them to attend the church."

While Francisco labored by day at his carpentry shop, Dora sold food and clothing in a stall she rented in a local market. Everyday she left her little girls at home while she went to work. Arminda remembers that the sons of one of the families they lived with were rough and mean. She was afraid of them, and many times she wished her mother were home to protect her. In many ways Arminda's young girlhood repeats her mother's, staying home to work. She remembers trying to do the family washing by herself, without instruction. It didn't work well; her hands were too small to wring out the clothes.

But Arminda's girlhood was also significantly different from her mother's. Both her parents encouraged their daughters to go to school as soon as they were old enough. In fact, for the first three years of primary school, Francisco helped Arminda in the evenings with her homework. But by the fourth and fifth grades, the math was already beyond Francisco's own educational level, and Arminda had to figure things out on her own. These were frustrating years, and Arminda remembers often not finishing her homework and being ashamed about it in school. On recitation days she often sat outside, feeling too embarrassed to participate. Her parents didn't come to talk with the teachers, mostly because of the prejudice shown to indigenous people. Her teachers demonstrated that prejudice. These are hard years to remember.

Arminda's natural intelligence and her determination to succeed served her well. She finished both primary and high school and in the 1980s entered the new Bolivian

Evangelical University as a student in the department of communications. She graduated in 1990.

Arminda doesn't remember a specific time when she decided to become a Christian. She does remember that her parents, especially her father, gradually led her to a relationship with Christ. Francisco was firm with both girls about church attendance. They accompanied their parents to every meeting on Sunday and during the week, with the understanding that these meetings were sacred. Their father made them carry their own Bibles and hymn books. "Otherwise," he told them, "why show up?" Arminda's life revolved around home, school, and church. There was no room for "the world."

"God protected my heart," she says. "In my adolescence I finally began to understand what it was all about." By the time she was fifteen years old, her faith in God was firm and growing.

While Arminda was still a young teen, missionary Mark Roberts began an extension Bible school center in the central Friends Missionary Church, and she signed up. She attended faithfully, did the assignments, and easily passed the courses. She remembers being excited about Bible Geography, the History of Israel, and the rest of the courses. A vision for ministry began to grow, along with a hunger to understand the Bible.

Pastor Eugenio Ramos, seeing her capacity, decided to make her a Sunday school teacher for the adult class. The teenaged Arminda didn't feel ready, but "he forced me to do it," she claims with a laugh. He provided her with bilingual materials (Aymara/Spanish) and mentored her. She remembers her first class on Paul of Tarsus. She had the resources but no contextual background. She told the class that Paul's last name was Tarsus, and Eugenio corrected her publicly. She began copying Eugenio's teaching style—loud and emphatic. She even pounded the table a time or two. Later her father advised her to teach "less forcefully." But she learned by doing and discovered a gift as a teacher.

David and Arminda Tintaya, Pastoral Couple

Meeting David Tintaya in 1978, their eight-year long-distance friendship, and their marriage in 1986 proved turning points in Arminda's life. Although they had taken time to get to know one another, Arminda says they were too immature to get married. They didn't yet know where they were going or what they wanted out of life. Moving to Santa Cruz, they lived with Arminda's parents in a second-floor apartment. Anabel was born during their second year of marriage, another event for which Arminda claims they were not prepared. She still remembers the feeling of panic at having to care for a baby, wishing there was someone to advise her.

But little by little the couple found their way, nurtured by family and a local church that appreciated their gifts. While David found work in APRECIA, Arminda finished her university degree and began working for the same university, eventually being given the position of registrar, a role she continues to fill today.

A large part of their story and their identity comes from their experience in the Friends church known as the *Congregación Cristiana Amigos* (Friends Christian Congregation), or CCA.[29]

During David's growing up years, we've seen how he imbibed a spirit of servanthood and ministry from his parents, but at no time in those years did he envision himself as a pastor. Likewise, Arminda grew up in a Quaker family heavily invested in the church, and as she studied in the extension Bible school program and taught Sunday school, she developed as a Christian education teacher, but with no intention of pastoral ministry.

As a young married couple, David and Arminda were members of the central Friends Missionary Church in Santa Cruz. In 1988 the Missionary Church became involved in a new church plant in a lower-class *barrio* of the city. Actually, the church there began because two of the member families of the Missionary Church moved to two *barrios* that were part of Santa Cruz known as Los Lotes. Simón Gómez and Fernando Nina, along with their families, found the distance from their new homes to the church too far and asked if a church could be planted in their area. The home church responded positively, and Eugenio Ramos accepted a call to pastor the new group that met in the Gómez home. At the time, David was president of the local church council. The vision was simply to plant a new church.

Ramos and several other older members of the congregation began meeting with the new group, and the *Congregación Cristiana Amigos* was officially inaugurated on January 22, 1989. They met in the Gómez home for several years, until a gift from visiting missionary Roscoe Knight made it possible to purchase property in the *barrio*, and within a short time the new church building had been erected.

The young church had three different pastors during its first five years, and in 1994 the group found itself searching for another pastor. David, still the president of the Missionary Church council, felt a sense of responsibility to provide for the needs of the congregation the church had planted, so the church council approved releasing the Tintayas for three months. David had no formal pastoral training for this assignment, but he brought with him years of teaching in the Sunday school and youth programs of the church, as well as the influence of his parents. Arminda was backed by her Bible school courses and experience as a Sunday school teacher.

The couple poured themselves into this new assignment, traveling out to the *barrio* on weekends. David preached, Arminda taught, and they both began to get to know the families of the church. Something clicked. They loved the people and the

29. Much of this section comes from an interview conducted via Skype with David and Arminda Tintaya, in Santa Cruz, on May 27, 2017; from a document entitled "Congregación Cristiana Amigos" by D. Tintaya and sent to Nancy Thomas on May 27, 2017; and from interviews conducted by Harold Thomas and Nancy Thomas, February 11, 15, 2016, Santa Cruz.

people loved them back. At the end of the three months, the group pleaded with them to stay. Now, after twenty-three years of ministry, both David and Arminda see clearly the hand of God in bringing them as a pastoral couple to this church.

Through the years David and Arminda have grown into the pastorate, learning by doing, and also by taking short courses and reading widely. Along with pastoral practice, vision has developed. David bases his vision of the church on a model he learned from missionary Hal Thomas; it balances three basic purposes of worship (a God-ward focus), community life (an inward focus), and mission (an outward focus). David has adapted and taught this in the church, and now all planning and activities revolve around what he has called the three Cs: communion, community, and commission. Discipleship and leadership training form an important part of the vision, and this has become Arminda's specialty. A complete five-year curriculum for all age groups fleshes out the "three Cs" vision, and young people actively serve in the church and community, as they learn to become leaders.

Involvement in the *barrio* has become another focus. One of the church's first efforts was to plan for the *barrio fiesta* held every year on October 12. The church, under David's leadership, used one of the community playing fields and organized all-day sports activities, musical programs, food, and a time to get to know their neighbors. It soon extended to other *fiesta* days, and the church gained a reputation for being there to serve the community.

Programs to tutor school kids, sponsorship of all-day medical clinics, marriage and family classes, combined with street evangelism and a lively Sunday school program especially for neighborhood kids. All this has formed part of the church's community outreach focus.

Gradually, the vision of reaching the *barrio* grew to include a missionary vision for the whole world. But before we tell that story, we need to introduce the next generation of the Tintaya family.

THE DAUGHTER

The fourth generation of Tintaya Quakers carries the story of the INELA into the future. INELA's young people have inherited the church from their ancestors, but they face new challenges and have a higher level of educational preparation. Anabel Tintaya, David and Arminda's firstborn, came into the world in 1987. Anahí was born in 1991, and Joana joined the family in 2004. All three were born in Santa Cruz. Their parents have never regretted not having a son. They've encouraged their daughters to make the most of their gifts, freeing them to stretch toward leadership positions and become the persons God created them to be.

By the time Anabel graduated from high school, there was no question about her attending a university, and she chose her mother's alma mater, the Bolivian Evangelical University. A bright student, she majored in the science of nutrition and graduated at the head of her class in 2009.

Anabel has been exploring ways to express her commitment to mission through her profession as a nutritionist. Before and since her graduation from the university, she has gained professional experience working for NGOs and in international petroleum companies, as staff nutritionist. She was employed by the Bolivian Ministry of Sports as head nutritionist for the 2018 South American Games, an Olympic-level event. As such she headed a team of ten professionals who oversaw more than three thousand employees, charged with the task of feeding the athletes, judges, and others who gathered in the city of Cochabamba for two weeks in May and June. It was a position of tremendous responsibility, and Anabel flourished under the challenge.

Anabel sometimes dreams of creating her own business in the nutrition industry. Other times she thinks she would like to participate on the government level of life in her country, working to improve health and nutrition through better laws and national norms. She remains strongly committed to the church and to the vision of a holistic mission outreach.

Joana is the youngest of the three sisters. Her joining the family some seventeen years after Anabel was born surprised everyone. Joana is growing up active in the local Christian school as well as in the congregation her father pastors. She loves playing the violin. She dreams of traveling; she wants to know the world and is especially interested in Egypt and India. Professionally she plans on studying either architecture, auditing, or medicine. She still has time to decide. She has no doubts that she will graduate from a university.

Anabel and Joana, along with their sister Anahí, are the face of the new generation of Quakers in Bolivia.

David and Arminda's middle daughter, Anahí, was born in 1991. She affirms that growing up in the Tintaya home in Santa Cruz was a blessing and a privilege. She claims that her parents encouraged her in her education and preparation for a profession. They helped her grow spiritually and gave her opportunities to help in the church. Most of all, she says, they provided her with examples of servant leadership in the work of the church.[30]

Her experience in the local church as the daughter of the pastor was not quite so positive. Although the members of the church respected her, expectations sometimes felt too high. And sometimes, she felt, along with her parents, that their position meant they could not ask for help when they needed it. She experienced loneliness in the midst of the congregation.

As a little girl in Sunday school, her mother and her Aunt Rufina were her teachers. They taught the kids the need for a personal relationship with Jesus, but Anahí says she heard it so often, the impact was minimal. But she attended a private Christian school, and through the influence of one of her teachers, she asked Jesus into her heart at the age of nine. When she told her mother about it, both of them cried for joy.

---

30. Much of the material for this section comes from a Skype interview with Anahí Tintaya, conducted by Nancy Thomas, June 3, 2017.

Another of the formative moments of Anahí's childhood came through an informal event. It was around the time of her conversion, and missionaries Hal and Nancy Thomas were living in an apartment in the Tintaya family complex, directing a program in the UEB for training Latin American missionaries. The Thomases had just returned from a visit to their son David and family, now serving as Friends missionaries in Rwanda. They brought with them a DVD presentation that David had put together of the Friends work in that African nation.

The family gathered one evening to watch the DVD. Anahí was too young to remember David, but her parents were recalling him and his sister growing up in Bolivia. They were moved and impressed that this missionary kid was now an adult and serving in Africa. As Anahí watched the DVD, she was deeply moved, even without understanding the English script. She watched David Thomas, a lone white man worshipping in a congregation of black Quakers, singing, dancing, obviously loving the worship and loving his Rwandan brothers and sisters. She thought to herself, "I want to be like him. I want to do what he is doing." The other aspect of the DVD that impacted her was seeing the exuberance of Rwandan Quakers at worship. "I didn't know Friends could be like this!" she marveled.

The images of that worship service would come to her again and again during the next years, and, without her realizing it at the time, this small experience would constitute the beginnings of God's call on her life to missions.

As Anahí finished primary and then high school, her question was not, "Will I attend the university?" but rather, "What will I study?" Now strongly drawn to missions, she wondered how she could best prepare. Another informal conversation help set her course. This time visiting missionary Ron Stansell was asking about her dreams and plans. Anahí told him of her growing interest in China, and Ron proceeded to tell her about the NWYM's program of sending people to China to teach English in the local schools. He shared his hope than one day Bolivian and North American Friends could join in similar mission endeavors.

Anahí caught the vision and enrolled in the UEB with a double major in English and music. She figured music was a universal language that she could use wherever in the world she went, and she realized that English was a world language that unlocked doors and might make future cooperation with NWYM or other organizations possible.

Concurrent with her university studies, Anahí became involved with the local branch of Youth With a Mission (YWAM), one of the largest missionary sending agencies in the world. In the Santa Cruz branch, she interacted with people who were passionate about missions, took classes that prepared her for future work, participated in street ministries, and experienced deep personal growth.

Several things converged to stoke her interest in China. When her grandmother (Francisca de Tintaya) died her parents passed on to her two books that had belonged to her grandparents, *The Small Woman* and *Hudson Taylor's Spiritual Secret*, both

Spanish translations of missionary stories set in China. The underlined portions spoke to her of her grandparents' heart for mission work and interest in China, something they had kept secret, not figuring they could ever fulfill a dream like that. This thought moved Anahí and she wondered if she might be the answer to the missionary calls of her ancestors.

In 2008 she raised money to participate in a YWAM trip to China where she worked with a team in a village that had been affected by an earthquake. She especially loved working with the Chinese children. Then again in 2009, she went to Paraguay to study with YWAM. As part of her practical work, she served in a Chinese church in Asunción, working with adolescents in music, drama, dance, and evangelism. Her love for the Chinese people deepened.

She held on to the vision of working under NWYM with their Teaching Abroad program in China. In 2012, she began a regular correspondence with Shawn McConaughey, superintendent for global outreach for NWYM, and he encouraged her to finish her university education and continue preparation for mission service. She completed her coursework in the UEB in 2016 (finishing her thesis in 2018) with a degree in music and continued her classes in English in a local institute. News of the division within NWYM forced her to put that particular dream on hold, which involved some personal struggle. When she thinks of herself as one day fulfilling the missionary dreams of her grandparents and parents, she asks, "How long do I wait and hope? I don't want God to fulfill his promises to me in my kids and grandkids. I want to be the one to go and serve."

Anahí Tintaya (A. Tintaya)

When asked about her dreams for the INELA, she says, "I would like to see the church convert and become a missionary church in all senses: a church capable of giving financially, of calling and sending people, and of going throughout the world. This is a great dream we hope will one day be fulfilled."

There is something else Anahí wishes she could do in the near future. "I want to go to the United States to express my gratitude," she says. "I wonder if the young people in NWYM know how much their church in mission has impacted the church in Bolivia. This is a debt I want to pay. I want to go and tell them." Then, ever the perfectionist, she adds, "I'll do it as soon as I learn how to speak English better."[31]

THE STORY CONTINUES: THE TINTAYA FAMILY IN MISSION

In this chapter we've seen how the story of the Tintaya family reaches back to the beginnings of the INELA, both around the shores of Lake Titicaca and in the *altiplano* community of Laja. It accompanies and exemplifies the story of the church up to the present day. But it doesn't stop there. The Tintaya family represents the future of the church as it reaches forward with a missionary vision.[32]

For David and Arminda, their awakening to mission occurred when the UEB extended an invitation to Hal and Nancy Thomas to come and begin a masters-degree program in missiology. The NWYM board of missions approved and sent the Thomases to begin working with the UEB, which they did from 1999 to 2006. The *Centro de Estudios Interculturales* (CENESI, Center for Intercultural Studies), the first legally recognized graduate program in the university, opened its doors to the first cohort group in 2000.

The Thomases lived in Santa Cruz, part of that time in an apartment on the Tintaya property. As David and Arminda were both serving in the university, they were crucial to the Thomases in setting up the program. In turn the Thomases encouraged the Tintayas to take advantage of the courses, as students or auditors. Many visiting professors stayed with the Thomases and enjoyed interacting with the Tintayas. People like Antonio Carlos Barro, Chuck Van Engen, Pablo Deiros, and Betty Sue Brewster, through both classes and informal conversations, exerted their influence. A new world was opening up.

Concurrently, Anahí was becoming more involved in Youth With a Mission (YWAM), another powerful influence. Her parents realized she was having problems finding a place in the church, partly because of the expectations people put on her as the pastor's daughter, and they sought a way to encourage her in her Christian experience. A friend who worked in the UEB registrar's office with Arminda had connections to a local YWAM program called "King's Kids," where Christian youth were trained to work with children in the city. She suggested this might be a good fit for Anahí.

Arminda persuaded Anahí to go with her one afternoon, and Anihí loved it. She continued going on her own and in time became deeply involved, gradually imbibing YWAM's passionate commitment to missions. As we've seen above, in time Anabel also took YWAM training, as well as their Aunt Rufina. The whole family acknowledges a debt of gratitude to this mission organization.

---

31. In December 2018 and January 2019, Anihí visited Oregon and was able to worship in four congregations in NWYM, plus meet with many of the former missionaries to Bolivia.

32. Information for this section comes from an interview conducted by Harold Thomas and Nancy Thomas with David Tintaya and Arminda Quispe via Skype, May 27, 2018.

In 2012 David and the family began organizing annual missions conferences for the Santa Cruz Friends churches. These caught on slowly at first, but now are an event people look forward to.

In 2014, almost out of the blue, David announced to the family one day that he felt God calling him to India, at least for a visit, to see how missions were affecting this country. He said he had no idea what he was supposed to do there or how he was going to get there. The family was a bit surprised, to say the least, but one by one they all responded, "I'm going, too!" They took the "call" seriously and began preparing by checking out books and watching videos on life in India.

The YWAM base in Argentina had just developed a short-term mission program to India, taking Spanish-speaking pastors to this country to minister to their Latin American missionaries. The Tintayas applied, but communication broke down and the trip fell through. That was a big disappointment, but in the meantime, Evangelical Friends Mission (EFM) missionary Roy Twadell had been invited to the YWAM base in Santa Cruz to teach a course. The Tintayas met him, and when Twadell found out about their thwarted trip to India, he said, "Friends have a work in India. Why don't you go with your own denomination?"

Twadell made the connection between the Tintayas and Dan Cammack, director of EFM, and plans began forming. As director, Cammack frequently traveled to visit the various EFM fields. As the son of Peruvian/Bolivian former missionaries Ed and Marie Cammack, raised in Peru, and former missionary to Peru himself, Cammack spoke Spanish and could serve as an interpreter for the Tintayas on a short-term mission trip. He told them to raise their funds, buy their tickets, and he would include them in a trip early in 2016.

The family decided they all should go. Anabel was working and volunteered to pay her own way. The *Congregación Cristiana Amigos* committed to pay for David's ticket. That left tickets for three family members. They all got to work to raise the money through bake sales, a concert in La Paz (where their musical friends volunteered), and fund-raising among churches, friends, and family members. By the end of 2015, they had raised almost $13,000 (US) and David was able to purchase five tickets on an economical Ethiopian airline that traveled between Sao Paulo and Kolkata once a week.

The whole experience lasted a month, with two weeks in India. After an eventful journey, Dan Cammack met the Tintayas in Kolkata. Indian Pastor D. K. Sarkar and his wife, Choity, also welcomed them with open arms. David and Arminda's first lesson in Indian culture was that they were not to give Latin American *abrazos* (huge hugs) to Indians. Having been trained in the need for cultural sensitivity and adaptation, the Tintayas quickly learned.

The Sarkars had arranged an extensive schedule of visits to around twenty churches, most of them in rural areas and all part of the growing Northwest India Yearly Meeting of Friends. This sometimes meant visits to three churches in a single day. The pace was rigorous, but the Tintayas found the people so loving and welcoming (even without hugs), that they scarcely felt tired. They discovered that they were a novelty to the Indian Friends, with their strange language (Spanish) and customs. But everyone managed to find common ground in their faith in Christ. It turned out to be a life-time highlight for the whole Tintaya family.

Tintaya family and Dan Cammack ministering in India, 2016 (D. Tintaya)

They managed to find time to visit the William Carey center, remembering from their studies the story of Carey's missionary adventures in India and the contribution he made to Christianity in this huge country.

Back home in Bolivia, some people asked David and Arminda if it was worth it to spend so much money to send the whole family to India for only two weeks. The Tintayas have no hesitancy in answering in the affirmative, such was the impact of the trip on their lives. Arminda notes that it was the whole experience that served as a school of missions for them, beginning with the raising of their funds. They noted that over half of the $13,000 came from Bolivian churches and individuals, the other half coming from their own savings over several years. And then the process of getting legal permission, finding the best airline rates, arranging their schedule, securing the visa—they consider all this valuable experience.

And the time in India relating to their new brothers and sisters, receiving their loving welcome, sensing how much people appreciated the visits, and understanding how firmly the church has been planted on Indian soil—this has served to deepen their commitment to the cause of world mission, even though no one in the Tintaya family senses a specific call to go back to India. David and D. K. Sarkar remain in contact.

David and Arminda consider this adventure their actual "launching pad" in mission. They now have a stronger sense that Bolivians can send out their own missionaries and support them. Arminda says, "We need to open our eyes to the needs in the world, and the funds will come to and through our hands."

The route home took the Tintayas through Sao Paulo where several Bolivian Friends had migrated for better work opportunities. David had already made contact through the Internet with Sara Tito, daughter of INELA leader Enrique Tito, and with Marilyn Ayala, a former UEB student. The family stayed in the home of Ayala, a nurse who had been trained in the graduate missions program, CENESI, and was in Sao Paulo as a missionary to Bolivians in this huge Brazilian city. They followed her in her routine and learned from her way of being a missionary in this context.

Once again in Santa Cruz, David continued his Internet search for Bolivian Friends in Sao Paulo. In May of that same year, David and Arminda returned to Sao Paulo with a team of sixteen people from their congregation, this time to participate with the Baptist Church in a campaign to reach out to Spanish-speaking people in the city. The Tintayas wanted to learn this particular missionary strategy by participating, but they were simultaneously trying to locate Friends who had migrated. They managed to find Octavio Vargas, relative of the current INELA president Timoteo Choque Vargas. A small group was already meeting in his home.

Octavio was excited to meet the visiting Friends from Santa Cruz and invited them back when they could dedicate more time to his group. That happened in November, still in 2016, when David, Arminda, Anahí and Joana returned to Sao Paulo and, with Octavio's help, visited all the INELA Quakers they could find, inviting them to become part of a new Friends church in the city. Before the end of their trip around eighty Bolivian Friends had gathered to begin the church.

David and Arminda report that offerings from the Santa Cruz Friends covered the costs of the November trip. Then again in 2017, another group of INELA Friends took a short-term missions trip to Sao Paulo to learn about urban mission strategies and to encourage the new church. The new church is definitely Friends, but the members have not yet (as of this writing) decided whether to associate with INELA or with Holiness Friends. Either way, David sees the number of Bolivians in Sao Paulo and their needs and is dreaming about beginning other Friends churches in Brazil.

The adventures of the Tintaya family in mission don't end with India and Brazil. In 2017, the New Jerusalem Friends Church in La Paz asked David to help them plant a Friends church in the city of Tarija. Tarija is the capital of the department of that name in the south of Bolivia. This fits with the INELA's goal to have Friends churches in every department of Bolivia.

David and Arminda decided that they could cooperate with the New Jerusalem Church in some way. They made two exploratory trips to Tarija in 2017 and found a former INELA leader from the Caranavi District already living there and wanting to begin a Friends church. Pablo Flores was eager and willing to work under the INELA again.

After David's last visit, some twenty-five people began meeting with Flores in his home. The church plant continues under the supervision of the New Jerusalem Church in La Paz.

Another of David's deep concerns is for the Chimane and Mosetén ethnic groups within Bolivia, among which national missionaries have begun a work. David and others sense that this effort needs special attention and training in cross-cultural mission.

The greatest challenge for the Tintayas is to raise a vision for missions in the whole INELA, along with the training to make that vision a reality. They both realize they are growing older, but they still have much to give. They feel their experiences up to this point have prepared them for how God wants them to spend the last part of their lives in mission. They're ready to go or ready to stay and motivate.

And who knows where God will take their daughters?

12

Higher, Ever Higher

Conclusion

This book has come to its conclusion, but the Bolivian Friends Church continues its long journey to maturity. As we observed in chapter 10, the INELA is now a fully independent national church with its own leaders, administrative processes, and roster of ministries. Its worship services vibrate with life and it is beginning to cast a missionary vision that stretches to new cultures and even countries. Many people have experienced transformation and personal growth.

Yet in this book we have tried not to paint an idealistic portrait of Bolivian Quakers. The church clearly struggles in many areas. Leaders are now trying to face the fact of plateaued growth, the loss of second- and third-generation persons and families, and the need for a more effective program of leadership development. They are attempting to learn from the weaknesses in their mission outreach in the past as they consider entering new areas in the future.

As the book draws to a close, the INELA has just celebrated its centennial. Some seven thousand Aymara Quakers gathered in a coliseum in the upper city of El Alto to thank God for one hundred years of God's faithfulness. They chose Easter weekend, April 19–21, 2019, as an appropriate time to celebrate.

In the year prior to the celebration, choosing the date for the centennial was a source of conflict. When can we consider that the INELA began? Many people opted for 1919, the date William Abel came to Bolivia, interacted with Juan Ayllón, and then died of small pox. They considered this the seed planted in the ground of Bolivia that would one day grow up as the church. Others insisted that 2024 is the right date to celebrate; this would focus on 1924, the year the first INELA Friends church was planted by Juan Ayllón in the Tembladerani *barrio* of La Paz.

Representatives in the 2017 annual meeting voted (such an un-Quakerly thing to do!) for 2019 as the centennial celebration. I wouldn't be surprised to see another celebration in 2024. Celebrate is something this church does well.

As people have come through the celebration, a key word is gratitude. Leaders and planners are focusing not only on understanding their history, but also on being grateful for all God has done. This gratitude includes the work of the Friends Mission, with all the ups and downs of this relationship, and reaches back to their own grandparents and even great-grandparents, men and women God raised up from Bolivian ground to build the church.

Leaders also want to learn from the mistakes and conflicts of the past as they continue to walk that mountain trail. This will be a challenge.

UNDERSTANDING BOLIVIAN FRIENDS

One of our purposes in writing this history has been to help English-speaking Christians understand the Bolivian Friends Church. We hope you can see this group as a people who have overcome cultural barriers to become a Christian Quaker church. We hope you can also see them as Aymara Christian Quakers, reflecting the values of their cultural tradition even as they struggle with other aspects of the culture. In many ways, this church seems more Aymara than Quaker. That might be one of its strengths.

This history has made clear that the Bolivian Friends Church is not a peaceful church, which, considering the worldwide Quaker peace testimony, is an irony.

In a gathering of INELA leaders in February 2018, Elías Mamani presented a talk entitled "Biblical Foundations of Friends Principles of Conduct." In other Quaker contexts, the word "principles" would be "testimonies." Mamani presented the five Quaker testimonies of peace, honesty, equality, simplicity, and solidarity with the poor, noting that around the world Quakers have earned a reputation for upholding these values.

The hour-and-a-half presentation focused on the peace testimony and engendered lively discussion. Elías was scarcely through his introduction, when one of the pastors raised his hand and his voice, insisting on expressing himself. He proceeded to vigorously argue, in a most unpeaceful manner, saying, "How can you present these as our values? INELA does not follow the way of peace or honesty or equality or simplicity. Maybe we practice some solidarity with the poor, being poor ourselves. But we are not a peaceful people!" At this point others spoke up, mostly in agreement. People recognized that the conflicts inherent in the Aymara culture exist also in the church.

Elías Mamani then very gently summed up and affirmed what people had been observing. He focused on peace, admitting that the INELA has problems with the lack of internal peace. "We hurt each other," he said. "We criticize each other. We don't preach on peace. INELA leaders end up wounded, damaged and in pain. We need to change!" Around the room, people nodded in agreement.

After an admonition to continue discussing the issue peacefully, "speaking the truth in love," the group went forward with some painful but honest evaluation, exploring the possibilities for change. Elías closed his presentation with a reference to perhaps the most controversial area of Friends doctrine and practice, the spiritual interpretation of the sacrament of baptism. He pointed out that the fact that the church does not practice water baptism is NOT one of its testimonies. The testimony, and the theology behind it, is the baptism of the Holy Spirit, he told them. And it's the presence of the Spirit in the life of the church that enables living out the testimonies of peace, honesty, equality, simplicity and solidarity. As heads again nodded in agreement, it was clear that Mamani had expressed the sense of the meeting.

Mamani went on to admonish the leaders to encourage peace in their local, district, and national *directivas*, and also to be influences for peace in their city zones and rural communities.

Discussions like this are happening more and more as people enter into a healthy evaluation of the church. They strongly identify with the Friends movement around the world but are also struggling to find their own identity within that movement. This struggle is positive.

The churches in Oregon, Washington, and Idaho who supported the Friends Mission in Bolivia for so many years need to continue in relationship with the INELA. Just as it is good and needful for parents to continue in a changed relationship with their adult offspring, so the national church needs to know that the group of believers who were involved in their development still cares about them.

The benefits would be mutual, of course. We can encourage the INELA through cooperative projects in holistic mission, through visits back and forth, through times of reflection together on issues where Friends can still make a contribution to meeting the needs of the world. We can receive their ministry as we learn from them how to live holistically, how to care for the earth, and how to learn the ways of peace in a context of conflict. We can let them teach us how to worship and celebrate.

Friends in the United States, especially the Northwest, need to recognize the INELA as family and to relate as a family should.

Jim Le Shana, NWYM superintendent, with Hector Castro, INELA president, at the 2019 centennial celebration in El Alto (Jonathan Le Shana)

UNDERSTANDING AND LEARNING FROM
THE MISSION'S ROLE IN THE STORY

A second purpose in writing this history for English-speaking audiences was to arrive at an understanding of the role of the mission in the church's development and from that to draw out applications for an ongoing missiology.

We can learn from biography, from some of the outstanding stories of the actual missionaries. We can learn from the rugged pioneers, those like Carroll Tamplin and Roscoe and Tina Knight, who by their dedication and hard work opened up works in new territory. While these sometimes seemed more consumed by zeal for the holiness movement than by Quaker convictions, perhaps this type of missionary is necessary during the beginning phases of a work.

We can learn from missionaries like Helen Cammack, also an early pioneer, but one who was more patient and reflective, in a sense, more "Quakerly," than her fiery brothers and sisters. Cammack came to Bolivia first of all as a learner, and only later developed as a minister. She lived out the Quaker theology of recognizing that of God in every person and, by extension, in every culture. She focused on relationships, even while dedicating herself to the tasks at hand. She was the first to gain fluency in the Aymara language.

We can learn from missionary statesmen like Ralph Chapman and Jack Willcuts, whose quieter gifts of administration and teaching were key in the development of the INELA. They both embodied peacemaking during times of intense conflict. We can learn from Quaker educators like Ron Stansell and Jerry Clarkson, from pastoral ministers like Mark Roberts and Ed Cammack. We can learn from anthropologists and reflective theologians like Hal Thomas. We can learn from the ways God took so many different personalities and gifts and forged them into a team that worked together to plan strategy, work with the national church, know when to move forward and when to pull back. And who discerned when to go home.

One outstanding aspect of the story of the mission is its adoption of the indigenous principle at the very beginning of its involvement in Bolivia, long before this was being widely taught in seminaries and training schools. The indigenous principle at its best holds that the purpose of a foreign mission is to plant a national church that will eventually be an independent expression of Christianity appropriate to its context. The old formula stated that the national church must be "self-governing, self-supporting, and self-propagating." The mission, of course, would then leave.

The first missionary sent out by Oregon Yearly Meeting, Carroll Tamplin, insisted on this policy and persuaded the mission board to also buy into it. Throughout its seventy-two years of relationship with the INELA, the mission held to the indigenous concept as its policy and eventual goal for the national church. In this aspect, the mission was clearly ahead of its times.

And yet this history of the development of the church has shown how complex and how difficult the indigenous policy was to actually live out. From the early days of the Tamplins, in spite of good intentions, a subtle paternalism crept into the relationship between mission and national church. Frankly non-indigenous practices such as salaries for national workers grew with time to become a major cause of dependency. Much missionary time was spent trying to deal with the realities caused by this dependency, seeking for ways to correct it and encourage the church toward independence.

One curious situation from the 1940s and 1950s stands out. This was the purchase by the mission of Copajira, a hacienda on the *altiplano*, a large farm complete with the Indians that belonged to it. And this during a time ripe for revolution, when haciendas in other parts of the country were being attacked. One wonders today if the mission staff and mission board back home understood fully the implications of a hacienda-owning mission, working exclusively among the Aymara population. It seems a miracle that the mission was able to hold onto Copajira in the years following the 1952 revolution, and that the end of this chapter was not more violent and tragic.

We can't doubt the good things that resulted from the ownership of Copajira. The Indians attached to the hacienda were, of course, given their freedom, along with land, in as short order as possible. The Bible school on the farm—the reason for its purchase—prepared a whole generation of pastors, teachers, and leaders for the national church. And the demonstration of effective farming methods and vocational classes were instructive for both the Bible school students and the surrounding communities. Yet one wonders how the Aymara Friends of the era saw the missionaries, set in the same role as the Spanish landowners who had exploited them for so many years. The mission could not have chosen, however unconsciously, a more paternalistic model.

That all of this took place in a "culture of conflict" adds to an understanding of the tensions between mission and national church. In a culture where mistrust and suspicion of the outsider are the norm, one can see that the building of trust relationships would be difficult at best.

And yet, in spite of the negative factors, trust was built, leaders received training, and a church arose in the highlands of Bolivia. Nationals and missionaries worked together to open new territories to the gospel message, to learn how to administer the church, to bring education to children in remote areas, and to worship in ways appropriate to the culture. That the process was never smooth or easy just goes to show there were human beings involved at every level.

There is much we in the Western world can learn from this story as we continue to reach out in mission at home and around the world. It's an obvious understatement to note that the world has changed since 1930 when Oregon Yearly Meeting agreed to take on Bolivia as its mission field. While today there are a few Friends missions doing pioneer church planting in other cultures, many yearly meetings are sending out people to places of limited access to the gospel, places where overt evangelism and preaching are against the law, and could even result in death for either expatriate or national believer. Mission strategies necessarily must adapt to these situations. NWYM has wisely done away with the word "missionary" and adopted the neutral term, "Friend serving abroad" (FSA). In some areas of the world, the work of such Friends is referred to by phrases such as "being Friends of Jesus in Palestine [or Russia or China, or . . .]."

Yet, despite the differences, there are still lessons to be learned from the Bolivian experience. Today the "indigenous principle" would probably be replaced by the term "contextualization," meaning that whatever expression of Christianity might emerge should reflect the culture and setting. It would not necessarily be a traditionally organized church or denomination and would certainly avoid any kind of long-term dependency on foreign funding or personnel. The Friends view of that of Christ in every person and context is as vital in these situations as it was in the Andean setting of the 1920s and 1930s. Today's witness to the presence of Christ would necessarily be a gentle witness, and one that focuses on relationships. And just as the Bolivian Friends have shown a growth toward a more holistic gospel, mission endeavor today must include justice, mercy, stewardship of creation, as well as a patient pointing to the reality and authority of Jesus.

Mission endeavor today is also about building trust in situations where trust is not natural or a way of life. It's living as witnesses in realities where so many voices are shouting their perspectives that it becomes vital to get quiet enough to hear the still small voice of the Spirit. And then to be brave enough to follow the voice. It implies going out in humility, as learners, expecting that those we go to will end up being our teachers as well.

Quaker mission endeavor today is also about community. Teamwork among the staff (both field and mission board) was necessary to the work of the mission in Bolivia, and it's necessary today. The lone-ranger missionary hero has no place in Quaker theology or practice and is rarely what the Spirit asks of the sent-out ones. We are family, community, the people of God even when we disagree (which we frequently do), and the Spirit gives discernment to listening communities. And this community life needs to intentionally include those to whom we are sent.

Undoubtedly, there are many other lessons to be gleaned from the story of church and mission in Bolivia.

THANKS BE TO GOD!

Our third purpose in writing this history was to encourage a sense of gratitude for all God has done. We recognize God as the chief protagonist of this story, the Spirit behind the scenes and events and persons, both expatriate and national. We recognize that Christ is the Head of the church.

The INELA faces difficult issues in her current setting, yet there is One who walks with her on those difficult but life-giving mountain trails. Our desire is that this look to the past will inspire courage for the present and hope for the future

If I were to direct my remarks to the INELA, I would borrow from the Apostle Paul when he wrote to the believers at Philippi, "I thank my God every time I remember you. In all my prayers for all of you, I always pray with joy because of your partnership in the gospel from the first day until now, being confident of this, that he who began a good work in you will carry it on to completion until the day of Christ Jesus" (Phil 1:3–6).

Thanks be to God.

Appendix A

Maps

Pacific Ocean

**Map of South America
with Bolivia highlighted**

Atlantic Ocean

**Map of Bolivia
with Departments (States)**

PANDO

PERÚ

BENI

BRAZIL

LA PAZ

Lake Titicaca

La Paz/El Alto   COCHABAMBA   SANTA CRUZ

ORURO

Sucre

POTOSÍ

CHUQUISACA

CHILE

TARIJA

PARAGUAY

ARGENTINA

Map of the Department of La Paz, Bolivia with INELA Quarterly Meeting Districts

INELA Districts

1955	Cordillera
1955	Península
1955	La Paz
1955	Frontera
1958	Yungas
1967	Caranavi
1975	Pacajes
1980	Lago Norte
1981	Santa Cruz*
1984	Sud Yungas
1984	Nor Yungas
1988	El Alto
1988	Altiplano Sud
2000	La Asunta
2000	Alto Beni
2004	Camacho

*The Santa Cruz District is in the department of Santa Cruz. All other districts are in the department of La Paz.

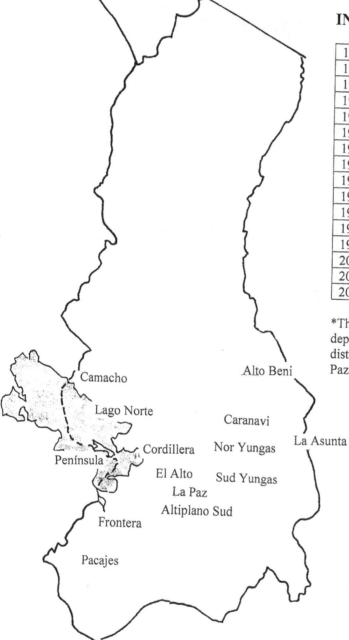

Appendix B

Highlights of the History of the INELA

1915–1924	The church in Amacari begins.
1919	William Abel comes to La Paz, preaches on the streets, disciples Juan Ayllón and dies.
1924	Juan and Tomasa Ayllón begin their missionary service in Bolivia under the sponsorship of the Central American Mission and Friends Church. The church in Tembladerani is established, the first officially recognized church of the INELA.
1930	OYM accepts Bolivia as their new mission field. They also accept Juan and Tomasa Ayllón as their first missionaries.
1931	OYM sends Carroll and Doris Tamplin to Bolivia as their first North American missionaries.
1938	The La Paz Friends Church meeting house built on Max Paredes Street.
1944	Helen Cammack dies of typhoid fever.
1944	Juan Ayllón leaves the church and mission; later begins his own denomination.
1947	The Friends Mission changes from a field superintendent to a mission council system of administration.
1947	The mission buys the Copajira farm, begins the Helen Cammack Memorial Bible School.
1947	The *Sociedad Evangélica de Amigos Bolivianos (SEAB,* Evangelical Society of Bolivian Friends) is created, with Máximo Loza as president, as a step toward self-government.
1948	The *Sociedad Evangélica de Amigos Nacionales (SEAN,* Evangelical Society of National Friends) is created, with Feliciano Sirpa as president, the next step toward self-government.
1952	On April 13, the *Iglesia Nacional Evangélica de Los Amigos (INELA,* National Evangelical Friends Church) is born, with Mariano Baptista as first president.
1953–1955	The Yungas valleys open to a church planting effort by the national church and the mission, led by Mariano Baptista and Roscoe and Tina Knight.
1956	On March 16, the Bolivian government signs the document that gives the INELA official recognition and approves their constitution, the *Estatutos.*
1961	The Copajira farm is lost.

1963	A crisis of relationship between the mission and the INELA sends most of the missionaries back to the US.
1964	The INELA is reorganized under the leadership of Carmelo Aspi. The way opens for the missionaries to return.
1965	A school opens in Batallas that includes 5th and 6th grades.
1965	The national women's organization, *Unión Femenil de INELA (UFINELA,* Feminine Union of INELA) is organized.
1966	The Patmos Bible Institute in La Paz is founded under the INELA leadership of Carmelo Aspi.
1968	The national youth organization, *Unión de Jóvenes Evangélicos de Los Amigos de Bolivia (UJELAB,* Union of Evangelical Friends Youth of Bolivia), is founded.
1972	The mission begins the Extension Bible School. Cooperating missions in La Paz form the San Pablo Seminary.
1972	The first church in the city of Santa Cruz is established.
1973/74	INELA is recognized as a Yearly Meeting.
1973	INELA begins its first national missionary society (1973–1978).
1979	The medical clinic on the Max Paredes property opens.
1981	INELA begins to send national missionaries to Peru.
1982	The *Universidad Evangélica Boliviana (UEB,* Bolivian Evangelical University) in the city of Santa Cruz is founded.
1982–1987	The greenhouse project brings relief and training to people on the *altiplano*.
1983	Young leaders in the INELA found the *Sociedad Evangélica de Tecnología Apropiada Los Amigos (SETALA,* the Friends Evangelical Society for Appropriate Technology).
1984	INELA becomes a member of the *Comité Organizador para América Latina (COAL,* the Organizing Committee for Latin America, part of the Friends World Committee for Consultation).
1987	A Friends church in Buenos Aires is established by INELA members.
1991	The school on the Max Paredes property is re-opened.
1992	A national missionary program begins again.
1998	The revision of the *Estatutos* is accepted, dividing the church into a national *mesa directiva* and two regional *directivas*.
1998	The project to build a medical clinic in Amacari begins (1998–2010).
1999	The INELA celebrates seventy-five years since Juan Ayllón founded the first Friends Church in 1924.
2002	The *Instituto Superior de Educación Teológica Los Amigos (ISETA,* Friends Higher Institute for Theological Education), for the training of pastors and leaders, is founded by the INELA.
2002	The Friends Mission retires after seventy-two years of working with the INELA.

2010	The *Buen Amigo* (Good Friend) organization begins.
2012	A reorganized national missionary program begins again, with cooperation from NWYM.
2017	A new revision of the *Estatutos* is accepted.
2019	The INELA celebrates its centennial.

Appendix C

INELA Presidents

1947	Máximo Loza, SEAB
1948–1950	Feliciano Sirpa, SEAN
1951–1954	Mariano Baptista, INELA
1955	Pedro Guanca
1956–1958	Vicente Yujra
1959–1960	Antonio Mamani
1960–1961	José Acero
1962–1963	Timoteo Condori
1964–1965	Carmelo Aspi
1966–1967	Antonio Mamani
1967–1968	Felipe Apaza
1969–1970	Antonio Mamani
1971–1973	Pascual Quispe
1974–1975	Carmelo Aspi
1976–1981	Francisco Tintaya
1982–1984	Pascual Quispe
1985	Humberto Gutiérrez

1986	Venancio Quispe
1987–1989	Francisco Mamani
1990–1991	Patricio Medrano
1991–1994	Remigio Condori
1995–1997	Sabino Chipana
1998–1999	Sabino Chalco
2000–2001	Cirilo Aruquipa
2001	Ezequiel Chipana
2002–2004	Silver Ramos
2005–2007	Mario Chávez
2008–2010	Félix Nina
2011–2013	Daniel Limachi
2014–2016	Timoteo Choque
2017–	Hector Castro

Appendix D

OYM/NWYM Missionaries to Bolivia

1930–1933	Juan and Tomasa Ayllón	From 1924 to 1930, the Ayllóns were supported by the Friends mission and national church in Guatemala.
1931–1943	Carroll and Doris Tamplin	The Tamplins returned to Bolivia in 1944 under the National Holiness Missionary Society, at times on loan to the Friends Mission, along with Marshall and Catherine Cavit.
1932–1944	Helen Cammack	
1935–1939	Esthel Gulley	
1936–1950	Howard and Julia Pearson	
1944–1958 1963–1965	Ralph and Marie Chapman	
1945–1962 1978–1979	Roscoe and Tina Knight	In 1962 and again in 1979, they transferred to Peru.
1947–1958	Jack and Geraldine Willcuts	
1948–1961	Paul and Phyllis Cammack	In 1961, they moved to Peru to begin a new work.
1951–1959	Leland and Iverna Hibbs	
1953–1963 1974–1978	Mark and Wilma Roberts	
1956–1958	Forest and Orpha Cammack	
1957–1971	David and Florence Thomas	

1958–1964	Everett and Alda Clarkson	In 1964, they transferred to Peru.
1958–1959	Chuck and Charlotte Scott	
1960–1963	Oscar and Ruth Brown	
1960–1972	Eugene and Betty Comfort	
1962–1963 1972–1974	Quentin and Florene Nordyke	In 1963, they transferred to Peru.
1963–1965	Paul and Martha Puckett	In 1965, they transferred to Peru.
1968–1985	Ron and Carolyn Stansell	
1970–1973	Mary Bel Cammack	In 1973, she transferred to Peru.
1972–1989 (1999–2019)	Hal and Nancy Thomas	The Thomases served part-time with the INELA while seconded to other organizations (1999–2014) and on the history project (2013–2019).
1976–1978	Gil and Louise George	In 1979, they transferred to Peru.
1980–1988	James and Gail Roberts	
1981–1982	Randy and Mary Morse	Previous service in Peru.
1985–1988	Dwaine and Becky Williams	Previous service in Peru.
1985–1987	Steve and Janelle Baron	
1988–1989	Wayne and Bev Chapman	Previous service in Peru.
1989–2001	Ed and Marie Cammack	Previous service in Peru
1995–2002	Jerry and Keri Clarkson	

Bibliography

Ajnota, Esteban. "Volviendo para servir a Dios" [Returning to serve God]. In *De encuentro a ministerio: La vida y fe de los Amigos latinoamericanos* [From encounter to ministry: The life and faith of Latin American Friends], edited by Nancy Thomas, 65–69. La Paz: CALA, 2012.

Albo, Xavier. "La experiencia religiosa Aymara" [The Aymara religious experience]. In *Rostros indios de Dios* [Indian faces of God], edited by Manuel M. Marzal et al., 81–136. La Paz: CIPCA, 1992.

———. "La paradoja aymara: Comunitario e individualista" [The Aymara paradox: Communitarian and individualistic]. In *Los Aymaras dentro de la sociedad boliviana* [The Aymaras within Bolivian society], 25–34. La Paz: CIPCA, 1976.

Albó, Xavier, et al. *Chukiyawu: La cara aymara de La Paz. III. Cabalgando entre dos mundos.* [Chukiyawu: The Aymara face of La Paz. III. Traveling between two worlds]. La Paz: CIPCA, 1983.

Arguedas, Alcides. *Raza de bronce* [Race of bronze]. 4th ed. Buenos Aires: Editorial Losada, 1968. First published 1919.

Aspi, Carmelo. *Los Amigos en marcha* [Friends on the move]. La Paz: Filigrana, 2007.

Beck, Charles Darrell. *On Memory's Back Trail: A Story History of Ramona and the Backcountry of San Diego County.* Ramona, CA: Backcountry, 2004.

Beebe, Ralph K. *A Garden of the Lord: A History of Oregon Yearly Meeting of Friends Church.* Newberg, OR: Barclay, 1968.

Brown, Michael L. *Sent to the Heart: The Story of World Gospel Mission in Bolivia.* Marion, IN: World Gospel Mission, 1995.

CALA. *Breve historia de Publicaciones CALA en sus 50 años: 1957–2007* [Brief 50-year history of CALA publications]. La Paz: CALA, 2007.

Carrico, Richard. *Strangers in a Stolen Land: Indians of San Diego County from Prehistory to the New Deal.* San Diego: Sunbelt, 2008.

Carrillo A., Ramiro. *Los Amigos en la historia: Una visión después de Cristo* [Friends in history: A vision of the times since Christ]. La Paz: INELA, 1999.

Carter, William, and Mauricio Mamani. *Irpa Chico: Individuo y comunidad en la cultura aymara* [Irpa Chico: Individual and community in Aymara culture]. La Paz: Juventud, 1982.

Contreras, Manuel E. "A Comparative Perspective of Education Reforms in Bolivia:1950–2000." In *Proclaiming Revolution: Bolivia in Comparative Perspective*, edited by Merilee S. Grindle and Pilar Domingo, 259–86. London: University of London, 2003.

Dunkerley, James. *Rebellion in the Veins: Political Struggle in Bolivia, 1952–1982.* London: Verso, 1984.

Foster, George M. *Traditional Cultures and the Impact of Technological Change*. New York: Harper & Row, 1962.

———. *Traditional Societies and Technological Change*. 2nd ed. New York: Harper & Row, 1973.

Gisbert, Teresa. "Libro I: Período prehispánico" [Book I: Prehispanic period]. In *Historia de Bolivia*, edited by José de Mesa et al., 3–74. 7th ed. La Paz: Gisbert, 2008.

Gotkowitz, Laura. *A Revolution for Our Rights: Indigenous Struggles for Land and Justice in Bolivia, 1880–1952*. Durham, NC: Duke University Press, 2007.

Grindle, Merilee S. "Shadowing the Past? Policy Reform in Bolivia, 1985–2002." In *Proclaiming Revolution: Bolivia in Comparative Perspective*, edited by Merilee S. Grindle and Pilar Domingo, 318–44. London: University of London Press, 2003.

Gutiérrez, Gustavo. *La teología de la liberación: Perspectivas* [Liberation theology: Perspectives]. Lima: Centro de Estudios y Publicaciones, 1971.

Hertzog, S. K., et al. *Algunas aves de Bolivia: Guía del campo* [Some birds of Bolivia: Field guide]. Santa Cruz: Armonía, 2017.

Hesse, Alan, et al. *Algunas aves del Chaco: Un paseo en el Isoso* [Some birds of the Chaco: A walk by the Isoso]. Santa Cruz: Armonía, 2005.

Hittson, Paul A. *History of Peniel Missions*. Homeland, CA: Peniel Missions, 1975.

INE. *Características de la población: Censo de población y vivienda 2012, Bolivia* [Charcteristics of the population: Population and housing census, 2012]. La Paz: INE, 2015.

———. *Censo de población, 1992* [Population census, 1992]. La Paz: INE, 1993.

Jackson, Sheldon. *Azusa Pacific University, 1899–1999: One Hundred Years of Christian Service and Scholarship*. Whittier, CA: Azusa Pacific University, 1999.

Jammes, Lois, et al. *The Salar de Tunupa*. Santa Cruz: Armonía, 2000.

Kearney, Michael. *World View*. Novato, CA: Chandler and Sharp, 1984.

Klein, Herbert S. *Bolivia: The Evolution of a Multi-ethnic Society*. New York: Oxford University Press, 1982.

———. *A Concise History of Bolivia*. 2nd ed. Cambridge: Cambridge University Press, 2011. Kindle edition.

———. "Social Change in Bolivia since 1952." In *Proclaiming Revolution: Bolivia in Comparative Perspective*, edited by Marilee S. Grindle and Pilar Domingo, 232–58. London: University of London Press, 2003.

Knight, Tina. *On Down the Trail*. Mountain Terrace, WA: WinePress, 1995.

Kraft, Charles H. *Anthropology for Christian Witness*. Maryknoll: Orbis, 1996.

———. *Christianity in Culture: A Study in Dynamic Biblical Theologizing in Cross-Cultural Perspectives*. Maryknoll: Orbis, 1979.

Las Casas, Bartolomé de. *A Brief Account of the Destruction of the Indians*. New York: Penguin, 2004. First published in Seville, Spain, 1552.

Libermann, Kitula, et al. "Mundo rural andino" [The rural Andean world]. In *Para comprender las culturas rurales en Bolivia* [Understanding Bolivia's rural cultures], edited by X. Albo et al., 18–156. La Paz: Ministerio de Educación y Cultura, CIPCA, UNICEF, 1989.

Mesa, José de et al. *Libro II: El choque de dos culturas, 1492–1600* [Book II: The clash of two cultures, 1492–1600]. In *Historia de Bolivia*, edited by José de Mesa et al., 75–142. 7th ed. La Paz: Gisbert, 2008.

Morales, Juan Antonio. "The National Revolution and Its Legacy." In *Proclaiming Revolution: Bolivia in Comparative Perspective*, edited by Merilee S. Grindle and Pilar Domingo, 213–31. London: University of London Press, 2003

Nordyke, Quentin. *Animistic Aymaras and Church Growth*. Newberg, OR: Barclay, 1972.

Orta, Andrew. *Catechizing Culture: Missionaries, Aymara, and the "New Evangelization."* New York: Columbia University Press, 2004.

Payne, Frances R. *They Make Us Dangerous (Bolivia 1964–1980)*. Bloomingdale, IN: Xlibris, 2012. Kindle edition.

Peet, Mary Rockwood, ed. *San Pasqual: A Crack in the Hills*. Ramona, CA: Ballena, 1949.

Quisbert Ramos, Elizabeth, and Ana Ramos. "El espíritu de hacer misiones: breve biografía de Eugenio Ramos Tenorio" [The missionary spirit: Brief biography of Eugene Ramos Tenorio]. In *De encuentro a ministerio: La vida y fe de Los Amigos latinoamericanos*, edited by Nancy Thomas, 96–98. La Paz: CALA, 2012.

Quispe Jahuira, Rufina. "Mi historia, con gratitud a unas mujeres valientes" [My story, with gratitude to some brave women]. In *De encuentro a ministerio: La vida y fe de los Amigos latinoamericanos*, edited by Nancy Thomas, 88–91. La Paz: CALA, 2012.

Raser, H. E. "Holiness Movement." In *Dictionary of Christianity in America*, edited by D. G. Reid et al., 543–47. Downers Grove: InterVarsity, 1990.

Ritchie, John. *The Indigenous Church in Peru*. London: World Dominion, 1932.

Roberts, Elizabeth Judson. "Indian History." In *San Pasqual: A Crack in the Hills*, edited by M. R. Peet, 17–38. Ramona, CA: Ballena, 1949.

Shaw, R. Daniel. *Transculturation: The Cultural Factor in Translation and Other Communication Tasks*. Pasadena, CA: William Carey Library.

Smith, R. Esther. *In Aymara Land*. Chiquimula, Guatemala: Corazón y Vida, 1930.

Thomas, Harold R. "Bolivia." In *Evangelical Dictionary of World Missions*, edited by A. Scott Moreau, 136–37. Grand Rapids: Baker, 2000.

———. "Cultural Themes, Worldview Perspectives, and Christian Conversion among Urbanizing Evangelical Aymaras." PhD diss, School of World Mission, Fuller Theological Seminary, 2003.

Thomas, Nancy. "Alto Lima: A Landmark for the Bolivian Church." *Evangelical Friend*, January 1979, 7–9.

———. "Hard Hats in a Friends Church." *Evangelical Friend*, July–August 1985, 11–12.

Tintaya, David. "Mi escuela de liderazgo" [My leadership school]. In *De encuentro a ministerio: La vida y fe de los Amigos latinoamericanos*, edited by Nancy Thomas, 99–101. La Paz: CALA, 2012.

Tippett, Alan. *Introduction to Missiology*. Pasadena, CA: William Carey Library, 1987.

Union Bible College and Academy: A Heritage to Remember, a Heritage to Keep. Westfield, IN: Union Bible College and Academy, 2011.

US Census Bureau. US Census of 1880: Township of Ballena, San Diego County, State of California. Taken June 7, 1880.

———. US Census of 1900: City of Whittier, Los Angeles County, State of California. Taken June 6, 1900.

Wagner, C. Peter. *The Protestant Movement in Bolivia*. South Pasadena, CA: William Carey Library, 1970.

Index

Made in the USA
Monee, IL
11 December 2019